_____

DICKENS STUDIES ANNUAL

Robert B. Partlow, Jr., *Editor*

DICKENS
STUDIES
ANNUAL

VOLUME
I

Edited by

ROBERT B. PARTLOW, Jr.

SOUTHERN ILLINOIS UNIVERSITY PRESS

Carbondale and Edwardsville

FEFFER & SIMONS, INC.

London and Amsterdam

COPYRIGHT © 1970 *by* Southern Illinois University Press
All rights reserved
Printed in the United States of America
Designed by Andor Braun
ISBN 0–8093–0473–2
Library of Congress Catalog Card Number: 78–123048

Contents

List of Illustrations

Preface

THE CENTENARY year is an especially auspicious time to launch a new series devoted to the publication of research and criticism of Charles Dickens. Public and scholarly interest in The Inimitable has been growing steadily since the 1930's, fostered by the Dickens Fellowship and the editors of *The Dickensian* and taken up in the last twenty years by dozens of younger scholars who feel that the true dimensions of Dickens are still to be discovered. They are demonstrating that he is a far more subtle writer than most earlier critics had suspected. It is true, of course, that a few critics like G. K. Chesterton knew that Dickens was England's finest and most rewarding novelist and that a corporal's guard of the faithful have always loved and appreciated Dickens, but it has remained for an increasingly large and dedicated group of scholars to expand that love and appreciation to formal analysis, research, and criticism.

Even a superficial investigation reveals that more than a hundred and fifty doctoral dissertations, more than twenty major books, and literally hundreds of fine articles on Dickens have appeared in the last two decades—all deepening and broadening our understanding of Dickens the man, Dickens the writer, and the age he lived in. Some of the most valuable work might be called "traditional scholarship," for example the classic biography of Edgar Johnson, K. J. Fielding's edition of the speeches and Harry Stone's edition of the uncollected writings in *Household Words,* the superb edition of Dickens' letters by Madeline House and Graham Storey, Kathleen Tillotson's definitive edition of *Oliver Twist*—all of which are not only monuments of scholarship but the indispensable tools for the development of further critical study. Much recent publication, especially by some of the younger investigators, might be called "experimental," at least in the sense that the approaches, techniques of analysis, angles of vision, and results have no exact parallels in earlier work. No one could possibly do justice to all those who have contributed to our knowledge of Dickens as a journalist, editor, public speaker, actor, social reformer, traveller, confidant; as a writer of novels, short stories, plays, editorials, speeches; as a man for all times and a man of his time. There have been perceptive analyses of the influence on Dickens of fairy tales, the stage, other novelists, his audience, his friends, his illustrators. Brilliant work has been done on Dickens as a creator and craftsman, notably the seminal studies by John Butt and Kathleen Tillotson. Equally informative have been studies of his reading, his knowledge of the science, politics, art and literature of the period, his involvement in reform movements, his iconographic eye. Such books and articles (and many others not mentioned) have immeasurably extended our knowledge of Dickens and the Victorian age. Even more, they both extended and sharpened study of the novel-as-genre. Thus the Dickensians are serving not only other Dickensians but all students of literature.

The *Dickens Studies Annual* was established by the editors and the Advisory Board to provide a major American outlet, open to scholars everywhere, for this activity. In part this is a response to the need for more space than can be provided in *The Dickensian* and *PMLA*, and in journals founded more recently, notably *Victorian Studies, Nineteenth-Century Fiction, Victorian Newsletter, Critical Quarterly, Review of English Literature,* and others. It seems generally agreed that Dickens scholars and critics of the novel can benefit from an annual which will accept articles of considerable length on any aspect of Dickens; there has been almost universal encouragement of the editors' intention to solicit and publish the finest examples of research and criticism of Dickens.

We hope this initial volume fulfills our intentions. Quite deliberately we selected for inclusion the work of both established scholars and the early work of yet unknown writers, articles on broad aspects and tight studies of single elements, iconographical and psychoanalytic studies of Dickens' mode of creation and his problems of structuring— attempting to provide a cross-section of modern critical work. Future volumes will continue to present articles which seek to discover the true dimensions of Charles Dickens.

Robert B. Partlow, Jr.

Carbondale, Illinois
16 March 1970

Notes on Contributors

ROBERT BARNARD is Universitetslektor at the University of Bergen, Norway, after having taught at the University of Australia. He has published previously in the *Review of English Literature* and is now at work on Mrs. Trollope and Mrs. Gore.

J. MIRIAM BENN is Lecturer at the Australian National University. She is completing studies of *Barnaby Rudge* and *Great Expectations*.

TREVOR BLOUNT is Professor of English at the University of Southampton. He has published many articles, especially on *Bleak House,* and his *Dickens: The Early Novels* appeared in 1968.

JANE RABB COHEN is an Instructor at Radcliffe. She has published articles on Keats, *Edwin Drood,* Dickens and Cruikshank, Dickens and Seymour, and is completing a book-length study of Dickens and his illustrators.

DUANE DEVRIES is an Assistant Professor at New York University. His edition of *Bleak House,* based on the first edition in parts, is scheduled for release in late 1970. He is also working on book-length studies of *Sketches by Boz* and the writing of *Bleak House.*

ANGUS EASSON, after completing his dissertation on *Little Dorrit,* became Lecturer at the University, Newcastle upon Tyne. His editions of *The Old Curiosity Shop* for Penguin and *Hard Times* for an experimental school series will probably be available when this volume appears.

MARGARET GANZ, Assistant Professor at Brooklyn College of the City University, has already published a fine book on Mrs. Gaskell and several articles on Dickens. She is at work on an extended study of Dickens' humor.

PAUL A. GOTTSCHALK is Assistant Professor at Cornell University. His chief interest is Shakespeare: he has published several articles, has just completed a full-length study of *Hamlet,* and has begun an analysis of the internal mimetic structures in Shakespeare.

LOUIS JAMES is Senior Lecturer at the University of Canterbury, but was serving as Visiting Professor of English at the University of South Carolina when he wrote this article. His best known book is *Fiction for the Working Man, 1830–1850,* but many readers know his articles on various phases of Victorian life. He is now preparing a book on Carlyle for the Routledge Critics Series, a nineteenth-century popular reader for Penguin, and a life of G. W. M. Reynolds.

LEONARD MANHEIM is Professor at the University of Hartford, and founder and editor of *Literature and Psychology* and the *Hartford Studies in Literature.* He has published numerous papers on the psychoanalytic theory of literature and is presently working on analyses of Dickens and Hawthorne.

JEROME MECKIER is Associate Professor at the University of Kentucky, former sub-editor of *Dickens Studies,* and present sub-editor of the *Dickens Studies Annual.* He has published articles on Aldous Huxley, T. S. Eliot, and Dickens, and his book on Huxley's novels has been released by Chatto and Windus.

ANNABEL M. PATTERSON, Associate Professor at Victoria College, the University of Toronto, has published articles on both Renaissance and Victorian literature. Her *Hermogenes and the Renaissance: Seven Ideas of Style* is on the fall list of the Princeton University Press.

JAMES R. REED, Assistant Professor at Wayne State University, has published articles on *Great Expectations* and *Nicholas Nickleby.*

LANCE SCHACHTERLE, now Assistant Professor at the Worcester Polytechnic Institute, was a doctoral candidate when his present article was accepted. He is now at work on the serial novel before Dickens.

MICHAEL STEIG, Associate Professor at Simon Fraser University, has published articles on Dickens, Samuel Warren, and the grotesque in fiction, much of which is embodied in his full-length study of the grotesque in Dickens, publication date not yet established. His next book will be an analysis of the relationship between Dickens and Phiz.

HARRY STONE, Professor at the San Fernando Valley State College, has authored more than forty articles on Dickens, edited *Charles Dickens' Uncollected Writings from "Household Words,"* contributed to *Charles Dickens (1812–1870): A Centenary Volume,* and is a member of the Advisory Board of the *Dickens Studies Annual*. He is currently working on a book entitled *Dickens and the Fairy Tale*.

HENRI A. TALON, Professor of English Literature at the University of Dijon, is the author of eight major books, including his works on Bunyan, Thackeray, D. H. Lawrence, and D. G. Rossetti. He has also produced editions of Bunyan and Byron and has contributed regularly to Continental and American journals. At present he is working on extended studies of Tennyson and of Thackeray.

DICKENS STUDIES ANNUAL

Harry Stone

THE UNKNOWN DICKENS

With a Sampling of Uncollected Writings

TO WRITE on Dickens at this particular moment is exciting and frustrating. It is exciting because so much that is fundamental—textually, critically, historically—remains to be done. It is exciting also because we are at last sufficiently distanced from Dickens' impact upon his era to assess his writings with dispassion. This new assessment—one might think of it as the first definitive phase in Dickens' ultimate historical fame, the first phase free from the taint of mere submission or rebellion—has been going on for a generation now and has not yet culminated. I am not implying that this phase will fix Dickens' fame. Future ages will read his writings with different eyes and different needs—after all, that they should want and be able to do so is a *sine qua non* of the kind of fame I am talking about. I am simply stating that to have a part in this first fundamental reassessment of a very great writer, a writer of worldwide reputation and importance, to contribute to the documents and judgments upon which that assessment is based, perhaps even to help shape the character and outcome of that assessment, is a very exciting thing for a critic and scholar.

But what appears as an exciting opportunity from one perspective can loom as a frustrating difficulty from another point of view. What is opportunity for the editor—the chance to establish the text of a major novel, or to produce a definitive edition of the letters—is frustration for the reader or critic or biographer who must make do without these essentials, or try as best he can, by an inordinate expenditure of time and effort, to make up for these lacks. We are now in the very slow process of getting a reliable (but unannotated) text of the novels, and a comprehensive, well-annotated edition of the letters. There are many other major projects, projects that would be of incalculable benefit to students of Dickens, that should be undertaken: a definitive bibliography, for example, and a concordance to the writings. But strange to say, an even more basic task remains to be completed: we have not yet established the canon of Dickens' writings.

Most literary experts—indeed many Dickens experts—are astonished to learn that there is an unknown Dickens, a Dickens who has never been identified or collected. If I may be forgiven for using a personal experience, I should like to relate an anecdote about this unknown Dickens which underscores what I have been saying. Last year I published a two-volume edition entitled *Charles Dickens' Uncollected Writings from "Household Words" (1850–1859)*. This edition contains some seventy-eight hitherto unidentified or uncollected pieces, more than a quarter of a million words written by Dickens or by Dickens and a collaborator during the period when he was also writing *David Copperfield, Bleak House, Hard Times,* and *Little Dorrit.* These anonymous pieces, covering virtually every subject that interested him and displaying virtually all his modes and moods, were no mere scraps and jottings; they were full-fledged articles published under his own supervision and cachet, and they contained passage after passage of vintage Dickens.

When I originally approached a publisher with the idea of collecting these pieces, my proposal was received with incredulity. "You mean," he said in amazement, "there are writings by Dickens—really substantiated writings by Dickens—that have never been identified or collected?" I assured him there were. "I can't believe it," he said. I then showed him some of the pieces, read him passages that no one but Dickens ever could or did write, told him about the *Household Words* Office Book that put the identification beyond any doubt. His attitude changed from incredulity to suspicion. "Why," he asked, "haven't they been collected before? You mean to tell me they have been sitting there for over a hundred years and no one has bothered with them? You mean there is a new book by Dickens here and it's just been sitting here? You mean *Dickens.* . . . I mean, after all, *Dickens.* . . . You know, *Dickens.* . . ." His voice trailed off in disbelief.

When the book came out it received prominent attention in the mass media—in the major newspapers and the great national magazines. *Look* magazine, which devoted most of its book section to the edition, began its review with the following sentence: "Disgruntled readers who complain that they haven't read a good book since Dickens thoughtlessly died in the middle of *Edwin Drood* will be glad to hear that, his death notwithstanding, Mr. Dickens has a new book on the market." Now this attention in these quarters connoted, I think, two things. First, it was a testimony to the wide and enduring interest in Dickens' writings. Second, it was a sign of astonishment—of astonishment that had real news value —that major new writings by Dickens could still turn up. They could, and they still can. Indeed I shall devote the rest of this paper to describing where some of these lost writings are to be found, and to retrieving another sampling of them from their century-long languishment. That this can still be done is one reason why it is exciting to work on Dickens at this time. Think how Shakespeare scholars would feel if they could still turn up tens of thousands of new lines from the master's prime.

— 2 —

Most examples of these lost writings are to be found in Dickens' periodical works. In the earlier years the writings are likely to be unidentified contributions to newspapers and magazines—in the 1830's contributions to the *Morning Chronicle* (which employed Dickens as a reporter); in the late 1830's and the 1840's contributions to the *Examiner* (which was edited during this period by Dickens' closest friend, John Forster); and in the mid-1840's contributions to the *Daily News* (which was founded and briefly edited by Dickens). In the later years—the 1850's and 1860's—the new writings are more likely to emerge from what Dickens called his "composite" or collaborative writings. They will be found for the most part in *Household Words, All the Year Round,* the Christmas writings (mostly the extra Christmas numbers of *Household Words* and *All the Year Round*), and a variety of dramatic pieces (such as Wilkie Collins' *The Lighthouse*).[1] There are undoubtedly unidentified pieces elsewhere—stray contributions, squibs, and the like—but the above are the main locations where such lost writings are to be found in abundance.

In the case of the very early journalism, some contributions can be identified by references in Dickens' letters, and many have been so identified by the editors of the Pilgrim *Letters*. With the *Examiner* the letters are also helpful, but since most of the externally identifiable pieces have already been collected, internal evidence here takes on more importance.[2] In fact, meticulous use of internal evidence is likely to pay dividends in recovered writings from a variety of sources, and on many occasions such evidence leads to external verifications which would otherwise go unnoticed. This is not surprising; nor is the fact that some veritable writings by Dickens are unaccompanied by external evidence. Much of Dickens' contact with his early editors, with Forster, and with staff members of *Household Words* and *All the Year Round* was through weekly, sometimes daily, conferences and conversations. Assignments would be agreed upon verbally, copy turned in by hand. Casual pieces identifiable through letters or manuscripts or proofs are the chance exceptions rather than the rule, and while utmost caution must be observed when external evidence is lacking, there are unquestionably gems as well as workaday efforts waiting to be discovered.

Some of the early pieces which have been and will be recovered are brief notices or passing observations—short reviews of plays, sketchy accounts of performances, comments on topical trends or problems. They are not deathless masterpieces, but they are often more important than they seem at first glance. At the very least they are part of the canon; they also add to the store of Dickensian phrasings or observations, and they frequently put him on record in respect to people, issues, or ideas where before the record was blank. But aside from these considerations, we have all come to realize how the most ordinary evidence—a stray allusion, a casual remark, even when inconsequential in its own context—can solve a long-standing riddle in some other context or provide the answers to questions that only the future will ask.

Dickens' many uncollected reviews of dramatic performances, mostly from his early years, are a good example of what can emerge from such stray pieces. Such reviews locate him on particular nights and give us details about specific performances, but, much more important, they provide us with early examples of Dickens' critical values and judgments. This evidence is invaluable, for Dickens was chronically loath to theorize about art; he felt that works of art should be self-contained and should speak for themselves. With his own writings it was only when challenged or gravely misunderstood, or when discussing his work in progress with Forster or a fellow novelist, that he dealt with the theoretical considerations that motivated his artistic choices. But in these early reviews and pieces of set criticism, his critical principles emerge directly, and such writings, along with his prefaces, his many letters of private criticism, and his manuscripts and proofs can help us understand Dickens' aesthetic—an area of great importance that has received very little attention.

So much for just one use to which these early pieces can be put. My primary task here, however, is to discuss where these new writings are to be found and how they may be identified, and to reprint a sampling of them. The process of identifying the new writings of the middle period—mainly pieces published in *Household Words*—is comparatively simple. The official ledger of *Household Words,* usually called the "Office Book" or "Contributors' Book," is extant, and this ledger identifies the author or authors of virtually every article in the periodical and gives other information as well. With the publication of my edition of Dickens' uncollected writings from *Household Words,* what can be further recovered from this periodical is probably small, though new letters and other sources may clinch the identification of interpolated paragraphs here or there and perhaps some longer passages as well. The possibility of additional discoveries, even with *Household Words,* always remains, owing to Dickens' ubiquitous editorial intervention, an intervention that often went unrecorded. In those situations in which Dickens' changes were significant and yet were not deemed extensive enough to warrant his being entered in the Contributors' Book as joint author, one must depend upon surviving accidental evidence—in letters, proofs, memoirs, or what not—in order to make definitive identificaton possible.

Similar difficulties occur when making specific passage, word, or phrase attributions in the many "composite" articles that Dickens contributed to *Household Words*. The extent of Dickens' contribution to such articles varies, though in articles planned for joint authorship it usually runs to roughly one half. The gross fact of such authorship is not a problem, for the Contributors' Book lists all authors in each collaborative piece. But more specific internal attribution is often made very difficult by Dickens' practice of going over the entire proof, not simply his own sections, deftly weaving all portions together, and changing his collaborators' sections or adding to them at will.

With *All the Year Round,* the problems of identification and attribution are even more difficult, for its Contributors' Book has apparently been lost or destroyed. Fortunately most, possibly all, of Dickens' solo contributions have been identified, and some of his composite pieces as well. Dickens himself collected many of the former in his two *Uncommercial Traveller* volumes (1861 and 1868). After his death, a number of additional contributions were collected and included in editions of his *Works*. Then in 1900, Frederic G. Kitton, who had access to a marked office set of *All the Year Round*—this set too has disappeared—identified in his *The Minor Writings of Charles Dickens* presumably all of Dickens' additional solo contributions, almost all of which were collected by B. W. Matz in the *Miscellaneous Papers* (1908) issued in conjunction with the National Edition of Dickens' *Works*. There are undoubtedly interpolations and some composite articles yet to be identified, and it should be possible, by virtue of extant proofs, memoirs, Dickens' correspondence, the correspondence of contributors, and the documents recorded in the Letter Press Books of business correspondence for *All the Year Round* (one volume of which survives in the Huntington Library), to track some of these writings down.[3]

There remains one other important source from which hitherto unidentified writings by Dickens may be retrieved—the extra Christmas numbers of *All the Year Round*. These numbers, like the Christmas numbers of *Household Words*, usually consisted of a framework into which a series of self-contained stories could be inserted. Dickens always conceived the framework, wrote most of it, wrote one or more of the interpolated stories, and wrote all or most of the introductory, concluding, and transition passages which integrated the interpolated tales. After the first few extra Christmas numbers of *Household Words*, Dickens gave a good deal of attention to the framework, sought to make it an outstanding feature of the number, and tried to make the interpolated stories carry out—or at least blend with—the scheme of the framework.

He attempted to achieve this end by sending identical memos to a group of regular contributors. These memos outlined the framework situation, suggested the kinds of narrators and stories that would be appropriate, and solicited contributions. When the stories came in Dickens would select the best, edit them very freely, fit them into the framework by writing introductory and bridging passages, and bind the whole together by other interpolations or modifications. In some of the later frameworks he wrote sections, sometimes whole chapters, in collaboration with Wilkie Collins, and in two instances, *The Perils of Certain English Prisoners* (1857) and *No Thoroughfare* (1867), he and Collins wrote the entire number, dispensing with the interpolated stories altogether.

Except for *Mugby Junction* (1866) and *No Thoroughfare* (1867), all the extra Christmas numbers of *Household Words* and *All the Year Round* were issued without any indication on the numbers themselves as to who wrote what, or even as to who contributed. However, in 1858, in *Reprinted Pieces*, Dickens collected his contributions to three Christmas numbers, and in 1867, in connection with the preparation of the American Diamond Edition of his *Works*, he extracted his chief contributions to seven additional numbers, making such adjustments in his segments as would enable them to stand alone. These extracts, plus similar extracts from other Christmas numbers, usually all collected under the generic title *Christmas Stories*, were later reprinted in standard editions of the *Collected Works*. But in making his extracts Dickens abandoned much that he had written: the introductory and concluding bridges, the transitions, the interpolations and additions, and a number of long composite sections, sometimes whole chapters.

In the case of *Household Words*, the Office Book enables one to determine not only the author or authors of each article in each regular number, but the author or authors of each major segment of each extra Christmas number—and one can use other means to identify the bridging, transition, modifying, and composite sections that are by Dickens.[4] For the extra Christmas numbers of *All the Year Round*, on the other hand, one must depend for primary identification upon an erratic secondary source: the information Kitton gleaned from his perusal of a marked office set and his unsystematic transmittal of that information. But as it happens there is another source which can be used to identify the authors of these pieces, a source which bears Dickens' own cachet. In December 1868 Dickens collected the extra Christmas numbers of *All the Year Round* and reissued them in a single volume, reprinted from the original stereotype plates. This volume, now quite rare, bears the conjoint imprint of the Offices of *All the Year Round* and Chapman & Hall, and was entitled *The Christmas Numbers of All the Year Round Conducted by Charles Dickens*.[5] What makes the edition so valuable, how-

THE HAUNTED HOUSE.

THE EXTRA CHRISTMAS NUMBER OF **ALL THE YEAR ROUND.**

CONDUCTED BY CHARLES DICKENS.

CONTAINING THE AMOUNT OF TWO ORDINARY NUMBERS.

CHRISTMAS, 1859.

Price
4d.

INDEX.

THE MORTALS IN THE HOUSE.

UNDER none of the accredited ghostly circumstances, and environed by none of the conventional ghostly surroundings, did I first make acquaintance with the house which is the subject of this Christmas piece. I saw it in the daylight, with the sun upon it. There was no wind, no rain, no lightning, no thunder, no awful or unwonted circumstance, of any kind, to heighten its effect. More than that: I had come to it direct from a railway station; it was not more than a mile distant from the railway station; and, as I stood outside the house, looking back upon the way I had come, I could see the goods train running smoothly along the embankment in the valley. I will not say that everything was utterly common-place, because I doubt if anything can be that, except to utterly common-place people—and there my vanity steps in; but, I will take it on myself to say that anybody might see the house as I saw it, any fine autumn morning.

The manner of my lighting on it was this.

I was travelling towards London out of the North, intending to stop by the way, to look at the house. My health required a temporary residence in the country; and a friend of mine who knew that, and who had happened to drive past the house, had written to me to suggest it as a likely place. I had got into the train at midnight, and had fallen asleep, and had woke up and had sat looking out of window at the brilliant Northern Lights in the sky, and had fallen asleep again, and had woke up again to find the night gone, with the usual discontented conviction on me that I hadn't been to sleep at all;—upon which question, in the first imbecility of that condition, I am ashamed to believe that I would have done wager by battle with the man who sat opposite me. That opposite man had had, through the night—as that opposite man always has—several legs too many, and all of them too long. In addition to this unreasonable conduct (which was only to be expected of him), he had had a pencil and a pocket-book, and had been perpetually listening and taking notes. It had appeared to me that these aggravating notes related to the jolts and bumps of the carriage, and I should have resigned myself to his taking them, under a general supposition that he was in the civil-engineering way of life, if he had not sat staring straight over my head whenever he listened. He was a goggle-eyed gentleman of a perplexed aspect, and his demeanour became unbearable.

It was a cold, dead morning (the sun not being up yet), and when I had out-watched the paling light of the fires of the iron country, and the curtain of heavy smoke that hung at once between me and the stars and between me and the day, I turned to my fellow-traveller and said:

"I *beg* your pardon, sir, but do you observe anything particular in me?" For, really, he appeared to be taking down, either my travelling-cap or my hair, with a minuteness that was a liberty.

The goggle-eyed gentleman withdrew his eyes from behind me, as if the back of the carriage were a hundred miles off, and said, with a lofty look of compassion for my insignificance:

"In you, sir?—B."

"B, sir?" said I, growing warm.

"I have nothing to do with you, sir," returned the gentleman; "pray let me listen—O."

He enunciated this vowel after a pause, and noted it down.

At first I was alarmed, for an Express lunatic and no communication with the guard, is a serious position. The thought came to my relief that the gentleman might be what is popularly called a Rapper: one of a sect (some of) whom I have the highest respect, but whom I don't believe in. I was going to ask him the question, when he took the bread out of my mouth.

FRONT PAGE OF *The Haunted House*

Showing how the contents were listed with no indication of authorship.

ever, is the fact, apparently unknown to Kitton, that most copies of the volume contained a Contents page which listed the author or authors of each section of each number.[6]

In the case of *The Haunted House* (1859), the first extra Christmas number of *All the Year Round,* and the number I shall concentrate on in what follows, both Kitton and the Contents page identify Dickens as the sole author of "The Ghost in the Corner Room," the concluding segment of *The Haunted House*—yet this segment, for reasons which will soon become clear, has hitherto been excluded from Dickens' *Collected Works.* Kitton labeled other excluded passages—the passages which introduce the interpolated stories, for example—as also solely by Dickens, but he failed to notice still other excluded passages which are assuredly by Dickens. I shall identify and reprint all these uncollected passages in a moment, but first I should like to put them and the whole of *The Haunted House* in context.

– *3* –

The Haunted House tells the story of how the narrator, Joe, and his sister, Patty, accompanied by servants, go down to a decaying, reputedly haunted house with the purpose of living in it and demonstrating that it is not in the least bit haunted. The experiment does not work. The servants are soon hearing strange noises and seeing strange sights, and they so infect one another with fears and fantasies that the narrator sends them packing and invites in their place some stalwart friends who agree to form a self-contained society and test the house rigorously by living in it for three months. The friends arrive late in November, each is assigned a bedroom, and each agrees to watch in his room every night from then until Twelfth Night, communicating what he sees during the interval to no one. On Twelfth Night, in accordance with their agreement, they gather together, disclose what they have seen—in this way the interpolated stories are introduced—celebrate the conclusion of their adventures, live out the remainder of their term in the house, and then go their separate ways.

The Haunted House was suggested to Dickens by a curious succession of incidents. In August 1859 there appeared in *All the Year Round* a series of three articles entitled "A Physician's Ghosts." These articles, while accepting certain kinds of psychic phenomena as authentic, took a skeptical position on ghosts, spirits, hauntings, and the like. Early in September 1859, William Howitt, an acquaintance of Dickens, a spiritualist—Dickens dubbed him the "arch-rapper of rappers"—and earlier a fairly frequent contributor to *Household Words,* wrote Dickens a letter objecting to the articles and asking him what he thought of the War Office Ghost—the reputed ghost of an officer killed in the Crimea who

CONTENTS.

THE HAUNTED HOUSE.

A MESSAGE FROM THE SEA.

TOM TIDDLER'S GROUND.

SOMEBODY'S LUGGAGE.

MRS. LIRRIPER'S LODGINGS.

MRS. LIRRIPER'S LEGACY.

DOCTOR MARIGOLD'S PRESCRIPTIONS.

MUGBY JUNCTION.

AND

NO THOROUGHFARE.

By CHARLES DICKENS AND WILKIE COLLINS

THE CONTENTS PAGE

Issued as part of the collected edition (1868) of the extra Christmas numbers of *All the Year Round*. This page, hitherto neglected, is the primary record of authorship for the Christmas numbers in question and the only record publicly sanctioned by Dickens.

had supposedly forced the War Office to correct its erroneous record of the date of his death. In his reply to Howitt, Dickens wrote (6 September 1859) :

> My own mind is perfectly unprejudiced and impressible on the subject. I do not in the least pretend that such things are not. But I positively object, on most matters, to be thought for, or— if I may use the odd expression—asserted down. And I have not yet met with any Ghost Story that was proved to me, or that had not the noticeable peculiarity in it—that the alteration of some slight circumstance would bring it within the range of common natural probabilities. I have always had a strong interest in the subject, and never knowingly lose an opportunity of pursuing it. But I think the testimony which I cannot cross-examine, suffi- ciently loose, to justify me in requiring to see and hear the modern witnesses with my own senses, and then to be reasonably sure that they were not suffering under a disordered condition of the nerves or senses, which is known to be a common disease of many phases.[7]

Upon receiving this letter, Howitt responded in a way that Dickens deemed inexcusable—he published his own letter and described Dick- ens' reply. To compound matters, Howitt chose the *Spiritual Telegraph* as his instrument of response, and the *Spiritual Telegraph,* so Dickens wrote his brother (2 November 1859) , was nothing more than a "periodi- cal curlpaper." But Howitt was not yet done. In a subsequent letter to Dickens, he apparently sought to meet Dickens' demand for "modern witnesses" by citing the evidence of haunted houses, for on 31 October 1859 Dickens wrote him again, and said, "if you know of any haunted house whatsoever within the limits of the United Kingdom where no- body can live, eat, drink, sit, stand, lie or sleep, without spirit-molesta- tion, I believe I can produce a gentleman [John Hollingshead] who will readily try its effect in his own person." The correspondence continued and became more and more farcical, Howitt pursuing the subject earnestly, Dickens responding with growing impatience and satire. When Howitt sent Dickens a list of haunted houses, including a public house in London, Dickens asked for the exact address, and pledged (8 Novem- ber 1859) "to try to get the landlord's consent to the House's being ex- orcised," adding that he had hopes of succeeding, since "I suppose the restoration of the Goodwill to be worth something to him." Hollings- head went to the tavern in question and found it a "tumble-down pot- house." The house was haunted truly enough, but only "by the claims of brewers and distillers." [8]

By 15 November, the correspondence with Howitt was concentrat- ing on another area, Hertfordshire, and Dickens was writing about "an idea of taking the haunted House at Cheshunt altogether." Kitton, without giving his source, says that Dickens, accompanied by W. H. Wills, Wilkie Collins, and John Hollingshead, went to Cheshunt, visited the house, and that Dickens subsequently wrote Howitt to say that the house had been greatly enlarged, commanded a high rent, "and is no more disturbed than this house of mine." [9] This visit is corroborated by Hollingshead who gave an account of the adventure many years later and added a number of details.[10] Collins and Wills, according to Hollingshead, went down to Cheshunt in a brougham, and took with them a supply of fish, "as Dickens did not care to trust altogether to the local hotel or inn." Meanwhile, Dickens and Hollingshead set off to walk the distance, sixteen miles at a swift Dickensian clip. When they arrived at Cheshunt, they foregathered with Collins and Wills and proceeded with their quest, but they could find no one who had ever heard of a haunted house. Then, after much enquiry, they unearthed an old resident who recalled dimly that thirty years earlier a certain house had a vague reputation for unspecified ghosts, but alas, the house had long since been pulled down and a semidetached villa, "worthy of Bayswater," stood in its place. Dickens listened to this testimony, treated his Cheshunt informant to a "friendly quart," and then went off to dine elaborately with his three companions—"the ale," adds Hollingshead, "was nectar."

Unpublished letters make it clear that Dickens visited Cheshunt about 12 December 1859, but whether or not he entered the "haunted" house is unrecorded.[11] On 17 December 1859, he wrote and told Howitt that he had been to Cheshunt. Then he continued: "I can hear of no one at Cheshunt who ever heard of anything worse in it [the house] during Mr. Chapman's occupancy, than rats, and a servant (one Frank by name), said to have had a skilful way of poaching for rabbits at untimely hours." Shortly after the middle of December 1859, Howitt read *The Haunted House* and wrote Dickens an indignant letter protesting, among other things, his use of the Cheshunt residence in the Christmas number. Dickens replied (21 December 1859) that the house in *The Haunted House* was quite distinct from the Cheshunt house, that he had not gone to Cheshunt to make enquiries until the day before the Christmas number was published, that he cannot oblige Howitt by saying that he found a house with a reputation of *once* being haunted, for he found nothing of the sort; he found instead that the house in which Mr. Chapman had lived for four years was now "altered, enlarged, increased in rent, and prosperously inhabited"—nothing else.[12] Howitt countered by publishing a letter in the December 1859 *Critic* in which he quoted from Dickens' letter of 17 December 1859 and defended the authenticity of the Cheshunt house as a haunted house. He also allowed Thomas Shorter, the editor of the *Spiritual Magazine,* to combine a partisan account of the dispute, entitled "Mr. Howitt and Mr. Dickens" (January 1860), with an attack on *The Haunted House* and a challenge to Dickens to conduct further investigations. Dickens did not deign to reply, and there the matter seemed to rest, but it had an interesting coda.

Four years later, Howitt produced a two-volume work of more than nine hundred pages entitled *The History of the Supernatural in All Ages and Nations, and in All Churches, Christian and Pagan: Demonstrating a Universal Faith* (1863). In his book he expatiated unrepentantly on haunted houses, but worse still, from Dickens' point of view, he testified blithely to the veritable hauntings of the Cheshunt house. According to Howitt, the disturbances in the Cheshunt house were so pervasive and so persistent that they drove out tenant after tenant. The final result was that the house had stood empty for years. Howitt's only concession to Dickens' evidence came in his concluding sentence. The Cheshunt house, he admitted, "has recently been partly pulled down and rebuilt, and it would seem that this alteration has broken the spiritual spell, for it is now inhabited and reported free from haunting." [13] Dickens, thoroughly provoked by this intransigence, returned to the attack. In *All the Year Round* for 21 March 1863, in an article called "Rather a Strong Dose," he castigated Howitt and his book. In his article he pointed out that a "champion" haunted house "represented to have been closed and ruined for years" proved, after "one day's inquiry by four gentlemen associated with this Journal, and one hour's reference to the local Rate-books," to be a figment of Howitt's imagination. Obviously Dickens' antagonism and exasperation were still fresh.[14]

In September and October 1859, those feelings were fresher still. It is clear that the series of antihaunting articles in *All the Year Round*, Howitt's demurrers regarding them, the ensuing correspondence, Howitt's violation of that correspondence, and the negotiations regarding a prospective visit to a haunted house, provided Dickens with the motivation, the idea, and much of the material for *The Haunted House*. The gestation of the number was exceedingly rapid. Long before the end of November, long before the visit to Cheshunt actually took place, the idea for the Christmas number had been fixed upon and the plan of the work circulated to prospective contributors. By late November Dickens was complaining to Forster: "As yet not a story has come to me in the least belonging to the idea (the simplest in the world; which I myself described in writing, in the most elaborate manner); and every one of them turns, by a strange fatality, on a criminal trial!"

Ultimately two criminal trials appeared in *The Haunted House*: one trial, rather peripherally, in Sala's contribution; the other trial, much more importantly, in Mrs. Gaskell's story. How Dickens accomplished this winnowing—whether by prescription, cutting, rewriting, substitution, or a combination of these methods—is unclear. What is clear is that the published version of *The Haunted House* consisted of eight sections, as follows: "The Mortals in the House" by Dickens, "The Ghost in the Clock Room" by Hesba Stretton (pen name of Sarah Smith), "The Ghost in the Double Room" by George Augustus Sala, "The Ghost in the Picture Room" by Adelaide Anne Procter, "The Ghost in the Cupboard Room" by Wilkie Collins, "The Ghost in Master B.'s Room" by Dickens, "The Ghost in the Garden Room" by Mrs. Gaskell, and "The Ghost in the Corner Room" by Dickens. Only "The Mortals in the House" and "The Ghost in Master B.'s Room" are included in editions of Dickens' *Collected Works*. Dickens' introductions to the other segments, his interpolation of certain transitional passages, and his concluding contribution to the entire number—all these have been lost to the Dickens canon.

That the concluding contribution, "The Ghost in the Corner Room," is by Dickens and solely by him is beyond reasonable doubt, identified as it is both by Kitton and Dickens' own 1868 Contents page. Dickens almost certainly left this segment uncollected because much of it was germane to segments of *The Haunted House* not by him. Similarly there can be little question but that the introductory passages are solely by him. Kitton, presumably basing his assertion on the vanished office set, states categorically that this is so. There is other evidence as well. The introductory passages are different in style and function from the stories they introduce and are isolated from the stories typographically, both through spacing and by being set in full-page lines instead of double columns. It is hard to believe that Dickens, the virtuoso "Conductor," delegated these crucial sections to someone else and then underlined their importance by emphasizing them typographically, but there are other, less psychological reasons (if reasons beyond the testimony of the office set are needed) for believing that Dickens himself composed these introductory passages. The passages are written in the guise of the narrator, Dickens' role throughout the number; they provide the integrating framework for the number, a framework that Dickens usually conceived and wrote himself; they are brief and yet central to the whole—they would require more effort and more explanation on Dickens' part to delegate than to write himself; and finally, they are written in a style that is everywhere thoroughly Dickensian.

The first of these lost writings, a transition rather than an introductory passage, occupied the last few lines of "The Mortals in the House," Dickens' opening contribution to *The Haunted House*. Dickens excised this passage when he collected his Christmas stories, obviously because the transition was pertinent to the scheme of *The Haunted House* and not to the scheme of his two contributions. The passage bridged the time between late November, when the occupants of the house began their watch, and Twelfth Night, when they recounted their experiences; it also set the stage for the introduction of the first interpolated story. Here is the passage, the first of Dickens' uncollected contributions to *The Haunted House*:

> Christmas came, and we had noble Christmas fare ("all hands" had been pressed for the pudding), and Twelfth Night came, and our store of mincemeat was ample to hold out to the last day of our time, and our cake was quite a glorious sight. It was then, as we all sat round the table and the fire, that I recited the terms of our compact, and called, first, for

THE GHOST IN THE CLOCK ROOM.

The next uncollected segment, the first of the lost introductions by Dickens, preceded "The Ghost in the Clock Room," Hesba Stretton's contribution to *The Haunted House*. Owing to a seemingly unnecessary contrivance, "The Ghost in the Clock Room" is told by John Herschel rather than his wife, though the story is hers and she is present at the telling. Dickens himself was probably responsible for this complication, and his motivation in introducing this artificiality requires a few words of explanation. It seems clear from what Dickens said in his note to Forster already quoted, from the evidence of the stories themselves, and from the introductions that Dickens wrote for them, that the memo he circulated to prospective contributors to *The Haunted House* had not been well understood. The stories which came in were ordinary stories, not stories which exemplified that the house, if haunted at all, was haunted by the imaginations and remembrances of its present occupants. The latter notion seems to have been what Dickens was striving for: that ghosts and haunted houses are claptrap, that we are all haunted, but haunted by our past, by our selves, not by wandering spirits. This is the burden of Dickens' opening contribution ("The Mortals in the House") which, among other things, lampoons the gullibility and banality of spiritualists —a ludicrous Howitt-like spiritualist appears in the opening pages; and this is why at the outset Dickens offers naturalistic or psychological explanations for all of the supposedly supernatural phenomena connected with the "haunted" house; finally, this is the burden, as we shall see, of the last line of *The Haunted House*, a line that occurs in Dickens' hitherto lost conclusion.

Dickens' own story for *The Haunted House*, "The Ghost in Master B.'s Room," carries out his idea superbly, for the ghost that haunts the narrator's bedroom proves to be a montage of living memories rising up from the narrator's dead self (actually autobiographical vignettes from Dickens' life). These memories are glimpsed in Master B.'s mirror as the narrator (who occupies Master B.'s room) shaves himself. But the other contributors simply told conventional tales and failed to link them effectively to subsequent "hauntings" or present surroundings.

This unexpected discontinuity galled Dickens ("not a story has come to me in the least belonging to the idea . . . which I myself described in writing") and he struggled in his introductions, and probably in his editing of the stories themselves, to relate each contribution to his central idea. This attempt, as already suggested, sometimes heaped artificiality upon artificiality. Dickens' introduction to Hesba Stretton's story is a case in point. Of necessity his introduction had to posit (since Miss Stretton's story demanded it) that the spirit "haunting" the Clock Room was the former wayward spirit of John Herschel's wife. But for a Victorian audience this idea introduced a potentially dangerous, or at least an indelicate, situation: a formerly wayward woman brazenly telling about her own waywardness. As a consequence, though the story is the wife's and is told in the first person, Dickens has the husband, to save his wife embarrassment, stipulate that he will recount her story in the guise of her spirit. Danger was averted, but only at the expense of narrative simplicity. Here is Dickens' introduction to "The Ghost in the Clock Room," hitherto uncollected:

THE GHOST IN THE CLOCK ROOM

MY cousin, John Herschel, turned rather red, and turned rather white, and said he could not deny that his room had been haunted. The Spirit of a woman had pervaded it. On being asked by several voices whether the Spirit had taken any terrible or ugly shape, my cousin drew his wife's arm through his own, and said decidedly, "No." To the question, had his wife been aware of the Spirit? he answered, "Yes." Had it spoken? "Oh dear, yes!" As to the question, "What did it say?" he replied apologetically, that he could have wished his wife would have undertaken the answer, for she would have executed it much better than he. However, she had made him promise to be the mouthpiece of the Spirit, and was very anxious that he should withhold nothing; so, he would do his best, subject to her correction. "Suppose the Spirit," added my cousin, as he finally prepared himself for beginning, "to be my wife here, sitting among us."

And at this point the wife's first-person story—told by her husband—begins with, "I was an orphan from my infancy, with six elder half-sisters."

The next uncollected introduction is to the second interpolated story, a story contributed by George Augustus Sala. This story is told by Alfred Starling, the occupant of the Double Room. Dickens introduced the story as follows:

THE GHOST IN THE DOUBLE ROOM

WAS the next Ghost on my list. I had noted the rooms down
in the order in which they were drawn, and this was the order we
were to follow. I invoked the Spectre of the Double Room, with
the least possible delay, because we all observed John Herschel's
wife to be much affected, and we all refrained, as if by common
consent, from glancing at one another. Alfred Starling, with the
tact and good feeling which are never wanting in him, briskly
responded to my call, and declared the Double Room to be
haunted by the Ghost of the Ague.

"What is the Ghost of the Ague like?" asked every one, when
there had been a laugh.

"Like?" said Alfred. "Like the Ague."

"What is the Ague like?" asked somebody.

"Don't you know?" said Alfred. "I'll tell you."

Hereupon Sala told a light, amusing story about a young man who
boards a train on Christmas eve to visit his betrothed and is suddenly afflicted with the ague. He tries to explain his predicament to everyone
he meets but finds that the world attributes his infirmity to drunkenness,
cowardice, and the like, with the result that he undergoes a series of
ludicrous adventures. Ultimately Sala brought his hero to trial for supposed robbery, but solved his hero's dilemma and ended the story by
having him wake up—he had fallen asleep on the shaking train and
dreamed his ague-filled adventures. The moment of awakening is separated from the rest of the text and emphasized typographically, thus:

I WOKE.

After awaking, the protagonist gets off the train, visits his beloved, mar-
ries her, and is about "to live happy ever afterwards when"—he wakes
again, an awakening accompanied by a second typographical separation
and emphasis.

The idea of the second awakening and the text following the second
typographical break were probably by Dickens, for the story proper ends
with "happy ever afterwards"; what follows returns the reader to the
haunted house and sets the mood for the next interpolated story—in
other words, the second awakening is all framework. But aside from this,
and aside from the unlikelihood that Sala would have planned to over-
turn the conclusion of his story twice using the same device, the second
awakening is different in tone, tendency, and style from all that comes
before it. Here is the final conclusion, probably by Dickens, and hitherto
unidentified:

WILLIAM HOWITT C.1859, AGE 67

Showing Howitt about the time of his controversy with Dickens regarding
haunted houses (Harry Stone, "The Unknown Dickens").

CHARLES DICKENS IN 1858, AGE 46

Showing Dickens about the time of the haunted-house controversy.
(Harry Stone, "The Unknown Dickens")

I WOKE AGAIN

—really did wake in bed in this Haunted House—and found that I had been very much shaken on the railway coming down, and that there was no marriage, no Tilly, no Mary Seaton, no Van Plank, no anything but myself and the Ghost of the Ague, and the two inner windows of the Double Room rattling like the ghosts of two departed watchmen who wanted spiritual assistance to carry me to the dead and gone old Watch-house.

The next segment of *The Haunted House,* told by Belinda, the occupant of the Picture Room, is a poem by Adelaide Anne Procter. The poem opens with Belinda looking at the portrait of a nun which is hanging in her room. The portrait reminds her of an old miraculous saint's legend, and soon she is retelling the old story. Dickens launched this segment of *The Haunted House* with a single sentence, hitherto, of course, also uncollected:

THE GHOST IN THE PICTURE ROOM

BELINDA, with a modest self-possession quite her own, promptly answered for this Spectre in a low, clear voice:[15]

Miss Procter's poem was followed by Wilkie Collins' story, told in the guise of Nat Beaver, the captain of a merchantman, and comrade to Jack Governor, a naval officer. Mr. Beaver, who occupies the Cupboard Room, and sometimes has "a curious nervousness about him, apparently the lingering result of some old illness," tells a horrific Poe-esque tale of being tied in the black hold of a ship and made to watch as a slowly burning candle, fused to an explosive charge, consumes the last hours of his life. Dickens prefaced the story with the following uncollected introduction:

THE GHOST IN THE CUPBOARD ROOM

MR. BEAVER, on being "spoke" (as his friend and ally, Jack Governor, called it), turned out of an imaginary hammock with the greatest promptitude, and went straight on duty. "As it's Nat Beaver's watch," said he, "there shall be no skulking." Jack looked at me, with an expectant and admiring turn of his eye on Mr. Beaver, full of complimentary implication. I noticed, by the way, that Jack, in a naval absence of mind with which he is greatly troubled at times, had his arm round my sister's waist. Perhaps this complaint originates in an old nautical requirement of having something to hold on by.

These were the terms of Mr. Beaver's revelation to us.

At this point, without further ado, Wilkie Collins' narrative commences.

The next story, "The Ghost in Master B.'s Room," is told by Joe, the narrator of *The Haunted House*. Dickens himself, of course, undertook this role and also wrote this story; I have already mentioned the series of autobiographical vignettes he chose to tell. The prologue he wrote for his contribution is the briefest of all the introductions in *The Haunted House*, and consists simply of the following uncollected sentence:

THE GHOST IN MASTER B.'S ROOM

IT being now my own turn, I "took the word," as the French say, and went on.

"The Ghost in Master B.'s Room" was followed by Mrs. Gaskell's contribution, told by Mr. Undery, the occupant of the Garden Room. Mr. Undery is friend and solicitor to the narrator of *The Haunted House*. Dickens' choice of the name Undery was an inside joke, for Dickens' own solicitor, also a good friend, was Frederic Ouvry.[16] Mrs. Gaskell's story was by far the longest of the interpolated tales, accounting for over a third of the entire Christmas number. Mrs. Gaskell told the story of a farmer's son slowly growing up and slowly going wrong, a story strongly reminiscent of Wordsworth's "Michael," both in subject matter and emotional impact. Dickens prefaced the tale with the following uncollected introduction:

THE GHOST IN THE GARDEN ROOM

MY friend and solicitor rubbed his bald forehead—which is quite Shakespearian—with his hand, after a manner he has when I consult him professionally, and took a very large pinch of snuff. "My bedroom," said he, "has been haunted by the Ghost of a Judge."

"Of a Judge?" said all the company.

"Of a Judge. In his wig and robes as he sits upon the Bench, at Assize-time. As I have lingered in the great white chair at the side of my fire, when we have all retired for the night to our respective rooms, I have seen and heard him. I never shall forget the description he gave me, and I never have forgotten it since I first heard it."

"Then you have seen and heard him before, Mr. Undery?" said my sister.

"Often."

"Consequently, he is not peculiar to this house?"

"By no means. He returns to me in many intervals of quiet leisure, and his story haunts me."

sued the phantom : never with this man's stride of mine to come up with it, never with these man's hands of mine to touch it, never more to this man's heart of mine to hold it in its purity. And here you see me working out, as cheerfully and thankfully as I may, my doom of shaving in the glass a constant change of customers, and of lying down and rising up with the skeleton allotted to me for my mortal companion.

THE GHOST IN THE GARDEN ROOM.

My friend and solicitor rubbed his bald forehead—which is quite Shakespearian—with his hand, after a manner he has when I consult him professionally, and took a very large pinch of snuff. "My bedroom," said he, "has been haunted by the Ghost of a Judge."

"Of a Judge?" said all the company.

"Of a Judge. In his wig and robes as he sits upon the Bench, at Assize-time. As I have lingered in the great white chair at the side of my fire, when we have all retired for the night to our respective rooms, I have seen and heard him. I never shall forget the description he gave me, and I never have forgotten it since I first heard it."

"Then you have seen and heard him before, Mr. Undery?" said my sister.

"Often."

"Consequently, he is not peculiar to this house?"

"By no means. He returns to me in many intervals of quiet leisure, and his story haunts me."

We one and all called for the story, that it might haunt us likewise.

"It fell within the range of his judicial experience," said my friend and solicitor, "and this was the Judge's manner of summing it up."

Those words did not apply, of course, to the great pinch of snuff that followed them, but to the words that followed the great pinch of snuff. They were these:

Not many years after the beginning of this century, a worthy couple of the name of Huntroyd occupied a small farm in the North Riding of Yorkshire. They had married late in life, although they were very young when they first began to "keep company" with each other. Nathan Huntroyd had been farm servant to Hester Rose's father, and had made up to her at a time when her parents thought she might do better; and so, without much consultation of her feelings, they had dismissed Nathan in somewhat cavalier fashion. He had drifted far away from his former connexions, when an uncle of his died, leaving Nathan—by this time upwards of forty years of age—enough money to stock a small farm, and yet to have something over to put in the bank against bad times. One of the consequences of this bequest was that Nathan was looking out for a wife and house-keeper in a kind of discreet and leisurely way, when, one day, he heard that his old love, Hester, was—not married and flourishing, as he had always supposed her to be—but a poor maid-of-all-work, in the town of Ripon. For her father had had a succession of misfortunes, which had brought him in his old age to the workhouse; her mother was dead; her only brother struggling to bring up a large family; and Hester herself, a·hard-working, homely-looking (at thirty-seven) servant. Nathan had a kind of growling satisfaction (which only lasted for a minute or two, however) in hearing of these turns of Fortune's wheel. He did not make many intelligible remarks to his informant, and to no one else did he say a word. But, a few days afterwards, he presented himself, dressed in his Sunday best, at Mrs. Thompson's back door in Ripon.

Hester stood there in answer to the good sound knock his good sound oak stick made; she with the light full upon her, he in shadow. For a moment there was silence. He was scanning the face and figure of his old love, for twenty years unseen. The comely beauty of youth had faded away entirely; she was, as I have said, homely-looking, plain-featured, but with a clean skin, and pleasant, frank eyes. Her figure was no longer round, but tidily draped in a blue and white bedgown, tied round her waist by her white apron-strings, and her short red linsey petticoat showed her tidy feet and ankles. Her former lover fell into no ecstasies. He simply said to himself, "She'll do;" and forthwith began upon his business.

"Hester, thou dost not mind me. I am Nathan, as thy father turned off at a minute's notice, for thinking of thee for a wife, twenty year come Michaelmas next. I have not thought much upon matrimony since. But Uncle Ben has died, leaving me a small matter in the bank; and I have taken Nab-end Farm, and put in a bit of stock, and shall want a missus to see after it. Wilt like to come? I'll not mislead thee. It's dairy, and it might have been arable. But arable takes more horses than it suited me to buy, and I'd the offer of a tidy lot of kine. That's all. If thou'lt have me, I'll come for thee as soon as the hay is gotten in."

Hester only said, "Come in, and sit thee down."

He came in, and sat down. For a time she took no more notice of him than of his stick, bustling about to get dinner ready for the family whom she served. He meanwhile watched her brisk, sharp movements, and repeated to himself,

---

FORMAT OF AN INTERIOR PAGE FROM *The Haunted House*

Showing the way in which Dickens' introductions (hitherto uncollected) were set off from the text typographically.

We one and all called for the story, that it might haunt us likewise.

"It fell within the range of his judicial experience," said my friend and solicitor, "and this was the Judge's manner of summing it up."

Those words did not apply, of course, to the great pinch of snuff that followed them, but to the words that followed the great pinch of snuff. They were these.

At this point Mrs. Gaskell's story begins.

Dickens concluded *The Haunted House* with a section entitled "The Ghost in the Corner Room." For reasons that have already been discussed, this section, though entirely by Dickens, has never been collected. It is, nonetheless, a very characteristic piece of writing, both structurally and stylistically. In accordance with Dickens' usual practice in such conclusions, he ties up loose ends and sounds some Christmas chords:

THE GHOST IN THE CORNER ROOM

I HAD observed Mr. Governor growing fidgety as his turn — his "spell," he called it — approached, and he now surprised us all, by rising with a serious countenance, and requesting permission to "come aft" and have speech with me, before he spun his yarn. His great popularity led to a gracious concession of this indulgence, and we went out together into the hall.

"Old shipmate," said Mr. Governor to me; "ever since I have been aboard of this old hulk, I have been haunted, day and night."

"By what, Jack?"

Mr. Governor, clapping his hand on my shoulder and keeping it there, said:

"By something in the likeness of a Woman."

"Ah! Your old affliction. You'll never get over *that,* Jack, if you live to be a hundred."

"No, don't talk so, because I am very serious. All night long, I have been haunted by one figure. All day, the same figure has so bewildered me in the kitchen, that I wonder I haven't poisoned the whole ship's company. Now, there's no fancy here. Would you like to see the figure?"

"I should like to see it very much."

"Then here it is!" said Jack. Thereupon, he presented my sister, who had stolen out quietly, after us.

"Oh, indeed?" said I. "Then, I suppose, Patty, my dear, I have no occasion to ask whether *you* have been haunted?"

"Constantly, Joe," she replied.

The effect of our going back again, all three together, and of my presenting my sister as the Ghost from the Corner Room, and Jack as the Ghost from my Sister's Room, was triumphant—the crowning hit of the night. Mr. Beaver was so particularly delighted, that he by-and-by declared "a very little would make him dance a hornpipe." Mr. Governor immediately supplied the very little, by offering to make it a double hornpipe; and there ensued such toe-and-heeling, and buckle-covering, and double-shuffling, and heel-sliding, and execution of all sorts of slippery manœuvres with vibratory legs, as none of us ever saw before, or will ever see again. When we had all laughed and applauded till we were faint, Starling, not to be outdone, favoured us with a more modern saltatory entertainment in the Lancashire clog manner—to the best of my belief, the longest dance ever performed: in which the sound of his feet became a Locomotive going through cuttings, tunnels, and open country, and became a vast number of other things we should never have suspected, unless he had kindly told us what they were.

It was resolved before we separated that night, that our three months' period in the Haunted House should be wound up with the marriage of my sister and Mr. Governor. Belinda was nominated bridesmaid, and Starling was engaged for bridegroom's man.

In a word, we lived our term out, most happily, and were never for a moment haunted by anything more disagreeable than our own imaginations and remembrances. My cousin's wife, in her great love for her husband and in her gratitude to him for the change her love had wrought in her, had told us, through his lips, her own story; and I am sure there was not one of us who did not like her the better for it, and respect her the more.

So, at last, before the shortest month in the year was quite out, we all walked forth one morning to the church with the spire, as if nothing uncommon were going to happen; and there Jack and my sister were married, as sensibly as could be. It occurs to me to mention that I observed Belinda and Alfred Starling to be rather sentimental and low, on the occasion, and that they are since engaged to be married in the same church. I regard it as an excellent thing for both, and a kind of union very wholesome for the times in which we live. He wants a little poetry, and she wants a little prose, and the marriage of the two things is the happiest marriage I know for all mankind.

Finally, I derived this Christmas Greeting from the Haunted House, which I affectionately address with all my heart to all my readers:—Let us use the great virtue, Faith, but not abuse it; and let us put it to its best use, by having faith in the great Christmas book of the New Testament, and in one another.

THE END

Dickens' conclusion to *The Haunted House* speaks for itself, but if we compare it to his other Christmas writings, and in particular to his prototypical Christmas Books, one or two continuities and departures emerge very clearly. The Christmas dance is still there, even as it was in *A Christmas Carol, The Chimes, The Cricket on the Hearth,* and *The Battle of Life.* The Christmas marriages are there too, as in *The Chimes* and *The Cricket on the Hearth,* though Dickens' comment about the marriage of Belinda and Alfred perhaps owes as much to the recent breakup of his own marriage as it does to his Christmas philosophy. There are other Christmas consanguinities. In *The Haunted House* the machinery (hauntings), atmosphere (pressure of the past), and message (have faith in one another), recall their correlatives in virtually all Dickens' Christmas writings. Finally, and again in accordance with his custom, the concluding Christmas sentiment of *The Haunted House* is both traditional and topical. If it harks back to the *Carol* formula and the *Carol* philosophy, to "God bless Us, Every One!" (in *The Haunted Man* it is "Lord Keep my Memory Green"), it also performs the *Carol* or the *Chimes* function of attacking the abuses of the day: in 1859 the target is Howitt and the abuse of faith.

All this underlines a central paradox. The unknown Dickens, as we might have expected, and as we soon came to see, is known—or at least partly known—after all. The passages retrieved in this article enforce that reassuring lesson. We find in these lost writings themes, phrasings, and techniques that we have encountered elsewhere in Dickens' works. We mark the family resemblance, but we mark the freshness and individuality as well. For Dickens' genius was protean: each new paragraph, each new line, both confirms and extends our comprehension of his achievement. That is, after all, why we seek to define his canon and why we rejoice at each new discovery.

Margaret Ganz

THE VULNERABLE EGO

Dickens' Humor in Decline

THE REVIEWER of *Blackwood's Magazine* who in 1857 greeted *Little Dorrit* by lamenting that "in the wilderness we sit down and weep when we remember thee, O *Pickwick!*" would not today find many critics to sympathize with him. Nor would Henry James' estimate of *Our Mutual Friend* in 1865 be any more popular since he could find, besides the creation of Mrs. Wilfer, only "a dozen more happy examples of the humor which was exhaled from every line of Mr. Dickens's earlier writings" to make up "the list of the merits of the work." [1] Indeed, while the Victorians hailed the auspicious beginnings of Dickens' comic talent, celebrated its fulfillment, and mourned its decline,[2] a consideration of his humor is hardly fashionable in our time. Basically it has been eclipsed by the prevailing preoccupation—so germane to the psychologically oriented modern temper—with the somber and symbolic aspects of Dickens' art. The fear that analyzing humor may dissipate its essence, may "empty the haunted air," is of course an abiding obstacle. In any case the recent critical point that "taking his humour for granted comes after a time to suggest a failure of response" [3] is well taken.

Whatever the cause, we have conspired to accept Dickens' humor as *sous entendu* and in so doing have almost lost sight of what constitutes perhaps his most striking and original contribution to fiction. Critical evaluations of the early novels clearly reflect this present attitude. Sergeant Buzfuz's fantastic prosecution of Pickwick gets less appreciation than the symbolic significance of legal corruption entrapping an innocent man; the delightful idiocy of Mr. Bumble becomes irrelevant to the central problem of Oliver Twist in search of his identity; Dick Swiveller's grotesque diversions are overshadowed by the image of Nell—the embodiment of Dickens' memory of Mary Hogarth or the agent of his denunciation of Victorian materialism.[4]

[23

Interestingly enough, while Dickens himself could be as readily charmed by his humorous creations as his contemporary critics (or for that matter such later ones as Chesterton, Gissing, or Cecil [5]), yet, under the stress of irrelevant critical demands, he sometimes felt impelled to minimize, as many modern critics have done, the originality of perception that underlies his humor. Late in life he thus apologizes to Bulwer-Lytton for his comic extravagance:

> I think it is my *infirmity* to fancy or perceive relations in things which are not apparent generally. Also, I have such an inexpressible enjoyment of what I see in a droll light, that I dare say I pet it as if it were a spoilt child.[6] (*Italics mine*)

Whatever qualms Dickens may have developed about his "inexpressible enjoyment" of incongruity, he both spontaneously and skillfully expressed this enjoyment in his early works by exercising his extraordinary *ability* "to fancy or perceive relations in things which are not apparent generally."

As our ability to respond and do justice to the originality of Dickens' humor increases, our involvement with the thematic, symbolic, and sociological aspects of his works may well lessen. We may come to recognize that he has no peer in his exercise of a comic vision of seemingly unrelated phenomena, whereas in craftsmanship, psychological insight, and social profundity many of his contemporaries and later novelists could better him. Even the often arresting symbolic treatment of his themes has some serious limitations. The very imagination which so uniquely fitted him as a humorist to explore the incongruous was not wholly suited to the demands of symbolism—paradoxically enough because that imagination so easily transcended the bounds of realism. He lacked that peculiar sensibility which effortlessly produces emblematic overtones from a realistic treatment of action and passion. Moreover, his symbolic expression is too often self-consciously wedded to a didactic purpose. In such works as *Bleak House, Little Dorrit,* and *Our Mutual Friend,* he seems rather too deliberately to be forging emblems suited to convey dramatically the social disorganization and corruption of Victorian England—and is perpetually at the reader's side, reminding him of their significance, as in the treatment of the Circumlocution Office.[7] His humor on the other hand is an organic part of his whole vision of reality which spontaneously manifests itself from the beginning and whose gratuitous power is never wholly dissipated.

Few would deny that T. S. Eliot's vision of the waste land has more universal significance for us than Dickens' symbol of the dust heap in *Our Mutual Friend;* beside the Circumlocution Office of *Little Dorrit* we can now place Kafka's castle. But the greatest modern humorist cannot duplicate the particular perception of incongruity which set Alfred

Jingle, Sam and Tony Weller, Mr. Pickwick, Mr. Mantalini, Mrs. Nickleby, and Dick Swiveller on the scene of Dickens' early novels and, better still, created their amusing modes of trafficking with reality—their inspired *conversation*. Fresh insights into the incongruous are offered to us when Jingle apologizes for not paying because he is short of change and "Brummagem buttons won't do—no go—eh?", Sam Weller depicts the London poor desperately rushing out to eat oysters, Mr. Mantalini renders his verdict that the dowager he charmed had a "demd outline," Mrs. Nickleby recalls her vision of the Bard of Avon, and Dick Swiveller bids a funereal farewell to Sophy Wackles. All humorists perceive the world "in a droll light" (to use Dickens' already quoted words) ; the richness of their achievement, however, essentially depends on the quality of the imagination that does the perceiving, as Louis Cazamian reminds us,[8] and on their ability to transmute those creative impulses of the imagination into verbal art.

The very originality of Dickens' humor is evident in the fact that *expression* rather than *action* is his best mode of celebrating the absurd clashes and triumphs that mark the encounter of fancy with fact in the human world. The real activities of Alfred Jingle in *Pickwick Papers* (his elopement, for instance) hardly concern us, but his conversation (which so often celebrates imaginary heroic achievements and romantic conquests) arrests our attention and provokes our laughter. The movements of Sam and Tony Weller are not as diverting as the quaint meditations and pronouncements that can encompass marriage licenses and meat pies. Mr. Mantalini's denunciation of Nicholas to Ralph Nickleby is not half as memorable as his "droll" insight and complaint that "yolk of egg does not match any waistcoat but a yellow waistcoat, demmit." Mr. Crummles most easily wins our amused attention when he champions the decorative attractions of "a real pump and two washing tubs" to be worked into a new theatrical showpiece. That Mrs. Nickleby walks the streets of London, visits Mrs. Wititterly, and goes to the theatre has little import for us; her mental confusion between the activities of a hairdresser and a bear is absolutely pertinent to our enjoyment of her.[9]

In fact the truly humorous character cannot be made subservient to action; he transcends it. Since he serves the viewpoint which derives laughter from the incongruous aspects of life, he must remain consistently unaffected by the often tragic events of existence if he is to preserve his *raison d'être,* his identity. Such capacity to rebound endows him with a permanence of existence which, even as it runs counter to reality, triumphs over it by the sense of immortality it conveys. As Chesterton puts it, "especially in the comic literature . . . the characters are felt to be fixed things of which we have fleeting glimpses; that is, they are felt to be divine. Uncle Toby is talking for ever, as the elves are dancing for ever. We feel that, whenever we hammer on the house of

Falstaff, Falstaff will be at home." [10] If the humorous character is forced into realistic action, especially to illustrate a moral viewpoint, his authenticity is immediately endangered and with it his power to induce affirmative laughter. We are as reluctant to accept the reality of a repentant Jingle and a sentimental Sam Weller in the prison scenes near the conclusion of *Pickwick Papers* as we are unprepared to countenance a Falstaff rejected by Hal. Most often, however, the humorist spares us glimpses into the vulnerability of existence. Thus the very immortality of Dickens' humorous character, an attribute he so largely owes to the versatility and charm of his gratuitous expression, guarantees his capacity to evoke spontaneous laughter. With that laughter man challenges mutability as he responds to what Freud terms the "fine" attribute of humor: "the ego's victorious assertion of its own invulnerability." [11]

Dickens' appraisal of his own tendencies, which was quoted above, reinforces one's feeling that he never fully appreciated the originality of his gift. To a certain extent, indeed, the history of Dickens' artistic development chronicles the negation of the greatest natural talent he possessed. From the very beginning, other concerns vitiated some of his best efforts. His indignation at social ills provoked satirical descriptions and pronouncements that contrasted strangely with his humorous viewpoint—a scene such as the Bardell vs. Pickwick trial incorporated a somewhat awkward mixture of indignation and high-spirited amusement. His fascination with the macabre and the sensational—with the nature of crime, rebellion, and death—and his indulgence in pathos and sentiment at times overclouded or minimized the importance of the genial delight in things seen (as Dickens termed it) "in a droll light." His desire to achieve mastery as a weaver of plots made him too often renege on his humorous characters, though the indestructible appeal of these gratuitous figures only managed to point up the irrelevance of the stories in which they made their memorable appearances.

It would of course be absurd to expect Dickens, who was so peculiarly suited by his upbringing to know the anguish of human deprivation, the prevalence of evil, and the lures of sentiment and self-pity, to excise one part of his temperament from his works, simply because his most inspired vision is a comic apprehension of the paradoxes of human behavior which transcends moral, sentimental, and social considerations. Yet, when he wants to, he is in fact much better able to do justice to these considerations as a humorist than as a serious social commentator, satirist, or sentimentalist.

For if the projection of a comic vision of incongruity in man's character and actions is Dickens' most original contribution as an artist, the early novels demonstrate that this vision often functions not only to provoke laughter at the eternal discrepancy between human aims and achievements, claims and performances, illusions and realities, but also to reconcile joy and sadness, pity and contempt, anger and indulgence. Dickens charms us by the spectacle of such appealing oddities as the "angel in tights and gaiters" which is Pickwick. But he also makes us accept human weakness and error by proving that imaginative eccentricity can flourish in the pedestrian and tawdry world of the shabby-genteel class (with the Crummles' histrionic exertions and Mrs. Jarley's waxwork wanderings as appropriate emblems of the conjunction of romance and reality). Finally he allows us to detect symptoms of an imaginative life in the minds of his embodiments of hatred, greed, and malice. Through humor, he succeeds not only in making the ludicrous aspirations, petty snobberies, and cheap sentiments of the lower middle class worthy of our tender and tolerant amusement (as in his portrait of the Kenwigs), but he injects reality into such studies of evil as those of Fagin, Bumble, Squeers, Quilp, and Brass. He enables us to dissipate their threat by laughing at absurdities of behavior in those whose very irrationality marks them creatures as authentic in their vulnerability as the rest of mankind.

That capacity of Dickens the humorist to effect a reconciliation between the tragic and comic elements in our life—robbing evil of its destructive potential by emphasizing its grotesqueness, for instance— is one of his most significant achievements. For it makes possible through laughter the pleasurable transcendence of the threats and perplexities in man's existence. As the decline of Dickens' humor marks the dying out of "the ego's victorious assertion of its invulnerability," we miss what Freud calls "the . . . magnificent rising superior to the real situation" through the affirmation of laughter, "the triumph not only of the ego, but also of the pleasure principle, which is strong enough to assert itself . . . in the face of . . . adverse real circumstances." [12]

Despite his early achievements and acclaim, Dickens moved consistently away from what he seemed suited to do so effortlessly. What happens to his humor in his later works is in a sense the chronicle not only of a supplanting of a great gift by other considerations but also of a qualitative decline in the very nature of Dickens' comic vision. The exact relation between these two phenomena remains to a certain extent a mystery. But an examination of certain manifestations in that decline helps to clarify one's reservations about Dickens' later artistic achievements and by contrast to denote the peculiar distinction of his earlier efforts.

The decline of humor in Dickens' novels is a gradual and infinitely subtle process that forbids convenient divisions into early, middle, and later phases. The humorist's talent which fashioned Mrs. Jarley and Dick Swiveller in *The Old Curiosity Shop* (1840–41) is hardly on the wane when it can produce such whimsical figures as Mrs. Gamp in *Martin Chuzzlewit* (1843–44) and Mr. Toots in *Dombey and Son* (1846–48).

Barnaby Rudge (1841), which immediately follows *The Old Curiosity Shop,* is indeed largely humorless, but such a phenomenon has little meaning, since we know that the novel was started quite early in Dickens' career, that it cost him great pains and conflicts with his publishers to terminate it,[13] and that he was attempting a different genre altogether, a historical recounting of the Gordon riots—to which serious purpose his humor would inevitably become subservient. (This argument would to a certain extent also account for the dearth of humor in *A Tale of Two Cities.*)

Because of the sustained study of a character trait—pride—in *Dombey and Son,* this novel has often been seen as a departure from Dickens' previous work and as marking a new trend in his development as a serious artist. Yet in the preceding novel, *Martin Chuzzlewit,* Dickens was already attempting, though without much success, a similar psychological study of certain aspects of character: of selfishness as the attribute of the Chuzzlewit family and of hypocrisy as incarnated in Mr. Pecksniff. Undoubtedly, in the larger part of *Dombey and Son* which follows after the death of Paul, there is a notable decline of high spirits and whimsy, a ponderous gravity in the elaborate chronicle of the evil ways of parents with their offspring, and a melodramatic stylization in the portrayal of the villain Carker.[14] But what are we then to make of *David Copperfield* (1849–50) with its exuberant spirit, the originality of its observation, and the profusion of its eccentric figures?

In none of these novels can we truly assert that the breaking point has been reached, that the humorous affirmation is clearly receding before the weight and emphasis of other concerns. Yet we do find in all of them indications that the old "inexpressible enjoyment" is no longer an unalloyed delight in humorous invention, and that the invention itself shows signs of becoming strained. Such a recognition prepares us for an entrance into the "wilderness" in which the *Blackwood's* reviewer looked back nostalgically at *Pickwick Papers;* and *Bleak House* (1852–53) is our first complete introduction into that wilderness. The texture, the atmosphere, the tone of the first few chapters of this novel seem indeed dramatically to ring down the curtain on the career of the greatest humorist of the Victorian age. Neither *Hard Times* (1854), *Little Dorrit* (1855–57), *A Tale of Two Cities* (1859), nor *Our Mutual Friend* (1864–65) would lead one to controvert this judgment, yet in a late work like *Great Expectations* (1860–61) the presence of Joe Gargery and Mr. Wopsle shows that the fresh perception of things "in a droll light" has not altogether died out.

While there is thus no absolute shift in Dickens' artistic development, there is also no exact reason for the disappointing decline of his humor. True, Dickens did not sufficiently value his most original gift, and his quoted apology to critics in search of realism is ample evidence of this underestimation of his humor. With the paradoxical attitude of so many artists, he made light of the native talent so effortlessly exercised and sought achievements for which he was not so happily predisposed. Moreover, he may have felt that his prominent position was being threatened in the late 1840's by new writers who were commended for their technical proficiency and understanding of psychological and social problems. Indeed, he faced "the first serious literary competition of his career" from writers like Emily and Charlotte Brontë, Mrs. Gaskell, Charles Kingsley, and—more formidable still—Thackeray, whose *Vanity Fair* (1847–48) won far more praise from the critics than *Dombey and Son*.[15] Two more factors must be taken into consideration: the progressive unhappiness of his private life, which might well have thrown a somber cast over his later works, and a general decrease in the spontaneity of his invention reflected in his use of notations before the actual writing and his complaints of the arduousness of composition. In itself the increased care in preparation could mean no more than a greater striving to achieve technical proficiency and psychological probability but, as John Butt and Kathleen Tillotson remind us, John Forster used the notes to *Little Dorrit* to demonstrate "the labour and pains" (as he put it) involved in the writing of it.[16] The best evidence comes from Dickens himself who in February 1856 writes to Miss Coutts:

> Your note finds me settling myself to Little Dorrit again, and in the usual wretchedness of such settlement—which is unsettlement. Prowling about the rooms, sitting down, getting up, stirring the fire, looking out of window, tearing my hair, sitting down to write, writing nothing, writing something and tearing it up, going out, coming in, a Monster to my family, a dread Phenomenon to myself.[17]

It would be as much an oversimplification to account fully for the perceptible change in Dickens' art as a novelist as it is to establish sharp contrasts between his early humorous novels and the works that followed. Yet one can indicate the main aspects of his decline as a humorist, and by so doing measure the extent of the loss so deeply felt by many Victorian readers and critics.

The success of Dickens' humor, as we have seen, depended largely on his capacity to forge the mode of *expression* by which his characters revealed incongruities of personality and behavior rather than the ability to create amusing *situations* and *actions*. The latter, as *Pickwick Papers* clearly reveals, are all too often *farcical* rather than humorous in their dependence on physical action and traditional mishaps and misunderstandings in which the life of the imagination may have no part. Such farcical episodes evoke our laughter, but as a visceral reaction rather than a cathartic response. Pickwick mistaking the room of the lady in the yellow curlpapers for his own diverts us as he re-enacts a *faux pas* consecrated by comic tradition; Pickwick mistaking the callow and slovenly medical students for thoughtful and inspired professionals allows us a rich and complex amusement. To be victimized by a faulty sense of direction is a commonplace fate; to be victimized by an optimistic imagination almost guarantees an original experience: Pickwick's *words* on the subject of the medical students are worth a dozen Pickwickian *actions* which reveal some grotesque *quid pro quo*. Undoubtedly expression in Dickens is the best clue to the imaginative life which lies beneath the surface: Winkle as an impostor is a failure, for his actions neatly belie his silly claims, but Jingle as an impostor is wholly convincing, for his imaginative speeches sustain and transfigure his impudent pretensions.[18] The decline of that fertile invention which buttresses the expression of Jingle and Mrs. Jarley, of Vincent Crummles and Mr. Mantalini, and of Mrs. Nickleby and Dick Swiveller, is the clearest instance that the humorist's vision has been obscured or obstructed by other preoccupations.

In the character of Mrs. Gamp in *Martin Chuzzlewit,* we see the final flowering of Dickens' gift of humorous expression, its last triumph over those concerns which will conspire to subdue the author's spontaneous delight in exploring incongruity. These will bring to the fore his social indignation and his mingled revulsion and attraction for the sentimental and sensational aspects of human passion. We never again witness such a complete affirmation of humor both in inspiring gratuitous laughter and in reconciling us to human weakness. In creating Mrs. Gamp, Dickens was striking a blow at the profession of nursing which he considered to be sorely in need of reform.[19] Mrs. Gamp is not merely inefficient; she is a drunkard who is both careless and rough in the treatment of her patients; her unction, which thrives on the presence of disease and death, is at best heartless and at worst depraved:

> "Wishin' you lots of sickness, my darling creetur," Mrs. Gamp observed [to Mrs. Prig], "and good places . . . and may our next meetin' be at a large family's, where they all takes it reg'lar, one from another, turn and turn about, and has it businesslike." [20]

Yet, despite her many vices, Mrs. Gamp is a monumental humorous figure whom we greet with amusement, indulgence, and tenderness. It is not surprising that we tend to compare her with the vice-ridden but eternally appealing Falstaff.[21] For she shares with the great knight, not only a perception of the vulnerable condition of man—the recognition that when one is "born into a wale" and exists "in a wale" one "must take the consequences of sech a sitiwation" [22]—but the ability to vanquish depravity, anguish, and loneliness by countering their claims with those of the poetic imagination. Just as Falstaff perpetually dispels tedium or shame by juggling reality and, for instance, indulges so freely in play-acting with Hal that he seems to live the role he has assumed for the diversion of the moment, so Mrs. Gamp transfigures her world by casting the glow of the imagination over its sordidness and solitude. She creates "Mrs. Harris" not just to serve as a perpetual testimonial to her own talents as a nurse, but to fill the void in her life and enable her fertile invention to exercise itself on the vicissitudes of such a friendship. Her creativity takes hold of our imagination as does the inventiveness of Falstaff, or that of Alfred Jingle, and if, where Jingle is concerned, we are willing to suspend our disbelief in the matter of Spanish donnas and the perceptive dog Ponto, we accept with even greater conviction the particulars of Mrs. Harris' family life and the travails of her offspring Tommy, who, Mrs. Gamp informs us,

> "calls me his own Gammy, and truly calls, for bless the mottled little legs of that there precious child . . . his own I have been, ever since I found him . . . with his small red worsted shoe a gurglin' in his throat, where he had put it in his play, a chick, wile they was leavin' of him on the floor a looking for it through the ouse and him a-choakin' sweetly in the parlour!" [23]

The transcending power of humor is perhaps nowhere more evident than in its ability to transmute the degradation of (the now deceased) Mr. Gamp into an irresistibly amusing eccentricity. His "wooden leg" which, as Mrs. Gamp says, "in its constancy of walkin' into wine vaults, and never comin' out again 'till fetched by force, was quite as weak as flesh, if not weaker," [24] is, like Mantalini's "two countesses and a dowager," a humorous leitmotif which, sustained by Mrs. Gamp's versatility of expression, makes the most heart-rending situations seem diverting. Mrs. Gamp literally *talks* us out of pity and sentimentality as she muses on her family life:

> "the blessing of a daughter was denied me; which, if we had had one, Gamp would certainly have drunk its little shoes right off its feet, as with our precious boy he did, and arterwards send the child a errand to sell his wooden leg for any money it would fetch as matches in the rough, and bring it home in liquor: which was truly done beyond his years, for ev'ry individgle penny that child lost at toss or buy for kidney ones." [25]

Whether wishing that the "Ankworks package" about to carry Merry away were "in Jonadge's belly," or denouncing the "Bragian words" of "that perfeejus wretch"—Mrs. Prig—Mrs. Gamp is perpetually recreating the language and the reality which that language represents and assisting us through laughter to enshrine imagination above the reason and logic which constantly restrict our lives.[26]

Though the gift of expression reaches its culmination in Mrs. Gamp and never again flourishes with that magnificent expansiveness, it never totally disappears. Almost every novel after *Martin Chuzzlewit* shows some evidence of it,[27] but in the last works it can hardly sustain itself against the weight of sarcasm, irony, and heavy-handed didacticism.

One might think that the fertile rhetoric of Mr. Micawber in *David Copperfield* could surely put Mrs. Gamp to shame, and yet a careful examination of his speech shows that it lacks the inventiveness and subtlety of the Gamp style, and, more significant still, that a didactic purpose on Dickens' part is steadily at work behind it.[28] Whereas Mrs. Gamp is intoxicated with imagination, Mr. Micawber is intoxicated with words; while she manages to conjure up for us the incongruous actions and sentiments of live or fictitious people, Mr. Micawber merely adorns commonplace or sordid considerations with a heavy brocade of prose; while she is busy coming to terms with the regrettable situation of being forced to endure life "in a wale," Mr. Micawber is perpetually running away from the disagreeable reality of his parasitism into the emptiness of pompous protestations. There is a stylization in his remarks which contrasts unfavorably with the freshness of Mrs. Gamp's *aperçus* on her condition and on the behavior of others. Dickens lets Mrs. Gamp exert her spell unaided, but is obviously eager to point up the contrast between Micawber's ornate style and the pedestrian reality to which it corresponds.

> "Under the impression . . . that your peregrinations in this metropolis have not as yet been extensive, and that you might have some difficulty in penetrating the arcana of the Modern Babylon in the direction of the City Road—in short . . . that you might lose yourself . . ."
> "Copperfield . . . has a heart to feel for the distresses of his fellow-creatures when they are behind a cloud, and a head to plan, and a hand to—in short, a general ability to dispose of such available property as could be made away with." [29]

With a few exceptions, the effusions of Mr. Micawber and of Mrs. Micawber (who is equally endowed with the power of ornate circumlocution) lack the spontaneity of invention which individualized Dick Swiveller, Lillyvick Kenwigs, or Vincent Crummles. The Micawbers are perpetually working and reworking elegant clichés of conversation into an elaborate patchwork of prose; indeed their contributions to the dialogue are at times indistinguishable one from the other. We need only compare Squeers' burlesque epitaph: "The coat of arms of the Squeerses is tore, and their sun has gone down into the ocean wave!" or Mantalini's assertion that he "has gone to the demnition bow wows" with Micawber's "The canker is in the flower. The cup is bitter to the brim. The worm is at his work, and will soon dispose of his victim" [30] to gauge the alteration of the humorist's technique. Dickens' judgments of Mantalini and Squeers provide a conventional moral ending for his plots, but his depiction of Micawber's "relish in [the] formal piling up of words" culminates in a scathing attack on private and public morality:

> We talk about the tyranny of words, but we like to tyrannise over them too; we are fond of having a large superfluous establishment of words to wait upon us on great occasions; we think it looks important, and sounds well. . . . The meaning or necessity of our words is a secondary consideration, if there be but a great parade of them. And as individuals get into trouble by making too great a show of liveries, or as slaves when they are too numerous rise against their masters, so I think I could mention a nation that has got into many great difficulties, and will get into many greater, from maintaining too large a retinue of words.[31]

Yet, despite the reservations suggested by Micawber's expression, he is undeniably still a great humorous creation. But the humor resides now less in expression than in situation: in Micawber's *behavior* towards the young David as if the boy were a mature counsellor (his reference to David in later years as "the companion of my youth" reminds us of this quaint assumption) ; in the *spectacle* of Micawber's alternating between careless jollity and abysmal despair; in his *action* of writing lengthy missives on the slightest occasion rather than in the content of these epistles; and in the *description* of his imaginative tendency to assume different roles upon the shortest notice. The appealing eccentricities which would have been conveyed to us through the medium of conversation are now often left for us to envision. Thus we are not treated to an inspired discussion on kangaroos or on the merits of the bullocks of Canterbury, but must take David's words for the quaint behavior of his friends soon after the project of emigrating to Australia has been suggested to them:

> Shall I ever forget how, in a moment, [Micawber] was the most sanguine of men, looking on to fortune; or how Mrs. Micawber presently discoursed about the habits of the kangaroo! Shall I ever recall that street of Canterbury on a market day, without recalling him, as he walked back with us; expressing, in the hardy roving manner he assumed, the unsettled habits of a temporary sojourner in the land; and looking at the bullocks, as they came by, with the eye of an Australian farmer! [32]

Along with the alteration of Dickens' humorous style in *David Copperfield,* surely a loss of the distinctive creativity of the early writer, we also notice in this novel an accentuation of the tendency first evident in *Oliver Twist* and more pronounced in *Martin Chuzzlewit* and *Dombey and Son:* the tendency to substitute one particular expression for a general eccentricity of expression, to determine personality not through inspired conversation but through the repetition of one idea or item of speech which serves as a tag of character. (Appearance and behavior Dickens had from the beginning used as tags, often for farcical effects, as in Joe's tendency to doze off in *Pickwick Papers*.) This facile and unsubtle method of provoking amusement easily becomes tedious to the reader if used too frequently. Just as mechanical tendencies in appearance and behavior soon lose their comic appeal, so obsessions which repetitive words invariably revealed to be rigidly uniform become tiresome, whereas there are perpetual discoveries to be made when the eccentric applies his versatile imagination to the world around him.

If Dickens in the early novels rarely deserved his own condemnation of petting a droll idea "as if it were a spoilt child," in his later works he frequently vitiated the whimsy of such an idea by incorporating it in recurrent modes of expression. In *Martin Chuzzlewit*, Mark Tapley's incongruous feeling that comfort and well-being are to be shunned because they present no challenge to his desire to "come out strong" is at first appealingly comic; by dint of repetition, it becomes a wearisome obsession. We tire quickly in *Dombey and Son* of Mrs. Chick's gospel of "effort"; of Major Bagstock's references to himself as "Old Joe," "J. B.," "Joey B." and of the continual reminder of his "purple visage" and his "lobster eyes"; of Captain Cuttle's snatches of the ballad of "Old Lovely Peg," of his injunctions to "overhaul" texts for quotations one should then "make a note on," and of his nautical terminology; of Mrs. Blimber's desire to have known Cicero; even of the winning Toots' pathetic excuse that "it's of no consequence." Dickens manages at times to use this technique of the tag line in *David Copperfield* with delicacy and tender humor (as in "Barkis is willin'") and the idea behind some of the obsessions can be delightfully odd (the relentless influence of King Charles' head on Mr. Dick, for example). Yet throughout the novel there is too heavy an emphasis on recurring ideas and modes of expression: Mr. Micawber's reliance on something "turning up," Mrs. Micawber's vow that she "never will desert Mr. Micawber," Mr. Peggotty's mention of "the old 'un," Mrs. Gummidge's complaint of being "a lone lorn creetur'," Traddles' assurances that he is engaged to "the dearest girl," Betsey Trotwood's warning shout of "Donkeys," and Mr. Spenlow's allusions to the obduracy of Mr. Jorkins.

In the novels that follow *David Copperfield*, the use of such mechanical means to provoke laughter becomes even more noticeable, not so much because of its incidence, but because of the frequent absence of inventive humor which could counteract its disappointing poverty of imagination. Too frequently the obsessive mannerism of speech is the only means by which the character can arouse our laughter; it is not, as in the earlier novels, only one manifestation of his eccentric view of the universe. We do not get tired of Mrs. Gamp's request for a bottle of spirits to which she can put her lips when she is so "dispoged," because she gives us other instances of imaginative expression. But in *Bleak House,* Mrs. Badger's references to her two former husbands, Mr. Snagsby's apologetic "not to put too fine a point upon it," Mr. Bagnet's reluctance to praise his wife because "discipline must be maintained," and Mr. Guppy's allusion to his blighted love for Esther as "there are chords in the human mind—" fail to amuse us because they do not spring from an organic incongruity of perception in the characters but seem to have been superimposed on them to make them diverting. The same deplorable lack of invention is evident in *Hard Times,* in Mrs. Sparsit's assumed forgetfulness of the married name of her rival, Louisa Grad-grind. *Little Dorrit* exhibits this unfortunate technique in Mr. Meagles' assertion that all the generous deeds he and his wife perform merely show that they are "being practical people," and in his injunction to Tattycoram to count to "five-and-twenty" to recover her good temper; in Mrs. General's insistence on the gospel of "Papa, Potatoes, Poultry, Prunes, and Prism" to keep "the setting of her face" and soul in a state of perpetual "varnish." Mr. Pumblechook's request to shake hands with Pip and the monotonous reiteration of his claims to have been the boy's benefactor are flaws in the vigor and inventiveness of *Great Expectations;* they are devices almost as forced as Silas Wegg's references to "Miss Elizabeth, Master George, Aunt Jane, and Uncle Parker" in *Our Mutual Friend.*

The obsessive, mechanical mode of thought and expression has not only become a poor substitute for the humorous conception of eccentricity; it has also, in the novels that follow *David Copperfield,* been made subservient to the same didactic purpose which provoked Dickens' judgment of Micawber's rhetoric. The use of this rather artificial technique is indeed well suited to the increased stylization of Dickens' satirical writing, which is first perceptible in *Bleak House,* and is most marked in *Our Mutual Friend.* Carker's white-toothed mechanical smile was in *Dombey and Son* only a melodramatic token of his villainy, but Harold Skimpole's insistence that he knows nothing about money, Bounderby's references to his early indigence, Mr. Dorrit's self-satisfied allusions to the Testimonials, and Podsnap's wave of the hand and rejection of what will "call a blush to the cheek of the young person" are consistently presented so as to evoke our moral judgment. Eccentricity has been enlisted in Dickens' attack on the vices of nineteenth-century England.

Didacticism is indeed often responsible in those later novels for the stifling of that humorous invention which had flourished in the early works. In *Bleak House,* the creation of Mrs. Jellyby posits an incongruous idea closely allied to Dickens' earliest humor: the lady who is striving to reform the world, but cannot keep her own home in order. But

Mrs. Jellyby does not exhibit that originality of expression which had atoned in Mantalini and Jingle for their distasteful lack of responsibility; she is clearly the embodiment of Dickens' indignant appraisal of misguided philanthropy. Were his description of her home and the misery of her husband and children not sufficient indications of his moral purpose, the comments of Ada Clare and Esther Summerson and the bewilderment of the kindly Mr. Jarndyce would convince us of the attitude Dickens wants us to take towards her behavior.[33] Nothing so testifies to the heavy-handedness of Dickens' satire as his failure to convince us that, even for a short while, anyone might be deceived by the seemingly charming, carefree, whimsical, droll nature of Harold Skimpole's evasions. What he never succeeds in doing is to match Skimpole's *expression* with the ecstatic *descriptions* of his quaintness which invariably follow upon his conversation. Moral indignation vitiates the novelist's intention and causes the reader to view Skimpole from the start as a tedious humbug rather than a dangerous charmer; in driving too hard at his point, Dickens undercuts even his moral purposes. The tolerance and indulgence of the humorist have disappeared. Dickens could still be amused by Micawber's parasitism, but he severely judges the shiftlessness of Skimpole: Micawber enjoys nothing so much as testifying to his indebtedness by the elaborate concoction of I.O.U.'s, but Skimpole is perfectly willing to take money from two wards in Chancery to cancel his debts.

Other comparisons with earlier characters clearly illustrate the change that has taken place in Dickens' artistic intentions. The peculiar charm of Dick Swiveller was that he transcended moral judgments and won our allegiance mainly by gratuitous eccentricities. Mr. Guppy in *Bleak House* has some of Dick's quaint self-sufficiency but his impudence lacks the redeeming touches of Dickens' humorous viewpoint. Dick's aspiration to the hand of Nell is an aspect of the plot which Dickens soon discards; Mr. Guppy's sentiments towards Esther Summerson consistently illustrate the arrogance of the parvenu. Though she has not given him the least encouragement, he has the insolence to inform her of his changed feelings after her disfigurement (all the well-bred people still love her as much as ever!) and then to foist his condescension upon her in renewing his demand for her hand. Dick Swiveller escaped vulgarity; Mr. Guppy is perpetually demonstrating it, and at the last the picture of his coarse and querulous mother is created to further convince us of his upstart strivings.

If a comparison of Skimpole with Micawber, and Mr. Guppy with Dick Swiveller assists us in understanding the decline of Dickens' humor, the characterization of Bounderby in *Hard Times*, if we view it in conjunction with that of Mrs. Gamp in *Martin Chuzzlewit,* is the clearest instance of Dickens' sacrifice of the humorous viewpoint to the expres-

sion of his social indignation. Like Mrs. Gamp, Mr. Bounderby is a humbug in that he foists a false conception of himself on others; like her he
shows himself not invulnerable to the claims of the imagination—indeed
the memories of his supposed childhood possess a graphic power somewhat reminiscent of Mrs. Gamp's description of Tommy Harris. It is
with a real relish that Bounderby recalls the "egg-box" that served as his
cradle, evokes the picture of himself as "a ragged street-boy, who never
washed his face unless it was at a pump, and that no oftener than once a
fortnight," who "didn't want a shoeing-horn, in consequence of not having a shoe," and whose only artistic "possession" was "the engraving of a
man shaving himself in a boot, on . . . blacking bottles." [34] But where
Dickens intends us to greet Mrs. Gamp's deception with laughter and
tenderness, he asks us to view Mr. Bounderby's concealment of his orderly and comfortable upbringing as a crime against society: his is not
an individual deviation into humbug, but the emblem of that wide-
spread and senseless glorification of the self-made man which Dickens is
angrily satirizing. Mrs. Gamp, though nearly detected, is never made to
reveal the nonexistence of Mrs. Harris, but Mr. Bounderby is publicly
humiliated by being brought face to face with his good-natured mother
whom he had accused of abandoning him (as Mr. Gradgrind puts it)
"in . . . infancy . . . to the brutality of a drunken grandmother." [35] Not
content with the judgment he has passed upon his character in this situation, Dickens goes on sententiously to explain Bounderby's state:

> Detected as the Bully of humility, who had built his windy repu-
> tation upon lies, and in his boastfulness had put the honest truth
> as far away from him as if he had advanced the mean claim
> (there is no meaner) to tack himself on to a pedigree, he cut a
> most ridiculous figure.[36]

It is the same tendency to moralize which robs the circus people—the
spiritual adversaries of Gradgrind and Bounderby—of some of the absurd charm inevitably associated with their profession and so characteristic of Vincent Crummles and his troupe in *Nicholas Nickleby*. E. W. B.
Childers and Kidderminster must be shown to judge Bounderby severely, and the lisping Sleary twice delivers himself of a sermon to Gradgrind whose purport would have seemed strange indeed in the world of
Vincent Crummles:

> "Don't be croth with uth poor vagabondth. People mutht be
> amuthed. They can't be alwayth a learning, nor yet they can't
> be alwayth a working, they an't made for it. You *mutht* have uth,
> Thquire. Do the withe thing and the kind thing too, and make
> the betht of uth; not the wurtht!" [37]

Though it is largely Dickens' growing concern with social evils
which quenched the high-spirited exploration of incongruity, his preoc-

cupation with plot and with the delineation of serious character (a concern which deepened in the later novels) likewise conspired to mute the
power of his humor. In the far more solid structure of his late works, the
gratuitously humorous character is indeed a rare phenomenon. But that
Dickens was still capable of such invention when he chose to exercise it
is proven in *Little Dorrit* by the appeal of Mr. F.'s Aunt, whose portentous irrelevancies transcend the mechanical nature of a tic. One never
really knows what provokes her wrath (though at times she seems to be
directing it at Arthur Clennam), but one is delighted to have her
"malevolent gaze" followed by the "fearful remark" that "when we lived
at Henley, Barnes' gander was stole by tinkers"; to see her (as Flora requests of Arthur "a glass of port for Mr. F.'s Aunt") provoked into the
momentous statement that "the Monument near London Bridge . . . was
put up arter the Great Fire of London; and the Great Fire of London
was not the fire in which your uncle George's workshops was burned
down"; to be met (as Flora and Arthur struggle with the embarrassing
past) with the "inexorable and awful statement": "There's mile-stones
on the Dover road!" [38]

Like the old eccentric who is perpetually at her side, Flora Finching
suggests that Dickens' power as a humorist may well have been largely
displaced by other considerations, not extinguished by the waning of his
imagination. Her forte, like that of the early humorous characters, is expression and, at times, she equals (if she does not excel) Mrs. Nickleby
in the forging of odd comparisons and the yoking together of incongruous ideas. In keeping with what we have already noted about gratuitous
humor, her most amusing inventions are the free coinage of an unleashed
imagination. Thus little Dorrit's sudden wealth leads Flora to assume
that the Dorrits now have "a coat of arms of course and wild beasts on
their hind legs showing it as if it was a copy they had done with mouths
from ear to ear good gracious." [39] She envisions Amy in Italy "that favoured land with nothing but blue about her and dying gladiators and
Belvederas" and concludes her musings with an absurd appraisal of two
Italian cities:

> "Venice Preserved too . . . I think you have been there is it well
> or ill preserved for people differ so and Macaroni if they really
> eat it like the conjurors why not cut it shorter, you are acquainted
> Arthur . . . acquainted I believe with Mantua what *has* it got to
> do with Mantua-making for I never have been able to con-
> ceive?" [40]

Her memories of the past to which she constantly refers are as ab-
surdly graphic as those of Mrs. Nickleby and Mrs. Gamp for she brings
before us Mr. F. with "his slippers on the mat at ten minutes before six
in the afternoon and his boots inside the fender at ten minutes before

eight in the morning to the moment in all weather light or dark" who "proposed seven times once in a hackney-coach once in a boat once in a pew once on a donkey at Tunbridge Wells and the rest on his knees," and with whom on their honeymoon she "went upon a continental tour to Calais where the people fought for us on the pier until they separated us though not for ever that was not yet to be." [41] Her persistent recollections of the tragic parting from Arthur are invested with humor through a similar obsessive emphasis on detail:

> "You must be very well aware [she tells Arthur] that there was Paul and Virginia which had to be returned and which was returned without note or comment, not that I mean to say you could have written to me watched as I was but if it had only come back with a red wafer on the cover I should have known that it meant Come to Pekin Nankeen and What's the third place barefoot." [42]

Yet the effect of Flora's ruminations on the past is not that of liberating the kind of laughter which greets the vagaries of Mrs. Nickleby and Mrs. Gamp. Our appraisal of Flora closely resembles that of Arthur Clennam, who, viewing her attempts at "grafting" her youthful wiles "on to the relict of the late Mr. P.," reacts 'with feelings where his sense of the sorrowful and his sense of the comical were curiously blended." [43] Whereas Mrs. Nickleby and Mrs. Gamp play but a minor role in the story in which they appear and derive most of their reality as characters from their imaginative life, Flora is an emblem of the disappointments which life holds in the world of *Little Dorrit,* of the dismaying triumph of sordid reality over the claims of the imagination: the wispy, charming girl who had inspired Arthur's youthful passion has become a blowsy matron who lacks the grace fully to understand that that early passion can never be recaptured.

Thus the humorous aspects of Flora's temperament and behavior are overshadowed by the tragic nature of her predicament and that of Arthur Clennam; indeed, disappointment and the loss of illusions are such central aspects of the novel that we sense the close kinship between Arthur's brooding dejection and the state of mind of his author.[44] But Dickens' attempts to give Flora dimensions as a character further negate the imaginative play in some of her pronouncements. For by emphasizing her kindness and generosity, Dickens invests with pathos her erratic attempts to come to terms with the death of romance; by stressing the sordid details of her drinking habits and of her yearning for some physical expression of Arthur's interest, he annihilates the humorous effect of her self-delusion. Her "stream of consciousness" style, which can at times be so charmingly imaginative, at other moments—as it becomes erratic and muddled—seems to reflect Dickens' feeling that Flora's inconsistent behavior and lack of self-knowledge are not only the symptoms of a distasteful failure of judgment but of an irrationality that borders on madness. Like Bounderby's, Flora's imagination does not earn her immortality, but punishment, for it is seen as a ridiculous or frightening irrelevance in the dismaying reality that surrounds her.

In judging her, Dickens is in a sense passing a judgment on his former self, and the roots of that judgment lie in his earliest artistic efforts. From the beginning, his humorous viewpoint had been threatened by a somber appraisal of human misery, by a vulnerability to sentiment and pathos, by a fascination with the morbid aberrations of human behavior. The desire to extend his technique in fiction, the search for a greater complexity and seriousness in the portrayal of character, and the deepening of his anguish at the human condition inexorably led him to reject that spirit of humor which had negated suffering and gilded misery by imaginative creations that triumphed over human transience. Had this rejection led to the flowering of a satirical or tragic art which had far surpassed his achievements in the early works, the decline of Dickens' humor might not have been such a great loss. Yet, the impressive moral fervor and the insight into social conditions which Dickens revealed in his assault on Chancery, Circumlocution, Prison, Finance, and Public Charity never quite matched the originality of his insight into the incongruities of man's condition which can be enjoyed and endured through laughter. The delineation of weakness and passion in Lady Dedlock, William Dorrit, and Bradley Headstone never quite endowed them with the authenticity which a humorous approach to thought and behavior had stamped upon the figures of the early novels.

One must agree with modern critics that many Victorians did not appreciate the full extent of Dickens' artistic powers. But, despite the limitations of their viewpoint, Dickens' contemporaries understood the originality of his contribution to fiction. And that originality, even after we have duly recognized the growth of his psychological insight into characters and of his craftsmanship in the later novels, will still be found to lie in the humorist's imagination which fashioned Pickwick, Sam Weller, Alfred Jingle, Mr. Bumble, Vincent Crummles, Mrs. Nickleby, Mrs. Jarley, Dick Swiveller, and Sairey Gamp and endowed them with a gift of expression that transcended temporal concerns and vindicated man's "invulnerability" to the precariousness of his condition.

John R. Reed

CONFINEMENT AND CHARACTER IN DICKENS' NOVELS

DICKENS' obvious utilization of imprisonment and confinement as literary themes represents more than social criticism. It indicates the crystallization of character. What may have begun as an unconscious or fortuitous theme in his writing, soon enough became a conscious and polyvalent emblem. To some extent, it is possible to locate the dynamism of Dickens' novels in the conflict between confinement and liberation, between constraint and freedom. But this dynamism has a direction consistent with Dickens' attitude toward writing itself, since the freedom toward which characters are impelled in his novels is not an absolute freedom of the untrammelled will, but a disciplined liberation of governed impulses resembling the command of the artist.

The Pickwick Papers reveals an increasing atmosphere of confinement. It is possible to see the novel's movement in terms of contracting space with Pickwick's conversion from innocence to knowledge located in the Fleet experience.[1] The Pickwickians set out on their adventures with no restraints, though the interpolated tales hint at the destructive nature of self-indulgent and unrestrained behavior while suggesting the need for humility and self-control. Above all, it is self-knowledge that is lacking to the characters of this novel, good and bad alike. Only Sam Weller draws upon a certain, disciplined character. In this regard, he is the touchstone for all of the other characters, especially for Pickwick himself. Sam's anti-type is Jingle, who, early in the novel, appears with "an indescribable air of jaunty impudence and perfect self-possession" (ii). But Jingle is merely a skillfully selfish and exploitive individual who lacks genuine self-discipline. Consequently, when he is finally imprisoned, the energy that he has been expending is exhausted and he appears "without one spark of his old animation" (xlv). Winkle is an innocent variation of Jingle. He too is an imposter, but his ineptitude saves him from the consequences that overtake Jingle.

Pickwick himself is not thorough innocence embodied as some have supposed, for he is not beyond offering a timely bribe, and, what is more, it is his failure in self-discipline that initiates the contracting action of his world. Mr. Pickwick's vain and unwarranted assumption of authority regarding the discovery of the "rune stone," a discovery supported by extremely doubtful appearances (xi), leads directly to his embroilment with Mrs. Bardell which results from equally superficial appearances (xii). Not much later, Pickwick finds himself enclosed in the village pound after he has taken too much cold punch (xix), and before long he is again in custody at the hands of the foolish magistrate George Nupkins (xxiv). These encounters with external forces of constraint directly anticipate Pickwick's confinement in the Fleet, which is to a great extent voluntary.

From early in the novel, Dickens provided random but increasingly orderly signs of what the nature of confinement was; two of the interpolated tales indicate the general direction of his thoughts. In "The Madman's Tale," "thoughtless riot, dissipation and debauchery" have led the madman to "fever and delirium." His delusions occasion crimes which cause his imprisonment, but, for him, this confinement is spectral and internal. In his "grey cell where the sunlight seldom comes," the moonlight illumines "that silent figure," the spectre of his conscience, in a dim corner (xi). Self-indulgence and the lack of restraint result here in the same spiritual or imaginative constraint as in the more sophisticated case of Miss Wade in *Little Dorrit*. The tale of Gabriel Grubb, the tippling sexton, is an equally grotesque, but comic, version of the same lesson. Grubb's morose inebriation evokes a goblin who draws him down into a goblin cave and forces him to witness alien scenes of human affection and dignity much as the Spirits of Christmas instruct Scrooge. Once Grubb has seen that life is good for those who bear "in their own hearts an inexhaustible wellspring of affection and devotion," he is freed from the goblin cave and the dreamlike figures disappear (xxix).

These and similar hints prepare us for Pickwick's prison conversion. Pickwick's confusion at the Inn at Ipswich is a forecast and emblem of the manner in which the kind but undisciplined gentleman wanders into error. The Inn is a "multitude of tortuous windings," stairs after stairs, "passage after passage," and "rows of doors" (xxii). In this instance, Pickwick's confusion ends innocently enough, but the mazelike Inn cannot be forgotten when Mr. Pickwick is wandering "along all the galleries, up and down all the staircases" of the Fleet (xlv). It is at this point, appalled by a world turned dreamlike in the "crowding and flitting" of indistinguishable forms that Pickwick makes his "inflexible resolution" to "be a prisoner in my own room," thereby drawing his world to its furthest constraint.

The external pressures of society, irrational as they are, nonetheless provide the model for Pickwick's inner conversion. Having carried the contracting process to its limit with his inward discoveries, Pickwick is lured forth once more through the opportunity for "sympathy and charity" toward Mrs. Bardell, the Winkles, Mr. Jingle, and others (xlvii). Mr. Jingle's achievement of humility through confinement echoes, in fact, the more profound transformation in Mr. Pickwick. However, Pickwick, after his release from prison and the conclusion of the Winkle affair, does not resume his unrestricted travels, but establishes a "little retreat" at Dulwich, remarking that, as a result of his travels, "numerous scenes of which I had no previous conception have dawned upon me—I hope to the enlargement of my mind and the improvement of my understanding" (lvii). Pickwick is set at large when his mind is. Like Gabriel Grubb, he acquires freedom when he recognizes the dimensions of a disciplined and generous heart. Henceforth random expenditures of force appear unwise and consolidation seems the better course. Consequently, Pickwick, freed from the Fleet, elects a life that is still circumscribed, but voluntarily so. Armed with his new knowledge, he spends his later days "in his new house, employing his leisure hours in arranging the memoranda" which constitute the novel.

Confinement, then, can be a limitation or the means of liberation. For Mrs. Steerforth, Mrs. Clennam, and Miss Havisham, voluntary confinement is negative and useless, while for Heep, Compeyson, or Fagin, involuntary constraint is a cessation of selfish activities. But, as we have seen, for virtuous characters confinement leads to self-awareness. The difference between fruitful and barren constraint becomes clearer through a parallel notion in "George Silverman's Explanation." George Silverman scrupulously observes, "I had never been alone, in the sense of holding unselfish converse with myself. I had been solitary often enough, but nothing better" ("Silverman," iv).

Constraint of any kind is a means toward freedom when it forces the individual to hold "unselfish converse" with himself. Fagin's meditations in his cell bring him to no self-knowledge; they are, like the thoughts and dreams of the condemned man in the sketch, "A Visit to Newgate," little more than fantasy. But Arthur Clennam's enforced confrontation with himself does induce a consolidation of his character that constitutes freedom. So Wemmick, in *Great Expectations*, leaves the offensive constraints of his work with Jaggers for the ornamentally fortified house in Walworth where the "ingenious twists of path" in the garden mimic the many involved twistings of chambers, corridors, and paths throughout the novel, particularly those associated with Satis House (xxv). But also in a profounder way they mimic what Pip calls the "poor labyrinth" of his life (xxix), for, whereas Wemmick's withdrawal from social and externally controlled pressures and constraints to willed confines "brushes the Newgate cobwebs away" (xxv), Pip, though completely accepting pressures from without, still wonders why he "should be encompassed by all this taint of prison and crime" and why he feels "Newgate in [his] breath and on [his] clothes" (xxxii).

Pip, of course, does eventually free himself from the imprisoning forces of the world that has fettered him with false ideals, but only after he has passed through real and metaphorical constraints. Saved from Orlick's entrapment, Pip must also liberate himself through selfless action. While recovering from his salubrious illness, Pip dreamed that he "was a brick in the house wall, and yet entreating to be released from the giddy place where the builders had set me" (lvii). If we recall that Pip, observing Satis House—the symbol of a selfish and money-enslaved society—notes mainly "its seared brick walls, blocked windows," and ivy "clasping" the structure "with sinewy old arms," we will understand what it is that Pip is freeing himself from. It is selfishness and false values that he sheds in favor of the selfless offerings of a disciplined heart, for Pip devotes his subsequent life to disciplined and frugal labor. Like other heroes he moves from unwilled constraint to a willed control.

That Pip would break free from the confines of his false world is guaranteed by his name. Early in the novel, before Pip has made his first visit to Miss Havisham's, he discovers seeds tied in packets and kept in drawers in Mr. Pumblechook's shop and wonders "whether the flower-seeds and bulbs ever wanted of a fine day to break out of those jails, and bloom" (viii). When we reflect that a pip is a small seed, we instantly realize that Pip is destined from the beginning to "break out of" the imaginative jails that others have constructed for him. What is more, Pip's course appears as the natural course. Men are meant to be unimprisoned and free; but they only come to ultimate freedom through self-command and "unselfish converse" with themselves.

That the worst confinements are spiritual is evident throughout Dickens' novels, though perhaps the most graphic example of this fact is in the case of Mr. Dombey. Dombey is not self-aware, and when his son dies, carrying with him Dombey's cherished dreams, he roughly excludes his daughter Florence from his affections. Locking his feelings in, he locks Florence out and "what the face is in the shut up chamber underneath, or what the thoughts are, what the heart is, what the contest or the suffering, no one knows" (xviii). Florence, seeking to draw near to her father, if only in spirit, would creep to his room in the lonely nights and crouch "upon the cold stone floor outside it," but the "door was ever closed, and he shut up within" (xviii).

When Dombey's "old indifference and cold constraint" toward his innocent daughter becomes evident hostility, the narrative voice intones: "Let him remember it in that room, years to come" (xviii) —and indeed years later, in that room, Dombey will remember it, for "that room" is the "shut-up chamber" of his heart. Left alone, ruined and morose in the room that has become his "cell," Dombey finally engages in a semblance of converse with himself (lix). He perceives his failings as strictly as Gabriel Grubb or Mr. Scrooge, though without supernatural assistance. What Dombey sees in his mirror is a "spectral, haggard, wasted likeness of himself." The furniture of Dombey's shut-up heart now overwhelms him. He is powerless while the "likeness" takes up poison and prepares to end forever its terrible lonely imprisonment. But Florence arrives opportunely and opens the door to the long-shut-up chamber. Dombey begs his daughter's forgiveness and thereafter comes to a limited self-knowledge through humility and love. His confinement has not redeemed but it has improved him.

Hablôt K. Browne's illustration for this scene, entitled, "Let Him Remember It in That Room, Years to Come!" is, like many another, remarkably in keeping with Dickens' intent.[2] The room in Phiz's illustration has a strongly claustrophobic atmosphere. It is emblematic of Dombey's shut-up heart not only because of the mirror into which he is gazing, nor because his right hand rests upon his heart, but also because the picture of his lost wife peeps over the room divider that fails to hide it. Florence, in entering the room, admits a broad stream of light which has not yet, but is about to transform the prisoning room to a shared intimacy between father and daughter.[3] In entering the room, Florence enters Dombey's heart.

This illustration derives much of its power from allusions to earlier drawings. In the drawing, "The Dombey Family," Florence is again barely entering a doorway from the right while her father's stiff back is turned to her. In "Mr. Dombey introduces his Daughter Florence," she is entering the same doorway that she will enter so dramatically later, and is making a slight bow before Edith. In this same illustration, the painting of Dombey's first wife is largely shrouded, just as she is largely shut out of his mind. In "Mr. Dombey and the World," it will be Edith's portrait that is covered: the same portrait that later succeeds in raising its eyes over the room divider. In "Mr. Dombey and the World," Dombey has his back to the mirror, as he does in the much earlier "The Christening Party." These signs show that Dombey's room in the late illustration is the shut-up chamber of his heart where he must finally reflect upon himself. Only now does he turn toward the mirror. And strive as he may to exclude by drapery or other means the woman who has wounded him, she cannot be wholly hidden. The room's disorder suggests the chaos beneath Dombey's superficial order and constraint. Dombey will assume some capacity for selfless action only when he has admitted into his heart the broad beams of love symbolized by Florence's entrance.[4]

As Lionel Trilling has indicated, *Little Dorrit*, more than any of Dickens' novels, makes the extended meaning of confinement evident.[5] Life, it is remarked again and again, is a "labyrinth," [6] and it "appeared on the whole, to Little Dorrit herself, that this same society in which they lived, greatly resembled a superior sort of Marshalsea" (II, vii). Bleeding Heart Yard is "a maze of shabby streets" (I, xii), taking its name from an archetypal constraint upon love; the neighborhood near Park Lane, where Miss Wade "put her arm around [Tattycoram] as if she took possession of her for evermore," is another "labyrinth" and Miss Wade's dwelling a "close black house" (I, xxvi), while the theatre where Fanny Dorrit performs is a "maze" that seems to be "on the wrong side of the pattern of the universe" (I, xx).

This incarcerated world suggests that all of society has got on the wrong side of the pattern of the universe. The frequent association of Society—especially as represented in the Merdles—with disease indicates this reversed order of things. The diseased go free and spread their infection, though a "blessing beyond appreciation" would be conferred on mankind if the tainted elements "could be instantly seized and placed in close confinement (not to say summarily smothered) before the poison is communicable" (II, xiii). This is Dickens' solution for moral disease: absolute containment. Blandois must be crushed, Quilp drowned, Fagin hung, Headstone and Riderhood smothered in the mud, and so forth.

There are, on the proper side of the pattern of the universe, uses for constraint and confinement. Voluntary constraint, we have learned, can be a means to liberation of the spirit, but this purpose may also be abused. Miss Havisham's retreat proves destitute; Mrs. Clennam's willed infirmity grows into genuine paralysis (II, xxxi). Utter denial is not the answer.

From the beginning of *Little Dorrit* the differing purposes of constraint and confinement are made evident. In the Marseilles prison "the imprisoned men [are] all deteriorated by confinement" (I, i), while at the port travellers are held in quarantine to protect society against disease. Mr. Dorrit's deterioration in prison results from his acceptance of a condition which makes no demands upon his will and character (I, vi). Arthur Clennam admits that his severely constrained upbringing left him with a "void in [his] cowed heart" and "no will, . . . or next to none" (I, ii). Having met Mr. Dorrit, Clennam observes: "He has decayed in his prison; I in mine" (I, viii). But Clennam's decay is not the same as Dorrit's. Outside the security of the prison, Dorrit gradually caves in under the pressure of liberty. He is driven back through his inner emptiness to his one certainty: the world of stipulated rules and regulated spaces, the Marshalsea. Clennam, on the other hand, constrained, exiled, and finally forced into prison by the moral diseases of his society (represented by Mrs. Clennam's religion and Merdle's swindles), falls physically ill in the room of the Marshalsea where Dorrit so subtly decayed. But this incarceration is Clennam's quarantine and his illness brings him to self-awareness and strength.

Clennam's imprisonment forces him into an unselfish converse with himself, instead of leaving him to speculate upon "Nobody." In what he supposed to be his empty heart, Clennam dreamt of possible joys with Pet Meagles, but this fancy along with "Nobody" vanished when Pet married (I, xvi, xxvi). When Clennam relinquished Pet, he correspondingly applied himself to useful labor in partnership with Doyce. He had bid farewell to the Nobody within him and had begun to shape his identity anew. In this regard, it is significant that he meets another dream face to face only to experience disillusionment. Meeting his youthful love again, he discovers that "Flora, whom he had left a lily, had become a peony" (I, xiii).

Little Dorrit, like Clennam, is a dreamer. Confined in her garret, she fashions dreams which she does not imagine will conclude well. But this "small bird, reared in captivity," does not suffer deterioration through confinement (I, ix). Instead, she exploits her conditions, exercising self-less devotion for her family and others, and thereby reaping the reward of a full and bestowing nature. There is no void in Little Dorrit's heart, though there may be pain.

It is when Clennam is imprisoned that he discovers what a model Little Dorrit has been and "how much the dear little creature had influenced his better resolutions" (II, xxvii). Despite his upbringing, Clennam has preserved the virtues of humility, hope, and charity, and has always held as "the first article in his code" that he must "begin in practical humility." He has always known that "strait was the gate and narrow was the way" (I, xxvii). But it is only in prison that the value of his self-discipline and selflessness manifests itself. His incarceration facilitates the intimacy with Little Dorrit that will free his spirit. When Little Dorrit comes to him in the Marshalsea where he lies ill and thought-ridden, he sees in her "dear face, as in a mirror, how changed he is," changed both physically and spiritually, for, as Little Dorrit's nature pours out "its inexhaustible wealth upon him," Clennam is "inspired . . . with an inward fortitude that [rises] with his love" (II, xxx).

If Florence Dombey freed her father's smothered spirit by bringing light and love into the shut-up chamber of his heart, Little Dorrit too pours her riches into Clennam's vacant heart, whose boundaries have been established by his own noble code, and is therefore prepared to convert this love to new and generous expenditure. Accordingly, the powers of evil that have forced him into the most contracted space now retreat before his expanding nature. The Merdles, Mrs. Clennam, and Blandois wither, leaving the dimensions of the fictional world to Clennam and Little Dorrit who fill the entire space. When the old clerk of records observes that Little Dorrit has passed through the first volume of her birth, the second volume of her ordeal, "and she's now a-writing her little name as a bride, in what I call the third volume," he is, by allusion, conferring upon Little Dorrit and her spouse the entire space of the customary three-volume Victorian novel. Appropriately, the novel now ends as its hero and heroine leave the church, destined for "a modest life of usefulness and happiness," and the reader may close up the volume that is Little Dorrit (II, xxxiv) .

For Edgar Johnson, "the great and successful effort of [Dickens'] career was to assimilate and understand the blacking warehouse and the Marshalsea, and the kind of world in which such things could be." [7] It would be possible to argue that Dickens' entire outlook was spatially determined.[8] But my aim is not to attempt a psychological portrait of Dickens, presenting his entire life as a fascination with confinement and a struggle toward freedom. It is in Dickens' "career," in his fashioned utterances, that we may discover his use of what was undoubtedly a psychological preoccupation for esthetic purposes.

George H. Ford observes that Dickens' novels create their effects more through characters and their atmosphere than through teleology of plot. "Dickens' lavish use of settings is one more indication of his predominant concern for spatial realities rather than for time realities." [9] If Dickens' fictional world is essentially spatial, then prisons will be only the most obvious centers of confinement. In a world where all things press against one another, confinement may be defined as the sense of that pressure. And in a world that, like nature, abhors a vacuum, every space represents potential confinement. Moreover, each individually defined space may serve, though less obviously than the Marshalsea in *Little Dorrit,* as an emblem of larger concepts of constraint or control. In this way, Todger's, with its incalculable chambers, becomes "all of London, as London is the whole world." [10]

Dickens' fictional world presents not merely a maze (though the image recurs frequently in his novels) , but a series of enclosures and spaces. Sometimes all of existence seems to crush inward upon the space of the novel, as in *Oliver Twist,* of which J. Hillis Miller remarks, "no novel could be more completely dominated by an imaginative complex of claustrophobia." [11] At other times, objects within the cluttered fictional world exert an awesome pressure outward. It may be a boiler that threatens to burst, or characters who are themselves pressurized vessels in *Barnaby Rudge,* or Mr. Krook in *Bleak House,* who finally explodes as violently as do the Gordon riots.[12]

Dickens' novels present a dynamic plenum wherein parts move in response to exertions of force, and where the displacement of one barrier, through a species of moral isostacy, merely occasions another. They contain numerous shifting enclosures of variable natures, consequences, and values. What is more, characters themselves are not separable from objects or from one another and they respond to the same laws of force and resistance. Dickens thus exploits the opposition of constraint and freedom as a principal source of energy in his novels.

CARICATURE SHOWING DICKENS AND MEMBERS OF HIS STAFF
"CONCOCTING" THE CHRISTMAS NUMBER OF *All the Year Year Round*
FOR 1861
The caricature shows from left to right George Augustus Sala, Wilkie
Collins, Charles Dickens, William Henry Wills (possibly), and John
Hollingshead. Dickens, Collins, Wills, and Hollingshead went down to
Cheshunt to investigate Howitt's "champion" haunted house.
(Harry Stone, "The Unknown Dickens")

"Let Him Remember It in That Room, Years to Come!"
(John R. Reed, "Confinement and Character in Dickens' Novels)

Not all confinement is valuable. It is, in fact, highly ambiguous and its virtues depend upon the individual subjected to it. Even in cases of voluntary circumscription, certain choices are preferable. Alice, in the tale, "The Five Sisters of York," urges her sisters, who consider withdrawing into a convent for a life of meditation and virtue, to look upon "the bounds which God has set to his own bright skies, and not on stone walls and bars of iron!" Alice prefers her "green garden's compass" to the "gloom and sadness of a cloister" (vi). Confinement becomes what the individual confined will make it—a genuine prison, or a strait gate that leads to salvation. Mr. Merdle remains confined regardless of his physical situation, while Little Dorrit's spirit is forever free and growing; Arthur Clennam discovers and escapes his spiritual constriction only when he is physically confined.

The obvious means of indicating constraint is the outright image of physical confinement, the opposition of an inanimate object to a human being. Thus the Fleet in *Pickwick,* Newgate in *Barnaby Rudge* and *Great Expectations,* the Marshalsea in *Little Dorrit,* and the Bastille in *A Tale of Two Cities* serve as massive emblems of a universal condition where constraint has subtler forms, involving the oppositions of humans to one another. Mrs. Murdstone wears bracelets like fetters and her purse snaps things up as though imprisoning them. Her manner and appurtenances evoke the sense of constraint. Like Mrs. Joe in *Great Expectations,* she functions as a jailer.

The vilest forms of constraint are personal, wherein one individual imposes his will upon another. It is this that makes Uriah Heep so repulsive, Estella so awesome, and Bradley Headstone so frightening. The constraints imposed by institutions, such as Chancery or the Office of Circumlocution, are more debilitating, but less terrible.

The most serious constraints arise less from the force of external pressure than from the failures of the individual. Subordination to or dependence upon others is a form of constraint. *Nicholas Nickleby* presents a regular scheme of such dependencies, from the Nicklebys' dependence upon Ralph, to the children of Dotheboys Hall's dependence on Squeers, to the Kenwigses' dependence upon Mr. Lillyvick and his upon Miss Petowker, or the ignoble and confused dependency of the Mantalinis upon one another. After all, the most severe constraint is that imposed by oneself. An extreme of unwise self-constraint appears in the story of Miss Wade, though other willful limitations of freedom occur in characters such as Richard Carstone, Pip, or Podsnap. In every case, the circumscription of action and feeling is the consequence of a jaundiced vision which perceives the world only in terms of its own preoccupations. Freedom from self and the hungers of the self would be freedom in fact.

Imposing constraints upon the self is both the profoundest tyranny and a means to liberty. Liberty follows the clarification of identity through control; tyranny is self-ignorance. Most characters in Dickens have no means of defining themselves. Even Squeers tries to persuade others and himself that he is what he is not. Is he not, after all, tender with his family? Usually, characters employ fantasy or lies to image a history and a personality. Some, like Jingle, do this by design; others, like Sarah Gamp, through excess of spirit; and yet others, like Miss Knag, from frustrated necessity.

Dickens' villains rarely enjoy self-knowledge. Their inner world is void or chaotic, yet their strongest drive is to impose their will upon others. They seek always to be the movers in the pressurized space of their fictional world. Even when other motives seem weak or improbable, as with Monk in *Oliver Twist* or Quilp in *The Old Curiosity Shop,* the urge to compel is paramount.

Such flawed characters are all the more frightening when they begin to perceive that the will to power is their *only* form of identity. Mr. Merdle, aware of the limits of his financial strength, holds himself in presumptive custody until, this outward power failing, the more authentic pressures of the closed space in which he exists crush him. Similarly, Ralph Nickleby retreats into the tiny enclosure of the room where his crime against his son began, ultimately extinguishing himself, unable to counteract the predominant force of justice that is usurping the space he once controlled. Silas Wegg is the parodic version of this brand of villain, since all the while that he seeks to gain power over others, he is literally unable to pull himself together. Calling upon Mr. Venus to recover his lost leg, Wegg describes his excellent prospects of "elevating himself," and announces: "I tell you openly I should *not* like—under such circumstances to be what I may call dispersed, a part of me here and a part of me there, but should wish to collect myself like a genteel person" (OMF, I, vi). In the same novel, Eugene Wrayburn admits, "I know less about myself than about most people in the world. . . . I bored myself to the last degree by trying to find out what I meant" (II, vi). Yet, empty and powerless as he is within himself, it excites him to discover that he has "gained a wonderful power" over Lizzie Hexam (IV, vi).

"Power (unless it be the power of intellect or virtue) has ever the greatest attraction for the lowest nature," Dickens declared (OMF, III, vii). Both noble and ignoble natures exert power. Both can be motive forces in the claustral Dickens' world and it is the opposing pressures of these two powers that determine the shape of that world. The difference between the power of virtue and the power of evil is in the nature of their constraints. For the virtuous, each constraint and confinement serves as a means to discipline the chaotic world within; it is a constructive limitation. Thus, when Martin Chuzzlewit has returned from Eden where, despite the illusion of America's supposed freedoms, men worked "as hopelessly and sadly as a gang of convicts in a penal settlement" (xxxiii), he is ready to declare that he "should have best remembered [himself] by forgetting" himself; he is no longer "self-willed, obdurate, and haughty," for he has "been disciplined in a rough school" (xliii).

Admirable characters, such as Lizzie Hexam, Joe Gargery, Esther Summerson, and Nicholas Nickleby, are distinguished by their capacity for selflessness. Just as villains consciously exert power upon the world around them for their own ends, heroes and heroines exert a similar force for the benefit of others. In one case energy boils from an uncomprehended inner chaos, exploding upon the world like a fearsome escape of gas. In the other, a stream of power wells from a disciplined inner plenitude. In the first case, there is expenditure without renewal; in the latter, constant replenishment. Villainy spends itself and must eventually collapse, its internal space empty and void. But virtue, by continued restraint and control, holds in a regenerative power and thereby constantly expands. Thus, although most of Dickens' novels begin with virtue cornered, bullied, or oppressed, they end with the virtuous liberated. Dickens is employing the device of shifting pressures to vitalize his narratives. As virtue stores up its energies, it swells; villainy drains its chaotic substance. Accordingly, the available space of the novel is gradually appropriated by the representatives of virtue, while evil is depleted and forced out of the spatially disciplined world into undistinguished slime or to the undisciplined elements.

This dynamism of virtue and villainy is evident in the emblematic sea wreck of *David Copperfield*. The sea imagery of the novel reaches its climax in this scene. David's inner turmoil is germane to the tempest which wrecks the ship that Steerforth, despite his name, has been unable to control. David had been set "adrift" as a young boy in London, sojourning with the "shipwrecked" Micawbers (xii), and later, disturbed by his unpromising prospects, "was always tossing about like a distressed ship in a sea of bed-clothes" (xxxv). Thus, what happens at Yarmouth is not only the melodramatic extinction of Steerforth and Ham, but the culmination of David's own maturation. It is a painful liberation. Steerforth tossed about wildly by the elements is a graphic extension of the young man who confessed to David that he was afraid of himself, exclaiming, "I wish with all my soul I had been better guided! . . . I wish with all my soul I could guide myself better!" (xxii). Finally his unguided soul is claimed by the ungovernable elements. But Ham, steadfast, faithful, and selfless, also dies in the storm. However, he dies courageously contending with the roaring sea. The lifeline he carries indicates his awareness of danger and aptly represents his self-control and his acknowledgement of the unbreakable bond among all men. Ham achieves apotheosis; Steerforth dies.[13]

Earlier, in a difficult period of his career, David recognized that "what [he] had to do, was, to turn the painful discipline of [his] younger days to account, by going to work with a resolute and steady heart" (xxxvi). In doing so, he discovered the valuable attributes of character in "perseverance," "patient and continuous energy," "punctuality, order, and diligence," and "earnestness" (xlii). Now he must turn even sorrow to account. Agnes knew that David's nature could "turn affliction to good. She knew how trial and emotion would exalt and strengthen it" (lviii). It is David's "undisciplined heart" that must undergo the final constraint and have the vestigial selfishness squeezed from it through the pressure of steadfast work and a growing command of his emotions until he can offer an outwelling love from a full and disciplined heart to Agnes with the words, "There is no alloy of self in what I feel for you" (lxii).[14]

David has moved from the constraint of the Murdstones, through the control of Aunt Betsey, to self-direction, which comes only with self-knowledge. It is not accidental that David's final liberation in his elected bondage to Agnes (as distinguished from his "captivity" with Dora) follows the prison scene in which the false penitents, Littimer and Heep, are supposedly benefiting from the principle of solitary confinement. David has passed his confinement and will spend the remainder of his life in disciplined joy.

Earlier I said that the dynamism of constraint and freedom in Dickens' novels is consistent with his attitude toward writing itself, and *David Copperfield* is the novel that most clearly indicates this relationship. Unlike David, Dickens never fully achieved proportion in his generous and governing impulses though he certainly recognized the need for such proportion.[15] He was aware that proportion was achieved through self-control, through looking into the self and discovering the truth residing there. For Dickens, maturity was discovering the boundaries of one's nature and suitably arranging its attributes. In life as in art impulses require constraints which govern without quelling.[16]

David Copperfield says little about his art, though, as we have seen, he recognizes the function of self-discipline as a means of self-awareness.[17] For Dickens, art was more clearly a discipline leading to self-awareness. The novel's web of incident controlling its characters was the constraint by which he confronted himself, thereby approaching a truer perception of his own identity. How like one of his own characters Dickens may have felt when, deep in the regions of his own created world, he discovered his own mirror image. Like Yeats' anti-self, calling up its opposite and producing a sharper consciousness, David Copperfield or Charles Darnay could evoke a sharper self-image for Charles Dickens.[18]

If Dickens' fiction was a means of self-discovery, then it is not at all surprising that "not one of his novels was ever written out before publication."[19] Instead, Dickens conceived of large designs, frameworks, boundaries, which established an ideal space, subsequently populated with living characters and incidents. It is equally understandable that, if Dickens depended strongly upon the use of names in creating, defining, and advancing character, he should be equally concerned with the "identity" of the fictional space that he was creating.[20] As a result, Dickens could not start writing a novel until he had found it a name. In a sense, each novel became a character that Dickens was forming.[21]

There is something else, however, that led Dickens to conceive of literary composition in spatial terms, that made him dream of his story, *The Battle of Life*, as "a series of chambers impossible to be got to rights or got out of," [22] or that inspired him with the notion of a journal in which a kindly narrator keeps a supply of manuscript tales "in the old, deep, dark silent closet where the weights are in an old clock." [23] Undoubtedly, Dickens' experience in the blacking factory was critical and emphasized his sense of a world composed of varying constraints, for, upon being set free from this onerous experience, it was "with a relief so strange that it was like oppression, [he] went home." [24] But there had been an earlier experience which had made of confinement no evil suppression, but a joyful deliverance. In what is agreed to be an autobiographical passage in Dickens' most autobiographical novel, David Copperfield describes "a small collection of books in a little room upstairs, to which [he] had access" and where he read the tales that remained with him for life and which he declared "kept alive my fancy, and my hope of something beyond that place and time." Moreover, young David, consoled himself under his troubles "by impersonating [his] favorite characters in" these novels (iv). This consolation became a capacity for extending himself imaginatively into the surrounding world (v). At Salem House, it was David's "story-telling in the dark" that made him the intimate of J. Steerforth and gained him the respect of his schoolmates (vii).

David's imagination provides an escape from an increasingly sordid existence, but it is an undisciplined escape. Eventually David learns to discipline his heart and this control is mirrored in the discipline of his art (lxi). But *David Copperfield*, autobiographical or not, is Dickens' creation, not himself, and the "old unhappy loss or want of something" (xliv), if it left David, did not leave Dickens, who, apparently unsatisfied to confine his imaginative creations in the substantial form of his novels, yearned to *become* those fictions in the way that young David impersonated his own favorite characters. Thus he acted out on the enchanted space of the stage the very characters his imagination had engendered.[25]

In his maturity, David returns to the source of his imaginative strength—books. But, whereas the reading in the little room represented an unrestrained liberation from physical constraints, writing books is a nobler confining of experience in the discipline of art, which permits the artist's self-awareness. "I search my breast, and I commit its secrets, if I know them, without any reservation to this paper," David says, and, at last, his identity crystallized through the constraint of art, his life confined in the space of his book, David's "written story ends," and he may "close these leaves" (lxiv), as we close the leaves of Pickwick's papers, of Little Dorrit's last volume, and of Charles Dickens' *David Copperfield.*

Duane DeVries

TWO GLIMPSES OF DICKENS' EARLY DEVELOPMENT AS A WRITER OF FICTION

WHILE Charles Dickens was naturally elated and even tearful when he saw his first story, "A Dinner at Poplar Walk," in the December 1833 issue of the *Monthly Magazine,* he had recovered sufficiently by mid-1836 to make numerous revisions in the tale before reprinting it in the Second Series of *Sketches by Boz.*[1] But he seems to have responded objectively much earlier; his fourth story, "The Bloomsbury Christening" (*Monthly Magazine,* April 1834) , was enough like his first and yet a decided enough improvement upon it to suggest not only that he had already discovered deficiencies in his earlier piece but that the later tale was essentially a completely redesigned version of the first. Thus a study of the revisions that he made in "A Dinner at Poplar Walk" and an examination of the improvements evident in "The Bloomsbury Christening" should provide two important glimpses of Dickens' early development as a writer of fiction.

The revisions that Dickens made in 1836 are largely attempts to achieve fluency and clarity of style, to create a fuller, more chronologically consistent scene, and to give the whole story greater form. The revisions in style dispense first of all with a number of literary affectations (but by no means all of them) , such as the frequent use of italics and quotation marks to indicate the author's cleverness ("Mr. Minns . . . was always exceedingly clean, precise, and *tidy,* perhaps somewhat priggish, and the most 'retiring man in the world' "—*Monthly Magazine,* XVI, 617). Dickens also deleted a number of extravagant, even grotesque, figures of speech (for example, Minns "looked as merry as a farthing rushlight in a fog," his boots "were like pump-suckers," had he "been stung by an electric eel, he could not have made a more hysteric spring through the door-way"). But he left several others (Minns "leaped from his seat as though he had received the discharge from a galvanic battery," he was "looking forward to his visit of the following Sunday with the feelings of a pennyless poet to the weekly visit of his Scotch landlady," he was as happy as "a tom-tit upon bird-lime") and added yet another ("the first gleam of pleasure he had experienced that morning, shone like a meteor through his wretchedness"). He made numerous other stylistic revisions to clarify meaning, eliminate wordiness, and in a few instances sharpen the humor, as in the description of a poodle who, "with his hind legs on the floor, and his fore paws resting on the table, was dragging a bit of bread and butter out of a plate, preparatory to devouring it, with the buttered side next the carpet" (*Sketches by Boz,* Second Series, pp. 262–63). In the original version, the dog "was dragging a bit of bread-and-butter out of a plate, which, in the ordinary course of things, it was natural to suppose he would eat with the buttered side next the carpet" (*Monthly Magazine,* XVI, 618).

F. J. H. Darton associates such changes, even what he characterizes as "a more self-conscious, dramatised system of stops" (76), with an undesirable shift in the narrative tone of voice. They show Dickens, he claims, "now, ever so slightly, looking at the effect of his words, instead of writing fluently," trying, "not too successfully, to feign an artlessness which was merely natural a little earlier in his career" (75). I think Darton is mistaken. As I believe the examples above and the longer one below illustrate, the stylistic revisions help to produce a tone of voice that is, instead, at times somewhat more mannered than that of the original, but perhaps therefore more appropriate to the artificiality of farcical characterization and plot. If the story suffers even in revision— and it does not compare favorably with the much less fully revised versions of Dickens' other early tales—it is not because the style is ostentatiously artless or too artfully mannered but because it is neither with any great consistency. Although Dickens was enough of a craftsman by 1836 to recognize some of the stylistic weaknesses in the original version, he was still not sufficiently experienced as an artist to know how to make or even to be aware of all the changes requisite to creating a consistent, appropriate, and artistically satisfying tone of voice.

In addition to stylistic changes, Dickens made two other important alterations in 1836 that illustrate his development as a craftsman. The first of these is a thorough revision of a scene in a coach. Having waited an excessively long time for the coach that will take him to Poplar Walk for dinner with the Bagshaws to get underway (the coachman is attempting to find additional passengers), Minns, the tale's protagonist, voices his irritation. The two versions proceed as follows:

Original

"Going this minute, Sir," was the reply;—and, accordingly, the coach trundled on for a couple of hundred yards, and then stopped again. Minns doubled himself up into a corner of the coach, and abandoned himself to fate.

"Tell your missis to make haste, my dear—'cause here's a gentleman inside vich is in a desperate hurry." In about five minutes more missis appeared, with a child and two bandboxes, and then they set off.

"Be quiet, love!" said the mother—who saw the agony of Minns, as the child rubbed its shoes on his new drab trowsers— "be quiet, dear! Here, play with this parasol—don't kick the gentleman."

The interesting infant, however, with its agreeable plaything, contrived to tax Mr. Minns's ingenuity, in the "art of self-defence," during the ride; and amidst these infantile assaults, and the mother's apologies, the distracted gentleman arrived at the Swan, when, on referring to his watch, to his great dismay he discovered that it was a quarter past five.

(Monthly Magazine, XVI, 620)

Revision

"Going this minute, Sir," was the reply; —and, accordingly the machine trundled on for a couple of hundred yards, and then stopped again. Minns doubled himself up into a corner of the coach, and abandoned himself to fate—as a child, a mother, a bandbox, and a parasol became his fellow passengers.

The child was an affectionate and an amiable infant; the little dear mistook Minns for its other parent, and screamed to embrace him.

"Be quiet, dear," said the Mamma, restraining the impetuosity of the darling, whose little fat legs were kicking, and stamping, and twining themselves into the most complicated forms, in an ecstasy of impatience. "Be quiet dear, that's not your Papa."

"Thank heaven I am not"—thought Minns, as the first gleam of pleasure he had experienced that morning, shone like a meteor through his wretchedness.

Playfulness was agreeably mingled with affection in the disposition of the boy. When satisfied that Mr. Minns was not his parent, he endeavoured to attract his notice by scraping his drab trousers with his dirty shoes, poking his chest with his Mamma's parasol, and other nameless endearments, peculiar to infancy, with which he beguiled the tediousness of the ride, apparently very much to his own satisfaction.

When the unfortunate gentleman arrived at the Swan, he
found to his great dismay, that it was a quarter past five.

(Sketches by Boz, Second Series, pp. 269–71)

In the revision, it is, I think, evident that Dickens not only creates
a more artfully mannered narrative voice but also fills in the confusing
gaps in the continuity of the narrative and produces humor that is less
strained, more the natural if slightly exaggerated outgrowth of reality.
He reports the child's behavior more directly and in greater descriptive
detail and allows his narrator to indulge in humorous irony, hyperbole,
and litotes—and even a touch of anthropomorphism as the bandbox
and parasol, along with mother and child, become Minns' fellow passengers. Finally, he gives the scene more of a reason for its existence: it
effectively dramatizes an earlier description of Minns' character and
becomes less a transitional scene and more noticeably one in a series of
frustrating encounters for Minns.

The other important change that Dickens made in 1836—a thorough revision of the conclusion—gives the story the focus that the original version lacks. The conflict in the tale, as we know from a brief scene
between Mr. and Mrs. Bagshaw, Minns' cousin and his wife, revolves
around their plan to persuade Minns to make their son the heir to his
modest fortune. In the original version, Dickens soon loses sight of
this plot line while trying to derive as much humor as possible from
Minns' harassment by Bagshaw and his undisciplined poodle, by the
cabman and the child in the coach, and by the adults and young Bagshaw at the dinner party. This series of humiliations for Minns provides a secondary structure for the story along a line tangential, though
not contradictory, to what seems to be the announced direction of plot
movement. Toward the conclusion of the story, Dickens makes a crude
attempt to regain his initial emphasis by having the Bagshaw child, in
the confusion resulting from Minn's attempt to make a hasty departure
from the party, cry out, "Do stop, godpa'—I like you—Ma' says I am to
coax you to leave me all your money!" *(Monthly Magazine,* XVI, 624).
But he fails to maintain the focus at the very end:

> Never from that day could Mr. Minns endure the name of
> Bagshaw or Poplar Walk. It was to him as the writing on the
> wall was to Belshazzar. Mr. Minns has removed from Tavistock
> Street. His residence is at present a secret, as he is determined not
> to risk another assault from his cousin and his pink-eyed poodle.
> *(Monthly Magazine,* XVI, 624)

The revision, however, while still structuring the major portion of
the story as before, brings the focus back at the end to the main conflict.
Minns makes a definite decision about his will, and the reader, if not the
Bagshaws (Dickens changed their name to Budden in 1836), is aware
that the scheme of Minns' cousins has failed:

> He made his will next morning, and his professional man in-
> forms us, in that strict confidence in which we inform the public,
> that neither the name of Mr. Octavius Budden, nor of Mrs.
> Amelia Budden, nor of Master Alexander Augustus Budden,
> appears therein.   (*Sketches by Boz*, Second Series, p. 282)

It seems likely that Dickens made these specific changes in the tale's
resolution because he realized that in its main outline the original version was essentially formless. It did not take much to give form to the
story, for the secondary structure held most of it together, but once
again the alterations show Dickens learning to write better fiction.

Despite the young author's obviously greater awareness of his craft,
and a developing ability in using the techniques of it, the revised version
of "A Dinner at Poplar Walk" is not a completely effective story. It still
contains many stylistic crudities and much uninspired writing. Though
somewhat more fully developed in one scene and better structured overall, it is, like the original version, little more than a farcical and rather
sterile *jeu d'esprit*. However, in revising the tale in 1836, Dickens must
have found himself considerably hampered not only by time (he was,
after all, writing *Pickwick Papers* in monthly parts as well as holding
down a full-time position as a reporter for the *Morning Chronicle* and
doing other writing besides) but also by his original conception of the
work. To have made anything more of the story would have involved a
thorough redesigning and a complete rewriting of it.

In several important respects, "The Bloomsbury Christening," Dickens' fourth tale, can be considered as the very redesigned and rewritten
tale that perhaps the young author should have made of "A Dinner at
Poplar Walk" in 1836. The stories themselves are very much alike. Each
has as its central character a grumpy, ill-natured, fastidious bachelor-
misanthropist (Minns, Dumps). He is visited by a relative (Bagshaw,
Kitterbell) who invites the man to his home for a special occasion from
which the host hopes to benefit tangibly. The bachelor accepts with reluctance. Following a disagreeable ride in a public conveyance, he arrives at the home, where he spends several boring hours replete with
arid conversation and long-winded dinner speeches, in the company of
people who only exacerbate his misanthropic inclinations. In the end
he manages to escape, vowing to have nothing more to do with his
relatives. Dickens was at least reusing a standard plot structure of the
sort encountered in the theatrical farces and the comic magazine tales
with which he was perhaps too familiar, a kind of farcical story that he
knew his editor liked.[2] But he made important changes and refinements
in writing "The Bloomsbury Christening" that seem to point specifically
to a dissatisfaction with "A Dinner at Poplar Walk" and to a new insight into the potentialities of the basic story. While little improvement
in the more technical aspects of style is to be noted—or expected—in
"The Bloomsbury Christening," the very *telling* of the story is a bit

smoother, more continuous, perhaps because of the greater length of the tale (twelve pages as opposed to seven). But, whether the cause or the effect of the additional pages, the interlinks between scenes and between actions and speeches within scenes are better developed, the main characters are presented in fuller detail and the minor characters somewhat more colorfully, the conflict is more evident throughout, and characterization, plot, and tone of voice work together to produce a much more structurally unified story.

A scene in an omnibus provides examples of some of these improvements. It is three times as long as the parallel coach scene in the original version of "A Dinner at Poplar Walk," and more effective. The narrative transitions within it are smoother and the progression of events more naturally sequential and a bit more dramatic. Beginning with a long description of a rainy, miserable London day, the narrator then introduces us to Mr. Dumps, who, pausing at the corner in search of transportation to his nephew's, is immediately stolen by an omnibus "cad," or conductor, from beneath the noses of two others, and unceremoniously thrust into the middle of an already crowded vehicle. The discomfort of the wet passengers, newly augmented by the addition of Dumps, quite naturally becomes the subject of conversation and leads to the bachelor's argument with the cad. As a result, the young man deliberately allows the omnibus to dash past Dumps' stop. Losing the altercation with cad and driver over the fare, Dumps departs for the Kitterbells' in a vile mood. It is true that narrative progression in the 1836 version of the coach scene in "A Dinner at Poplar Walk" is handled at least as effectively, perhaps even more so. But, of course, when Dickens completely revised this scene then, he was able to utilize everything that he had learned about writing fiction in the two and one-half years between early 1834 and mid-1836.

What is particularly important about the scene in "The Bloomsbury Christening" is that Dickens is working in it with a larger number of characters—the scene is conceived on a slightly grander scale than is that of "A Dinner at Poplar Walk" and requires that the author exercise greater control over his materials. The result is not perfect, but it is a notable accomplishment for a young writer's fourth story and a striking improvement over the scene in the original version of his first tale. Actually, several of the characters in the Bloomsbury-bound omnibus momentarily spark into life, and all the occupants of the vehicle, operating as a group in one of life's numerous petty conflicts, produce a scene whose humor, arising largely out of consistency of character, is at least suggestive of what the more experienced author would produce a few years later.

The techniques of characterization are necessarily simple—a descriptive touch, a suggestion of dialect, a mannerism, a gesture, an action briefly sketched—but the result is surprisingly good. A lawyer's clerk (possibly a satirical self-portrait of the author) is concisely depicted as a damp, constantly smirking young man in a red-and-white-striped shirt. His contribution to the conversation consists of two atrocious puns. For example, when one of the passengers requests that Dumps sit anywhere but on his chest, the clerk replies, "Perhaps the *box* would suit the gentleman better" (*Monthly Magazine,* XVII, 379). The description is sketchy, the characterization flat, *à la* E. M. Forster, but when combined with the comic tone of voice in which the clerk delivers and reacts to his own witticisms (he chuckles audibly at his second effort, blithely oblivious of the discomfort of Dumps that occasioned it), the result is a young man bursting with self-satisfaction and *joie de vivre.* The omnibus driver appears in one brief paragraph, but his speech, apparently an accurate reproduction, and the brief description of his nonchalant stance on the box that belies at the same time that it reinforces the determination of his remarks reveal more than one might expect about the confidence of the man. The Cockney omnibus cad, who is the major antagonist in the scene, is a notorious troublemaker, as is revealed by the false solicitousness of his tone of voice and by actions clearly expressive of his independence: slamming the door once he knows it bothers Dumps, deliberately allowing the omnibus to go far past Dumps' corner, and joining with the driver in demanding full fare nevertheless. After each incident he appears all innocence—and all arrogance.

Like its counterpart in "A Dinner at Poplar Walk," this scene in the omnibus provides a transition between the two main episodes in the story and is an important structural element if the story is viewed largely as a character sketch. Here again "The Bloomsbury Christening" is an improvement upon the original version of the first tale. Dickens, flexing his new authorial muscles, builds onto his earlier characterization of Minns by making Dumps, though basically similar, a more colorful, more fully conceived, more humorously depicted, more complex character than Minns. A cross, cadaverous, odd, ill-natured, tall, fifty-year-old bachelor, Dumps is initially described as delighting in being miserable and in making others miserable, too. He takes a perverse pleasure in cemeteries, funeral services, fretful and impatient whist players, and King Herod's massacre of the innocents—and hates children, cabs, old women, doors that will not shut, musical amateurs, harmless amusements, people who find comfort in religion, and omnibus cads. The scene in the omnibus helps to dramatize this description by showing Dumps confronting unsuccessfully (thus contributing to his love of misery) two of the antipathies listed, as well as rain, wet umbrellas and people, a crowded omnibus, a window that will not shut, annoying passengers, and an unsympathetic coachman.

And this takes us beyond an examination of the scene in the omnibus for its own sake to a more general consideration of the importance of Dickens' characterization of Dumps to the structure and purpose of the entire story. Unlike Minns, Dumps is aggressive; thus the rudeness with which he is treated during his ride in the omnibus, and his failure to reciprocate fully, reinforce his misanthropy and, what is more important, further motivate him to unleash the full force of his frustration on the Kitterbells, who he believes beguiled him in some way into serving as their infant's godfather. In "A Dinner at Poplar Walk," Minns' mild triumph over the Bagshaws is an unexpected windfall, for he is predominantly a victim, a passive receptor of the incivilities of others. Even in deciding finally to have nothing more to do with his relatives—and in the revised version to leave the Bagshaw boy out of his will—he is not acting in a way contrary to how he might have behaved under less harassing circumstances. As a result, even the 1836 version of the story contains very little dramatic tension. Mr. Dumps, on the other hand, does not have such an easy time of it. There is no immediate question of whether or not the godson is to be Dumps' heir. So far as tangible benefits are concerned, Kitterbell desires only the traditional silver christening cup, and he is understandably upset when it is discovered that a thief has deftly removed it from his uncle's coat pocket.

But this is a minor disappointment; the story does not end here. Dumps must himself take steps to upset the family and guests at the christening party, to make them at least as miserable as he feels they have made him. He consciously sets about this through his understanding of the psychology of newly-made parents, dwelling at great length in his toast at supper upon such sensitive matters as infant mortality, wasting childhood diseases, and filial ingratitude. Mrs. Kitterbell goes into violent hysterics, her husband is almost as greatly upset, the christening party ends in shambles. Thus Dumps is a far more effective protagonist than Minns, and the plot of the story, held together by the reader's desire to see whether or not Dumps will behave in a way consistent with his early established character and whether or not he will manage to revenge himself upon the Kitterbells, has a greater suspense, force, and vitality to it. Again, Dickens elaborates upon the basic plot line used in his first tale, makes slight changes, shifts emphases, develops a closer relationship between character and structure, and comes up with a noticeably improved and redesigned version in "The Bloomsbury Christening."

In connection with the improvements already described, Dickens makes a basic change in the narrative tone of voice that produces a noticeably consistent satiric effect in "The Bloomsbury Christening." The change is largely achieved through a shift in the attitude of the narrator toward the characters in his tale. In "A Dinner at Poplar Walk," the Bagshaws are crude, boorish, unattractive fortune-hunters, but Minns, their victim, is entitled to some sympathy. Even though the reader is not particularly attracted by the man's irritability and fastidiousness, he is inclined to respond favorably to the bachelor's triumph at the end because of the indignities to which the Bagshaws have subjected Minns. The narrator himself seems to be a young man who thinks he is terribly clever, and more often is not, but whose sympathy for Minns' desire to be left alone and whose even more intense dislike of the Bagshaws' greed and provinciality guide the reader's response to the characters and to the final working out of the story.[3] While the narrator of "The Bloomsbury Christening" shares an often tasteless cleverness with Minns' narrator, he is a more objective observer of human behavior; as a result, the reader is not allowed to extend his sympathy, at least not for any length of time, to any one character in the tale. If at one moment he feels that Dumps has been unduly subjected to a series of indignities, a page later he encounters Dumps inflicting similar insults on others. If on occasion the reader is inclined to sympathize with the Kitterbells (it is their child's christening day, after all, and Dumps' vindictiveness seems a bit of an overcompensation), he must recall their greed, smug middle-classness, unattractive physiognomies, unpleasant mannerisms, silliness, and general dullness.

What Dickens much more successfully and much more intentionally produces in "The Bloomsbury Christening" than in "A Dinner at Poplar Walk" is a satire on human relationships. Through his obvious lack of sympathy for either man and his insistence upon the misanthropy of Dumps and the stupidity of Kitterbell, the objective and aloof narrator of the tale forces the reader to see clearly that both men are foolish, foible-ridden, and at times disgusting human beings, that in the end neither man triumphs, that no good, no human understanding, results from their interaction. This conscious satiric intent of the author is most evident in the ironic juxtaposition of the reactions of each man to the other in the last two paragraphs of the story, Dumps gloating in mad triumph, Kitterbell happy to be rid of "the most miserable man in the world." Certainly the final effect of this tale comes much closer than that of "A Dinner at Poplar Walk" to what its youthful author considered to be an accurate picture of life (in the Preface to the First Series of *Sketches by Boz,* he proudly characterized the pieces in the collection as "little pictures of life and manners as they really are"). This picture is surprisingly dark, as dark in some respects as that in the novels of his maturity, and darker than that in his early novels. Mr. Pickwick, Mrs. Nickleby, and Mr. Micawber, for example, are products of a far more sympathetic understanding of man's frailties than are Dumps, the Bagshaws, the Kitterbells, and even Minns. Compared with the satirical effectiveness of the short pieces that Dickens wrote in the next two years and certainly of *Pickwick Papers* itself, the satire in "The Bloomsbury

Christening" is relatively crude. Nevertheless, the emphasis that it gives to Dickens' early impression of reality is, it seems to me, another important if still primary stage in the young man's progress as a writer.

Thus, in the slightly greater vitality and import of its subject (a christening as opposed to a Sunday dinner), in its more fully and more colorfully realized characters, in its greater dramatic tension, and in the satirical suggestiveness produced by improvements in structure and tone of voice, "The Bloomsbury Christening" stands as a significant early work in Dickens' career. It seems likely that such improvements in conception and technique came earlier and more easily than might otherwise have been the case largely because the tale was conceived and worked out from the beginning essentially as a redesigned version of Dickens' first story.

As his work on these two tales illustrates, Dickens' early development was largely associated with a search for effective style and form. We get intimations (particularly, of course, in the 1836 version of "A Dinner at Poplar Walk") of the style that, from *Pickwick Papers* on, would be recognized as "Dickensian." We see Dickens working conscientiously with various stylistic elements to improve the quality of humor, to redeem characters from utter flatness, to create fuller and more colorfully detailed scenes, and to maintain a more consistently satiric tone of voice. At times his attempts are reasonably successful. But Dickens was always, I think, less troubled by style than by form. As his novels became increasingly complex, reflective of his developing artistic facility and maturity but also of a more serious assumption on his part of the responsibilities of social critic and moral philosopher as well as artist, the structural problems demanding solution merely increased in number and difficulty. In these early tales, his problems with form are of a lower order—nevertheless, basic in importance—and certainly as troublesome for the young writer to resolve satisfactorily. In "The Bloomsbury Christening" and the 1836 revision of his first tale, he manages to correct some of the flaws in structure that mar "A Dinner at Poplar Walk," both in regard to the development of individual scenes and, especially in "The Bloomsbury Christening," to the artistic unity of the entire tale. He was not, however, as successful with most of the other tales that he wrote in 1834. While it is obvious that Dickens would need to improve considerably before *Pickwick Papers,* the writing of the fifty-seven other tales and essays that comprise the two series of *Sketches by Boz* would continue to provide him with the necessary experience. In the two attempts that he made to improve "A Dinner at Poplar Walk" we can observe at least the beginning of a major author's journey to greatness.

Louis James

PICKWICK IN AMERICA!

THE PLAGIARISMS of *The Pickwick Papers* are a curious phenomenon. The Pickwick chintzes, cigars, coaches, songbooks and knickknacks are nothing unexpected: similar exploitation has surrounded popular novels from Richardson's *Pamela* (1740) to the present. But the literary plagiarisms, while they trade on the popularity of Dickens' work, and are closely derived from it, also take on a certain life of their own. They can be longer than Dickens' *Pickwick*. Edward Lloyd's publication *The Penny Pickwick* by "Bos" (1837–39) ran weekly for two years, comprising some five hundred thousand words. Mimic Pickwicks gyrated through mimic Pickwick plots but also into new adventures at home and overseas. During the first year of *The Penny Pickwick* its readers could follow G. W. M. Reynolds' *Pickwick Abroad; or, the Tour in France* (1837–38); during the second they could buy *Pickwick in America!* (1838–39), also by "Bos." Yet the qualities of a major novel often preclude extended imitation. In this paper I wish to argue that in *The Pickwick Papers* Dickens fused together various popular cultural elements, and a semi-literate hack like "Bos" could modify certain of them back into a minor subliterature of its own. Dickens himself was unsuccessful when he tried to resurrect Pickwick and the Wellers in *The Old Curiosity Shop*. Even during the writing of *Pickwick,* Dickens developed as a novelist. Masterpiece as it is, it was written in a mode to which he could never fully return.

The title page of the plagiarism I wish to examine in some detail suggests a rag-bag performance at a popular theatre. The Pickwickians would entertain. It reads: PICKWICK / IN / AMERICA! / DETAILING ALL THE REMARKABLE / ADVENTURES OF TAAT [sic] ILLUSTRIOUS INDIVIDUAL / AND HIS LEARNED COMPANIONS, / IN THE / UNITED STATES. / EXTRAORDINARY JOHNA-THONISMS, / COLLECTED BY / MR. SNODGRASS, / AND / THE SAYINGS, DOINGS AND

[65

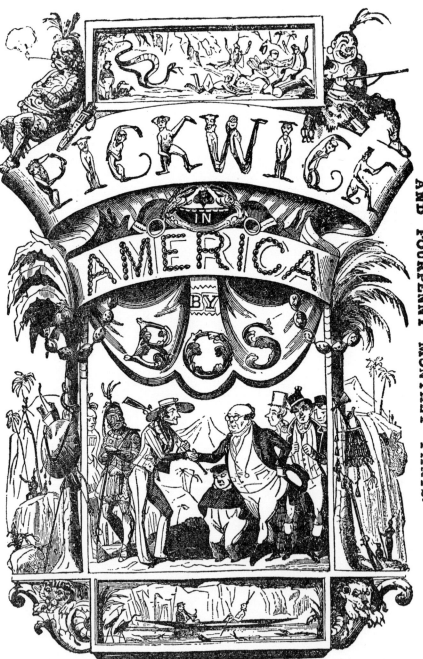

PUBLISHD BY E. LLOYD, 62, BROAD STREET, BLOOMSBURY

COVER FOR *Pickwick in America*

MEMS, / OF / THE FACETIOUS SAM WELLER, / EDITED BY "BOS" / ILLUSTRATED WITH FORTY-SIX FINE ENGRAVINGS. / LONDON / PRINTED AND PUBLISHED BY E. LLOYD, 62, BROAD ST. BLOOMSBURY. The "fine engravings" were lively if crude half-page woodcuts, in the theatrical style, printed on the front of each weekly number of eight pages of small double-column print, and covered in a brown or blue wrapper. The wrappers announced monthly issues at fourpence, which presumably would contain four, and periodically five, numbers. It ran from either April or May 1838 (contemporary advertisements cannot be relied on for an exact date), for forty-four numbers, three hundred and fifty pages plus four which comprise title page and advertisements. "Bos," from the internal style and other evidence, was almost certainly Thomas Peckett Prest (18–(?)–1859), a prolific penny-issue novelist, dramatist, song writer and literary hack of the forties and fifties. The idea of sending Pickwick overseas probably came from the success of Reynolds' *Pickwick Abroad;* the plot may have been suggested by M. G. Lewis's popular *Journal of a West Indian Proprietor* (1834). Although Lewis goes to Jamaica, both Lewis and the Pickwick of "Bos" go out to see to the management of their plantations, and hear the complaints of their slaves. Weller contrives to cross the Atlantic, together with many of Dickens' *Pickwick* characters. One exclusion is Jingle: his boasting and imposture were perhaps felt to be too close to those of a standard American stereotype, who is presented in a Mr. Johnathon Junket.

In North America, the Pickwickians see New York, and Pickwick is attacked by rats and "muskatoes," which, being American, are gigantic. They see a Negro theatre, and are nearly lynched when Weller insists on treating a Shaker meeting as a dance, grabs a Shaker woman, and joins in. Pickwick ousts his delinquent plantation manager Squabbs, and favourably receives a Negro petition asking for better conditions. Debts to *The Pickwick Papers* are constant. Occasionally there is word-for-word piracy. "New" plots are often adaptations, e.g., a love affair between Tupman and a Miss Jemima Slumkey is a reduplication of the Winkle / Arabella Allen story. Weller at a Negro ball sings a song about Dick Turpin (101–2). The song is different from that which Dickens' Sam sings in the inn by the Insolvent Court (xliii), but "Bos" remembered Sam sang songs about Turpin. Even ideas for variations may come from Dickens. When the Pickwick of "Bos" goes to plead the case of Tupman, he goes disguised as a woman (181). In the parallel passage in *The Pickwick Papers* (xxxix) there is no mention of woman's dress: Pickwick does, however, tell Sam to get "his great-coat and shawl" ready. A shawl more usually indicated woman's dress; "Bos" may have pondered, then given Pickwick a shawl, with dress and petticoats as well. In characterization, the Pickwick of "Bos" in part existed vicariously, drawing life from Dickens' original. But, as any readers of the penny-issue version probably would not have read this, the Pickwickians of "Bos" had to have some life of their own. The imitator relies on the stereotypes that Dickens transforms, and they show through. Dickens never mentions his debt to Goldsmith's perennially popular *The Vicar of Wakefield;* "Bos" explicitly compares his Pickwick to Dr. Primrose (167). "Bos" also holds closer to the comic types of Winkle the cockney sportsman, Tupman the aged but still aspiring Don Juan, and Snodgrass the inarticulate poet. In particular he and his illustrator (probably C. J. Grant, though the cuts are not signatured) rely on Dickens' visual dimension of characterization.

A new phase in the interaction between the graphic and the verbal arts began with the work of William Hogarth (1687–1764) at the time of the rise of the novel in England. This has to do both with Hogarth's "realistic" attitude to life and with his technique. Lamb declared, "His graphic representations are indeed books: they have the teeming, fruitful, suggestive meaning of words. Other pictures we look at—his pictures we read." [1] And, if his details have the complex meaning of words, his work opened the eyes of writers to the wealth of significance in detail, in the next century to no one more than the young Dickens. "The Soul of Hogarth has migrated into the Body of Mr. Dickens," said Sydney Smith; [2] and after relating Boz to Smollett and Fielding, *The Edinburgh Review* declared, "We would compare him rather with the painter Hogarth. What Hogarth was in painting, such very nearly is Mr. Dickens in prose fiction." [3]

If Dickens was noted as a Hogarthian writer, the original proposal that he write text for Seymour's etchings places him in a graphic / verbal genre that includes as an important element the frequent reissues of Hogarth's prints with written commentary. A new turn to this tradition came when from 1809 to 1811 William Combe wrote "The Schoolmaster's Tour" as text for Thomas Rowlandson's etchings in *The Poetical Magazine.* Published revised in monthly parts as *The Tour of Dr. Syntax in Search of the Picturesque,* this continued work was highly popular, going through five editions in 1812–13. It was still being reprinted as late as 1903, when it appeared with its two sequels published by Methuen and Company. Combe and Rowlandson later collaborated on their grotesque masterpiece *The English Dance of Death,* which was brought out in twenty-four monthly numbers, 1814–16. (The etching of the clown in this serial may possibly have prompted "The Stroller's Tale" in *Pickwick,* where the dying clown is directly compared to "the spectral figures of the Dance of Death." The Dance is also referred to in the 1847 Preface to *Pickwick.* Dickens, however, also knew Holbein's work.) In 1821 the popularity of *Dr. Syntax* was surpassed by the acclaim given to the serial *Life in London* written by Pierce Egan, Sr. for the etchings of George and Isaac Robert Cruikshank. Dickens was to turn to George Cruikshank for illustrations to his own grimmer "life in London," *Oliver Twist*.

The content of *Dr. Syntax* and *Life in London* is directly relevant to *Pickwick*, and more will be said on this below. Their linking of text and illustration also makes them part of the increased visualization of mass communications that was to be a feature of Victorian culture in media ranging from newspapers to the novel. I have suggested else-where [4] that the Pickwick characters are rooted in the visual dimension of cartoon, and in the convention of caricature or the selection and exaggeration of comic eccentricity. Round beaming face with green-tinted spectacles, stout body with tailcoat, white waistcoat, tights and gaiters, these are essential to the genesis of Pickwick and to the way he was enjoyed by his contemporary readers, however much modern criti-cism stresses rather the moral qualities that emerge as the story develops. This aspect is an important clue to the plagiarisms. The visual quality gave the Pickwickians a 'solidity" that carried them across barriers of class attitude and social sensibility, to where they were reinterpreted but kept an identity.

The first artist to draw the Pickwickians was Robert Seymour (?1800–1836). His most popular work was his series of 3d. etchings, *Sketches by Seymour* (four vols., 1833–36). No bibliography has traced the many editions of the series, which was reprinted until the blocks lost their definition. Although originally issued with only short sub-titles, at least two writers later provided it with text: R. B. Peake *Snob-son's Seasons* (c. 1838) and Alfred Forrester *Seymour's Humorous Sketches* (1843). As *Pickwick* was planned to follow the success of the *Sketches,* it is interesting to compare the two works. Seymour portrays cockney hunters in the style of Mr. Snodgrass (although they were also to be found elsewhere in contemporary literature); [5] a (female) drunk like Mr. Pickwick under the influence of the salmon carried in a wheel-barrow; a village cricket match; a comic coach-riding disaster and a pic-nic. But Seymour's style of humor is more important than are particular incidents. His visual interpretation of the new type of middle and lower-class cockney life emerging in London with its variety, its pre-tensions and its vitality, must have made Seymour particularly exciting to the future author of *Pickwick, Nickleby* and *Martin Chuzzlewit*.

Seymour held the attitude of a middle-class southerner towards the birth of a new and self-respecting working-class identity that took place in the first decades of the nineteenth century. He satirizes butchers and dustmen reading books and newspapers. Yet his awareness of class tensions underlies many of his cartoons. In one of them, for instance, a middle-class gentleman, his respectability emphasized as is Pickwick's by somewhat "old-fashioned" clothes, has wandered into a working-class eating house. Nervously he asks for "a portion of Veal and Ham, well done." "A plate o weal, an' dam well done," bellows the waiter to the kitchen, while the other diners stare and grin at the social intruder. Similar comedy of interclass embarrassment and malcommunication comes in chapter ii of *The Pickwick Papers* where Pickwick and the cabbie misunderstand each other, and the tensions blow up into a fight from which Pickwick is lucky to escape with a black eye. Class polarities emerge in other directions in the novel, as will be seen later.

"Embarrassing situations" were stock for Seymour's comic stew. Weller gives a close verbal rendering of this facet of Seymour with anecdotes such as "It's a great deal more in your way than in mine, as the gen'l'm'n on the right side o' the garden wall said to the man on the wrong un', wen the mad bull vos a comin' up the lane" (xxxvii). Up to a point, the plot of *Pickwick,* too, climaxes in comic tableaux of Pickwick in awkward situations—Pickwick set on by a cabbie, chasing his hat, discovered with Mrs. Bardell in his arms, drunk in the pound, or confronting the lady in the Ipswich inn bedroom—scenes which could be effectively focused in the monthly illustration. One cannot, however, make this more than a contributing factor to the writing of the book, particularly as such tableaux were also part of the modality of nineteenth-century theatre.

By the time he began *The Pickwick Papers,* Dickens had dramatized his short story "The Great Winglebury Duel" into the burletta, *The Strange Gentleman.* He had also largely finished an operetta, *The Village Coquettes.* He was to enter, with huge delight, into the production of both at the St. James' Theatre in 1836. Act Two, "Sc. second and last" of *The Strange Gentleman* is set on "A gallery in the Inn, leading to the bed-rooms." The inn Boots enters. He does not look like Sam Weller, being one-eyed and distinctly sinister, but he speaks cockney somewhat like Sam; in particular, he has a speech identifying the inn guests by their footwear. In chapter x of *Pickwick,* when Dickens introduces Sam Weller as a cockney Boots with a gift for boot-reading, he also sets him in a similar galleried inn. This makes the more interesting the highly theatrical construction of the scene that follows.

Mr. Wardle, Pickwick, and Mr. Perker have tracked down Jingle and Rachel Wardle. When Wardle opens the door, the trio do not file in. In good farce tradition they wheel in, three abreast, to confront Jingle in a perfectly-timed tableau at the precise instant he produces the marriage license. Collapse of stout lady into convenient chair, where she will not detract from the central conflict between Wardle and Jingle. The characters are perfectly cast as to appearance. The stout, choleric Wardle is played against the tall, gangly, imperturbable Jingle, with interpolations from the little bald-headed Perker. The scene gathers into a controlled crescendo, with the introduction of the voices of Weller, Pickwick, and the vociferous chamber-maid, of Arabella, kicking her heels on the way to "double hysterics," and of Jingle hamming it up threatening to call an officer. One notices the physical vigor with which actions are executed. This is true throughout *Pickwick*. On quick thumbing through two pages of chapter ii, I note "Mr. Samuel Pickwick *burst* . . . from his slumbers . . . *threw* open his chamber window . . . Mr. Pickwick and his portmanteau were *thrown* into the coach . . . *ejaculated* Mr. Pickwick . . . down *jumped* the driver . . . *flung* the money on the pavement." This intensity expresses the vital genius of Dickens, but it reflects also the heightened action of the nineteenth-century stage. "Gesture," the actor Dion Boucicault was to say, "is not a small thing." [6]

At the emotive climax of the Wardle-Jingle scene, Dickens suddenly changes dramatic direction. Up to this point, Wardle's outrage has been set against the cool amorality of Jingle. Suddenly the mild-mannered Perker emerges to take control. Passion and moral issues are answered by legal procedure and compromise. Dickens changes the scene, literally. A door is opened to a side room, and Perker, Jingle, Wardle and Pickwick enter it. There they make a dishonorable, rational settlement. The moral planes and dramatic handling thus have been perfectly fused. This relates the scene to the great trial of Bardell v. Pickwick (xxxiv). Here in this later episode, however, dramatic contrivance has a more complex effect. The trial is "staged" by Dodson and Fogg. Before, the "actors" are curiously casual, as before a performance. When a figure like the chemist, who leaves a potential poisoner attending his shop, enters the trial, he has to give up responsibility to the outside "real" world. The tableau of Mrs. Bardell and her children, complete with large umbrella, is straight theatre. Pickwick is audience. He is the person most affected by the trial, yet he says nothing throughout; and his slow, deliberate act of removing his spectacles at the end emphasizes his role of observer. Stage techniques not only provide the dynamics of the trial comedy, they highlight the contrived "pretend" system of the law, and indicate Pickwick exists on a different level of meaning.

The structural use of theatrical effects frequently can be found both in the narrative *Sketches by Boz* and other parts of *Pickwick*. Consider, for example, the use of the cluttered stage setting in the episode of Bob Sawyer's party. The claustrophobic effect ("Glad to see you—take care of the glasses," cries Bob to Pickwick) heightens the comic dynamic behind the scene. For immediately impending (literally) above the cramped party is Mrs. Raddle, with "her steam up," ready to explode the moment the occasion edges, against all dampening, into hilarity. One effect of dramatic techniques in *Pickwick* (clearer still in *Nicholas Nickleby,* which lacks a truly unifying hero) is to increase the imaginative autonomy of many of the scenes. This again aided the plagiarist with his scissors, paste and daub method of composition. More important, Dickens' sympathy with the drama immediately related his work to the new urban sensibility of "Bos" and his penny readers. The nineteenth-century city masses were finding a cultural focus in the theatres. By the eighteen-sixties, it has been estimated, some 150,000 Londoners alone were at a theatre on any one day. The urban community life, disillusioned yet sentimental, intimate yet impersonal, restless yet intense, created Victorian melodrama, with its rapidly alternating modes and moods, as its appropriate imaginative expression. Melodrama drew from and reinforced feeling and action in other spheres. As Robert Corrigan has written, it was not only "the prevailing form of popular entertainment, it was the dominant modality of all nineteenth-century British life and thought." [7]

The plagiarists therefore found Dickens' theatrical sense immediately accessible. In the penny version there is the same sense of staged scenes; again the physical vigor is heightened: "suddenly moved as though by an electric shock, [Tupman] bounded towards the amiable Pickwick . . . 'Then,' exclaimed Mr. Weller, striking a violent blow on the table with his clenched fist. . . ." Sam Weller, portrayed in the woodcuts with something of the handsome young actor about him, evinces an actor's talent. He insists on performing at the Negro Theatre, at a Shaker's meeting and at a Negro ball. Sam Weller was the most important character to many working-class readers; for them his theatricality heightened his fictional reality. Particularly interesting is the reliance of "Bos" on the dramatic performances of Charles Mathews the elder (1776–1835), whose "polymonologue" performances so delighted Dickens, and in one of whose parts the young Dickens intended to show himself worthy of the stage.[8] Earle Davis has shown that Dickens was indebted to Mathews for the use of verbal tags to characterize speakers, and in particular for the style, perhaps some of the Baron von Munchausen content, of Jingle's talk.[9] The imperfect way in which the "At Homes" were recorded makes it difficult to identify more precise verbal debts, but it would be surprising if Dickens, with his careful memorizing of Mathews, did not incur a few. For instance, in Charles Mathews' *Trip to America* we have

> "You are von—von"—"One what"—"Von individual"—
> "Well, and you're another." [10]

Dickens modifies the joke in chapter xv of *Pickwick Papers:*

> "Sir," said Mr. Tupman, "you're a fellow."
> "Sir," said Mr. Pickwick, "you're another."

"Bos" also takes up the idea in *Pickwick in America!:*

> "Why—why—" replied Winkle in a feeble voice, "I say you
> are—"

"What?"

"An *individual*," answered Winkle desperately.

"Then," said Tupman clenching his fist and looking awful upon Winkle, "I have not the slightest hesitation whatever in saying, sir, that you—you—are *another!*" (39)

"Bos" appears at first to be plagiarizing Dickens; his use of Mathews' "*individual*" rather than Dickens' "fellow," however, indicates he was going behind Boz to the dramatic monologue both were using.

"Bos" uses Mathews extensively also as a source of information about America. He portrays a scene of the Pickwickians visiting a Negro theatre at Philadelphia, which is an adaptation, often word for word, of a similar scene in Mathews' *Trip to America*. Both describe a "Sable Roscius," who, acting *Hamlet,* veers into *Richard III* with the line

"Now is him winter ob our discumtent,
Made de glorbius summer by him sun ob *New York!*"

which a partisan audience insists be changed to "sun ob Fill'emdelfy!" On which, in "Bos," Weller leaps onto the stage to render "Down in ther lowlands there lived a lov-er-ly damsel (110)." "Bos" also goes to Mathews for an account of a military muster and other incidents in his tale.

Theatrical debts are apparent throughout *Pickwick in America!* The Negro characters are generally based on the "Jim Crow" that the American entertainer T. D. Rice presented at the Surrey Theatre, London, in 1836, with enormous success, a presentation that was shown elsewhere and much imitated. In 1836 G. Smeeton published *Mr. and Mrs. Jim Crow's Collection of Songs,* and Negro songs were a well-established part of London music hall repertory by the time the indefatigable Mr. T. P. Prest edited *The London Singer's Magazine* (c. 1839). In *Pickwick in America!* the Negroes have "Jim Crow" as their "national ballad," and dance the shuffle-and-turn popularized by Rice. The steady stream of facetiae poured out by Weller, a Mr. Johnathon Junket and a Mr. Tristram Sparkles (which "Bos" clearly considered a bright feature of his serial) parallels W. T. Moncreiff's *Tarnation Strange* (first acted in 1838), which Moncreiff declared in his "Advertisement" to the printed version (London: J. Limbird, 1842) was to be "a framework in which a portion of the best of American jokes might be presented to the public." Moncreiff even provided the hero Johnathon Jonah Goliah Bang with two sets of jokes, so that those who came a second night would be regaled with a new supply. Behind this exploitation lay a fashion for American humor, sparked off in particular by Limbird's penny-issue serialization of *The Sketches and Eccentricities of Davy Crockett* (1834), but to be found everywhere filling short-fallen columns in cheap periodicals in the eighteen-thirties. American humorous journals following the success of Baltimore's *The American Turf Register and Sporting Maga-*

zine (1829–44) and *The Spirit of the Times* (New York, 1831–61) provided easy game for English paste-and-scissors editors, although the popularity of this humor meant some pieces were home-grown too—a long search for the items in R. Tyas' anthology *American Broad Grins* (1838) in their attributed sources met with no success.

These jokes do not bear repeating today, although the eighteen-thirties evidently found them irresistible. They are generally tall stories, either of the man-put-trousers-in-coal-bucket-and-sat-on-the-fire, "absent-minded" variety, or fantasy exaggerations, as when Johnathon Junket in *Pickwick in America!* recounts that his fever set the house alight, but his perspiration extinguished it (21). Yet these jokes should not be discounted. It is on such irrational bases that national attitudes are built up. "Bos" did not apparently read any of the available popular accounts of America by travelers such as Basil Hall, Frances Trollope, or Thomas Hamilton, or, if he did, he did not consider them a good basis for a popular story. The stereotypes of America and Americans came mainly from stage or humorous narrative. "Bos" was writing a "humorous" narrative. But confusion between humorous and serious narrative emerges. Tall tales are made to assume boastful Yankees. "Bos" holds the tall tales of Junket up for ridicule, yet has Pickwick chased by giant rats. There is also the incident of the slave petition.

On his plantation, Pickwick is confronted with a deputation of the slaves. Drifting into this situation (perhaps from his reading of M. G. Lewis's *Journal*), "Bos" found himself with conflicting attitudes. He had previously drawn the Negroes as sheer T. D. Rice comics, and the woodcuts had made great capital of their music hall frills and jackets and comic faces. But "Bos" was probaby aware of the popular Oroonoko complex of the noble, persecuted savage which emerges in another Lloyd serial about Negroes, *Lucy Neal* (1847). He may have known the part the Black Jacobins had played in radical movements, for the names of Pickwick's petitioners include Robespierre and Junius. "Bos" apparently held ambiguous attitudes toward Negro equality. Moreover, Pickwick's reaction must be pure benevolence. In this confusion "Bos" writes very curiously. One item of the petition requests "dat no nigger shall vork more den sixteen hours a day," then adds "an shall not hab less dan six meals *per diadem*." The next item asks "dat no nigger shall be flog more dan twite a day, namely, vonce in de mornin' and vonce at night." Demands to walk on the same side of the road as "de whitee gentlemen" and other apparently serious requests mingle with farcical petitions to wear eye-glasses up to frying-pan size, and for white silk stockings. Pickwick's attitude, however, is prescribed:

> "Gentlemen, . . . I have heard your petition with much pleasure and pain. Pleasure to see that the population of coloured

PICKWICK

IN

AMERICA.

EDITED BY "BOS."

"A Deputation Waiting on Mr. Pickwick with a Petition"

people begin at last to feel their independence, and to demand
their rights, and pain to think that they have so long endured
the greatest injustice and tyranny, the greatest cruelty and oppression from their masters, deprived of all those rights and
privileges which are not the property of one class of individuals,
only, but of all the human race!" (231)

The slaves respond to this (and much more like it) with a chorus from
"Jim Crow." The story does not include Pickwick *doing* anything to back
up his speech, but perhaps one is meant to assume that his words are as
good as deeds.

The conflict between crosscurrents of comic caricature and realism
is here explicit. If one impulse of nineteenth-century urban culture was
towards the formalization of experience in theatre, the grim conditions of
the cities, the hard, disillusioned quality of town life, led also to a demand for realism. Pierce Egan, Sr. (1772–1849) here played an important
part. With regard to Pierce Egan and *Pickwick,* most attention has been
paid to the "dash of grammatical Egan" noticed by the *Athenaeum* (3
April 1836). And indeed, Dickens at times echoes Egan's periphrastic,
Latinate style.

The first ray of light which illumines the gloom, and converts
into a dazzling brilliancy that obscurity in which the earlier
history of the public career of the immortal Pickwick would appear to be involved (i)

chimes with Egan's writing in such passages as,

Professors of the Royal Academy, let me entreat you not to avert
your microscopic eyes from my palpitating efforts; but second my
elevated wishes, if it seem good to your taste.[11]

But it is difficult to recapture the sense that this contrived style was the
expression of new vitality in English prose, that it is an elaboration of
the colloquial urban slang still to be caught in the few surviving English
Old Time Music Hall traditions. It reasserts a delight in sheer word-
play. Within its rhetoric—into which the reader must enter as into an
intimate game, or find it intolerable—there is a controlled tone and
attitude towards the subject which is partly ironic and partly serious.
Using epic style to describe a boxer or a horse, Egan does not mean his
subject *is* Homeric, but he does not deny it, either. It was the perfect style
for the post-Napoleonic years that suspected, and admired, the "heroic."
Dickens uses this stance and phraseology up to a point to create his own
comic/heroic figure, "the immortal Pickwick."

If the *Athenaeum* found a "dash of grammatical Egan," they found
a "handful" of Hook. This comment and the immense popularity of
Theodore Hook's *Sayings and Doings* (1826–29) have puzzled critics

who have not seen his style in its historical perspective. A dramatist and celebrated practical joker, Hook, like Dickens, contrives to direct his reader as a stage manager does his audience. His urbane style is relaxed, flexible, and vivid:

> The parsimonious youth proceeded to perambulate the streets, look at everything which was to be seen *gratis,* and having thrown a "portion" of tough roasted mutton into his stomach, upon the points of a two-pronged steel fork, at some economical dining-rooms near the Strand, he proceeded at half-price to the pit of the Adelphi Theatre, where he dissipated his evening in witnessing the freaks of Tom and Jerry, the exhibition of which filled him so completely with alarm and dread that, upon quitting the house, he ran home to the shelter of his bedroom.
>
> *(Sayings and Doings,* Second Series, 1825, p. 63)

There is a strong objective awareness—the scene is socially placed by the two-pronged steel fork (Bob Sawyer tried to get his oysters open with one *Pickwick,* xxxii), used in a shabby-genteel restaurant in the back streets behind the Strand. The words "economical" and "portion," and the roast *mutton* are exactly right, and the hero James's attempt to cut a dash as a man about town (he has elaborately dressed up as a dandy) culminates when a stage presentation of *Life in London* sends him home terrified. With his eye for the relevant comic detail, Hook also tended to compress characterization to the socially significant detail of dress, as did Dickens: "the tall gentleman in stockinet pantaloons" (Hook, p. 10), "the prim man in the cloth boots" (*Pickwick,* xxxii). Hook's rapid style, his objective comic vision, made his minor art one that Dickens could use for major.

Pierce Egan, Sr.'s *Life in London* (1821), seen dramatized by Hook's would-be dandy, was probably more important than his style, not only to Dickens, but to the course of the English novel. To understand the impact of *Life in London,* perhaps one must first consider *The Tour of Dr. Syntax in Search of the Picturesque* (1812) already mentioned. The gaunt, elderly pedant on his bony horse, was clearly modeled on Don Quixote: indeed, the French version was called *La Don Quixotte Romantique* (Tr. M. Grandais, Paris, 1821). But while Cervantes' hero went out to perform chivalrous deeds, Syntax went out, notebook in hand, to look for a Romantic ideal of scenic beauty and to *sketch.* Pickwick, also often compared to Quixote, does benevolent acts, and his tangle with the law could be remotely compared to Quixote's tilt with the windmills. But both at the beginning and at the end we see him as someone who wishes not to do chivalric deeds, but to see and note.

> "I shall never regret," said Mr. Pickwick in a low voice, "I shall never regret having devoted the greater part of two years to

mixing with different varieties and shades of human character; frivolous as my pursuit of novelty may have appeared to many. Nearly the whole of my previous life having been devoted to business and the pursuit of wealth, numerous scenes of which I had no previous conception have dawned upon me—I hope to the enlargement of my mind, and improvement of my understanding. If I have done but little good, I trust I have done less harm." (lvii)

If this shows an attitude related to that of Syntax, it is still closer to that of Egan's heroes. The title of the second book of *Life in London* runs "On the difference between what is generally termed 'Knowing the World' and 'Seeing Life.'" Chapter i begins, "with many persons, it should seem, to KNOW THE WORLD consists in knowing HOW to get money; . . . this sort of *knowledge,* however, was not the *forte* of CORINTHIAN TOM, nor of his friend LOGIC. . . . SEEING LIFE was their object." The process of "seeing life" and introducing the innocent Tom Hawthorne into it, was to become immersed in all the varieties and shades of London life. If Weller's knowledge of London was "extensive and peculiar," that of Logic, Jerry's mentor, is called "extensive and accurate." Informing Egan's work is his sense of the organism of the nineteenth-century city. Cruikshank's frontispiece of city life as a Corinthian column seems at first traditional in its view of society, but with its differentiation of "mechanic" and office worker, its acceptance of leisured class and "down-and-outs," and in the central position given to the prison, it was, as Jerry might have assured us, "Bang up to date." In *Life in London* and the darker sequel, *The Finish of Tom and Jerry* (1828), as in Dickens' *Pickwick* and *Oliver,* the city is also set against a rural haven and moral retreat. The demand for Egan's work was so great that etchings could not be colored fast enough; stage versions broke theatre records; newspapers emerged with *Life in London* in the title; it was pirated and imitated (over a hundred derivative works have been claimed) [12] and the phrase "Tom and Jerry" passed into the English language. It became a way of looking at external reality. In *Life in London* the picaresque hero changed his stance slightly, but significantly. He became the focus through which the inhabitant of the city sought a fuller awareness of his own complex identity as town-dweller.

Dickens satirized Egan's favorite type in the Game Chicken, and he makes fullest use of the fictional concept of the city as organism later, in *Bleak House, Little Dorrit* and *Our Mutual Friend.* Yet in *Pickwick* the models of *Don Quixote* and *Humphrey Clinker* are reinforced and modified by Egan's novel. Pickwick's quest to "see life," his city-initiated guide (with all that Weller's intimate knowledge of London implies), and Pickwick's movement across the extremes of the social organism, from the flunkeyed fashion world of Bath to the down-and-outs in the Fleet— these are all elements that reflect the impact of *Life in London.*

While *The Pickwick Papers* is not particularly about London, when Dickens is using the city as a setting his sense of its social structure and geography is unerring. The extended description of Lant Street before Bob Sawyer's party is humorous in tone, and allows Dickens to use the observations he had made when he knew it all too well lodging there across from the Marshalsea Prison in 1823. Yet without it, the episode would be crucially weakened. Bob Sawyer and Ben Allen, the guests, the landlady, the party itself are all given a sharper perspective by Dickens' succinct sketch of the social habitat. (Henry Mayhew was to show basically the same inquisitiveness about urban natural history in *London Labour and the London Poor* [1851, 1861–62]). When Pickwick scribbled his request to Mrs. Bardell for "Chops and Tomata Sauce," Dickens noted the address was Garraway's Coffee House, which looked out on the bustle of the commercial London City area. When Pickwick had left Mrs. Bardell and Goswell Street (unlike Lant Street, a socially respectable lodging house district), he fled back to the City inn, the George and Vulture. This inn still stands in quiet, like a dark, sawdusty womb, tucked within the bustling triangle of Cornhill, Lombard, and Gracechurch streets.

Pickwick's social status is also unobtrusively but carefully defined. We have noted the early scene where Pickwick is attacked by the cabbie, amid a hostile lower-class mob. His social position is made sharper even as he denies it by immersing himself in the low life of the Fleet. When he meets Mrs. Bardell in prison, it is important that we should be aware also of her lower-middle-class status. In this way her past presumption in aspiring to Pickwick's hand is emphasized, she is properly distanced from him in the tableau of his forgiveness, and we can fully appreciate Pickwick's magnanimity towards the social inferior who has wronged him. Immediately before this scene Dickens shows a tea party in which Mrs. Bardell is joined by Mrs. Cluppins and Bob Sawyer's raucous persecutor from Lant Street, Mrs. Bardell.

A further point about social awareness in *Pickwick* is suggested by one of the major differences in tone between it and *Pickwick in America!* The popular plagiarisms—and this includes that of Reynolds—are more physically violent than the original. Weller slashes the fat boy with a whip to make him dance. Winkle is dragged through a pond "full a dozen times" on a rope, then ducked in the mud again, "his body covered with wounds" (320). Dickens' *Pickwick* expresses violence only indirectly, through the *emotional* violence of interpolated stories or the unspeakable desires of the fat boy. It emerges most directly in the tags of Sam Weller, such as, "Wery sorry to 'casion any personal inconwenience, ma'am, as the housebreaker said to the old lady when he put her on the fire" (xxvi). These tags are comic, but with a distinctly sadistic streak of comedy. Dickens was accurately indicating a class difference in allowed taste. ("Bos" evidently found Weller's tags particularly easy to imitate.)

Sam has other moral characteristics which in Pickwick would be unthinkable. He comes to Pickwick with "one amiable indiscretion, in which an assistant housemaid had equally participated" (xii) ; although we are led to expect he will remain faithful to Mary, he believes Pickwick guilty of indiscretion both with the lady in the Ipswich inn and with Mrs. Bardell. He happily joins in manipulating the voters at Eatanswill, and counters Pickwick's stand for principle with a cheerfully anti-principle story about committing suicide to preserve the gastronomic reputation of crumpets. But while the middle-class Pickwick stands against strict ethical standards, morality for the *servant* Weller has a different basis: it stands on cheerfulness, efficiency, and reliability to his master. Now the social shift in moral expectancy enables the book to have two characters, of whom we approve entirely, yet who have complementary, different moral foci. We might call these innocence and experience. Weller exclaims against Pickwick's naïvety that he is *"half-baptised"* (xiii) . Without unduly elevating a casual Wellerism, (the phrase, however, is also used in chapter ii of *Oliver Twist*) , we may note it inverts the usual significance of baptism: instead of its transferring the initiated from sin into Christian innocence, Weller, brought up on the streets, sees baptism as initiation from innocence to experience. His is "life as it is." Pickwick has not properly made the transition. Even after the experience of the Fleet and the compromise decision that ends it, Pickwick can recover total benignity simply by shouting at Dodson and Fogg. Pickwick makes no subsequent action that bears out Auden's theory [13] that he has been changed by his descent into the depths of low life.

One might therefore say the novel has two attitudes to its age. In the Weller focus, it is "Life in London," knowledge of the fallen world, a zestful interest in its idiosyncrasies and variety. Weller's reaction to the ills of life is not moral speculation, but activity. "When a man is Down," writes Egan, ". . . he must get upon his pins how he can." [14] "It mustn't be," says Sam about Pickwick in the Fleet, not "how wrong." But through the focus of Pickwick it can simultaneously transcend this. It is the fairy-tale world of the guinea-laden god-uncle; where a man can end a successful business life uncompromised and innocent; where social injustice is "wrong"; but though it may temporarily distress the heart, kindness, feasting and laughter are the final virtues, and the Arcadia of Dingley Dell, garlanded with children, brings down the curtain, always. Because Weller can believe in Pickwick, Pickwick, improbably, exists. At its deepest, the triumph of *The Pickwick Papers* is a triumph of faith. To this level, *Pickwick in America!* never begins to penetrate.

CATTERMOLE'S FRONTISPIECE FOR *Master Humphrey's Clock,* I
(Jane Rabb Cohen, "Strained Relations")

CATTERMOLE'S "NELL DEAD" FOR *The Old Curiosity Shop* (1841)
Above, An early sketch; *below,* A later sketch
(Jane Rabb Cohen, "Strained Relations")

Jane Rabb Cohen

STRAINED RELATIONS

Charles Dickens and George Cattermole

GEORGE CATTERMOLE was the first of Dickens' illustrators whose initial ties to the author were social, not professional. Like Maclise, Frank Stone, and Stanfield, Cattermole's contributions to his writings were motivated by friendship, not ambition. In contrast to Cruikshank and Phiz, whose humorous interpretations of contemporary life and literature were far more appreciated by the public than by the *cognoscenti,* Cattermole was renowned by the time he illustrated Dickens' work in 1840. He was England's chief exponent of bygone-times, a full member of the Society of Painters in Water Colours, and one who had refused an offer of a knighthood. The "pure, earnest and natural" antiquarian feeling Ruskin perceived in Cattermole's works [1] never characterized those of Cruikshank. "Monks, cavaliers, battles, banditti, knightly halls, and awful enchanted forests," according to Thackeray's catalogue of Cattermole's favorite canvases,[2] were subjects foreign to Browne's pencil. Although Cattermole contributed only one-fifth of the illustrations for only one work, *Master Humphrey's Clock,* he elicited the author's deference, gratitude, and affection in ways his more prolific colleagues were never able to do.

Cattermole, as a spirited bachelor residing in Albany chambers previously occupied by Byron and Bulwer-Lytton, was welcomed by the various circles of the London art world. It was probably at Gore House, mingling among the fashionable visitors who gathered around the Countess of Blessington and the Count D'Orsay, that he met the author of *The Pickwick Papers* who took to him at once. Emerging from self-imposed isolation after the death of Mary Hogarth, Dickens hastened to further his acquaintance with Cattermole through their mutual friend, Forster. Did Forster think, the author inquired with unfeigned eagerness, that the artist would join them on their proposed tour of London prisons? He should also like to dine with Cattermole afterwards as he was already—

[81

"to use a Scotch expression—very fond of him." The two that very day
personally delivered the invitation which was duly accepted.[3]

Dickens saw Cattermole frequently in the subsequent months in
1837, but never as often as he wished. His regret when previous obliga-
tions prevented their meeting was unabashed. "Why do you always ask
me to dinner on days when I can't come?" Dickens complained, having to
decline the artist's invitation upon his return from inspecting Yorkshire
schools for *Nicholas Nickleby:* "I have been engaged for next Tuesday a
fortnight back, and you pick out that unfortunate day as if there were no
other days in the week and no other weeks in the year." The novelist took
this coincidence "exceedingly ill" as he wanted to tell the former pupil of
John Britton, a noted antiquarian draughtsman to whom Cattermole
had been apprenticed, about his visit to York Cathedral. Dickens had
"scarcely set foot in the Nave" when the Verger led him by the shoulder
to contemplate the "Five Sisters" window. "There!" said the old man,
"Mr. Britton the great artist and architect says that's the first window in
all Europe; and if Mr. Britton don't know a fine window when he sees it,
who does, as the Dean says." The novelist knew the encounter would
please his friend. The window pleased Dickens enough for him to im-
mortalize it in *Nicholas Nickleby* (65–66) .[4]

The following year, the artist's marriage to a distant maternal connection of the author promised to reinforce the growing friendship between the two men. Clarissa Elderton had never met her illustrious relation before the morning of her wedding on 20 August 1839. Yet Dickens
was "foremost" among the guests, who included Forster, the best man,
Thackeray, Macready, and the Landseers, in congratulating the couple.
As the newlyweds drove away from St. Marylebone, he energetically
pelted their carriage with rice while shouting "every joy and happiness
and *bon voyage.*" [5] The following day, the novelist wrote the couple,
honeymooning in Richmond, from nearby Petersham where he had
taken a cottage. Refraining from comment on the wedding or on the
bride's beauty on the "suspicion" that she might be reading over the
artist's shoulder, Dickens contented himself with saying—and sincerely
meaning—that he was "ever heartily, my dear Cattermole,—Hers and
yours." [6]

The author not only sent best wishes to the Cattermoles, but tangible
amusement while they waited for the completion of their home on Clapham Rise. His pony-carriage, his servant, and especially his library were
at their disposal. From Devonshire Terrace he sent down a carpetbag
full of novels, periodicals, and essays "convenient as being easily taken
up and laid down again"; the heavier works of Goldsmith, Swift, Fielding, and Smollett were "handy" at Elm Cottage should they be wanted.
Upon moving to Clapham Rise, Mrs. Cattermole received from Dickens
an exquisitely bound volume of *Nicholas Nickleby* together with a

charming letter of presentation.[7] Her husband was invited to "make one at the little table" at the *Nickleby* dinner, as he did in the novelist's "little circle," to add to the latter's pleasure of recalling this labor.[8]

Dickens extended his relationship with Cattermole beyond the social by asking him to join Browne in illustrating *Master Humphrey's Clock*, a periodical which was to appeal to popular tastes and purses by appearing weekly with woodcuts rather than monthly with engravings. But even the presence of Mr. Pickwick and Sam who joined Master Humphrey and his friends in linking the otherwise unconnected short pieces was not enough to steadily attract the public which wanted another novel by Dickens. Thus the author soon had to expand his story of Little Nell into *The Old Curiosity Shop* and revive his long-delayed *Barnaby Rudge* to rescue the faltering enterprise; most readers have forgotten that these two novels originally appeared as parts of *Master Humphrey's Clock*.

In propounding this "mightily grave matter," Dickens' jaunty tone belied how gratified he would be to have one of Cattermole's artistic stature contribute to his new venture; his unaccustomed deferential tone gives him away. Perhaps the artist would not "object" to making a specimen sketch of an old room with Elizabethan furniture and Master Humphrey's clock which might head the opening page. Cattermole would not have to bother copying and cutting the drawing on wood; the task could be done by others. Would the artist "like to repeat the joke at regular intervals," continued the self-deprecatory author, "and, if so, on what terms?" He and the publishers were justified by past experience in anticipating "enormous" sales and popularity. If Cattermole would dine with him within the next two days at Devonshire Terrace or the Athenaeum, Dickens could tell him more about the work. In the meantime, he had tried to make his written proposal "as business-like and stupid as need be."[9]

Cattermole agreed to join "the *Clock* works" as Dickens termed the venture. He submitted a sketch for the old "quaint" room which the author and publishers thought "most famous" (SBB, 699). The author placed Cattermole's name before Browne's on the title page. Far from acting "slighted,"[10] Phiz, also designated to copy Cattermole's drawings on the wood block, was anxious to do them justice. The publishers were to forward the block for the artist's approval before it was cut. If Cattermole preferred to select his own subjects for the future, the author would insure that he had the number to choose them from. "I ought to have done so, perhaps, in this case," Dickens apologized, "but I was very anxious that you should do the room." Finally, he assured the artist, Chapman and Hall "will never trouble you (as they never trouble me) but when there is real and pressing occasion; their representations in this respect, unlike those of most men of business, are to be relied on."[11]

Never had Dickens been so diplomatic in dealing with one of his illustrators. In constant communication with Cattermole concerning *Master Humphrey's Clock,* the author was never peremptory, irritable, or condescending as he had been occasionally with Cruikshank, Seymour, and Browne. The artist was treated as if he were doing Dickens an extraordinary favor and might suddenly back out of the project if not granted extreme consideration. Subjects mainly of a picturesque nature were sent by the author, "thinking" the artist would like them "best." Scenes were put in "expressly" with a view to Cattermole's "illustrious pencil." Suggestions were given with the understanding that the artist would realize them "a hundred times better" than the author could imagine. Dickens was not only greatly "obliged" to Cattermole for having altered "Little Nell Dead" (OCS, 575), but hoped that his wish in that respect didn't "go greatly against the grain." He strenuously regretted having "troubled" the artist by delaying the story of John Podgers and substituting another tale which would require a different illustration. When Dickens urged the "dear fellow" not to "forget dispatch," he never implied that the artist could be dilatory, rather that he or the publishers or the printers were "mortally pressed" for time. Dickens freely addressed Cattermole as "My Dear George"—even Kittenmoles—but he sprinkled his instructions with respectful references to "sir" throughout their correspondence.[12]

Contemporary readers, hardly aware that Cattermole had joined Phiz in embellishing *Master Humphrey's Clock,* did not engage in invidious comparisons between the two artists, though inevitably Cattermole's signature was sometimes confused with that of George Cruikshank.[13] Considering the obvious difficulties of mechanical and aesthetic coordination, Browne and Cattermole worked harmoniously together. His two artists endured with humor and patience the occasions when a subject meant for Cattermole was mistakenly sent to Browne or the times that Browne had to execute the tasks of his ill or pressured colleague. Considering "the material and the despatch," none, including the author, could have anticipated such good results.[14]

The "picturesque" subjects fell mainly to Cattermole: the time motif on the weekly wrapper (SBB, 697); the room of Master Humphrey (SBB, 699) which had come out "so admirably"; the stately bed of Master Graham (SBB, 715) of which Dickens heard such "glowing accounts"; the Cavalier who robs Hugh of his love and life (SBB, 720); and the ornate church in which Will Marks's burden is buried (SBB, 771). Cattermole's sole humorous scene, that of Mr. Pickwick and the Wellers on the frontispiece for the first bound volume of *Master Humphrey's Clock* (SBB, 688), was put by Thomas Hood to clever critical purpose. He pointed out, what Dickens also realized, that the club machinery of the *Clock,* as in *Pickwick,* was both inconvenient and unpopular. "Accordingly," wrote Hood, "whilst the two clubs are snugly housed

—the one in the kitchen and the other in the parlour, and, as the frontispiece hints, all fast asleep—the author quietly gives them the slip and drives off to take up characters, who really have business down the road."

The necessarily expanded "business" of these characters, especially that of Little Nell, captivated the hearts of contemporary readers. "Look at the artist's picture of the child, asleep in her little bed, surrounded, or rather mobbed, by ancient armour and arms, antique furniture, and relics sacred or profane, hideous or grotesque," noted Hood; "it is like an allegory of the peace and innocence of Childhood in the midst of Violence, Superstition, and all the hateful or hurtful Passions of the world" (OCS, 14).[15] Cattermole was given a disproportionate number of opportunities to portray the heroine. Browne was usually assigned to portray the villain.

If, by the time of William Dean Howells, Nell hardly brought tears to the eyes of anyone, the previous generation, "on both sides of the Atlantic, used to fall sobbing" at her name.[16] Dickens, though ignoring Macready's request to spare her life, confessed to Cattermole that he was "breaking" his heart over her demise, so fraught with memories of Mary Hogarth. The artist fully understood the author's mood in the last three scenes in which the heroine figured and incorporated the spirit as well as the letter of his endless suggestions. He sensitively rendered Kit running through the snow, bird cage in hand, to the parsonage whose lighted windows belie the fact that "the child (unknown, of course, to her visitors, who are full of hope) lies dead" (OCS, 568). Cattermole's portrayal of Nell lying alone with strips of holly and berries on her person and pillow manages to express "repose and tranquillity and even something of a happy look, if death can" (OCS, 575), though the print of "the dear dead child" gave Macready such a "chill" that he dreaded to read the accompanying text.[17] While Dickens concluded the story he could not "bear" to finish, the artist showed Nell's grandfather, "who cannot be made to understand that she is dead," repairing to her grave to await her arrival (OCS, 583). As a little tailpiece for the narrative, Cattermole drew three angels bearing Nell to heaven which certainly gave "some notion of the etherealised spirit of the child" (OCS, 593) if not the depressed spirits of the novelist, himself nearly "dead" with work and grief over her "loss."[18]

Dickens found strength, however, to express his gratitude to Cattermole. "Believe me," wrote the author, "this is the very first time any designs for what I have written have touched and moved me, and caused me to feel that they expressed the idea I had in my mind."[19] So attached was Dickens to this child of his fiction (and of his fantasy), that he commissioned Cattermole to make water colors of her home and grave. The author expressed rare pleasure upon receiving, after his return from America the following year, these "beautiful pictures, in which the whole feeling, and thought, and expression of the little story" were rendered "to the gratification" of his "inmost heart." [20]

This period of professional collaboration marked the height of Dickens' conviviality with Cattermole as well. Business matters could be just as easily discussed during a ride, a walk, or a "snug" dinner at Devonshire Terrace or the Athenaeum, or even during the periodic gatherings of the "Clock corps." "You have shewn your interest in the matter too well to leave me in any doubt of your joining us, and joining us heartily," teased Dickens, inviting the reserved artist to celebrate the completion of the first volume with *Master Humphrey's* staff.[21] In honor of the second of the three volumes, Cattermole was requested to "toast the Ali Babas, or wood-cutters," at the party.[22] If work sometimes made Dickens cancel leisure engagements with Cattermole, there were ample opportunities for fun. As friend, relative, collaborator, member of the Shakespeare Society, and the "Portwiners," [23] Dickens enjoyed many visits with the entire Cattermole family at Clapham Rise.

Cattermole's home on Clapham Rise perfectly suited the dignified artist, whom Thackeray could imagine "in possession of Windsor Castle." [24] Its neighborhood, still old-fashioned and rural, was reached from London by omnibus. It was Cattermole who first spotted the omnibus "tout," whose sphere of action was the Charing Cross tavern from which the Clapham cabs arrived and departed, dubbed him "Sloppy," and delighted Dickens with imitations of his Cockney speech. "It is amazing nonsense to repeat," Forster recalled, but to hear Cattermole as "Sloppy," speaking about an imaginary friend Jack, who represented his own youthful experience before converting to temperance, "in the gruff, hoarse accents of what seemed to be the remains of a deep bass voice wrapped up in wet straw" was unforgettable.[25] Cattermole's imitation inspired Dickens' invention of Mrs. Gamp and Mrs. Harris while the original's nickname became that of Betty Higden's "minder" in *Our Mutual Friend.* For the present, the real Sloppy heralded many congenial occasions.

Dickens, the Cattermoles, and the other "Portwiners," long recalled the splendid dinners served by white-gloved servants in the spacious dining room at Clapham Rise. After-dinner beverages were taken in the drawing room furnished with luxuriously thick drapes, golden-barred wallpaper designed by their host, and Byron's heavy carved furniture from the Albany. Cattermole would then lead his guests down a gloomy staircase and long corridor to his studio. Here, among dusky nooks, tapestried walls and ancient armor, illuminated by flickering brass oil lamps, the artist prepared his *Clock* illustrations and other canvases. While the Landseers and Maclise would peruse the latest work of their colleague, Lane studied Dickens for a portrait. His subject often held forth to Thackeray or Bulwer from one of Byron's armchairs, or brewed punch for the entire company, oblivious to the lemon juice squirting over his embroidered waistcoat. The host purchased Lane's portrait of the author. Mrs. Cattermole came to cherish it less for its artistic merit than for its association with happier days in a home "so frequently illuminated by, and associated with, the wit and vivacity of Dickens." [26]

Master Humphrey's Clock ticked on. Preparations for the illustrations to *Barnaby Rudge*, a story of "fifty years ago" like Scott's best novels, considerably antedated its public appearance on 13 February 1841. Conceived in 1836 as *Gabriel Vardon, the Locksmith of London*, the unwritten story became a major issue of contention throughout Dickens' association with Bentley, the publisher under whose auspices it was to have appeared. Having rescued "the Clock Works" from impending collapse with *The Old Curiosity Shop*, Dickens needed another long narrative to wind it up successfully. Reviving the skeletal Master Humphrey machinery for a few pages to bridge the gap, the author changed the title from *Gabriel Vardon* to *Barnaby Rudge* and commenced that long-postponed tale for which he had finally found motivation.

Cattermole found some aspects of this historical novel more congenial than others. He drew an ornate, many-gabled "Maypole Inn" for the opening scene (BR, 1) for which the author could not find enough words of praise; indeed, Dickens could not "bear" the thought of its being cut on the block, wishing he could "frame and glaze it *in statu quo* forever and ever." [27] Cattermole's feeling for picturesque buildings however, was not transferable to animals to judge from his response to Dickens' inquiry whether he similarly fancied "ravens in general and would fancy Barnaby's raven in particular." As Barnaby is an idiot, the author elaborated, "my notion is to have him always in company with a pet raven, who is immeasurably more knowing than himself." Dickens, having observed his own pet bird, was certain he could make a "very queer character" of him. Would Cattermole "like" the subject when this raven makes his first appearance? "I must know what you think about the raven, my buck," pressed the impatient author two days later, for he had given Browne no subject for the number and time was short. Dickens would be delighted if Cattermole would like to execute the raven's first appearance as well as "The Warren" (BR, 109) ; if not, he must "feed" Browne at once.[28] Cattermole declined the privilege of introducing to the world the immortal "Grip" (BR, 105), whom even Ruskin found "perfect—like all Dickens's animals" though it made him angrier with the rest of the novel, which he abhorred, "because I have every now and then to open the book to look for him." [29]

Cattermole had enough to preoccupy him on *Barnaby Rudge* without the raven. MS. slips, précis, and notes flew from Devonshire Terrace to Clapham Rise "upon each other's heels." After the artist finished Sir John Chester sitting before the monumental fireplace in the Maypole's "best apartment" (BR, 84) , the "very pretty scene" desired by the author, he was to turn his attention "first to the outside of The Warren" (BR, 109) and "secondly, to the outside of the locksmith's house, by night" (BR, 134). If the publishers were dilatory in sending Cattermole, now copying his own designs on wood, "a block of a long shape, so that the house may come upright as it were," he was to "put a penny pistol to Chapman's head and demand the blocks of him." [30] Even from Edinburgh in June, the socially beleaguered author dispatched chapters and subjects for illustration. The summer months found the artist depicting the mob, headed by Hugh and Simon, wrecking the Maypole bar as John Willet, fallen backward in his chair, looks on "with a stupid horror" as they turn his liquor taps, open his casks, drink out of his best punch bowls, smash his bottles, cut down his lemons, eat his celebrated cheese, and smoke his sacrosanct pipes (BR, 445). "John Willet's bar is noble," wrote Dickens upon receiving Cattermole's representation of the frenzied scene. [31]

If Henry Crabb Robinson was unwilling to subject himself to further anxieties, he was wise to vow to "read no more" until *Barnaby Rudge* was finished. [32] For Dickens, as he warned Cattermole, was in the "thick" of the story where the best opportunities for illustrations were "all coming off." From the destruction of one embodiment of the past, the rioters went right on to another, the Warren, which "they plundered, sacked, burned, pulled down as much of it as they could." Cattermole was to show one of the turrets "laid open" and among the ruins, Haredale, "excited to the 1st degree," clutching Rudge, still in cloak and slouched hat as Browne drew him (BR, 6, 19), while Solomon Daisy looked on from the ground below. "When you have done the subject," Dickens added, "I wish you'd write me one line and tell me how, that I may be sure we agree." Within the week, the artist sent a verbal explanation, fearful that Dickens could not "make much" out of the accompanying sketch. Cattermole's artistic vantage point was from the roof of one of the wings of the Warren towards which Rudge and Haredale rushed from a small door in the tower; below on the grass stood Solomon Daisy "in an ecstasy of wonder" while beyond were "clouds of smoke a-passing over and amongst many tall trees," and "frightened rooks, flying and cawing like mad." Dickens found the artist's representation "a queer picturesque thing" which wholly realized his intent (BR, 465). Less successful was the confused scene of Hugh and his cohorts driving from the Warren in a post chaise, though the scarf fluttering from the vehicle did indeed suggest the presence within of Dolly and Emma better than actually showing the captives (BR, 486). [33]

Cattermole understandably could not keep up with the pace of Dickens' instructions, which matched the rush of the narrative's conclusion. The author's final list of illustrations, "written in a scramble just before post time," necessitated not only disposing of "loves of cousin in a line" but apologizing to the artist. "Firstly," would Cattermole draw Lord George Gordon in his solitary prison in the Tower? (BR, 610); "secondly," would he delineate the duel between Sir John, exuding "most supercilious hatred—but polite to the last" and Mr. Haredale, "more sorry than triumphant" at his enemy's death? (BR, 677). The artist proved unable to execute the "Thirdly," a frontispiece for *Barnaby* (BR, vi), or the "Fourthly," a scene "representing Master Humphrey's Clock as stopped" (SBB, 817). It was well that Dickens decided not "to frighten" Cattermole with "a fifthly, sixthly, seventhly, and eighthly." But the author no sooner took "breath" than he recalled the "fifthly"; the artist duly drew Hugh being escorted to jail, with the old Fleet Market indicated in the background as well as the "foot soldiers firing at people who have taken refuge on the tops of stalls, bulkheads, etc." (BR, 756).[34] This scene was the last of Cattermole's contributions to the first of Dickens' two historical novels.

Cattermole, though he continued illustrating books, never again illustrated a work of Dickens. The novelist repeatedly told the artist how much he appreciated his efforts on *Master Humphrey's Clock*, how much he "wondered" at his "resources." Ruskin, however, doubtless alluding to Cattermole's association with the "profitless" woodcuts for the work, wondered to see an artist "of so great original power indulging in childish fanaticism and exaggeration, and substituting for the serious and subdued work of legitimate imagination monsters and machinations." For "no original talent, however brilliant," Ruskin continued more in sorrow than in anger, "can sustain its energy when the demands upon it are constant, and all legitimate support and food withdrawn."[35] Certainly book illustration, even by an artist as esteemed as Cattermole for an author as popular as Dickens, detracted from a serious reputation and added little to one's financial "resources."

Even the energetic novelist did not care to sustain the pace necessitated by weekly installments. With *Martin Chuzzlewit*, whose contemporary content would not have interested the antiquarian painter, Dickens returned to monthly issues illustrated solely by Browne. No longer professionally associated, Dickens and Cattermole saw less of one another socially. In contrast to the way strangers lionized the author both in Scotland and in America, the artist held himself "much aloof" from Dickens. Yet Dickens actively sought his company and his talents in other spheres in the years following *Master Humphrey's Clock*.

In 1845, after living in Switzerland and in Italy, where the Doria, an old palazzo, reminded him of "the most quaint and fanciful of Cattermole's pictures," Dickens invited the artist to play Downright in the opening production of *Every Man in His Humour;* the part had been vacated by Stanfield and turned down by Cruikshank. The author directed his appeal to Cattermole's innate sense of reserve and decorum.

Explaining that his small group was to act Jonson's play with "correct" costume and "good" orchestra before a "strictly private" audience admitted by invitation only, and that the cast included many mutual friends—Forster, Frank Stone, and Stanfield—Dickens urged the "kitten-molian Trojan" to participate. The artist, perhaps, regretted his refusal to be more than an onlooker at the overwhelmingly successful debut, which Tennyson and the Duke of Devonshire had come one hundred miles to see.[36]

When the role of Wellbred was vacated before the two remaining benefit performances, one of which Prince Albert planned to attend, Dickens overcame the artist's excuses of expense, illness, and inability to act. "You couldn't have done better," the author reassured Cattermole after his first rehearsal. "Heaven! *If* you had seen the other men when they began! The impression of everybody who spoke to me on the stage last night was that you were cool as a cucumber and safer than the Bank." He and his brother Frederick would rehearse the artist's role "over and over again, as often as you like"; Frederick was accordingly ordered to "produce" himself at Devonshire Terrace to help George Cattermole whom Dickens was pledged to "produce" for the benefit. The self-conscious artist not only played Wellbred in these 1845 productions, but retained the part when the play was staged again in 1847 to help Leigh Hunt and John Poole.[37]

After these performances, however, the increasingly nervous and self-effacing artist saw little of Dickens. The novelist's reaction to a birth announcement from the Cattermoles in 1852 indicates how infrequently the two men had seen one another, and how eager Dickens was to renew their intimacy. Kate and Georgina visited Clapham Rise, bringing with them a letter from the author which told of his pleasure in receiving the artist's note—"on account of the baby, on account of the mother, on account of the father, on account of the welcome I give your handwriting and any sort of communication with you however shadowy—on all accounts, and for all sorts of loving reasons." "Now don't you think," Dickens pleaded, "DON'T you think you *could* manage to dine here, at the family board, either next Sunday, or next Sunday after that, at 5 exactly? Couldn't we, if only for a novelty, meet as we used to do in bygone ages? Do let us try. How can it be that Clapham Rise gets so far off?" If Cattermole would come, Dickens would have "Sloppy" meet him and they would have "a leg of mutton from Tuckersesesesesesesesesesesesesz in the Strand" where, the author understood, "they are perpetually a hulloxinin of Devonshire Sassages round the corner." [38]

It is unlikely that Cattermole dined at Tavistock House "next Sunday" or any other day. If "cousin" Dickens has found a "genealogical poser" in his relationship to Cattermole's children, their father found the financing of both his growing family and his expensive tastes a serious perplexity. Cattermole understandably no longer had "enough and to spare of fun as well as fancy to supply ordinary artists and humourists by the dozen"; his lack of "ballast and steadiness," also observed by Forster, now became more pronounced.[39] The painter not only withdrew from Dickens' company but from the membership of the Water-Colour Society, whose presidency he earlier had declined, presumably to devote himself to oils. His award of the French *grande médaille d'honneur* and his election to the Dutch Royal Academy and to the Belgian Society of Water-Colour Painters enlarged Cattermole's reputation, but not his resources. When Dickens arrived to work on *Little Dorrit* in the summer of 1856 at the Villa des Moulineaux, he found the "unfortunate" Cattermoles stranded in another villa of their "more unfortunate" landlord who complained that the artist "promises always" but never paid his bills.[40]

Dickens never again encountered the artist abroad or in his picturesque home on Clapham Rise. In 1863, Cattermole moved his family down to Clapham Common. That autumn, the news of his eldest son's death, following that of his youngest daughter, precipitated him into a permanent depression over his double loss. In 1868, Dickens, during his trip to America, heard that Cattermole was ill; Mrs. Cattermole confirmed the bad news, but assured the author he was better. "My old affection for him has never cooled," her relative hastened to remind her. "The last time he dined with me, I asked him to come again that day ten years, for I was perfectly certain (this was my small joke) that I should not set eyes upon him sooner. The time being fully up, I hope you will remind him, with my love, that he is due." [41]

Dickens never saw Cattermole again. Although not unprepared for the news of the artist's death on 24 July 1868, he was nevertheless shocked. In his condolence note to the family, he tactfully enclosed £25, which he maintained he owed the widow. "Poor George Cattermole is dead," Dickens explained to Wills, "very, very poor. Family quite unprovided for; debt and distress." Mrs. Cattermole not only was aware of all that her illustrious relative would *say* to comfort her, but how much he might *do* to relieve the economic as well as the emotional distress of her loss.[42]

Even before Cattermole's death, his wife enlisted Dickens' aid in soliciting a pension for her ill husband from the Royal Academy. "Of course I will sign your memorial," Dickens had replied, certain that all painters would do "anything for George." [43] After the artist's death, the widow found Dickens' help indispensable in petitioning Parliament for a pension. The signatures of painters were most important, the novelist advised, knowing they would be the first names looked for in this case; any "literary" names could be added to the same document. She might write Disraeli, but Bulwer-Lytton was not in any position with the government to ask "favors" for her. The signatures of Parliament members were relatively unimportant: "do not, for Heaven's sake," he warned, "do such a foolish thing as think of giving your application a party air. Stark, Staring Ruin to your hopes would come of it, inevitably." Dickens, with the help of Frith and others, drafted the appeal, a copy of which he forwarded to the impatient widow to show he had wasted no time in representing her interests to Mr. Gladstone. Mrs. Cattermole meanwhile tried to convert the remaining works of her husband into tangible assets. Dickens received a catalogue of the artist's drawings to be sold, but as specimens of his skill were already hanging at Gad's Hill, he did not greatly regret his inability to attend the sale.[44]

Dickens' patience for the bereaved began to fray. Mrs. Cattermole's case was proving "most difficult and dispiriting." As he confided to Frith, "That vague evasiveness which was poor Cattermole's besetting sin, so wore out his friends for years and years, that it is impossible to kindle enthusiasm in the cause." Mrs. Cattermole herself inspired distrust; Dickens "hardly knew why," but he could not help "suspecting that when Mrs. Frith saw Mrs. Cattermole fireless, there was an uncommonly good fire in the next room." Even before Cattermole's death, he had been struck by the prosperous appearance of his two young sons, so at odds with their mother's forlorn description of them. Such discrepancies gradually eroded Dickens' own sympathy for the bereaved widow and her family.[45]

Dickens was certain that a public appeal would meet little response and he knew that the result of the private appeal was only "infinitesimally" helpful. He urged a meeting of the chief subscribers to decide the best course. The men who gathered at the office of *All The Year Round* on 13 April 1869, decided to hand the funds hitherto collected over to Mrs. Cattermole and to abandon solicitation and receipt of further contributions. Dickens, himself now ill from overexertion, was convinced nothing more could be done for the widow.[46] If persistent, Mrs. Cattermole was not ungrateful, having found the novelist a man of both "magnanimous and *practical* sympathy" as would so many of Dickens' illustrators and their families.[47]

Angus Easson

THE OLD CURIOSITY SHOP

From Manuscript to Print

THE MANUSCRIPT of *The Old Curiosity Shop* exists, complete, in the Forster Collection at the Victoria and Albert Museum (Forster 48 A 4). As bound up, the first five leaves (lettered A to E) consist of: (A & B) a letter to Forster, dated Monday, 17 January 1841;[1] (C) a Plan for Nos. XLI, XLII, XLIII and XLIV (the first extant number plan of a part of a Dickens' novel); (D) an outline of the relationship between the grandfather and the single gentleman; and (E) a list of characters, with ticks against many of them, presumably a check that all were accounted for in the final chapter. The number plan shows that Dickens' first thought was to have Kit's release before Quilp's death (lxvii, lxviii), while his concern with Nell as the central interest looms in "Keep the child in view" (No. XLII; repeated exactly in No. XLIII) and the single word for No. XLIV: "Dead."

The episodes of the novel then follow; they are written on one side of slips, at first irregular in number for each episode, but as the novel became Dickens' only concern in *Master Humphrey* they settle down to a regular size. The second episode was written out as part of the regular issue of *Master Humphrey,* numbered 12–20 (*not* a continuation of episode one, which is numbered 1–19); the only other episode so numbered is in No. X numbered 13–21, following "Mr. Weller's Watch" in *Master Humphrey.* Most of the following episodes (from the fifth, in No. X of *Master Humphrey*) are nineteen or twenty slips in length (except episode six, slips 1–14, and followed by the last considerable piece of *Clock* matter, "Master Humphrey from His Clock Side in the Chimney Corner"); until with episode twenty (No. XXV), the slips become eighteen in number, except episodes twenty-one (the last of Volume I, eleven slips), thirty-eight and thirty-nine (both seventeen, though the former was underwritten), and forty (nine slips), the final episode of the novel, which was followed by Master Humphrey's conclusion to the novel and introduction of *Barnaby Rudge*.

Proofs exist for twenty-three complete chapters and in part for eight others.[2]

In discussing the manuscript, I am interested both as an editor and a critic in Dickens' intentions and the significance of changes of all kinds. Of course, only a few examples can be given in this necessarily incomplete discussion.

— I —

As Dickens wrote, he numbered each chapter, but, relying upon memory, he was not always accurate. A whole sequence of chapters (xix to xxiv) is misnumbered ("Chapter The Eighteenth" and so on), chapter xxi being first numbered "Chapter The Nineteenth" before Dickens crossed the number out and confidently wrote "Twentieth." Chapter xxvi is again misnumbered, but after "Chapter The Twenty Fifth" another hand (presumably in the printing house) has added, in square brackets, "Twenty Sixth . . it ought to be." The proofs of chapters xlvi and xlvii show that the printers set up "CHAPTER THE FORTY—FIFTH" and "CHAPTER THE FORTY—SIXTH" as Dickens had written (Forster ff. 48 and 54), but the correct number appears in *Master Humphrey;* both were corrected in pencil on the proof, possibly in a contemporary hand, though proof-corrections are usually in ink. The early sequence of misnumbering suggests that Dickens may have written the section fairly continuously, ahead of the printer (the chapters cover Nos. XVII, XVIII and XIX of *Master Humphrey*); however, in No. XX, the misnumbered chapter xxvi follows the correctly numbered chapter xxv, so little definite can be gathered from these mistakes.

Normally, Dickens sent his first draft to the printers, relying upon them to read his writing and his corrections, but in a few places he apparently corrected so heavily that it was necessary to rewrite a particular passage; the new version was then pasted onto the slip over the original. It is possible that some of these represent changes of mind rather than radical reworking: unless the pasted slips could be removed there is no way of being certain. Some details in these additions are significant. Introducing the Bachelor, Dickens inserted the reason for his name ("Perhaps for some vague rumour of his college honours." II, 89, ll. 43–45 and 90, ll. 1–4) on a pasted slip; that he made much correction here is likely since the Bachelor was at one time to have been called the "doctor," the present title skillfully uniting the academic and the domestic. Other examples of this insertion occur in chapter liv (II, 101, ll. 36–4), when Nell is questioned by the schoolmaster about her sadness in the forgetfulness of the living; and chapter lxi (II, 140, ll. 23–26), which comments on the effect of a good conscience. The small number of these rewritings suggests the pressure on Dickens and the skill of his printers, who were prepared to set up the most involved copy; the wonder is not that they made mistakes, but that they were so largely correct.

Reading the manuscript confirms Dickens' reliance on his printers and his acceptance of their alterations. In editing any of the novels, it must always be a question how far we should return to Dickens' original readings. Certainly a great deal is lost if we do not, though his original spellings and heavy capitalization may be irritating rather than really useful. Yet I regret certain changes if only for their comic value. Spellings such as "favorable," "honorable," "shew," "staid" (for "stayed"), "attornies," "poney," "chaunt," and "accomodation" all appear in the manuscript. The printers indifferently accept or change the spelling and Dickens accepts the printed version. The only consistent spellings Dickens imposes are "favorable," "honorable," etc. (the so-called "American" spellings, though there is no question of trans-Atlantic influence), "chaunt" and "poney"; clearly any full edition would retain these forms, and either determine from the manuscript Dickens' preferred spelling for other words or else adopt some system of harmonization. Capitalization is more difficult, since, apart from difficulties in determining upper and lower-case letters in Dickens' handwriting, there is also a lack of consistency: the single gentleman always has small letters, but the Notary (Mr. Witherden) and the Bachelor vary. At times, Dickens seems indifferent between "Justice" and "justice," but when Trent's lodgings (I, 219) are placed "in an old ghostly Inn," the capitalization does remind us that this is one of those legal Inns of Court let out as lodgings, not a tavern or public house, a distinction *Master Humphrey*'s "inn" does not make. In chapter liv (II, 97–98) Dickens consistently wrote capitals for the Bachelor, Truth, Time, Fancy, Goddess, Tradition, and the Baron and the Priest of the church where Nell becomes custodian. Eighteenth century in its insistence, the capitalization gives a sense of the rhetorical figures used by the Bachelor, something lost in *Master Humphrey*'s reduction of all save Truth to lower case. A good joke is lost (II, 125) when Sally's looks bear a radiance "mild as that which beameth from the Virgin Moon," the manuscript capitals reminding us of the disparity between Sally and such symbols of chaste beauty, the disparity so slyly emphasized by her praise in amatory language.

Another loss is colloquial details that were smoothed out. Since no proofs exist for the two examples I have found, it is impossible to know whether the printer or Dickens is responsible. That Dickens did elsewhere intend colloquial effects is clear by his alteration in the manuscript of the "polite" "Plough and Harrow" to the colloquial representation "Plow an' Harrer" (I, 175), where of course the change Plough / Plow makes no more difference to pronunciation than "what" to "wot," though both changes are conventional ways of representing the educational or social level of speakers in printed texts. In chapter v (I, 108) when Nell comes to Quilp's countinghouse to collect money, he exclaims, "What, Nelly!" and " 'Yes,'—said the child, hesitating whether to enter or retreat." The manuscript reproduced her hesitation with "Ye-yes." A later and comic variant of this kind of speech form is also omitted. When, after the visit to Astley's, Kit commands the waiter, Dickens originally conveyed the speed and obsequiousness of the man by his answer, "Pot o'beer, sir? Yezzir," where *Master Humphrey* has a tame "yes, sir" (II, 12), the original compounding of the words suggesting the speed of the service; another example of this colloquial representation retained in print is Kit shouting " 'an-kor' at the end of everything" (II, 11).

Some of the compositors' difficulties are suggested in their guesses at Dickens' meaning. Miss Monflather's stronghold (I, 268) is more "obdurate than gate of adamant or bars" in proof (Dexter f. 6), a good association, though the final word proved to be "brass," as Dickens corrected it in the margin: even here the "br" might be a single letter and the "ss" a double letter or two different letters. Again, Dick says he has no "money; no credit; no beef from Fred" (Forster f. 8), though the association of credit and food proves to be only a guess, since "beef" is in fact "support" (I, 285). Dickens' writing was a stumbling block and so was his punctuation, which constantly represents a comma with a dash, many people in *Master Humphrey* breaking off speeches with apparent dramatic force when a comma will supply the correct effect. To take random examples: as Fred plans that Dick shall marry Nell (I, 118–19), *Master Humphrey* prints, " 'I don't mean marrying her now'—returned the brother angrily"; and " 'I suppose there's no doubt about his being rich'—said Dick." In both cases the manuscript has the short dash (placed after inverted commas) Dickens uses for, and which is elsewhere set up as, commas. Dickens does use dashes for rhetorical purposes, yet generally, where the printer has set up these "commas" as dashes, they are accepted (perhaps through lack of time) and so have passed into the text (both these examples remain in the Charles Dickens Edition, 34 and 35). In an edition, the original manuscript punctuation should be restored. When Dickens made insertions in the manuscript, confusion easily resulted in his crowded pages. When Brass is laying the ground for Kit's framing, the proof gives the following (Forster f. 81):

> "Oh certainly," replied Dick, shuffling among his papers.
> "And who," said Brass, "who is the lodger's visitor."

This is corrected by Forster on the proof to (II, 114):

> "Oh certainly," replied Dick.
> "And who, said Brass, shuffling among his papers, "who is the lodger's visitor."

The action is an addition which, being above the line (even though a line is drawn over it to associate it with Brass), could be read as belonging to Dick. It shows Dickens deliberately going back to insert details of the plot against Kit: this is the action Brass uses when putting the bank note in Kit's hat.

On occasions the text is slightly altered and I suspect the compositor of correcting something he felt was wrong, usually because the original sentence is rather complex. When Nell enters the race town with Codlin and Short (I, 197), *Master Humphrey* reads: "the streets were filled with throngs of people—many strangers were there, it seemed, by the looks they cast about"; the manuscript gives a harder but perfectly coherent reading: "the streets were filled with throngs of people—many, strangers there it seemed by the looks they cast about." If the compositor missed the comma, then he would feel the need for a verb, the change being accepted by Dickens in proof. Perhaps the most interesting misreading occurs when Nell passes through the churchyard (II, 88) and thinks of the dead lying there; Dickens comments that perhaps "not one of the unprisoned souls had been able quite to separate itself in living thought from its old companions," which is the version in both manuscript and *Master Humphrey*. However, the printer, no doubt mistaking the "un" and preferring to think of the buried as in prison printed "imprisoned" (Forster f. 72). Dickens, insisting that the soul is freed from the dead body, twice corrected this on the proof (i.e., crossed out "im," put "un" in the margin and then wrote "unprisoned" below it); yet ironically the reading in the Charles Dickens Edition (236), "corrected by Dickens himself," is "imprisoned" and so it has remained, for instance, in the National Edition and even in the Everyman, which largely reprints from the *Master Humphrey* text. Even an author may contribute to the deterioration of his own text.

Certain variations between manuscript and *Master Humphrey* are intentional rather than accidental or indifferent. The care with which Dickens pursued the right word is clear from changes in diction made between manuscript and print. Miss Monflathers, inspecting the waxwork figures (I, 254), originally "pronounced" on the correctness of Lindley Murray and Hannah More. On the proof this becomes "admitted" (Dexter f. 1), a nicely shaded sense of Miss Monflathers' essential reservation about the exhibition, of an admission wrung from her. A sense of distinction marks most of the other changes too. Dick, trying to pump Kit for information, originally called Mrs. Nubbles a "charming" woman but in *Master Humphrey* she is an "excellent" woman (II, 7), an ethical rather than physical approval; "charming" is more appropriate to Dick but tactless when trying to wheedle Kit. When Kit answers the charge at the Old Bailey (II, 152) it was at first in a "low and feeble voice," which in the manuscript itself became a "low and trembling voice." The physical weakness and age suggested by "feeble" are changed to the emotionally overwhelmed "trembling." Telling his children of his adventures, Kit originally explained "how poor he used to be," but this becomes "how needy he used to be" (II, 223) —Dickens may have wished to avoid a sense of complaint in "poor." Elsewhere the change is one of sense, since the Marchioness looking after Dick as though he were a very little boy and she "his grown up nurse" (II, 170) fits the comparison better han the manuscript "tender nurse." The Marchioness already *is* his "tender" nurse; so the parallel is not helped, is even spoilt, by the original idea. Obviously the tenderness of the Marchioness was uppermost in Dickens' mind, but the comparison needs to convey the disparity between her size and her ability, an ability prompted by her tenderness. A group of slight changes affect Nell. After watching the Misses Edwards, she "was alone with Heaven and Earth," whereas *Master Humphrey* simply states she "was alone" (II, 25; deleted on Forster f. 20), which stresses isolation and solitude better. With both Heaven and Earth, can one be alone? At the same point Nell gazes at the stars and "found new planets burst upon her view," which the proof (Forster f. 20) alters to "stars." Originally Dickens may have wished to avoid the repetition of "stars . . . stars," but decided that "stars" was more correct and more poetical than "planets." A case of what seems to be decorum occurs when the schoolmaster bids Nell goodnight (II, 96) ; as he kisses her cheek, the manuscript says "he felt a tear upon his lips," which is altered on the proof in pencil (Forster f. 77) to "upon his face." The meaning now is slightly ambiguous, since clearly it is one of Nell's tears if he felt it with his lips, but it is difficult to see how he could feel the tear on his face if he bent *down;* the change then seems deliberate, perhaps removing the particular and sexual associations of "lips" to the more general one of "face." A definite improvement comes by this kind of change when the Bachelor gives the history of the church (II, 97), he not being one of those who strip Truth of every little "shadowy vestment," which was originally "fairy vestment." The connection with shadowy types of truth is better than the debased fairy associations that Dickens normally has. A pointer to Nell's true state is the change in tone of her answer to her grandfather (II, 103), from "replied the child gaily" to "replied the child, with assumed gaiety," which indicates more clearly the true state of her feelings, showing how the child acts for the happiness of her grandfather though the underlying sense of sadness insists.

Dickens often consciously corrected his grammar and style, most clearly in the revisions for the Charles Dickens Edition. These changes have already begun in *Master Humphrey*, though often as stylistic rather than strictly grammatical revision, details picked up on the proofs that passed in haste of writing. What seem redundancies disappear ("the anxious child was unregarded and forgotten" becomes "the anxious child was quite forgotten" in I, 260). Ambiguities are resolved (the

Bachelor tells Nell of the monkish ceremonies, "and how, amid lamps depending from the roof," monkish voices chanted [II, 98], instead of the original "and how often amid lamps depending from the roof," the manuscript suggesting he showed exactly how many times, instead of "often" being a detached reference to a vague number). Repetitions are excised. Connections between subject and verb are made closer by the substitution of noun for pronoun or simply by omitting the pronoun altogether. Nell conducts the visitors round the church, grandfather listening to her voice (II, 105), "and when the strangers left it" he listens to their comments; "it" might refer to "voice" or "church" and so was omitted. Again, when fog hangs over the river shortly before Quilp's death, the boatman is bewildered and "the river itself might have been miles away" (II, 118); the original pronoun "it" (now "the river itself") had to hark back three lines to "river" and more naturally referred to the cry of the boatman.

Related to these revisions are examples of rephrasing, not so much for clarity as the desire to forge the best form. Dickens is shown working hard, improving in most cases and achieving some of his most characteristic felicities, not as momentary effects but as the result of thought. Some of these changes are made in the manuscript (see below); others take place at proof stage. The prosecutor at Kit's trial is in good spirits because (rather tamely in manuscript and on the proof, Forster f. 106) "he had very nearly got off a murderer in the last trial," which is transmuted to the characteristically Dickensian understatement that he "had, in the last trial, very nearly procured the acquittal of a young gentleman who had had the misfortune to murder his father" (II, 152). Then there is the Marchioness' splendid comment (II, 163) about pretending that orange peel in water is wine: " 'If you make believe very much, it's quite nice, . . . but if you don't, you know, it hasn't much flavour.' " Writing to Forster, Dickens gives the present version: " 'If you make believe very much it's quite nice; but if you don't, you know, it seems as if it would bear a little more seasoning, certainly.' I think that's better. Flavour is a common word in cookery, and among cooks, and so I used it" (*Pilgrim*, 166, ?16 or 18 December 1840). This correction is also made on the proof (Forster f. 109; [?] in Forster's hand rather than Dickens').

Other alterations at the proof stage probably show the corrections of both Dickens and Forster, changes of fact and minor detail, some for obvious reasons, others for no clear reason. When the single gentleman questions Codlin and Short about their itinerary, Short explains that they " 'take the East of London in the spring and winter, and the West of England in the summer time' " (I, 304), where the manuscript balanced the *West* of London with the *West* of England. Dickens presumably remembered that Bevis Marks is in the *East* of London and since the single gentleman has heard Codlin and Short in the street, their circuit must include that part of the city (on the proof, Dexter f. 9, the correction is in Dickens' hand). An interesting change of spelling (it could be a printer's change) that affects the meaning is in the description as Nell and her grandfather flee from Mrs. Jarley, through "the strait streets, and narrow crooked outskirts" (II, 31). Here "strait" evidently links with "narrow" as a Biblical allusion (Matt. 7:14: "Strait is the gate, and narrow is the way, which leadeth unto life"), but the manuscript gave "straight," linking with "crooked" rather than with "narrow." That the change "straight" / "strait" comes before the collocations "narrow" / "crooked" suggests not so much a printer's correction as an alteration by a reader who preferred the Biblical overtones (common is connection with Nell) rather than the more mundane connection of "straight" / "crooked." A clearer alteration of fact is in the description of the monks' ritual by the Bachelor, who imagines them "swinging censers exhaling scented odours" (II, 98), though the manuscript had them swinging "chalices" (a surrealistic touch), the change, I would suspect, being Forster's intervention. At one point there is a rather odd example of accuracy, when Dick's quotation from *Lalla Roohk:* "I never nursed a dear Gazelle" (II, 109) was at first "reared." The earlier (incorrect) version presented no problem in identifying the source of parody; it looks more like a change by a stickler for accuracy. A similar change on what may be grounds of accuracy is in the amount Brass pays annually for the right to practice, a right by which he is styled "gentleman." For the present round sum of twelve pounds (II, 137), the manuscript gave thirteen pounds two shillings, surely a very Dickensian detail in the odd two shillings which make up the precise sum by which one buys gentility; Forster's legal connections might make him more precise about the sum.

Other facts are changed for which no apparent reason can be suggested. Perhaps Dickens felt even as he wrote that a three-act piece at Astley's (II, 11) made for a shorter evening (or was a more accurate description) than a four-act one. But why should Mrs. Jarley, searching for a word to describe waxworks ("It's calm and—what's that word again—critical?—no—classical," I, 242) have originally called it "colossal" rather than "critical"? "Colossal" is closer to "classical," though "critical" is perhaps the better joke on classical taste. Again, some curious changes are made to the sexton, who originally had "crutches," altered in the manuscript to "a crutch" (II, 92). The plural might suggest a cripple rather than a rheumatic, aged man. More odd is Dickens' alteration of the sexton's age; from eighty-five, he dwindles to seventy-nine (II, 94), a change not made until proof stage, while in the next episode (Number XXXV), the manuscript has "seventy-four" four times but "seventy-nine" in the text (II, 99–100). Perhaps Dickens remembered, writing this episode, that he had altered the age, while not remembering what age he had come to; this change may account for the sexton's telling Nell that Becky Morgan was not more than sixty-four (II, 99) —exactly ten years younger than his own (manuscript) age, and her age is finally agreed to be eighty-nine (II, 101), though the manuscript had kept the correspondency of "eighty-four." Having made her "eighty-nine" in proof, there is no joke in agreeing finally that she had "almost reached the patriarchal term of ninety," and this term becomes "a hundred" (II, 101). Dickens (or his reader) can be seen checking on points of fact, but disregarding points like "sixty-four" which do not demand harmonizing. It is the care necessary for accuracy, though not an obsession with completeness; one might argue that it is more realistic to have the disparity "sixty-four" / "seventy-nine" than the symmetry of "sixty-nine" / "seventy-nine" / "eighty-nine."

— 2 —

By far the most significant group of changes between manuscript and *Master Humphrey* is the omission of material, usually on the grounds of lack of space. Several episodes were seriously overwritten (Nos. XXXIII, XXVI, XXVIII, XXXVII all had a page or more of material omitted, a page being 45 lines), and others had smaller amounts cut (Nos. XII, XXII, XXIV, XXIX, XXX, XXXIV, XL, XLI all suffered). Only Nos. XIX, XX, XXXIII, and XLV were at all noticeably underwritten. Dickens' early vitality of production was as unchecked as ever, and that so many late episodes were overwritten shows that it was no mere case of getting used to the size of weekly episodes, though clearly it was safer to write too much and cut than desperately try to expand at proof stage. Indeed, while his superfluous writing rarely shows signs of being spun out to make up space, the passages concocted to fill underwritten episodes are often singularly vacant, occasionally mere repetition.

Dickens employed a variety of cutting processes, and the evidence of manuscript, proofs, and *Master Humphrey* shows the care taken by Dickens and Forster, though both accepted the ruthless necessity that cuts had to be made. Where possible material was simply excised and instruction to "run on" given. Certain parts clearly were no loss: filler dialogue such as this between Quilp and the grandfather need not be regretted (I, 137, l. 7):

> *"I'm not quite small enough to get through keyholes. I wish
> I was; what a life it would be!"*
> "Why didn't you speak?" said the old man angrily.
> "So I did," replied Quilp.
> "You were not heard."
> "I know I wasn't."

It is scarcely necessary to remark that Quilp had not uttered a sound, but he was not particular, and it was his whim to say he had spoken.

"I know I wasn't heard, neighbour," he said, "but I spoke for all that. Shall I tell you what I said?"

"If you please," rejoined the old man.

"That I wanted *to have some talk with you,*" said Quilp, "*particularly, and in private.*"

The transition from one speech of Quilp's to another is made neatly and the seams joined without difficulty ("I wanted" becomes "I want"). In bigger cuts some slight rewriting was needed. At the end of the long comic passage describing events at the Wackleses' party (see below), Dickens returned to Mrs. Wackles and the two day-scholars. Since the cut meant they were now mentioned in successive sentences, a little rewriting was needed. Instead of continuing, as in the manuscript, "In the expression of this opinion, Miss Wackles smiled, and Mrs. Wackles smiled. The two little girls on the stools seeing this, sought . . . ," the reference to any definite reason for smiling is omitted, and Dickens has (I, 127): "On a couple of hard stools, were two of the day-scholars; and when Miss Wackles smiled, and Mrs. Wackles smiled, the two little girls on the stools sought. . . ." Again, a simple reference may be inserted, after a passage has been omitted, covering some essential point. When Brass proposes to take Dick as his clerk, the manuscript gives this conversation with his sister (I, 279 between ll. 27 and 28):

"*Is it my fault?*"

"Then why do you do it?" returned his sister.

"She asks me why I do it!" said Mr. Brass, looking up at the ceiling. "She asks me—this rascal asks me—why I am going to do it!"

"Well, what of that?" observed his sister coolly.

"She asks me," said Mr. Brass, striking his fist upon the table, "why I am going to do it, and she was consulting with me fully three hours last night whether I ought to do it, or whether I ought not! Now, there's a pretty fellow—there's a pretty fellow to drive a man crazy and beside himself!"

Miss Sally smiled, for she had a deep delight in irritating her brother; and presently said:

"*All I know is,*" said Miss Sally. . . .

Dickens goes back after striking this out on the proof (Forster f. 5), and inserts the italicized words in Brass's opening sentence: "What do you taunt me, *after three hour's talk last night,* with going to keep a clerk for?" The essential point about their relationship is thus retained.

At one point a section in the manuscript has been placed in brackets, as though it were originally to be cut. Quilp plots with Sampson and Sally to frame Kit: after urging them to listen (" 'A word,' said the dwarf . . ."), the following lines (II, 83, ll. 21–25) are bracketed, so that, if cut, the next words would be the description of Quilp, "glancing from brother to sister." Clearly it is one kind of cut Dickens does employ, linking one speech to another by the same character—yet the lines are both in proof (Forster f. 67) and *Master Humphrey*. It seems as though Dickens (or Forster) was prepared to indicate possible cuts as early as the manuscript (in the event No. XXXIII proved to be underwritten). Certainly in the letter returning the proofs of No. XXIX, Dickens was aware of excess in the manuscript, noting that for "number thirty there will be some cutting needed. . . . I have, however, something in my eye near the beginning which I can easily take out" (*Pilgrim*, II, 131, 4 October 1840). There is, however, only this one actual indication in the manuscript that I have found.

The proof was often corrected first and then gone over again to see which passages had to be omitted. The portrayal of Kit's feelings after the night at Astley's (II, 13) included the following:

> *usually endure until dinner-time or thereabouts!* To have drunk too much, to have had a great holiday, and to have fallen in love, are one and the same thing in their next day's consequences. A sense of something lost and gone, of a dim uncomfortable ghost perpetually haunting us, of a fire gone out which is never to be lighted any more, of water with its soul filtered away, of vapid air from half-extinguished ovens, of earth dull, dry, and arid; of a compounded moral and physical staleness, bleareyedness, consciousness of not being shaved, and feeling of utter discomfort—such is the common dust into which these three great things of earth resolve themselves next day.
> *Who will wonder . . .*

Originally only "blear-eyedness" was cut on the proof (Forster f. 12), and then the whole passage was scored through. Forster, having made necessary cuts in an episode, was prepared to indicate passages that might be removed if the cuts were still not drastic enough. The passage of speculation by the townsfolk about the single gentleman and Mrs. Nubbles, when they hope to find Nell (II, 60, ll. 31–37), was ringed round in the proof (Forster f. 56), with a marginal note: *"I hope I have / taken out / Enough*—but / if I have not, / You must / Cancel / this par. / Let it stand / if possible / J. F.* So narrowly were we saved the townspeople's eagerness to catch a glimpse of the single gentleman, 'though it were only of the tip of his noble nose." Other passages are deleted on the proofs and then marked "stet." This happens twice in chapter lviii (No. XXXVII, which was overwritten by one page—note on back of Forster

f. 94), where a brief description of Dick preparing himself for the day's duties and a passage of dialogue with Sally are thus reprieved (II, 125, ll. 7–10 and 25–34).

It is difficult to determine how many proof stages there were, though in one instance Forster preserves three sheets, all of them showing correction. That several stages existed is clear from a proof deletion which is then marked "stet," though the passage does not appear in *Master Humphrey;* it shows Brass in his best pietistic vein (II, 129), exclaiming on " '*a delicious picture of human goodness. It comes upon us who are in the law, Kit, like a refreshing breeze, mixing up violets and all that sort of thing with the fogs we live in—but I'm rather wandering from the point.—Put down your hat' "* (Forster f. 93), and so the trap is sprung. Other passages cut in proof still appear in the final version, again suggesting several proof stages. Just before Kit is trapped, Brass's reaction to Sally's revelation comes as a surprise, for, "instead of passionately bewailing the loss of his money, as Miss Sally had expected" (II, 126), he reveals he has lost money himself. This reaction is deleted on the proof (Forster f. 92), yet appears in *Master Humphrey.* Another curious intermediary stage is passages on the proof only, originally intended to appear but not in *Master Humphrey.* Two of these come in No. XXXIII, which was underwritten; this suggests that at some stage Dickens found he had added too much and the proofs were cut again— and further suggests that he kept his eye on the extra passages rather than cutting at random. The first of these passages is no loss; when Quilp confronts his wife after his return from "death," his wife insists she is glad to see him (II, 73 between ll. 25 and 26, Forster f. 61):

> *"I am glad to see you, Quilp; indeed I am."*
> *"You* glad!" echoed Quilp.
> "Yes, indeed. Very glad," replied his wife earnestly.
> *In truth Mrs. Quilp. . . .*

Then, a little later on in the proof, his speech is split (as elsewhere two speeches are linked by cutting), as he insists he is going away again (II, 73, l. 38; Forster f. 61):

> *"Yes again.* I tell you what, ma'am. I'll cure you of these tricks. If I die first (which I don't intend to do, Mrs. Quilp), you shall be in a delicious uncertainty about it for weeks, or months. I'll be a roaming, rambling blade. I'll go away for weeks together, perhaps. Perhaps not for minutes."
> "You're joking, Quilp."
> "Am I! *I'm going away. . . ."*

We might regret this second cut. One last method of omitting material, little used because of the effort involved, is to cut some words out of a paragraph, in effect précising it, retaining the essential outline while reducing the bulk. When the Marchioness, by Dick's direction, seeks for Mr. Abel Garland, her intelligence saves her, since the consequences of sending her *"out alone* through streets wholly unknown to her, and of despatching her in the first instance *from the very neighbourhood in which it was most dangerous for her to appear, would probably have been* her detention by some stray busybody who had seen the advertisement, and *the restoration of Miss Sally Brass to the supreme authority over her person. Not unmindful of the risk she ran, however,* but regarding it as a very important item of consideration, *the Marchioness . . ."* (II, 164, words in italics indicate the present printed text; deletions made on proof, Forster f. 112).

Though Dickens was careful in cutting to ensure smooth running on, and would add bridge phrases where necessary, he rarely checked through the whole section involved to make sure there were no anomalies. A small point, though one that might puzzle, comes when Mrs. Jarley's caravan is described as blundering on, "as if it too had been drinking strong beer" (I, 245), the associative "too" clearly being out of place, since no one has been drinking strong beer. But originally, on Mrs. Jarley's suggestion that they "have a bit of supper,"

> The motion being carried unanimously, the ham and bread and butter reappeared, flanked by a stone jar of beer like unto that which they had beheld in active service under the hedge; from which Mrs. Jarley took deep draughts of malt liquor in a most capacious mug. Indeed, she did no less justice to her supper generally, than she had done to her tea, and when the meal was over, fell into a slumber, accompanied with violent snoring.
> *In the meanwhile, the caravan blundered on. . . .*

The necessary excision of "too" was not caught up after the paragraph was deleted; it scarcely matters much, yet it does show Dickens cutting skillfully but not concerned to check closely whether everything harmonizes. A more extended revision which still shows through, like rock of an earlier stratum, is the treatment of the watcher by the furnace who befriends Nell in the industrial city (Birmingham). The man (II, 39 ff.) was originally a cripple and survived so to the proof stage (Forster ff. 33–39 and 42), where Dickens cut every direct reference to the fact. Perhaps he bore in mind that Master Humphrey was already a cripple, perhaps that the man has already sufficient suffering in his isolation from his fellows—certainly Dickens was sensitive about cripples, as his refusal to allow a stage Tiny Tim to wear leg-irons suggests.[3] The man's condition becomes generalized, his look of patient endurance "common to cripples (and he was one)" remains simply the look without the explanation. When he carries Nell, showing himself "both swift and sure of foot," he did so at first "notwithstanding his deformed and twisted shape." Other references are altered: "The cripple moved" > "he moved"; "her mis-shapen friend" > "her friend"; "the deformed man" > "the man"; "the untaught cripple" > "the labourer"—an interesting double shift of emphasis; "the poor crippled man" > "the poor man, their friend" (41, l. 5; 42, l. 37; 43, ll. 20 and 26; 46, l. 21). A direct reference to his original state, which obviously can refer to his present condition, takes on a new meaning in light of the original intention; speaking to Nell he says, "You may guess from looking at me what kind of child I was, but for all the difference between us I was a child" (42; cf. Master Humphrey's description of how he first became aware of his deformity, I, 4). The contrast between the physically perfect Nell and the crippled child has gone, and the idea of sanity set against grotesque companionship replaces it; the sharpness has gone and something more sinister, perhaps, intrudes.

— 3 —

Some of Dickens' changes in the manuscript as he was writing show the way his imagination was fired, how his creation is in a state of flux even as he sets down the words, and the comedy grows as he writes. As the single gentleman establishes himself in the Brass household, his trunk is brought in with difficulty, originally because the trunk was "pretty nearly as wide as the staircase"; then with a curly stroke of omission and a caret mark, Dickens makes it "nearly twice as wide" (I, 287), and the house of mysteries in which Dick finds himself is yet further established. No wonder such strange things exist in a trunk which enters the house like a Genie into a bottle only a fraction of his size. Again, when Sally in righteous indignation attacks the newly-arrested Kit but manhandles Chuckster instead, "rage being, like Love and Fortune, blind" (II, 139), "Love" is an insertion as Sally is given her appropriate language even in the course of composition. Sally's erotic style is remembered as Dickens' mind expands, the kind of expansion that occurs when the hamper sent by the Garlands arrives in Dick's room. The hamper becomes a cornucopia as Dickens inserts more and more, instead of the rather limited and more medically-based container of his first conception (pointed brackets enclose the manuscript insertions): "disgorged such treasures of tea, ⟨and coffee,⟩ and wine, ⟨and rusks, and oranges, and grapes, and fowls ready trussed for boiling,⟩ and calves-foot jelly, and arrow-root, and sago, and other delicate restoratives" (II, 172). The bounteous superfluity of Dickens' writing, that attention to detail so essentially part of his style, was no gift of Nature's child, but the accumulation of a conscious artist. Occasionally there are losses: the proprietor of the giant and the little lady staying at the Jolly Sandboys (I, 193) originally possessed also "a New Zealander's skull," crossed out in the manuscript. Manuscript changes can also remind the reader of a shift of emphasis. As the rescue party come closer to Nell, the single gentleman tells his story; arrived at the village and gaining no answer at the inn, " 'Let us go on,' said the younger brother" (II, 201). It is the first time this name has been given to him; in the manuscript Dickens wrote "the single gentleman" as he had been so long accustomed to do, then crossed it through, so stressing the new relationship established by his revelation to Mr. Garland.

A series of alterations between manuscript and *Master Humphrey*, amusing rather than portentous, is the omission of the name of God or at least its softening to "Heaven" (cf. the revision of *Sketches by Boz* discussed by J. Butt and K. Tillotson in *Dickens at Work*, 1957, particularly 57, fn. 4; and his letter to Forster, *Pilgrim*, II, 253, about *Barnaby Rudge:* "Don't fail to erase anything that seems to you too strong.") In the manuscript, Dickens is prepared to give the Devil his due and a capital letter, though it is printed with a small letter.[4] As an oath, "God" was apparently acceptable, providing it was suggested rather than printed in full: "Tom Codlin's the friend, by G——!" and "by G——, sir, there *is* offence" (I, 199 and 258). More usually it is omitted or softened, as when Mrs. Nubbles declares that "Heaven forbid that she should shrink" from the Garlands' examination of her character (I, 206).[5] "God" may be omitted altogether: "and God bless her" becomes "and bless her" (II, 16), though two pages later "the child, God bless her" (II, 18) is allowed to stand, as though someone had overlooked it. The two instances where Dickens made the alteration in the manuscript show he was concerned himself with this toning down, though his letter to Forster apropos of *Barnaby Rudge* already quoted suggests he sometimes felt the need of a nudge in the right direction. As a final example of this religious censorship (as though there was some objection to mingling fiction and the name of God, except when it was an oath), when Nell sees the dark figure stealing her money (I, 263), she is unable to "cry for help or commend herself to God," the last phrase being struck out on the proof (Dexter f. 4) by Dickens himself.

Although I have dealt with a number of vocabulary and stylistic changes between manuscript and *Master Humphrey*, it is convenient at this stage to consider a few of the minor changes between manuscript and *Master Humphrey* which do not really fall into those classes. Some of them seem significant, others to all appearances indifferent. Of this latter class, I suspect that some may be omissions by the printer, accepted by the proof readers. It is difficult to see why Dickens should want to drop single words or slight phrases (proofs do not exist for these examples; the omitted portion in each case is in italics): "with her *gentle* voice"; "if you think, my lad, *or if anybody thinks,* that I'm"; "for years *and years* to come"; "drew nearer *to* the ruined walls"; "the warriors, whose *mailed* figures"; "Hush! *hush!*" (I, 134; II, 4, 16, 31, 98 and 102). One must be cautious though; when the manuscript reading "One part of the edifice" becomes "Some part" (II, 95), I would suspect this to be a compositor's misreading, accepted in proof: in fact Dickens changed it in proof (Forster f. 77). Why the need of such a change?—it seems so slight. Again, when Nell asks the schoolmaster if he has many pupils, he "said with a smile that they barely filled the two forms." Does "with a smile" disappear in *Master Humphrey* (I, 230) because he must not appear cheerful at this point, or because a printer overlooked it? (It was introduced in the manuscript with a caret mark and so might the more easily be lost.)

Changes that have clear significance are easier to point to. When Quilp asks whether Tom Scott was standing on his head, Nell says no (I, 108). The manuscript has "replied Nell innocently," but the adverb might suggest a deliberate innocence on Nell's part, feigning she could not see because she did not want the boy to get into trouble. The removal of the adverb makes it a simple and positive assertion. When Nell starts out from Mrs. Jarley's, so that she may have no more dreams, she lost all other considerations "in the uncertainties" of their wild and wandering life, which *Master Humphrey* gives as "in the new uncertainties and anxieties" (II, 32; inserted on proof, Forster f. 25). The adjective stresses a *new* phase of their adventures, the new role of the child as the guide of her grandfather. A more extensive change, an interesting though rather mysterious one, comes when Miss Monflathers visits the waxwork with her charges. Mary, Queen of Scots, in male attire, makes such a complete Lord Byron that the girls

> screamed when they saw it, and asked each other who could mistake that Heavenly creature. But this expression Miss Monflathers sharply rebuked as bordering on impiety, requesting that she might not hear that word again in that room unless in connection with the Royal Family or some member thereof.

This is set up in proof (Dexter f. 1) but then Dickens began to change it; first he altered "the Royal Family or some member thereof" to "the Royal Family or at least with a Bishop," then crossed this and the whole section through, substituting the present version in the margin (I, 254, ll. 19 ff; perhaps "Bishop" suggested the Dean and Chapter). Was there particular excitement in 1840 about Byron's burial or memorial? or is it a sample of Miss Monflather's moral tone? This is one of the occasions when a new passage is substituted for an omitted one, and there could be no question of restoration in an edition.

In a few cases, Dickens added extra material in the manuscript. Sometimes this is slight and added on the main slips with caret marks; sometimes it is on a separate slip when it became clear either before or during the proof stage that the episode was underwritten. There is also a group of additions, apparently added during the writing of an episode as an idea expanded in Dickens' mind. To deal with this third group first: in the very first chapter, Dickens highlighted the character of Kit by giving him an appropriate exit, roaring himself out, insisting that if Nell *had* been lost, he would have found her (I, 43, ll. 37–46; on back of slip 14). The devotion of Kit is stressed, as well as his slightly demented air which suggests he may originally have been seen as a near-idiot rather than the upright lad he becomes. Again, when Nell stays with the schoolmaster, the description of the boys longing to be out of doors in the heat of summer is added on the back of slip 5 (I, 231, ll. 13–24 and 232, ll. 1–7). This might be a filler, added after Dickens calculated that the episode (No. XX) was underwritten, but the handwriting is more closely related to that of the rest of the chapter than even to that of the next chapter (xxvi) in the same episode. The incident of one boy managing to get out of the room, in this extra paragraph, seems to be illustrated in the woodcut (231), suggesting again that this addition was made early in the scheme of things. When the Nubbles go to Astley's, the description of the interior, "with all the paint, gilding, and looking-glass" (II, 10, ll. 30–42), was added on the back of slip 16; though Boz devoted a Sketch to Astley's and the two visits offer parallels, this addition is not one of them.

At the end of the manuscript, Dickens dashed off a conclusion, revealing Master Humphrey and the single gentleman as one and the same: "I am he indeed. And this is the chief sorrow of my life!" (on slip 9 of the final episode). Dickens wrote to Forster (*Pilgrim*, II, 190–91, 22 January 1841), explaining how he was trying to make up the last four pages of *Master Humphrey:* "I am at present in what Leigh Hunt would call a kind of impossible state—thinking what on earth Master Humphrey can think of through four mortal pages. I added, here and there, to the last chapter of the *Curiosity Shop* yesterday, and it leaves me only four pages to write." On slip 10 he then wrote (with underlinings): "Master Humphrey from his clock side in the chimney corner," and the conclusion follows as it now stands (II, 224–28), incorporating the first version and introducing *Barnaby Rudge*.[6]

Where an episode was clearly underwritten or where some necessary point had been overlooked, Dickens would include a separate sheet with the manucript, evidence that he checked over the episode before it went to the printers. No. XX was seriously underwritten (the handwriting on the first slip, for instance, is obviously occupying more space than normal); and on a sheet inserted between slips 18 and 19, written out in blue ink, different in color from his normal ink, are four passages, headed "A //," B, C, and "D //." These are: "A," the farewell to the schoolmaster; "B," a repetition of Mrs. Jarley's question about who won the Helter-Skelter Plate; "C," George's replies about the quality of the pie and beer; and "D," Mrs. Jarley's preliminary questions about whether they are too heavy a load (I, 236, ll. 9–14; 238, ll. 1–4; 239, ll. 32–43; 240, ll. 7–18). In No. XLIII, there is another manuscript sheet between slips 14 and 15, with two passages, headed "A //" and B //, but while the first of these may be extra material, it also is thematically important: Kit apologizes for rousing an ill and old man from his bed, and the added rejoinder by the man (II, 202, ll. 19–31) marks him out as the sexton (that favorite Dickensian device of someone reintroduced by a gesture or turn of speech rather than by name) with his association with death and his denial that his ills are real.⁷ The second addition is slight in length: "A strange circumstance, a light in such a place at that time of night, with no one near it" (II, 204). The sense of absence is stressed, the idea of isolation and death reinforced. Where an addition was necessary at proof stage, too long to be inserted on the proofs themselves, Dickens wrote it out on a separate sheet. The additions to chapter li are included amongst the proofs (Forster f. 69), the proof instructions reading: [Take in "A"] and a line drawn across (Forster f. 66); and: Take in "B //" (Forster f. 68). The first of these stresses Quilp's encounter with the Marchioness (II, 80, ll. 32–42 and 81, ll. 1–4), tying in with Dickens' original intention to make Sally the Marchioness' mother (hinting strongly that Quilp was her father), whereas the second, in no way instrumental to plot, shows Sampson stalling on Kit's identity and complimenting Quilp by calling him a Buffon of Natural History (II, 83, ll. 35–45 and 84, ll. 1–2). Additions may be for the sake of atmosphere; when Nell is shown to her room in the inn where grandfather has fallen in with List and Jowl, Dickens adds a description of the house on the proof: "It was a great, rambling house with dull corridors and [empty pass{ages}] wide staircases which the ⟨flaring⟩ candles seemed to make more gloomy" (I, 263; on Dexter f. 4). This sets the scene for the dark intruder who robs Nell, the addition of "flaring" even as Dickens writes suggesting the uncertain light and haunted ghastly aspect.

In the industrial unrest of the Black Country, Dickens added in proof to the night terrors illustrated by Phiz (II, 46, ll. 3–6). There are three proofs (Forster ff. 41, 44 and 45), each in a different state of correction, their relationship being problematical; f. 45 has the addition neither written on it nor inserted; f. 44 has the lines in manuscript, the crossings out and insertions suggesting that this is Dickens' original draft: "when [misguided] ⟨maddened⟩ men, armed with sword and [?fire] ⟨fire⟩brand, [and deaf to regardless of] spurning the tears and prayers of women who would restrain them, rushed forth [?to ?work] on errands of terror and destruction, [but worked] ⟨to work⟩ no ruin half so surely as their own"; f. 41 has the same passage added by (?) Forster but without deletions or insertions, and so may be the proof for the printer (the whole sheet—f. 41—has the deletions of ff. 44 and 45, and many additional corrections of punctuation). Dickens' shift of emphasis from "misguided" to "maddened" as he writes is interesting. A final example of extra material written at proof stage is Brass's speech on "human natur," which ran in the manuscript:

> *"And this,"* cried Sampson, *clasping his hands,* "is life! This is human natur! Oh natur, natur! This is the miscreant on whose account I've quarrelled with a sister, the tenderest in her affections and the toughest in her knowledge of business, that ever bloomed and blowed! *This is the miscreant."*

This episode (No. XXXVII) was "1 page over" (back of Forster f. 94), and cutting was necessary. The passage was omitted from the proof, but apparently Dickens found he had cut too much, for a new and expanded version appears in *Master Humphrey* (II, 132, ll. 32–35). Why Dickens did not restore the original is not clear; perhaps he had neither manuscript nor proof by him, or perhaps he felt he could improve what he had first written.

There are additions made both in manuscript and proofs, which seem calculated to fill space, and possibly show Dickens filling a page so as to leave no gap before a new chapter or else making up enough material to place some lines of text above one of the illustrations. An apparent example of this kind of page-filling comes at the end of chapter vi, where the last part of the paragraph that ends the page and the chapter together is not in the manuscript (I, 115):

> Some people by prudent management and leaving it [conscience] off piece by piece like a flannel waistcoat in warm weather, even contrive, in time to dispense with it altogether, but there be others who can assume the garment and throw it off at pleasure; and this being the greatest and most convenient improvement, is the one most in vogue.

Clearly this extends and rounds off with a general conclusion the point about Mrs. Quilp's tender conscience. But on the page, its absence would leave a gap of six lines (the heading of chapter vii clearly could not come in) and Dickens may have felt that the gap would sell his readers short. Another case may be in chapter xxiv (though this episode, No. XIX, was underwritten), where Nell and grandfather flee from Codlin and Short and encounter the schoolmaster. Three additions come in the chapter, of which two (I, 224, l. 29 to 225, l. 11, and 227, ll. 5–8) meet the simple need for extra material. A third passage, where grandfather urges Nell to speak to the schoolmaster (I, 225, l. 45 to 226, l. 9), now mostly comes at the top of 226, so giving a frame (with the type below) to the woodcut—there may be deliberate addition here (or in the first of the three passages) to ensure that the illustration is established below some type.[8] However, it is difficult to be certain between the needs of the whole episode for extra material and the need in page proof for a frame of type.

It has been pointed out (see, for example, John Butt, "On Editing a Nineteenth Century Novelist," *English Studies Today,* second series, Bern, 1961, pp. 190–91) that once a novel was printed, Dickens never reincorporated material cut during the serial issue. This is true, and is usually a result of printing from the same plates for serial and volume issue[9]; but within the manuscript there are passages which Dickens, forced to omit for reasons of space, reincorporated in a subsequent episode (usually in a modified form). Such passages could not be restored in an edition, since they lack internal harmony. Clearly, Dickens, proud of some of his strokes, was not prepared to let them go to waste simply because space demanded cutting. The most extensive (though most straightforward) of these shifts was the opening of chapter xxix, which now stands as the conclusion of chapter xxxii (I, 275, l. 26 to the end of the chapter). The passage fits perfectly well as it stands, with the ill-success of Mrs. Jarley's reopening by public demand suggesting how business is exhausted. The present opening of chapter xxix now follows from the close of the previous episode, which ends with a toast "to a flourishing campaign." Where originally there was an ironical juxtaposition to show how *un*flourishing the campaign was, now the toast is simply followed up. Originally the focus was upon Nell, since, when no one visited Mrs. Jarley's, she was sent out to stir up interest, caused a sensation "and began to draw people to the exhibition." It was not Mrs. Jarley or the waxwork but Nell that was the attraction. Her magnetic powers went, however, when Dickens, forced by the fact that the episode (Number XXII) was seriously overwritten, struck out the first three paragraphs and with them Nell's drawing power (Dexter f. 1). He then wrote (on the proof) the first sentence as it now stands ("Unquestionably Mrs. Jarley had an inventive genius"). When writing chapter xxxii, he wrote out the whole passage again in the manuscript; it may now perhaps be a surprise that no one comes, but there is comic poetic justice in disappointing Mrs. Jarley's expectations. Incidentally, this episode (No. XXIII) was again overwritten, but in cutting Dickens kept the transferred passage intact and hacked out a large section of social comment in chapter xxxi. Three examples of reincorporation in modified form occur. When Kit prepares to take service with the Garlands, he broaches Little Bethel to his mother, hoping not to see little Jacob looking (I, 213) "*grievous likewise* and brought up to consider that shirt-collars couldn't enter into the Kingdom of Heaven"; the omission of so brief a reference might look like a withdrawal on grounds of blasphemy or impropriety, but the hit at the idea that sanctity and dirty linen go together reappears when Kit asserts that "I don't believe, mother, that harmless cheerfulness and good-humour are thought greater

CATTERMOLE'S "NELL DEAD" FOR *The Old Curiosity Shop* (1841)
Published woodcut (Jane Rabb Cohen, "Strained Relations")

"Sloppy"
(Jane Rabb Cohen, "Strained Relations")

sins in Heaven than shirt-collars are" (II, 22). When Dick enters the Brasses' office, Sampson proposes looking for a secondhand stool and Sally originally volunteered that she knew of one (I, 282, l. 32):

> "*We'll look about for a second-hand stool, sir.*"
> "There's one in Whitechapel, nearly opposite the Hospital. At least, I saw one last week," said Miss Sally. "It's quite good enough. You had better make an offer for it if it's not gone."
> "Whitechapel, eh?" returned Brass, making a note of it in his pocket book. "I'll see about it today. *In the meantime, if Mr. Swiveller.* . . ."

This was omitted in proof, but the stool reappeared the following week (No. XXV, XXXV), when Brass greets Dick with the news that "Sally found you a second-hand stool, sir, yesterday evening in Whitechapel" (289–90). There is an element of contradiction here, since Brass was to have bought the stool, though now Sally is the one to find it by chance. Clearly an edition can only present the original passage in the apparatus. Another passage is treated similarly in chapter xxxiv (this episode, No. XXIV, was overwritten by "32 lines too many"—back of Forster f. 9), when Dick contemplated the beautiful Sally, weighing up whether she is mermaid or dragon (I, 284 between ll. 33 and 36):

> *in the client's chair and pondered.*
> "This is a blight. Richard Swiveller reduced to work, and to be guarded by a dragon—a she-dragon. *Is* she a dragon, though," argued Mr. Swiveller, "or is she a mermaid? Mermaids are fond of looking glasses, which she can't be, and have a habit of arranging their hair, which she hasn't. No, she's a dragon."
> This knotty point being adjusted to his entire content, Richard Swiveller *took a few turns up and down the room and fell into the chair again.*

Omitted in proof, a brief reference to Dick's state was added ("And the clerk of Brass's sister—clerk to a female Dragon"), but in chapter xxxvi Dick falls to wondering whether Sally is a dragon "or something in the mermaid way" (I, 298–99; added on Forster f. 8).

Finally, before looking at the major passages which have been omitted, two cases must be mentioned where the text provides a fundamentally different version of a manuscript passage. Master Humphrey's first encounter with Nell establishes the feeling of mystery about her mission, though in the manuscript the child was explicit about what she had been doing (I, 39, ll. 26–34 in *Master Humphrey*):

> "*And what have you been doing?*"
> "Selling diamonds," said the child quietly.
> Well! This was a startling answer. My face must have showed

pretty plainly that I thought so, for she added directly with a slight hesitation,

"You don't believe me I think, sir; but I have indeed."

"Do you know what diamonds are and what they are worth?" said I.

"Jewels, of course, and worth a great deal of money," she returned, smiling. "I would not tell anybody else where I have been, but I am sure there's no harm in telling you."

This was said with no appearance of cunning or deceit, but with an unsuspicious frankness that had the strongest impress of truth. I quite believed the child, I really quite believed her. *She walked on as before.* . . .

Dickens provides a plot function by the change, since we must wait for explanations of what Nell has been doing; and her innocence is further stressed, since now she does *not* know the value of diamonds. A less significant example is when Quilp, after keeping his wife watching all night, goes to refresh himself: in *Master Humphrey* he "proceeded to smear his countenance with a damp towel of very unwholesome appearance" (I, 105). It is a surprise to find that originally he "*withdrew to the adjoining room and* enlivened himself with a shower bath." The rewriting emphasizes Quilp's physical unpleasantness as when earlier, rubbing his hands together, he seemed to be "manufacturing, of the dirt with which they were encrusted, little charges for popguns" (I, 95).

– 4 –

For the final section of this brief account of the manuscript of *The Old Curiosity Shop* and its relationship to *Master Humphrey,* I want to present some of the more substantial omissions from the text. The way in which the novel suffers from enforced cutting can be seen clearly in No. XXVI (xxxvii) which gave Dickens a great deal of trouble. On the back of one sheet of the proofs (Dexter f. 8) is a note: "There is a page and a half too much here," that is, nearly seventy lines. The source of trouble was that this number, the last of Volume I, contained the dedication and preface to the whole novel, so that Dickens only presented one chapter instead of his more usual two, and the length was the more difficult to calculate. Much comic writing is lost, particularly details of the crowd and of the Brasses' reaction to Punch, Sally being so far moved as to quote verse. After the opening statement that the single gentleman took a remarkable interest in the exhibition of Punch (I, 301, l. 3), the manuscript adds:

Not that it is uncommon or at all unaccountable (Heaven forbid that it should be!) for persons of a reflective turn of mind and solitary life to feel a lively interest in that moral and just performance – indeed, to have been insensible to its attractions would have been to evince a peculiarity perhaps without parallel in the history of Mankind – but that the single gentleman displayed his fondness for the entertainment in an unusual and eccentric manner, extending his sympathy from the exhibition to the exhibitors, and bestowing upon them marks of his attention and regard which that peculiar class of social benefactors can rarely boast of receiving.

For instance, if the sound of. . . .

The opportunity to take a dig at political economists was not (originally) lost by Dickens (301, between ll. 29 and 30) :

fled from its precincts.

The reflection which forcibly presented itself to the more sober and meditative dwellers in this outraged spot, was, what an enormous family of Punches there must be in the land, since no Punch appeared twice – or if he did, he was never encouraged by the single gentleman – and yet these performances were constantly taking place by special desire and gave no sign of exhaustion. It must be left to political economists to deduce a new theory of supply and demand from these facts, or to cite them in support of an old one; but certain it is that as every day the single gentleman was ready for a new Punch, so a new Punch was every day ready for the single gentleman.

Nobody was rendered more indignant by these proceedings than Mr. Sampson Brass, who, having no very strong sympathy with the amusements of the public, and no particular taste for humour except in a rich client, was so exasperated that he once ventured, meeting his lodger upon the stairs, to address, with many compliments, a humble remonstrance to him upon the subject. Of this remonstrance the single gentleman, by word, look or gesture, took no notice whatever at the moment, but sending for Mr. Swiveller shortly afterwards, issued formal proclamation that if any person or persons resident in that house presumed to speak to him again without his speaking to him, her, or them first, the lodgings would be empty the next day. As Sampson *could by no means afford to lose. . . .*

Sally's declaration that she likes Punches shakes Sampson; is her rhyme the softening influence of Dick's quotations? (302 between ll. 20 and 21) :

"Is that no harm?"

"No, I don't think it is," answered Miss Sally. "I like 'em."

"She likes 'em!" exclaimed Brass. "She, that's always for quiet, and sticking to work by candle light out of term time, and never going out of the office except at meals—she likes 'em! Oh, you tantalizing villain!"

Miss Sally looked at her brother with extreme composure, and taking a pinch of snuff, replied with a little couplet to the effect that different people had different opinions, some preferring apples, other ingions (so pronounced for the sake of the verse); and added—yes, she liked them.

"And I suppose you like 'em too, eh, Mr. Richard?" said Brass spitefully. "No doubt you do."

"Why yes, sir," replied Dick, "I don't deny it. I should say, sir, that to hold the mirror up to Nature, show virtue her own image, vice her own deformity and all that, you know, Punch is about the best thing, in the way of a national stage—after the ballet at the Italian Opera House."

"Then, all I have got to say is," cried Brass, striking his fist upon the desk in a great passion, "that I'll consent to be broken alive upon the wheel if you an't a couple of the—"

The lawyer stopped short.

Dickens found comedy easy to write and easier to cut (it tends to be the pathetic episodes which are underwritten and which he is most reluctant to cut), and these losses are substantial. Although the other cuts in this episode, dialogues between Codlin and Short, are little loss in themselves, serial issue was a harsh taskmaster.

Dickens the social critic is present in *The Old Curiosity Shop,* most surely in the scenes of the Black Country, and there are plenty of small passing comments if not the insistence of *Nicholas Nickleby.* Yet a passage attacking the fatuous belief that the aristocracy are distinguishable by their very appearance originally stood when Miss Monflathers humiliated Miss Edwards for being intelligent and beautiful in contrast to the baronet's daughter (on Dexter f. 7, where it is corrected, then deleted; I, 271, l. 36):

> *It seems incredible.* There are divers writers of lofty prose and thrilling poetry—people who should know—ladies and gentleman of the world and of undoubted fashion too—who with a glance at his hands and feet, waist, nostrils, eyes, or neck, can tell old families from new and pick out nobility by marks of favour, never bestowed by Heaven without an earthly title. It seems incredible, and yet though almighty God does set His seal upon the acts of men and deal out pencilled eyebrows and chiselled noses only to those of high or noble birth, here was the poor apprentice of the school with a form as elegant, slight, delicate, and well-proportioned, an eye as bright, a heart as sensitive and true, and all the chiselling of nose, mouth, chin, and ankles too, to boot, and all the celestial sculpture which belongs to coronets, as perfect, as in any lady of the land. And this be it observed, though

an inscrutable vagary on the part of Providence, is not wholly without precedent either, for as camels have been seen with four humps and horses with six legs, so curious travellers now and then depose to having observed ankles and chins and even nostrils of perfect symmetry roaming about obscure places without any titles at their backs; and moreover it does sometimes happen that whereas this same Providence deigns from the first to chisel the noses and to pencil the eyebrows of great plebians who later in life by high desert win names and titles for themselves, it does un-pencil the eyebrows and unchisel the noses of their descendants who have a claim to be chiselled and pencilled in their own right. All of which premises, with many more suggested by them, would lead low minds, incapable of knowing better, to the conclusion that ankles, nostrils, mouths, and chins, are, like some other goods of fortune, pretty equally distributed by lot and cannot be en-joyed as the exclusive property and distinctive tokens of any class of mortals upon earth.

But leaving this question to be settled as it may, *here was Miss Edwards*. . . .

This looks back to *Nicholas Nickleby* and forward to the engrossing concerns (and more skillful handling) of *Great Expectations;* although Dickens feels strongly, it is not essential to the novel. A very minor gibe, yet one which involved Dickens in an old dislike, is his brief fling at Parliament. Talking of domestic virtue which springs from love of home, he declares it "no light matter—no outcry from the working vulgar, no mere question of the people's healths and comforts that may be whistled down on Wednesday nights" (II, 2). Wednesdays were free from govern-ment business, so Private Members' Bills could be debated, but many members either took the evening off (so the House was counted out), or prevented debates by claiming that a representative assembly was not present. Originally, Dickens wrote "whistled down by opera-going Sena-tors on Wednesday nights," and in answer to Forster's protest (appar-ently that it might give the wrong idea about opera rather than Members of Parliament), he wrote, "I have altered that about the opera-going. Of course I had no intention to delude the many-headed into a false belief concerning opera nights, but merely to specify a class of senators. I needn't have done it, however, for God knows they're pretty well all alike" (*Pilgrim,* II, 129, 21 September 1840). The social protest in this novel came from Dickens' own feelings, but he could see that it did not always function artistically. Facing the fact that No. XXX was over-written (the backs of Forster ff. 42 and 46 both have a note that the episode is "40 lines over"), he wrote to Forster that "there will be some cutting needed, I think. I have, however, something in my eye near the beginning which I can easily take out" (*Pilgrim,* II, 131, 4 October 1840). Such passages as the following (the one he had in mind) clearly come out easily because they are not involved with plot or character, are extraneous to the main business of the novel, interesting though they are (II, 38 between ll. 8 and 9) :

> *the very sight of which increased their hopelessness and suffering.*
> They had been used to stop at cottage doors, and beg a drink of water; and though these cottages were poor and small, they were often shaded by green trees, always in the free air, open to the sun and wind, and gay with the songs of birds. How different the stys, in which the working townsmen, women, children, babies—they all worked here—huddled together, and had their sickly homes! In courts so numerous as to be marked in every street by numbers of their own, for names for them could not be found—in narrow, unpaved ways, exhaling foetid odours, steeped in filth and dirt, reeking with things offensive to sight, smell, hearing, thought; shutting out the light and air; breeding contagious diseases, big with fever, loathsome humours, madness, and a long ghastly train of ills—in places where, let men disguise it as they please! no human beings can be clean or good, or sober, or contented—where no child can be born but it is infected and tainted from the hour it draws its miserable breath, and never has its chance of mirth (?worth) or happiness—in such noisome streets they, by tens of thousands, live and die and give birth to others, tens of thousands more, who live and die again, never growing better, but slowly and surely worse, and whose depraved condition—whose irreligion, improvidence, drunkenness, degeneracy, and most unaccountable of all, whose discontent, good gentlemen reprobate in Parliament tide, till they are hoarse; devising for their reformation Sabbath Bills without end (they would have General Fastings, but the name is awkward), and building up new churches with a zeal whose sacred fervour knows no limits.
> "Misery!" said a portly gentleman, standing in the best street of the town that very night, as he went home from dinner, and looking round him. "Where is it? A splendid Town Hall—a copy from the antique—the finest organ in Europe, a Museum of Natural Curiosities, a Theatre, some capital inns, excellent shops where every luxury may be purchased at very little more than the London prices; an elegant market place, admirably supplied— what would they have? Misery! Pooh, pooh! I don't believe a word of it."
> *The child had not only. . . .*

By this single cut, a large part of the overwriting was accounted for. A final curious passage (I have found no evidence for the custom referred to) should be quoted. Contemplating Kit in prison, Dickens stresses that the innocent suffer by confinement as well as the guilty (II, 140 between ll. 31 and 32) :

rendering them the less endurable.

There was—and may be now—a custom extant in England of waving flags with certain honourable ceremonies above the graves of those who had been wrongfully put to death by the law, being believed to be guilty, but whose innocence had been afterwards established. How many of these banners has society waved, in a mockery of reparation, above the graves of its greatest ornaments and benefactors, whose term of life its own injustice has abridged!

The world, however. . . .

Some of the cuts affect the minor characters. Among them is a clue about the Bachelor, the friend of the clergyman, "*a little old gentleman,* in whom the reader would have recognized a strong resemblance to another little old gentleman already familiar to these pages, but of that in its place—*who lived. . . .*" (II, 89, l. 33). This connection with someone else is only made clear in chapter lxviii (II, 192); perhaps Dickens' intention (the passage was an afterthought in the manuscript itself) was to connect the Bachelor and Master Humphrey; eventually he connects the Bachelor and Mr. Garland, but without preparation. Space seems an unlikely reason for omitting this, and when Dickens already had in mind some kind of revelation through the Bachelor, it seems strange that he did not retain a clue which commits him to so little. A simple omission loses us Mr. Chuckster on the pleasures of the country: summoning Kit to the Notary's, he gives Mrs. Garland his low opinion, establishing his character and perhaps making him too prominent (II, 16 between ll. 34 and 35):

"Delicious country, to be sure."

"You are fond of the country, sir?" said the old lady.

"Why, you know, ma'am, the pleasures of the town, ma'am, are, if I may venture to make use of a professional term, engrossing, quite engrossing. The country has its delights—partridges, pheasants, woodcocks, snipes, hares, wild rabbits—but as a general principle, and present company always excepted, I should say that all the desirable society is in town, and that the country is peopled with—in fact, with Snobs," said Mr. Chuckster, smiling agreeably.

"You are too hard upon us, really too hard," said the old gentleman.

"Why, you see, sir," returned Mr. Chuckster, "that here we come to a question of facts, and upon those facts issue is joined. If you only supported anything—when I say you, I mean the country in general, observe—I'd forgive you; but upon my soul you're slow fellers, dreadful dull, horrid. You've no taste for plays, no taste for (?) rows, no taste for smoking shops, no taste for harmonic meetings—no, no, you won't do. You oughtn't to be encouraged, that's the fact," said Mr. Chuckster pleasantly.

"You want to take Kit back. . . ."

One of the largest passages omitted (certainly the largest comic passage) is a description of the Wackleses' party (I, 127, l. 3).

were two of the day-scholars; and between the day scholars and the Wackleses and Miss Cheggs, the conversation proceeded thus:

"Mel, my dear," said Mrs. Wackles, "it don't signify. Don't let's have him here any more. I don't like him, and the sooner it's quite off, the better—That little Betsy Sparks's a trying to listen, I can see by her face."

"Nobody (?) desires to have him in this establishment less than I do, mother, for I abhor and abominate him as quite a monster," said Miss Wackles, "but if his being here accelerates Mr. Cheggs, and makes us more sure of Sophy, why then I repeat that it is politic, for a time, to encourage his approaches."

"There's reason for that, Mel," returned Mrs. Wackles. "Did ever anybody see such an inquisitive little creetur as that Betsy Sparks! Don't stare at me like that, miss, don't!"

While the offender was being anathematized by the old lady and promised sundry dismal punishments on the morrow, Miss Cheggs approached, skippingly.

"Oh, Mrs. Wackles, there never was such a case as it is, you know, between Alick and Sophy. Did you ever see anything like it? I am so glad. Could anything be nicer?"

The old lady responded with great vivacity to the glee of Miss Cheggs, and Miss Wackles responded to it also; but with a more grave and sober joy as being a disappointed one herself and predestined to a state of celibacy. Then Miss Cheggs departed—playfully as she had come—and Miss Wackles, looking after her with a disparaging air, remarked that it was a pity she was so very plain, and yet so very vain, which was an extraordinary contradiction in nature and one quite distressing to reflect upon. Before she had had any further time to reflect upon it, Mis Cheggs made a feint of approaching them again, but finding the pause not sufficiently long for the purpose, stopped halfway and returned to her partner in graceful confusion.

"Oh dear, her affectation is really too much!" cried Miss Wackles.

In the expression of this opinion, Miss Wackles smiled, and Mrs. Wackles smiled. The two little girls on the stools seeing this, *sought to curry favour by smiling. . . .*

Either because he wished to emphasize the role of Nell, or because he found invention flowed less easily in her part of the story, Dickens cut little material about Nell and her grandfather (necessary cutting is usually by brief omissions) ; the only considerable deletion (a kind of antiphonal elegy over Nell by the assembled bachelors) seems if anything an artistic gain. An early declaration by the grandfather that he will go on gambling would have been useful as an intimation of his later outbreaks (I, 138 between ll. 14 and 15), but is not essential since he repeats the substance elsewhere. The first encounter with the gamblers at Jem Grove's inn loses a little, and the encounter in the gipsy's camp loses a number of comments by List and Jowl as they inveigle the grandfather into robbing Mrs. Jarley. The only discrepancy is when Jowl "signed to the gipsy not to come between them" (II, 28), an unnecessary gesture since the gipsy has shown no sign of moving, except in the manuscript, where the "gipsy left the tree against which he had been reclining, and drew nearer under pretence of mending the fire" (28 between ll. 14 and 15). A more significant (though slight) omission comes earlier in chapter xlii, when the grandfather, withdrawing from Nell, "*evaded all inquiry,* avoided speaking with her if he could, and while he loved her no less than before, *maintained a strict reserve*" (II, 25, l. 34). The deleted passages concerned directly with Nell are often interesting, as in the stress on the morbid streak in her nature; she sees a coffin pass in the street (I, 134, l. 42):

> which made her shudder and think of such things until she was obliged to go close up to an old oaken table that stood in the middle of the room and turn its cover up to convince herself that there was no corpse or coffin there. After glancing carefully about the room, she would resume her station at the window, and looking out again and following the two long lines of lamps with her eye, wonder where her grandfather was, at which of those lamps he had turned off, whether to the right or to the left, whether he was far off or near, and what he could be doing. This *suggested afresh, his altered face. . . .*

Clearly space is one reason for this omission but the choice of the matter seems an attempt to avoid thoughts unsuitable to a child. A vision by grandfather of Nell's triumph would have colored the child's eventual fate when she enjoys no such progress (I, 267 between ll. 39 and 40):

> *"why was this blessed change?"*
> "Because I forgot the past, Nell," answered her grandfather, turning his head towards her for the first time; "because I forgot the love I owed thee—I am afraid I did. I'll be more mindful now though. Thou shalt be a lady yet, Nell. Poor as we are, I say thou shalt be a lady yet, and ride with jewels in thy ears and on thy neck, over the very ground we've travelled, spurning the hard stones that wounded thy tender feet, and rolling proudly by houses where we begged a drink of water. What are years of disappointment to such an end as this! Thou shalt have all the money for thyself, and I will be thy poor visitor; thou'lt use me kindly? I know thou'lt not forget the old man who toiled so hard for the only creature left to him to love, and she a patient child."

He stopped her with a motion of his hands as she was about
to speak, *and bade her talk to him. . . .*

Nell's determination to protect her grandfather was stressed by an effective image comparing her state with that of Nature (II, 32):

their condition roused and stimulated her; and the child of that
night was no more the child of yesterday, than the bleak bare
heath on which she stopped to rest, with the cold night-sky above,
were fitting couch and canopy for one so young and tender.
In the pale moonlight. . . .

The *King Lear* parallel is enforced by the grandfather's behavior in
Birmingham, exposed to the elements and despairing (II, 38 between
ll. 34 and 35):

"and all I had, for this!"
His hat fell off as he raised his hands, pressed convulsively
together, above his head, and with his white hair streaming in
the wind, uttered this complaint with a passion and energy that
shook him like an ague. Terrified to see him thus, the child clung
to him and besought him to be calm.
"Brought me to this! To what?" she said cheerfully, "one
night without a bed to lie on! What matters that! We shall laugh
at this one day; and when we are sitting before a good fire, we
shall feel glad to think how cold and wet we were tonight. Come,
let us find some corner where we can lie down to rest. There are
many, many poor creatures in this town, dear, who will not sleep
half so soundly as you and I tonight!"
For a moment she turned away her face. There was something in the action with which she pressed her hand upon her
drooping heart, sorely at variance with her speech, but next
moment she looked with a smiling hope into the old man's face,
and that was all he saw.
"If we were in. . . ."

Nell is Cordelia here; the reference to the "poor creatures" seems one of
several Shakespearean echoes.[10]
The revelation of Nell's fate in chapter lxxi shows Dickens hard at
work to produce his effects, most of all in the final pages (II, 209, l. 33
onwards; slips 1, 4, 7, 8 and 9 are all written with much revision). One
paragraph ("She was dead, and past all help . . . ," 210, ll. 15–19) was
added on the back of slip 8, catching up the ritual repetition of " 'She was
dead . . .' Traces of her suffering are all *gone*. That was the true death
before their weeping eyes" (210, l. 1), but this might seem to contradict
the idea that "peace and perfect happiness were born" and it was omitted. After Nell's burial, the bachelors, in a heavily sentimental passage,
the better for being omitted, speak solemnly of Nell (II, 214 between
ll. 19 and 20):

of light to Heaven.

They spoke of her as they crossed the churchyard on the way back, without reserve. "Let us not," said the schoolmaster, "bury all mention of her. It is a comfort to me to have her living even on my lips. And I am sure if she had been my own child, I could not have loved her more."

"It would seem a common practice," said Mr. Garland, "to bury the recollection of the dead in our daily intercourse with as much care as we bury them, or more."

"If I had friends," said the poor schoolmaster,—"I thank you, sir, for the check you give me"—to the Bachelor—"if I had had friends long ago, and had felt that I was dying, I should have desired to be remembered, sometimes, in their conversation. We —dear Nell and I, I mean—often spoke of a little scholar (my other favourite), who died—well, well—"

"I believe," said the Bachelor, after a short silence, "—Why do I say believe?—I know—that he was well-remembered by our sweet child. When she was a mere infant too, her grandfather would hold her on his knee by the hour together, as I have heard from himself, telling her stories of her poor lost mother."

"The lessons she had, dear girl, were not forgotten," said the younger brother, "neither will those be which she has left to us. You have spoken of her mother. I had heard that she resembled her. Indeed she did."

"Pardon me. I thought you had never seen her?" observed the Bachelor.

"Nor did I, ever. But I well remember her who gave her birth. I have had some cause to bear her in my mind. And when I went into yonder room upon that night of trial, I saw, in the pale face on the pillow, her breathless image. That face will be seen on earth no more, for the last of the race has passed away!"

(To the Printer. Leave a small space between this, and the next paragraph on following folio, as on last page of N°. 35.— The space should be a little wider—say by one line.)

Writing to Forster, who had been cutting No. XXXIX, Dickens noted with regret that the "part you cut out in the other number, which was sent me this morning, I had put in with a view to Quilp's last appearance on any stage, which is casting its shadow upon my mind; but it will come well enough without such a preparation, so I made no change" (*Pilgrim,* II, 166–67, ?16 or 18 December 1840). There are two passages in chapter lxii this might refer to; indeed, Dickens could intend "part" to cover both collectively. As Brass stumbles to Quilp's country-house, he thinks of death by drowning (II, 145 between ll. 15 and 16):

and over his shoulder.

"It is so cursed lonely—so dreary and so dark," he said, with a look of extreme distaste. "So out of hearing too! Suppose it was necessary to scream for help here, who would come to one's assistance? If anybody heard one, it would only be some coal-whipper or ballast-heaver, and much he'd care. He'd howl back again and there would be an end of it. These wretched old shells of houses and rotten places that are scattered about these banks," muttered Brass, looking pettishly round, "what the devil's the use of them, except to make men uncomfortable, and furnish opportunities for secret murders and buryings. Ugh! I never go down the river or along the shore on either side, but I believe Quilp must have built 'em, everyone."

Again, Sampson Brass turned his eyes distrustfully towards the light in the window and hesitated.

"What's he about, I wonder. . . ."

And Quilp himself sees it as a suitable way to become a widower (151 between ll. 43 and 44) :

and was out of hearing.

"Humph!" said the dwarf, looking round. "Gloomy and dark! If I took it in my head to be a widower, now, I need only invite Mrs. Quilp to take tea here one foggy night—the water's very near the door to be sure. If she took the wrong turning and her foot slipped—Ah!"

He stood musing for a minute or two on the very brink of the wharf, holding the lantern so that its light was reflected downward on the water, and resting one foot upon a great iron ring, sunk into the coping.

"Yes," said Quilp, knocking this ring with his heels, "it's a tempting spot. If anybody I hate, had fallen over, and was hanging by one hand to this, and screaming to me while I sat and smoked in Bachelor's Hall there, how very deaf I should be! I should hear the splash that followed though, for all that. Ha, ha, ha! I think I should hear the splash."

He walked away from it three or four times, and as often walked back to take another look. At last he *shut himself up again. . . .*

The *Pilgrim* editors (II, 167 fn. 1) seem to prefer the second of these passages as the one meant in Dickens' letter. Obviously one alone would have foreshadowed the death, and so the other be dispensable, but both have elements of Quilp's death—out of hearing, a kind of murder of himself, close to the suicide of which he is found guilty. In Quilp's last appearance, there is a comic passage between him and Tom Scott, which I do not much regret, since its humor is too mechanical in its use of contradiction (II, 182 between ll. 13 and 14) :

spend the evening.

"Do you like punch, you dog?" said the dwarf, stirring it up, and eyeing his attendant.

"No," replied Tom Scott.

"You lie, you dog, you do."

"I don't," roared Tom.

"Then you shall drink a pint," replied Quilp, smacking his lips. "If you had been very fond of it, you should have seen me drink it all, but as you don't like it, you shall swallow a pint."

"Come, you let me alone," said Tom, "and don't let's have any of your nonsense."

"Drink it every drop, you dog," returned his master, filling a pint pot to the brim and handing it to him, "or I'll pour boiling water down your throat and try if you like that better."

The truth is that the boy was very fond of punch, but that he knew his master much too well to say so. Therefore he took care to drink it with many wry faces, and strong expressions of disgust, which at once delighted Quilp extremely, and filled the lad himself with a secret joy; so that both parties were well satisfied.

The tankard was scarcely emptied, *when a low knocking at. . . .*

Dickens seems to have devoted as much care to Quilp's death as Nell's. There is a great deal of correction (especially on slips 7, 9 and 10—the chapter ends on the top of slip 11). The end of chapter lxvii was perhaps at one time intended to come where the river throws Quilp's body beneath the gallows "and left it there to bleach" (II, 187); there is a scrawl after the words (which come at the very end of a page—slip 10) rather like Dickens' page-filler. If so, he then crossed out "to bleach," wrote the words again on the next slip, and wrote the final pargraph, linking by its dark/light, death/life images with Kit's release. More probably, Dickens crossed out "to bleach" to avoid the idea that the slip and chapter ended together, and after he began chapter lxviii, he went back and made corrections (a newly sharpened pen is used for them) which encroach on the chapter heading.[11] In either case, we see the care with which Dickens links theme to theme in the novel; Quilp's death is involved in Kit's vindication.

As Dickens prepared for the framing of Kit, so he inserted details where necessary to prepare for the plot action. Mr. Chuckster's remark to Dick about Snobby, "you'll find, sir, that he'll be constantly coming backwards and forwards to this place" (II, 111) does not appear in the manuscript and points up the opportunity given Sampson to lay the groundwork in Bevis Marks. A deletion at the end of chapter lvi, using Dickens' favorite Arabian Nights, originally served to warn the reader of the future significance of events (II, 116 after l. 14):

"as good as done."

This mysterious dialogue quite satisfied Miss Brass. Mr. Sampson also appeared to be thoroughly satisfied, though one might have supposed (not being in his confidence) that his late employment had been one of a very needless and unprofitable kind. So thought the angry Sultan in the tale, of his, when his Vizier took him out of bed at night and carried him over rocks and mountains and through desert ways, only to cut a rope—by which, however, a great deal depended; as he learnt in the sequel.

Again in the same number (XXXVI, lvii) there is a long and not un-entertaining description of Sally's part in winning Kit's confidence (II, 117, l. 43):

> *is considering what he shall say,* when the gentle Sally appears at the door in the green gown and head-dress, and advances towards them for the purpose of taking notice of the poney, which she does, not in those timid and bashful advances or little fondlings and caresses in which the weaker portion of her sex are wont to coax dumb animals, but by boldly wrenching open his mouth to see how old he is or seizing one of his legs, and requiring him, in a hoarse and manly voice, to exhibit his shoe. The poney, unaccustomed to these impertinent familiarities from strangers, receives them in high dudgeon, and immediately commences a retreat from Bevis Marks with his tail first, which is an inconvenient way of traversing a narrow street as the carriage behind the tail does not under such circumstances run quite straight, but has a tendency to go sideways on the pavement, and to become entangled with area railings. Kit has a great deal to say and do, before the poney will listen to him at all, but by mild remonstrance he prevails upon him to remember the duty he owes, if not to his own character, at all events to his protectors and to society in general, and to come off the pavement, which he at length does (though by no means with a good grace) and so stands at the door again until *Mr. Garland appears. . . .*

The compositor's confusion over an insertion in the manuscript has already been mentioned; a similar insertion occurs when the trap is about to be sprung. The bank note to be used is displayed by Brass "somewhat ostentatiously," but the whole of this brief passage (II, 126, ll. 19–21) was an afterthought in the immediate writing. The action of the story presumably carried Dickens on, while the demands of the plot took him back to check that the necessary details were inserted.

A few deletions are made in the material connected with the Brasses, including passages stressing Sally's delight in seeing Sampson vexed. None of these is very important and none a great loss. The most important change is the omission of Sally's revelation that she is the Marchioness' mother and the consequent reorganization of No. XLI.[12] The omission of 43 lines (from II, 179), in an episode that was only "8 lines over" (back of Forster f. 121), meant a deal of new material. If Dickens wanted to conceal the Marchioness' origins entirely, he added some odd statements. Several hints of Sally's fear that the Marchioness may have revealed something are added. She now replies to the Notary "with a sudden flush overspreading her features" (173; added on Forster f. 118), which warns us to look more closely at her defiant speech (another addition in proof; Forster f. 118): " 'And now I *have* heard from you,' said Miss Brass, . . . 'what have you got to say? Something you have got into your heads about her, of course. Prove it, will you—that's all. Prove it. You have found her, you say. I can tell you (if you don't know it) that . . .' " (174). This seems a strong hint of mystery, a hint reinforced by the next addition: "Although her face was wonderfully composed, it was apparent that she was wholly taken by surprise, and that what she had expected to be taxed with, in connexion with her small servant, was something very different from this" (174; added on Forster f. 118). Read in connection with Sally's revelation, these seem like preparations for it, though they are all hints added after Dickens had determined to remove the direct statement. These additions, clearly important to Dickens, did not fill the space; more filling stressed Brass's motive of revenge against Quilp (176 and 177, though omitting another passage). On the proof (Forster f. 123) which he received with the revelation omitted and the passage run on as it now stands in *Master Humphrey* (and with a passage looking forward to Quilp's end; 179, ll. 38–43), the space still was not made up. So on the page proof (Forster f. 124; final page of chapter lxvi) he wrote out three passages to expand the disclosure of the Notary that Dick's aunt has left him a legacy (180, ll. 10–18, 23–25, 34–36). Sending a proof back to Forster (there is no certainty at which stage) Dickens wrote, "I think there is plenty inserted to fill the inclosed. I question, however, whether it will be necessary now to strike anything out" (*Pilgrim,* II, 175), which may suggest this very proof (Forster ff. 123 and 124). There are other changes concerned with the Marchioness. It is clear that, although Dickens no longer wished to be explicit about her mother, he did wish to hint pretty broadly. As Dick wonders whether Quilp could have given any information about the problem (II, 221, ll. 15–19), the manuscript shows Dickens evolving a form that hints and yet conceals: "but Mr. Swiveller, putting various slight circumstances together, often thought Miss Brass must know better than that; and, having heard from his wife of her strange interview with Quilp, entertained sundry misgivings whether that person, in his lifetime, might not also have been enabled to solve the riddle had he chosen." So the passage now runs; Sally and Quilp seem the possible parents, and Sophronia Sphynx (Sally was "the Sphynx of private life") remains a riddle. The connective "also," an addition in the manuscript, links Sally and Quilp—the Marchioness is a mystery, linked in her origins to the devilish pair, and out of evil comes forth good to confound the wicked.

Comparatively little of Dick and the Marchioness is lost, a happy situation, for can one have too much of a good thing? Early in the serialization Dickens wrote to Forster that he was glad "that what may be got out of Dick strikes you. I *mean* to make much of him" (*Pilgrim*, II, 70, ?May 1840), and towards the end he looked forward to "a great effort at the last with the Marchioness" (*Pilgrim*, II, 160, ?late November 1840). When Dick teaches the Marchioness what cribbage and beer mean, he describes the feelings of intoxication to her and offers her the chance of drinking again, adapting the words of Tom Moore (II, 121, between ll. 17 and 18):

> *choice drops of nectar.*
> "Marchioness," said Mr. Swiveller, handing her the tankard with profound solemnity, "if you feel that your thoughts are quite collected—if you have no sensation of giddiness, or vague desires to sing a song without knowing one—if you have undiminished confidence in your legs, and are sensible of no unusual thickness or hurry in your speech—I should feel personally complimented by your taking a little more. And if you will be kind enough at the same time to wreathe the bowl with flowers of soul, you will enhance the obligation materially."
> The Marchioness, who might understand, perhaps, of Mr. Swiveller's conversation, about one word in forty, grinned, accepted the tankard, grinned once more, drank a little, and still grinning in a modest confusion, returned it to her entertainer, who, feeling warmly towards it after its temporary absence, put it to his lips, and then, folding both his arms upon it, pressed it to his bosom.
> *"The Baron Sampsono Brasso. . . ."*

It is fitting that this sketchy survey of features of the manuscript and its progress towards the printed novel should end with a passage concerned with the triumph of the novel, Dick Swiveller and his Marchioness. This article has attempted to suggest the kind of work involved for Dickens at all stages of composition and publication. Working for certain effects, he was controlled by the form in which he was publishing and wrestled with the Protean shape of his material. In a letter he combines the conviviality of Dick (in his metaphor drawn from a brewer's barrel) with the tenderness he felt for Nell: "It is curious that I have always fancied the Old Curiosity Shop to be my XXX, and that I never had the design and purpose of a story so distinctly marked in my mind, from its commencement. All its quietness arose out of a deliberate purpose" (*Pilgrim*, II, 233, to Thomas Latimer, 13 March 1841). That sense of artistic concern emerges from a study of the first novel of Dickens for which the complete manuscript is preserved.

Jerome Meckier

THE FAINT IMAGE OF EDEN

The Many Worlds of Nicholas Nickleby

A GOOD deal has recently appeared about Dickens as a serial novelist, in particular Archibald C. Coolidge's book by that title and, earlier, the opening essay in *Dickens at Work*.[1] Yet no one today seriously reads the novels in their original serial installments except, as is the case here, in an academic exercise. There are few modern proponents of serial publication, unless one regards novel sequences, such as Anthony Powell's *A Dance to the Music of Time* and C. P. Snow's *Strangers and Brothers,* as contemporary equivalents of serial novels. Ultimately, it is a mistake to consider Dickens the serial novelist as though he were a separate person, distinct from the Dickens whose novels one can now read straight through. It seems evident that Dickens used what he learned about structuring the early serials as the basis of his technique throughout his later, more complex fictions, so that his ideas of the novel and of the serial novel are often remarkably similar. *Nicholas Nickleby,* the novel that is the subject of this essay, contains two different but related and overlapping patterns: a serial pattern and what might be called a posterity pattern. The first is geared to the serial reader and is concerned with such fundamentals as continuity and suspense. The second is aimed at future readers of the novel who can only artificially recover the experience of serial reading and must accept or reject the novel as an organic whole. The structural techniques that produce the posterity pattern are quite advanced in *Nicholas Nickleby* and lead directly to the complex interrelationships of characters, themes, and images handled masterfully in *Bleak House* and *Little Dorrit*. The posterity pattern in this novel had the additional advantage of abetting the serialization process, for a method emphasizing parallelism, variation, and counterpoint was to some extent dictated by the demands of serial publication while it was also another means of linking one number to another.

[129

Nicholas Nickleby is not among Dickens' better novels, but it constitutes a crucial stage in his development. In it he makes a determined effort to control the fecundity of his imagination and confine himself within the novel's design. J. Hillis Miller's insistence that the "individual scene" often "swells out of all proportion to its significance in the whole" is incorrect.[2] In *Pickwick Papers,* one has fecundity unlimited. But in this novel, as Forster noted,[3] the design restricts the fecundity, even if in the later novels there is a much happier marriage of invention and design. In a postscript to *Our Mutual Friend,* Dickens claimed that the "whole pattern . . . is always before the eyes of the story-weaver at his loom." So too in *Nicholas Nickleby,* especially since any installment contained in miniature the pattern of the work as a whole. The original preface to *Martin Chuzzlewit* speaks of Dickens' effort "to resist the temptation of the current Monthly Number, and to keep a steadier eye upon the general purpose and design." This too applies to *Nickleby.*

Chesterton's observation that Dickens could have published *Nickleby* as another series of sketches by Boz is an important one.[4] Some do read the novel this way, approving, as does Chesterton, of the Yorkshire sections and objecting, as did Huxley, to the Cheeryble Brothers. But *Nickleby* is Dickens' first novel. *Pickwick Papers* is a series of sketches. *Oliver Twist* is atypically Dickens in its concentration, in the manner of *Hard Times,* on one story line. *Nickleby* may look like a series of sketches: "A Yorkshire School," "A Provincial Theatre," "Sir Mulberry Hawk or High Life Revealed"; but it is, on the contrary, Dickens' attempt to convert sketches into a novel by imposing one overall pattern on apparently diverse materials. It is this ability that accounts for the range of a Dickens novel. Where *Little Dorrit* links different groups and situations by moving from prison (actual or psychological) to prison, *Nicholas Nickleby* progresses from circle to circle. Even within the novel one can watch Dickens mastering his craft. The second half is less digressive, more sure of itself in its use of pattern and in the liberties it takes with its own design.

Nicholas Nickleby is a novel in which a conventional ending is revitalized so that it becomes not only the meaningful goal of the novel but the controlling factor within each section or installment. In a Mrs. Radcliffe novel, such as *The Romance of the Forest,* the commendable characters band together at novel's end and set up a small ideal world or community of their own. Something quite similar happens at the conclusion of *Oliver Twist,* and Dickens was to end other novels, most noticeably *Dombey and Son* and *Our Mutual Friend,* in much the same way. But in *Nickleby* the establishment of an ideal world is not a conventional termination point imposed on the plot but rather a goal arduously sought throughout the novel in the face of constant opposition from a series of villains who are antidomestic rather than antisocial. The novel itself is best seen as a series of circles through which either Nicholas or Kate must pass in their mutual search for an ideal family circle in a better world. In any given installment, Nicholas and/or Kate generally take a step towards the ideal world or else encounter an obstacle that seems insurmountable.

The circles Nicholas and Kate pass through have much in common. Each is ruled by an ignorant, egotistic, petty tyrant who is usually inordinately proud of himself and of his wife and children as projections of himself. Squeers overrates Mrs. Squeers and Little Wackford as does Mr. Wititterly his wife and Crummles his wife and the Infant Phenomenon. Every nonbenevolent tyrant in the novel, whether comically villainous like Squeers, or harmlessly funny, like Lillyvick, has his slave whose revolt is instrumental in the smashing of the tyrant's world. Each circle is thus both a parody and a foreshadowing of the final community over which those benevolent but unbelievable tyrants, Charles and Edwin, will preside. Spanning the novel is Ralph Nickleby's circle, one that eventually includes, as his lieutenants, most of the other villains in the novel. Nicholas encounters his uncle Ralph first, Ralph introduces him to Squeers, and Nicholas' search for an ideal world and an ideal master begins. As Nicholas passes from one circle to another, he receives aid, sympathy, or encouragement from a number of individuals who are subsequently recruited for the ideal community. The world set up at the end of the novel is thus the outcome of a process of selection that operates throughout the book. No one whose heart and sensibility fails the test is admitted. All of the circles Nicholas or Kate pass through must somehow collapse or be destroyed as proof of their unworthiness. Each installment in the novel becomes itself a kind of circle in which the kingdom or dominion of some petty tyrant is introduced or overthrown as hero and heroine progress towards the pocket of compassion they will ultimately establish in a world Dickens portrays as being cruel and heartless.

In *Nicholas Nickleby,* the installments ran as follows: chapters i–iv, v–vii, viii–x, xi–xiv, xv–xvii, xviii–xx, xxi–xxiii, xxiv–xxvi, xxvii–xxix, xxx–xxxiii, xxxiv–xxxvi, xxxvii–xxxix, xl–xlii, xliii–xlv, xlvi–xlviii, xlix–li, lii–liv, lv–lviii, and the double number lix–lxv.[5] Each installment generally offers two or three chapters involving Nicholas and one featuring Kate, or, more rarely, two centering on Kate and one about Nicholas. The alternation from brother to sister is the simplest form of counterpoint in the novel. The rises and falls in the book are usually those of the successive groups that Kate and Nicholas pass through, so that tension within an installment or in the novel as a whole is similarly generated. But the main point here is that Dickens, as he moves from number to number, always has the overall design roughly in mind. Thus, through variations and reduplications, he links the installments to one another at the same time that he creates a posterity pattern that renders the novel

organic for readers who will later have to see it as a whole. Dickens may
very well have worked the way Coolidge and Butt and Tillotson contend
he did, but he also made sure that some of his methods for linking segment to segment would also give animated organic form to the novel once
it was completed and had to stand or fall as an entity.

CHAPTERS I–IV. Ralph Nickleby is to Dickens' third novel what Chancery
will be to *Bleak House:* a source of evil at the heart of the novel but one
that also reaches outward to each and every part. It is to Ralph's world
that one is introduced in this installment. Though later numbers move
on to, among others, Squeers, Mantalini, and Hawk, it is not until
Ralph's defeat in the closing chapters that the ideal community the good
characters strive for can hope for existence. Ralph's villainies thus span
the novel. He separates Nicholas and Kate at the start, and, as the enemy
of domesticity, he spends the second half of the novel trying to thwart
their attempts first to regroup and then to add allies to their number.
Every other villain in the novel, be it Squeers, Hawk, or Gride, is eventually tied to Ralph. As the others are defeated one by one, his own
position becomes increasingly precarious. As recommender of Squeers,
moneylender to Hawk, accomplice of Gride in the latter's bid for Madeline Bray, and ironically father and destroyer of Smike and therefore of
his own chances for domestic happiness, Ralph is the heartlessness of the
world personified.

It becomes clear upon rereading that *Nickleby* makes a full circle.
It begins here with the death of Nicholas' father (i) and ends with the
death of his uncle (lxii). The novel starts when Nicholas' father loses his
money and home, but it ends with Nicholas' acquisition of wealth,
through Madeline's legacy, and his repurchasing of the family home.
Nicholas' father, one is told, learned "to shun the great world and at-
tach himself to the quiet routine of a country life" (i). This is one lesson
that Nicholas and Kate have also learned at novel's end. The bubble that
bursts and ruins Nicholas' father has its echo in the business whose failure costs Ralph ten thousand pounds (liv). It is fitting that a novel
idealizing the family circle should also describe a circle.

The United Metropolitan Improved Hot Muffin and Crumpet Bak-
ing and Punctual Delivery Company is, one fears, an unpardonable
digression (ii). Yet it is a circle, or, more precisely, a monopoly; and it is
headed by Sir Matthew Pupker, the first of a series of tyrants in the novel
who have power and position out of all proportion to their capabilities.
Once Dickens has found his stride and sensed the pattern of his novel
more exactly, episodes of this kind disappear. The pace of the second
half of the novel is hectic by comparison with that of the early chapters.
With Squeers' initial appearance (iv), the first installment ends. It has
presented Ralph's world and prepared for Nicholas' transfer from

Ralph's dominion to that of the schoolmaster. It later becomes clear that characters will repeatedly circle into and out of the narrative. Squeers, for example, reappears again and again,[6] while Snawley, who here deposits two boys with Squeers, later returns to act the part of Smike's father (xlv).

CHAPTERS V–VII.   The second installment seems to go in three directions at once: it introduces two characters who are eventually recruited for the ideal world, namely the "good-natured" Miss La Creevy (v),[7] and the unfortunate Smike (vii); it displays Mr. and Mrs. Squeers at home in their absurd version of a family circle (vii); and it seems to pause for an unaccountable digression in which an optimist and a pessimist each tell a story. But all three movements are related to the governing design of the novel.

"Mr. and Mrs. Squeers at Home" is a chapter not about the ideal world Nicholas is in search of but rather about a private world set up by Squeers in which he reigns supreme and imposes his sense of reality on the other characters. At this stage in his career, Dickens does not see society as an intricate spider's web: *Bleak House* with its Chancery, *Little Dorrit* with its Circumlocution Office, or *Our Mutual Friend* with its dust heaps. Instead, society is a series of cells or circles that have at their centers egoistic tyrants dedicated to the suppression of good deeds and good feelings. This may seem relatively unsophisticated if one does not keep in mind that Dickens is purposely exaggerating his point. The cells he explores are meant microcosmically. Each is overdrawn and can be taken as society in miniature, just as each is a smaller-scale version of Ralph's more extensive domain of villainy. In later novels, instead of reproducing villain after villain, Dickens will take some larger force, person, or institution and show it victimizing all his characters. But whether he reduplicates tyrannies or creates an arch-villain, whether he follows Squeers with Hawk or traces the labyrinthian extensions of Chancery, he tries always to instill in the reader a sense of the pervasiveness of evil. Society itself is less atomistic in the later novels, owing perhaps to such inventions as the railway and the telegraph. The villains who rule as feudal lords in this novel can consolidate in the later ones into groups more maliciously oriented than the Muffin and Crumpet Company.

Dickens himself discloses the design of his novel at what is roughly the book's mid-point (xxviii). He insists that "most men live in a world of their own, and that in that limited circle alone are they ambitious for distinction and applause." This is quite true of Squeers, who is, in fact, permanently defeated only when he leaves Dotheboys Hall to conspire with Ralph in London (lvii). These villains prosper, Dickens continues, because they consult no opinion other than that "of their own little world." It is the atomistic state of society, the absence of an overall view, that gives each tyrant his unquestioned sway. Only Nicholas, after experiencing life in a series of these circles, has a nightmarish vision of "the huge aggregate of distress and sorrow" that is Dickens' synonym for the world (liii). Thus Nicholas, to succeed, must escape the many petty tyrannies that wait in the novel to trap him. He must fight evil on its own terms by setting up a little world of his own that will be a refutation of the pattern of nonbenevolent tyrannies Dickens sees in society and in fact reproduces in his novel. Perhaps Dickens should have suspected even here that, since the atoms of evil outnumber those of good, the advances of an industrial society, with its stress on merger and consolidation, would ultimately benefit Ralph's circle more than Nicholas'.

The stories told by the grey-haired man and the gentleman with the "good-tempered" face (vi) prove on examination related to the novel's progress. Unlike the inset tales in *Pickwick,* these stories, clearly related to the novel's central concerns, carry implications that a more thoughtful Nicholas could find comforting.

The "good-tempered" man tries to form a circle, a "little community," out of those who, like Squeers and Nicholas, are waiting for a coach to replace the one that overturned. At his urging, the grey-haired man tells the story of the Five Sisters of York. The tale proves that idyllic communities can survive.[8] Nicholas, who has been forced to leave Mrs. Nickleby and Kate, should find this encouraging. The sisters resist the Monk who insists that they dissolve their circle, take the veil, and, in effect, forfeit their freedom. Alice, the youngest, dies early and may therefore suggest Smike, while the Monk himself seems to be another version of Ralph. Though the sisters do marry and disband, they later reunite as widows and one by one join their sister, Alice. A moral, constructive community thus manages to survive outside the religious order, though in some ways it is a secular version of that order.[9]

The grey-haired man speaks sadly of the way "the faint image of Eden" that is stamped on hearts in childhood wears away in "rough struggles with the world." And yet, since the sisters who cling together "prepared themselves for a purer and happier world," it seems clear that their circle was itself an image, even if faint, of a lost paradise. Before he dies, Smike allegedly has a vision of "Eden" (lviii). The community that groups itself around his grave reminds one of Alice's sisters. In a world Dickens genuinely sees in *Nickleby* as a valley of tears, these little communities, no matter how sentimentally described, offer, for him, a foretaste of some sort of heaven.[10] Eventually, the Brothers become not only Nicholas' substitute fathers, not only his ideal masters, but also his temporal deities.

To counter the sadness in this story, the good-tempered man recites the adventures of Baron Grogzwig, whose jolly circle of hunting men dissolved upon his marriage. So complete was his subjection to the Baroness that he began to contemplate suicide. Instead, however, he revolted against her domination—as do Newman against Ralph and Nicholas against Squeers—and raised his sons to hunt with him in place of his former men. The tale illustrates that a circle once lost can be regained.

The two inset tales, the first sad in tone and the second its opposite, are a fine tour de force in the creation of contrapuntal moods. They also foreshadow the optimistic pessimism of the novel as a whole, a novel in which the circles of villainy outnumber but cannot defeat or engulf the one pocket of benevolence, headed by the Brothers, that opposes them.

CHAPTERS VIII–X.   In this installment, two would-be tyrants move towards their overthrow, while, contrapuntally, a third makes his initial appearance. Squeers and his daughter, Fanny, both try to enslave Nicholas, to subjugate him to whatever design for the world prevails in their minds. Fanny attempts to make Nicholas her slavish admirer (ix) so as to impress Miss Price and her future husband, John Browdie, both of whom will eventually be recruited for the ideal community (lxiv). Squeers wishes to absorb Nicholas into the little kingdom of Dotheboys Hall (viii), to absorb him so totally that he ceases to exist as anything more than an extension of Squeers himself.[11] As Squeers notes, a "slave-driver in the West Indies is allowed a man under him to see that his blacks don't run away, or get up a rebellion; and I'll have a man under me to do the same with *our* blacks." Almost all the circles in the novel are totalitarian enough to frighten Orwell. The relationship of Squeers and young Nickleby is one of many in the novel where good is forced to serve evil (Noggs and Ralph, for example, or Verisopht and Hawk). The revolt of Nicholas against Squeers is repeated by most of the other slaves in the novel. It foreshadows Dickens' subsequent concern with tyranny and revolt in such books as *Barnaby Rudge* and *A Tale of Two Cities.*

Mr. Mantalini is as unqualified to rule as were Fanny and Squeers. "He had married on his whiskers; upon which property he had previously subsisted, in a genteel manner, for some years" (x). Ralph introduces Kate into the realm ruled by this pretentious figure. Although she owns the dressmaking shop, Mrs. Mantalini is still a slave to her husband's histrionic professions of love. Admittedly less villainous, Mantalini is nevertheless another, less harmful version of Ralph and Squeers. He has managed what Fanny ardently desired to do: enslave an admirer. As a parasite, he becomes the first of several parasite-villains in the novel, among them Sir Mulberry and Arthur Gride.

Mantalini's world totters several times before its collapse. The bailiffs move in (xxi), but Sealey's question—"Is it only a small crack or a out-and-out smash?"—proves premature. Mrs. Mantalini threatens to confine her husband's spending (xxxiv) but he restores himself to favor.

Ralph, to whom the Mantalinis are in debt, "saw, clearly enough, that Mr. Mantalini had gained a fresh lease on his easy life, and that, for some time longer at all events, his degradation and downfall were postponed." Throughout the later sections of the novel, Dickens delights in postponing the inevitable, in taking liberties with the permeating pattern of rise and fall. Mantalini is finally defeated (xliv) when Miss Knag informs his wife of his philandering. Ironically, Mantalini calls his wife "enslaver," "captivator." The extent of his defeat becomes clearer when one sees him working the mangle as the slave of an unidentified buxom female (lxiv) and when one credits his own admission that he "has gone to the demnition bow-wows." In the second number, however, his circle makes it appearance as that of Squeers heads for an upset.

CHAPTERS XI–XIV. In addition to its division into installments, *Nickleby* seems to divide into four major sections, the first of which ends with this installment. The second section terminates after Nicholas thrashes Sir Mulberry Hawk (xxxiii). It is the departure for America of the Crummles circle that closes the third section (xlviii). The final division has two climaxes, one in which the designs against Madeline Bray collapse (liv), and one in which Squeers and Ralph are irrevocably defeated (lxii, lxiv). The sections thus comprise fourteen, nineteen, fifteen, and sixteen chapters respectively. But the sections, like the installments within them, are held together by a system of variations and reduplications that even an expert in counterpoint, such as Philip Quarles of *Point Counter Point*, would appreciate. For example, each section ends with the smashup of a private world. But the departure of Crummles means not the defeat of a villain, as is the case with the other sections, but the future unavailability of a refuge similar to that provided by Sleary's circus in *Hard Times*. The benevolent tyranny of Vincent Crummles foreshadows that of the Brothers at the same time that it is the core of theatricality in a novel whose entire cast seems drawn from melodrama. The downfall of Squeers and Hawk are variant forms and anticipations of the demise of Ralph. Crummles' departure, though somewhat similar to the falls of Squeers and Hawk, is yet quite different in the tone in which it is handled and in the bearing it has on the struggle in the novel between good and evil.

It is the third of four chapters in this installment (xiii) that chronicles the overthrow of Squeers. But the preceding chapter foresees this overthrow when the world of Fanny Squeers collapses. And the following chapter introduces a new circle—the Kenwigses—that will not be upset for twenty-two chapters (xxxvi).

Nicholas undercuts Fanny's pretensions and mortifies her ego when he declares his non-love for her in Miss Price's presence. All the pretenders or tyrants in the novel trump up their credentials, only to have them exploded by Nicholas or Kate. As the novel proceeds, these totalitarian kingdoms are blown up with increasing regularity. Fanny's catastrophe is followed by that of Squeers. Dickens builds up to it in a manner drawn from the stage, and even Nicholas' cry of "Stop!" (as Squeers beats Smike) and his talk of "the dastardly cruelties practised on helpless infancy in this foul den" seem part of a piece staged by Crummles. Squeers is specifically termed "tyrant" and he gives the boys "a look of most comprehensive despotism." Yet melodramatic or not, as Dickens permits Nicholas to "beat the ruffian till he roared for mercy," the toppling of Squeers has been carefully prepared for and comes as a genuine climax.

J. Hillis Miller's objection to the Kenwigses' anniversary party as a scene that distorts the novel's structure [12] becomes untenable once this family is recognized as another circle in the novel. Kenwigs himself, like Pupker, Mantalini, and Squeers, enjoys undeserved superiority. He is important because he "occupied the whole of the first floor, comprising a suite of two rooms" and because his wife's uncle, Mr. Lillyvick, collects water rates. Kenwigs functions as a dignitary for the other tenants, but, along with his wife and children, he is a slave to the irascible Lillyvick, whose will Kenwigs hopes may mention his children. After the serious villainy of Ralph, the comically serious maliciousness of Squeers, and the parasitic figure of Mantalini, Lillyvick appears as a domestic tyrant similar to his predecessors but different in that he belongs almost entirely to the world of comedy.[13] Lillyvick's marriage (xxv) signals the collapse of the Kenwigses' expectations, although they do not learn of the disaster for eleven chapters (xxxvi). Since the circle of the Kenwigses is a purely comic variant of other tyrannies in the novel, it recovers its former stability after the dictatorial Lillyvick is vanquished and enslaved by his wife, the former Miss Petowker. News of his enslavement (xlviii) is followed by his return, in chastened circumstances, to the Kenwigses (lii). No longer the man who acted "as if he had the world on his books and it was all two quarters in the arrear," Lillyvick makes a "return to the bosom of his family," thereby reconsolidating a domestic circle in which he reigns as "lion."

The design treated in detail through the first four numbers can be traced more cursorily in the remaining installments. As Nicholas moves from circle to circle seeking a bearable employer, the number of professions a young man can honestly pursue in nineteenth-century England is systematically reduced. In xv–xvii, the world of politics is ruled out as Nicholas decides not to enter the world of Manchester Buildings to work for Mr. Gregsbury, M. P. (xvi). Another unqualified tyrant, Gregsbury defies his constituency's attempt to unseat him. Like Squeers, Gregsbury expects Nicholas to have no mind or will of his own. As is the case with all the tyrants in this novel, he proves amazingly absorbent. Squeers confiscates the money and clothes of his charges, Lillyvick soaks up the praise of all in his company, and Gregsbury wants to "be crammed" by Nicholas with whatever facts are necessary for Parliamentary speeches. In this installment Nicholas enjoys his first glimpse of Madeline Bray (xvi), a candidate for the ideal world and Nicholas' future wife. The number ends with Kate encountering Miss Knag, despotic ruler of Mrs. Mantalini's showrooms. Kate, like Nicholas, is always a stranger in someone else's private world where she can never accept prevailing attitudes.

In xviii–xx, Dickens chronicles the collapse of Miss Knag's "little kingdom." It disintegrates when an old lord and his future bride, a preview of Gride and Madeline, request that Miss Knag be replaced by Kate (xviii). Miss Knag's defeat is followed by the appearance of a new circle, that of high life, in which Sir Mulberry is tyrant-parasite to Lord Frederick. As was true with education and politics, the aristocratic world also fails as a milieu where one can exist with integrity.

The subsequent installment (xxi–xxiii) records Mantalini's preliminary crash (xxi) and introduces two new circles. The first, that of Cadogan Place, contains people in the "middle station" (xxi). This level of society also fails as a potential ideal. The second is the world of the Crummleses (xxii), the circle that provides Nicholas with his only haven prior to the appearance of Charles Cheeryble (xxxv). Mrs. Wititterly, with her pretended fragility and her assumed aesthetic sensibilities, is another Mrs. Squeers, another Mrs. Kenwigs. Like them, she is hailed as a phenomenon by her equally hypocritical husband. Crummles is actually quite as absurd as Wititterly, particularly in idolizing his wife and daughters.[14] But he does exhibit "something between the courtesy of a Roman emperor and the nod of a pot companion." He is thus a friendly tyrant. Only in the benevolent tyranny of Crummles' theater does Nicholas find temporary safety, perhaps because here, like all the other villains in the novel and like Mr. and Mrs. Crummles offstage or on, Nicholas can act or dissemble, becoming whatever he chooses or a scene demands in an unreal world,[15] instead of being as before, innocence in a cruel one.

Lillyvick's marriage (xxv) in the next number (xxiv–xxvi) spells disaster for the expectations of the Kenwigses. In xxvii–xxix, Dickens explains the design of his novel (xxviii) while Kate fends off Hawk's attempts to subjugate her will to his (xxvii). Pyke and Pluck insist Hawk is Kate's "slave," but it is to rescue her from Hawk—the first of several rescues in the novel—that Nicholas circles back to London (xxix). Mrs. Wititterly's world is destroyed in the same chapter when she realizes that Hawk and Verisopht visit her only to facilitate their pursuit of Kate. When Smike asks if they will soon see Kate, Nicholas replies: "To be sure, we shall all be together one of these days—when we are rich, Smike" (xxix). In the second half of the novel, the prerequisites for an ideal community are one by one supplied: men of integrity, marriage partners, benevolent masters, homes, and, finally, the necessary income. In xxx–xxxiii, the climax of the second section arrives as Nicholas overhears Hawk talking freely about Kate (xxxii). As Hawk leaves the coffee-room and enters a carriage, Nicholas challenges him. In the ensuing scuffle, Nicholas gashes Hawk's face, the horse bolts, and Nicholas "could discern the cabriolet whirled along the foot pavement with frightful rapidity—then heard a loud cry, the smashing of some heavy body, and the breaking of glass." Hawk's world suffers its first collapse.

When Nicholas encounters the "old-fashioned" Charles Cheeryble (xxxv) in the next installment (xxxiv–xxxvi), the formation of an ideal world becomes imminent. Dickens lists the members of "the little circle" —Nicholas, Mrs. Nickleby, Kate, Miss La Creevy, Smike—in the chapter (xxxv) between one in which Mantalini nearly loses control of his wife and one in which the Kenwigses' hopes collapse upon news of Lillyvick's marriage. The world of the Brothers receives fuller treatment in the following number (xxxvii–xxxix), while the tyrant Squeers rises in one chapter with the recapturing of Smike (xxxviii) and topples again in the next as Browdie, honeymooning in London, rescues and frees Nicholas' friend.

Although the basic pattern of the novel does not alter, there is, from here on, a reverse in direction. Until this point, Nicholas and Kate have been avoiding absorption into the different private worlds in the novel. Now, with the aid of the Brothers, they begin to construct one of their own. The villains of domesticity now change their tactics and try to destroy this emerging community by kidnapping its members—the abduction of Smike—or by absorbing into their own designs the candidates slated for admittance to the new world—the attempt to marry Madeline to Gride. Thus even the old mad gentleman who presses his attentions on Mrs. Nickleby (xxxvii) is part of the pattern: he is a comic variation of Hawk's persecution of Kate and his efforts to crash into the new world, via the chimney (xlix), fits in as one of the many pressures the new community must withstand.

In xl–xlii, Madeline reappears and proves her suitability for the ideal society when her face offers Nicholas "a glimpse of some better world" (xl). The mad gentleman's world collapses, though he never notices, when Mrs. Nickleby declares her resolve to remain a widow (xli). In xliii–xlv, Frank Cheeryble arrives in London and one immediately recognizes him as the ideal marriage partner for Kate. The circularity of the world itself, a place where characters turn up again and again, becomes self-evident as Tom the clerk reappears (xliii) after an interval of twenty-seven chapters and Brooker returns to haunt Ralph (xliv) after an absence of seven years. The installment centers around the downfall of Mantalini and ends with the failure of Ralph, Squeers, and Snawley to remove Smike from the circle that now dwells in a cottage provided by the Brothers. Squeers feels it will be "the downfall and defeat of Nicholas" but Nicholas' world holds up.

The world of Crummles vanishes with his departure for America in the fifteenth installment (xlvi–xlviii). As Ralph and Gride formulate their plots against the defenseless Madeline Bray (xlvii), the loss of a haven that the departure of Crummles signifies is cleverly underlined. Madeline is central not only to Nicholas' hopes but also to the Brothers' desire to repair the past. Charles and Edwin never had the opportunity to form a faint image of Eden. Their mother, who, unlike Mrs. Nickleby, died too soon, the sisters they were to marry but did not, the faithful servant of the sisters whom Tim Linkinwater might have wed—all these were candidates for a circle that never materialized, perhaps because those intended for it were too syrupy to gel. Instead, one of the sisters married Mr. Bray. Madeline is thus the Brothers' link with a lost domesticity that they will recapture vicariously through Nicholas and Madeline, Frank and Kate.

In the sixteenth installment (xlix–lii), two worlds collapse: that of Mrs. Nickleby (comic) and that of Hawk (serious). One by one Ralph's outer perimeters fall apart as his fellow villains are defeated. Hawk's "dominion" ends (1) when Lord Frederick, sickened by Sir Mulberry's persecution of Kate, revolts, forcing Hawk into a duel. Although he wins, Hawk ironically destroys his own kingdom and the purse that supplied it. He flees England for a time, only to be arrested for debt on his return (xlv). As the exploder of his own kingdom, Hawk parallels Ralph, the destroyer of his own son. Verisopht, Dickens writes, might have "died with children's faces round his bed," but he expires, instead, outside any sustaining circle. Squeers' design against Smike, Gride's against Madeline, and Hawk's against Kate all crash to an end.

Mrs. Nickleby's private world, in which she sees herself as a paragon of attractiveness and common sense, is demolished when the old gentleman wooing her turns out to be fickle as well as mad. After his entrance down the chimney, Mrs. Nickleby can no longer pretend, as did Fanny Squeers, that she has a suitor. The old gentleman, who evidently proposes to every woman he meets, begins to woo Miss La Creevy (xlix). Mrs. Nickleby is the novel in miniature, for she is perpetually constructing dream worlds and unwittingly undermining them herself. She fabricates an excellent future for Kate on the basis of Mr. Watkins' assertion that Kate is an astonishing child (xviii). But she shatters her own daydream, without noticing it however, by adding: "I know it was he who said so, because I recollect . . . his borrowing twenty pounds of [your] poor dear papa the very moment afterwards."

The last installment before the traditional double number builds to a melodramatic climax in which the idea of collapse functions as both sound and sense (lii–liv). The number begins with Lillyvick's restoration to his former throne but ends with a resounding defeat for Ralph Nickleby and Arthur Gride. Gride, who wishes to enslave Madeline, is actually quite servile when with Ralph. But Nicholas and Kate, functioning virtually as two angels, appear in time to thwart the plot against Madeline. At the climactic moment, old Bray, who has forced Madeline to accept Gride, literally collapses. The sound of his body striking the floor overhead is also that of Ralph's designs falling apart. Miss Bray, formerly a "slave" to her father (xlvii) and potentially one to Gride, is rescued by members of the ideal world, the haven or heaven the good characters attain by the final installment.

The double number (lv–lviii, lix–lxv) contains a crescendo of crashes. Defeat becomes the pervasive motif. When Peg Sliderskew, Gride's slave, revolts (lvi), she causes the collapse of her master's world. Ralph, reenlisting Squeers, attempts to recover from Peg a document, stolen from Gride, that bequeaths a legacy to Madeline. But again Ralph fails, for as Squeers pockets the paper Newman brings the bellows crashing down on his head (lvii). Even Smike's death, a preview of the subsequent deaths of Little Nell and Paul Dombey, can be regarded as a defeat for Ralph (lviii). Smike will never enter the promised land along with the other commendable characters. Yet his defeat, different in tone from those in the previous two chapters, may be, Dickens insists, a victory. The vision of Eden Smike allegedly enjoys before dying indicates he is to enter the real paradise of which the ideal community at novel's end will be only a faint image. Unfortunately, neither Dickens nor the reader can put too much faith in the substantiality of Smike's compensating vision. In the later novels, utopia, whether in this world or the next, will be harder to attain. If ideal communities are but faint images of a paradise to come, that paradise will itself become fainter as the setting up of ideal communities becomes more difficult in the later novels.

From the moment Noggs overtly revolts (lx), Ralph realizes defeat is inevitable. Dickens' early villains, Ralph and Quilp, and even Dombey and Gradgrind, seldom oppose Church or State but bring the brunt of their villainy to bear on the domesticity of the decent characters. For this reason, the evil of a Dickens villain often seems too ponderous for its outlets. Nevertheless, the final blow for Ralph is the revelation that he is Smike's father. The domestic circle he has most effectively destroyed is his own. The last obstacle in the way of an ideal world disappears in the next chapter as the wealth of Madeline and the blessings of the Brothers guarantee that world money and benevolent deities. One should not miss the fact that the Brothers, like Squeers and Ralph, are also very much the tyrants, but benevolently so. They insist Nicholas marry Madeline. When Miss La Creevy, responding to Tim's proposal, asks what the Brothers will think (lxiii), Tim exclaims: "Why, God bless your soul! . . . you don't suppose I should think of such a thing without their knowing it!" The happiness of Nicholas and Tim forms a counterpoint with the despair of Ralph, who commits suicide in the preceding chapter.

The same chapter that records Mantalini's final ignominy (lxiv) also shows Nicholas journeying to Yorkshire to break the good news to Browdie about the forthcoming marriages. He will be a corresponding member of the ideal society firmly established in the last chapter. The novel has come full circle. It is now winter again as it was when Nicholas first journeyed to Greta Bridge. Squeers, the first of many enslaver-tyrants introduced in the novel, is technically the last to see his empire collapse, as revolution and rebellion bring about the "breaking up" of Dotheboys Hall (lxiv). The ideal world includes the houses of Kate and Frank, Nicholas and Madeline, a cottage for Noggs, Smike's grave, and, by extension, the London dwelling of Tim and Miss La Creevy. If utopia means stability for an ideal *status quo*, then, to Dickens at least, Nicholas' circle is a utopia: in Nicholas' house "none of the old rooms were ever pulled down, no old tree was ever rooted up, nothing with which there was any association of bygone times was ever removed or changed" (lxv). In a novel full of sentimentality and stock figures but masterful in construction, the final counterpoint to the rises and falls that give pattern to the installments and to the book as a whole is a utopian stability.

Unlike the later novels, *Nickleby* seems singularly lacking in recurrent metaphors, images, and symbols. The links between episodes are largely situational rather than verbal. Yet the words *world, heart,* and *home* reappear frequently enough to command attention, for the novel is about these three concepts. Dickens tries to determine in *Nickleby* if an individual with a heart can ever be at home in the world. He decides the world is, like Ralph Nickleby, essentially heartless and thus one cannot hope to be at home in it. The posterity pattern involving contrapuntal worlds is reinforced by the heart-home-world syndrome as almost every new world that appears proves inimical to heartfelt emotions or genuine domesticity.

It must be made clear that when Dickens uses the word *world* in this novel he means it to have the connotation it possesses when one speaks of the world, the flesh, and the devil. Nicholas and Kate are repeatedly described as being ignorant of the world, while Ralph is notorious for his "worldly manner" (iv). In passing from one circle to another, Nicholas and Kate exchange their ignorance for knowledge of the world. But what they learn only confirms them in what Dickens has suspected all along: that education, politics, high life, middle life, and even business (unless, as for the Cheerybles, business is benevolence) are not acceptable ways of life in a world that is pretentious, mechanical, and heartless. Acting does seem a possibility for a time, but that is chiefly because all the inhabitants of the other worlds in the novel are also actors or hypocrites whereas Crummles, by contrast, does most, but not all, of his acting on stage.

As Nicholas and Kate go from one little world to another, Dickens builds up a definition of the world at large: a place almost synonymous with evil, one where Nicholas and his sister seem too pure for any job that is offered. After Kate is fired from Mrs. Mantalini's, Dickens speaks of the "rough jostling" Kate has "already had with the world" (xxi). The implication is that one does not always live in the world but enters it towards the end of adolescence and, if one is wise, soon strives to become independent of it. *Nicholas Nickleby* is thus a Blakean song of innocence and experience in which Nicholas and Kate, at first ignorant of the world, acquire a knowledge of its workings only to attain a higher innocence in which one both knows and rejects the world. Nicholas and his sister live by humanistic principles whereas, notes Dickens, "most men unconsciously judge the world from themselves" (xliv). While Nicholas and Kate respond to the world by drawing on their principles, Squeers, Ralph, Mantalini, and others see the world as an extension of their egotistic selves. They are thus at home in a way that Nicholas can never manage until he too has a world that is an extension of his secularly Christian self. For Dickens, even this early in his career, the world is not redeemable. Late in the novel, Nicholas has a negative epiphany when he sees "how much injustice, misery, and wrong there was, and yet how the world rolled on, from year to year, alike careless and indifferent, and no man seeking to remedy or redress it" (liii). Nicholas realizes that "the huge aggregate of distress and sorrow" remains immovable. At best, the charitable operations of the Cheerybles create a pocket of benevolence in which Charles and Edwin can themselves live at peace even if no overall redress is possible.

What distinguishes the unworldly from the worldly in *Nickleby* is the possession of a properly functioning heart. The characters in this novel, both good ones and bad, speak of their hearts too frequently. Ultimately, it is ownership of a heart plus the capacity to sob in the face of another's sorrow or kindness that qualifies a candidate for the ideal world. Nicholas' father is said to have died of "a broken heart" (iii), the malady from which Smike also suffers (l). Miss La Creevy "had a heart big enough for Gog, the guardian genius of London" (xi), though London itself has none. John Browdie's major characteristic is "heartiness" (xliii), whereas Miss Squeers, says Nicholas, has "a virgin heart" (xlii), which means, one suspects, a heart unsullied by any unselfish feelings. By contrast with Kate's warm heart, "that of the old worldly man [Ralph] lay rusting in its cell, beating only as a piece of cunning mechanism" (x).[16] Ralph is thus on a par with the clock in Gride's house: it has an "iron heart" (lvi). Of all Sir Mulberry's friends, it is of course only Lord Frederick who "really had a kind heart" (xxxviii). Dickens is right in specifying old Bray's complaint as "one of the Heart" (xlvii). It is the failure of the feelings allegedly controlled by this organ that allows him to think of sacrificing his daughter. And it is the literal failure of his heart that frustrates his design. By contrast, Madeline's friends, Nicholas asserts, "would coin their hearts to save her" (liii). Those without hearts often seem on the brink of success in a world that has at its core something akin to the "cunning mechanism" in Ralph's breast.

Obviously, Nicholas and Kate cannot become domesticated in a world where Ralph desires to have Nicholas "stabbed to the heart and rolled into the kennel for the dogs to tear" (xxxviii). Couples such as Squeers and his Mrs., who are "at Home" in the second installment (vii), constitute so many parodies of domesticity. To Ralph, Kate exclaims: "I must have some place that I can call a home" (x). "When I speak of home," Nicholas tells poor Smike (xxxv), "I speak of the place where, in default of a better, those I love are gathered together." Though *Nickleby* is full of melodramatic situations and marred by sentimentality, its vision of the world is surprisingly bleak for one of Dickens' early comic novels. Establishing a home becomes, on the secular level, equivalent to entering a religious order or some other assembly of God's elect. Here is where, "in default of a better" world, some faint image of life as it should be can survive. The novel may be partially a fairy tale, as Bernard Bergonzi claims [17] and as Harry Stone would undoubtedly agree. But the Brothers seem more like deities than fairy godfathers. The pocket of benevolence they administer at novel's end is a haven or perhaps a secular heaven. The whole novel often becomes neither a fairy tale (Bergonzi) nor a romance (Chesterton) but rather a naïve reworking in a secular arena of situations drawn from the Old and New Testaments. Characters tested by the world, or by the series of worlds in the novel, are given their reward in a Conclusion chapter that operates as a Last Judgment. This is the "day of reckoning" Nicholas promises Ralph earlier in the novel (xx). As one tyrant's world after another crumbles, one imagines Nicholas, Kate, and their allies fleeing Lot-like from Sodom or else going off in the Noah's Ark of their ideal community. The "one black gloomy mass" that pursues Ralph as he passes the burial ground (lxii) seems to be the inverse of a pillar of fire.

It is difficult to understand why Graham Greene chose *Oliver Twist* rather than this novel as an example of the Manichean in Dickens.[18] The cast of characters in *Nickleby* can be easily divided into angels and devils and there is never any real question of the latter group's conversion. "Is there no Devil to help me?" Ralph cries before hanging himself (lxii). Dickens' answer is negative. Yet the world of *Nickleby* belongs more to the personage Ralph calls on than it does to the Brothers, Ralph,

LANE'S PORTRAIT OF DICKENS, 1840–1843
(Jane Rabb Cohen, "Strained Relations")

SOME PICTURESQUE BUILDINGS BY CATTERMOLE FROM *Barnaby Rudge*
Above, Maypole Inn; *below,* Locksmith's Shop
(Jane Rabb Cohen, "Strained Relations")

Squeers, and Gride, who, in their respective designs on Nicholas, Smike, and Madeline, are clearly aged and at times comical Satans pursuing youth and innocence as Quilp will pursue Little Nell. When Nicholas and Kate block the doorway that could take Gride and Ralph to Madeline (liv), they appear to be angels keeping evil out of paradise. Thus, at the center of the novel, one finds a contradiction, or perhaps a paradox. The good triumph, yet one feels it remains a Manichean world. The ideal community is achieved while almost all the other worlds collapse, yet one retains an impression of pervasive evil. The ideal world is the perfect ending for the pattern of the novel but is less successful as a thematic resolution.

The feeling that something more than a fairy tale is going on here is reenforced by the move from melodrama to Shakespearian tragedy. The origin of *Nickleby* may be Dickens' familiarity with the London equivalents of Vincent Crummles, but the ending just as surely stems from *Macbeth* and *Richard III*, plays the young Dickens saw at the Theatre Royal. The novel ends like Shakespearian comedy with a flourish of marriages, but these are structurally in counterpoint with Ralph's demise. All through the novel Dickens has been tempted to allow Ralph to develop a heart. The usurer warms slightly in the presence of Kate (xix) and, less credibly, laments the loss of his son (lx). Ralph is thus a forerunner of Scrooge, Dombey, and Gradgrind, particularly of Dombey, who does become a sort of Lear, while Ralph remains Macbeth. One thinks of the history plays when Ralph, tottering, declaims: "For the present I am firm and unshaken. Let me but retrieve this one small portion of my loss and disgrace" (lvi). And his exclamation, "Throw me on a dunghill, and let me rot there, to infect the air" (lxii), could come from any of several Shakespearian villain-heroes. The shift from melodrama to tragedy reflects the Manichean paradox. The good triumph as the world remains evil; the ending juxtaposes a flourish of marriages and the downfall of a pseudo-Shakespearian villain, a downfall for which the novel also offered several variations or anticipations. Surely Dickens is striving, albeit at times clumsily, for an unattainable inclusiveness that combines romance, melodrama, tragedy, Bible, and the different moods associated with each. One recalls Quarles' advice to the novelist employing counterpoint:

> Meditate on Beethoven. The changes of moods, the abrupt transitions. (Majesty alternating with a joke, for example, in the first movement of the B flat major Quartet. Comedy suddenly hinting at prodigious and tragic solemnities in the scherzo of the C sharp minor Quartet.) (xxii)

Dickens' conception of a comedy with a serious point, and thus of Squeers himself, is essentially contrapuntal. So too is his notion of construction for his novels whether those novels are examined serially or as entities.

The situation that one can call the Manichean paradox ceases to exist in the later novels that end with the formation of an ideal community. The houses Kate and Nicholas buy may be described as a "retreat" (lxv), thus suggesting withdrawal from the world, but it is a triumphant retreat earned by defeating the worlds of Ralph and Squeers. Good fights evil man to man, or perhaps as angel versus devil. In subsequent fictions, Dickens finds evil harder to personify and therefore more difficult to confront directly. Pegotty's world cannot keep out Steerforth. The shadow of Chancery falls across Jarndyce's world just as the Circumlocution Office entangles Clennam. The ideal community Nicholas sets up in Dickens' third novel is intended as a practical alternative to the other circles in the book. In the later novels, such communities are pure escapes rather than alternatives. The world of the Wooden Midshipman in *Dombey and Son* and Sleary's circus in *Hard Times* are communities of exiles whose chances for happiness cannot hide the general state of affairs. The struggle between good and evil is no longer simply one between individuals and the small world established at the end of these later novels and is thus of questionable durability. Nicholas and Kate attain heaven whereas the crestfallen Dombey exists in what one feels is only a temporary respite from trends and changes Dickens no longer pretends optimistically to combat. Surely Grandgrind cannot join Sleary's troupe, even if his son, Tom, can.

Seen from a post-1870 viewpoint, the little world at the end of this novel is an early installment or variation of the little worlds that survive at the conclusions of later works. But in these subsequent worlds the image of Eden becomes progressively fainter, even though the organizational techniques used in *Nickleby* are employed more skillfully. The secular arena proves less and less susceptible to infusions of Christianity as Dickens becomes surer in craftsmanship and less confident of the viability of his beliefs. In retrospect, the destruction of the worlds of Ralph and Squeers must have seemed to Dickens an instance of wish-fulfillment.

DOMBEY AND SON

A Closer Look at the Text

SEEN THROUGH modern criticism, Dickens has become a surprisingly many-faceted writer. For some of our contemporaries he is not merely a foe to injustice and the apostle of what Cazamian has called "Christmas philosophy," [1] but a lucid critic of capitalism and indeed a herald of socialism. It was in this guise that he was viewed last year by some of my students after they read *Dombey and Son*. Between them and Dickens this assumed community of political interest was probably the only tie, for I have found that young Frenchmen are not attuned to his art.

I should first like to make clear that the theme of this novel proceeds from moral, not political, certitude.[2] If Dickens was too intelligent to have, "properly speaking, . . . no ideas on any subject," as Santayana believed,[3] yet he had only a vague idea, if any, of capitalism as an economic system.[4] Nothing allows us to say that he ever thought doing away with private property would be a good thing because of the collective character of production. On the contrary, the *fabula* shows that property gives more scope to the individual's talents and enables him to actualize what is best in him. For the moment one example is enough: would Walter Gay, sensible and energetic though he is, have been appointed to "a post of great trust and confidence," and would he have mounted up "the ladder with the greatest expedition," if he had not been "assisted by his uncle at the very best possible time of his fortunes?" (lxii). For, as miracles are not exceptional occurrences in Dickens' fictional universe, Sol Gills has become a well-off man: "Some of his old investments are coming out wonderfully well" (lxii).

A DOMESTIC NOVEL. We must also remark that this novel, in which is expressed Dickens' profound uneasiness at the sight of the society of his time, is yet primarily a domestic novel. To a large extent disorder in public life and disorder in private relationships stem from the same causes: selfishness, pride, and the desire to assert one's superiority, all of which find in money the means one needs to rise above others, but, in the narrow framework of the family, better than in the social macrocosm, the evil is obvious: unconcern for others may lead even to the disruption of natural bonds. Mr. Dombey denies his daughter the love she craves. Mrs. Skewton and Mrs. Brown have both tried to turn their daughters' beauty into profit and made of them "a sort of property" (liii). Not only does James Carker humiliate his brother, but he would also like, if possible, to obliterate all kinship between them, and he disowns his sister: "I know no Harriet Carker. . . . *You* may have a sister; make much of her. I have none" (xxii).

Thus a number of things connected with family life, and more generally with the bringing together or the reunion of people, assume exceptional importance in this novel and serve as symbols, e.g., houses and meals, the human face, the handshake and the embrace. Dickens' philosophy of life must be sought for in the significance he attaches to the humble realities of daily existence. I suppose that readers who tax him with intellectual poverty can recognize "ideas" only when conveyed by discourse, whereas in Dickens' fictions they are most often and most vividly suggested by pictures. It is those pictures that reveal both the scope of his experience and its fruit: an art of living which makes him, in Santayana's words, "a good philosopher." [5] Philosophy, as Étienne Gilson reminded us recently, is not primary knowledge; philosophy is wisdom. [6]

THE HOUSE. Another French philosopher, Emmanual Lévinas, has written profoundly on a subject which (without forgetting either Bachelard [7] or Heidegger) [8] has seldom been considered a theme for philosophical meditation: the human significance of the house. [9] But many of the scenes created by Dickens show that he too had given much thought to that theme.

What a house ought to be we learn through the Toodles, that is to say, through the poor. Their house is a comment upon both Mr. Dombey's, which is but the place where his solipsism appears most noxious, and Carker's, which is only the shelter of his hedonism. For these businessmen the house marks the end of the day's activity from which it is cut off, in Mr. Dombey's case at least cut off in dreary silence. For the cheerful and noisy Toodles the house is the setting of an intense, affectionate life carried over into their kindliness outside the house and their contentment in the day's work. It is the warm intimacy of the home which moves them to greet and help others with pleasure. In the Dickensian world only when love prevails does the house cease to be a mere shelter and become a home. Moreover, it is always ready to give a welcome, and everyone knows the occupants. There is no need of a precise address to find the Toodles, as Susan and Mr. Toots learn: "He lived in the Company's own Buildings," they are told; "they couldn't mistake it; but if they did, they had only to ask for Toodle, engine fireman, and any one would show them which was his house" (xv). It is at the Toodles that Miss Tox, a snob but a kind heart, receives the warm sympathy she craves, once she has made up her mind to disregard class barriers. " 'How do you do, Mrs. Richards?' said Miss Tox. 'I have come to see you. May I come in?' The cheery face of Mrs. Richards shone with a hospitable reply, and Miss Tox . . . untied her bonnet strings, and said that in the first place she must beg the dear children, one and all, to come and kiss her" (xxxviii).

According to Lévinas, woman is "la condition . . . de l'interiorité de la maison." [10] Dickens goes so far as to say that a woman's face is a man's home: "the cordial face she [Harriet Carker] lifted to his to kiss him, was his home, his life, his universe" (xxxiii). There is no one like a woman, in Captain Cuttle's opinion, "to welcome a wanderer home" (lxi). Polly Toodle is the soul of the home and her husband forcefully conveys what she means to him when he says, "I should know her . . . anyhows and anywheres" (ii).

John Carker, who is single, has a house but no home. Mr. Dombey, a widower and then a married man without love, has no home; Florence compares "the bright house with the faded dreary place out of which it had arisen, and wondering when, in any shape, it would begin to be a home" (xxxvi). Mrs. Skewton does not have even a house of her own. Without any genuine love for anyone, without any inner life, she could not have transformed the initial loneliness of a modest dwelling into the rich solitude of true intimacy, for intimacy begins only with the birth of great affection for someone, and she has failed to win even her daughter's regard. Therefore she is condemned to a wandering life, going from seaside resort to watering-place, from one furnished apartment to another. In this novel the failure to make a home and (even more strikingly) voluntary itineracy are always the signs of a want of heart and of sins against the spirit.

With the symbolism of the house is associated the symbolism of cold and warmth, to which one resorts almost instinctively. Mr. Dombey's house is dismal and cold because he is a cold man. Houses are natural metaphors for their inhabitants of whom they are but one particular expression. Mr. Dombey, this "man of wood, without a hinge or a joint in him" (xxvi), lived encased in "the cold hard armour of his pride" (xl). It seems as though the mere presence of this man who "represented in himself the wind, the shade, and the autumn" of Paul's christening makes the cold church colder (v). It is enough for Florence to look up into his face for the tears in her eyes to be "frozen by the expression it wore" (iii). To this icy man Captain Cuttle's cordial handshake is unpleasant in a paradoxical manner: "at this touch of warm feeling . . . Mr. Dombey shivered all over" (x).

So much of the story takes place in Mr. Dombey's house that Dickens can touch up his picture time and again. Nothing in the world could be more solitary to Florence's fancy than "her father's mansion in its grim reality" with its curtains hanging "like cumbrous palls" (xxiii). For Florence, this house is truly what Bachelard has called "l'espace de sa solitude." [11] And, as Dickens' genius often destroys the anonymity of things, indeed often giving them a human countenance, Mr. Dombey's house has such a distinctive "personality" that it remains spiritually identical, whatever material improvements are made to it. (Parenthetically, it may be noted that the gloom of that house, which no costly embellishments can dispel, is one of the variations on the theme of the failure of wealth.)

Dombey's house does not belong to him as the Toodle's or Sol Gills's belong to them. He merely resides in it, or rather he keeps to a room or two, and thus appears to Richards "as if he were a lone prisoner in a cell, or a strange apparition that was not to be accosted or understood" (iii). His house is the symbol of his estrangement and solipsism, for he loves no one, not even his son: he never forgets himself in Paul, he pities himself through the child, and when he says "poor little fellow" one is to understand "poor me!" (ii).

There are several instances of houses as synecdochic expressions of human beings. Bagstock's and Miss Tox's reveal the foolishness, the inanity, of their class prejudices. They accept the discomfort of their dwellings because there is a fashionable street around the corner. "What a situation!" says Miss Tox. The Major swells with pride at his club when he can mention that "great" people are his neighbors. Princess's Place, which is not exactly "a court" and not exactly "a yard, . . . but the dullest of No Thoroughfares" (vii), is undoubtedly the symbol of nugatory snobbishness. Ironically, Dickens makes Mrs. Skewton speak the truth when she says that such social conventions cause the withering of life (xxv).

As we have seen, woman is the soul of the house, but the feminine principle is not represented by woman alone. Long before Freud some men had discovered this principle within themselves, so that a manly man like Luther could speak of his "feminine soul." Let me quote Lévinas again: "L'absence empirique de l'être humain de sexe feminin dans une demeure ne change rien à la dimension de féminité qui y reste ouverte, comme l'accueil même de la demeure." [12] This feminine principle is found in Sol Gills and Captain Cuttle: thanks to them the Midshipman is a welcoming home for Walter, Florence, and Mr. Toots. After the disappearance of Gills, Ned Cuttle "considered that the maintenance of 'a home in the old place for Walter' was the primary duty imposed on him" (xxv). To Florence he says: "When there's anything you want, my Heart's Delight, as this here humble house or town can offer, pass the word to Ed'ard Cuttle, as'll stand off and on outside that door, and that there man will wibrate with joy" (xlviii).

THE MEAL. But welcoming a friend does not only mean to open one's door to him with that joy of heart mentioned by Ned Cuttle; it also means to prepare a meal in haste for him and bring an old bottle out of its hiding place. Food is important in the world of Dickens (and those of Thackeray and Flaubert as well).[13] Other critics have remarked on this, A. O. J. Cockshut particularly, but it seems to me that he is wrong as regards the significance of this conviviality. Dickens, he says, "was born for festivity," but this is not a real awareness of corporate life. The idea that we are members of each other can only be imperfectly realized by festivity, because it implies that those who can never meet, never know of each other's existence, have, as we say, 'nothing in common.' "[14] But meals and festivity are not symbols of the withdrawal of friends and acquaintances from the wider community; they are symbols of one's regard for others, whether friends or strangers. The charitable characters never refuse to welcome an unknown visitor. What Aquinas calls "an avarice of the emotions" is foreign to them, and love is never "withheld from some stranger who . . . hungers for it."[15] Harriet Carker speaks kindly to that anonymous passer-by who later proves to be Mr. Morfin, and she shares her meal (and money) with a vagabond like Alice Marwood (xxxiii). Captain Cuttle cordially responds to the appeal of Mr. Toots: "You never *can* know me . . . if you don't give me the pleasure of your acquaintance" (xxxix). So strong is the Captain's sense of human fellowship that he naïvely imagines that a good little clerk like Walter must surely be "a member of Mr. Dombey's family" (xvii).

Indeed the meal is the symbol of the readiness to welcome, even more than of the actual welcome; and in this novel, which claims kinship with the fairy tale, there is always, miraculously as it were, food enough and to spare. Sol Gills, who has debts and no customers, manages to cook "a fried sole, with a prospect of steak to follow" (iv) for Walter's dinner. When Florence seeks refuge in Gills's little house, it does not take Captain Cuttle long to procure a chicken which he prepares "with extraordinary skill" (xlix), for the friendly meal, no matter how simple, is always a good one. In Dickens' anti-Malthusian universe there is always a "vacant seat . . . at Nature's mighty feast"[16] for anyone who is hungry. The starving man does not need to claim a "right" to be fed, for there is always a Sol Gills or a Ned Cuttle or a Harriet Carker to beg him to come in and to lay the table in no time.

Just as a house without love is but a caricature of the true home, so the egoist's repast or the sumptuous dinner given as a mere matter of convention distort the true meaning of the meal. Almost all the selfish characters are gormandizers. Mrs. Pipchin gives growing boys a dinner "chiefly of the farinaceous and vegetable kind" (viii), but orders mutton chops for herself, "buttered toast unlimited" for tea, and "a warm sweet-bread" for supper. Major Bagstock "always took the best possible care of himself" (xx): his face "with a complexion like a Stilton cheese and his eyes like a prawn's" (x) proclaim his gluttony.

Mr. Dombey's servants do themselves very well too, particularly when a great misfortune occurs in the house. For it is not wealth which poisons "human relations in the family and in society" [17] as Kathleen Tillotson says in her fine essay on *Dombey and Son*—it is filthy lucre.

Mr. Toots is wealthy, yet he is the incarnation of kindness. Sol Gills remains the same considerate man after he has become a "capitalist." Some poor folk, like Susan Nipper and the Toodles, are good because they are not greedy. Other poor folk, like Mrs. Brown and Dombey's servants, are bad because money is what matters most to them. They always have enough strength to bear their master's and Florence's grief, yet they confirm it by regaling themselves: Mrs. Pipchin "takes more table-ale than usual," cook "promises a little fry for supper," and all "make themselves dismally comfortable over bottles of wine, which are freely broached as on a festival" (xviii).

We may therefore conclude that, if *Dombey and Son* shows what Graham Smith calls "the alienating effect" of money,[18] it also makes clear that money may work either for good or bad according to who has it: a Dombey or a Toots.

Just as a house inhabited by united people is the happy norm, and a house without love is the deviation from the norm, in the same way the norm is to be found in a meal which at once reveals and deepens communion of thought and feeling (as when Sol Gills, Florence, and Susan take tea together to speak of Walter), and the deviation appears both in a Bagstock's gluttony and in a Dombey's ostentatious housewarming dinner, with sixty or so people together, but without togetherness.

In the moral world of Dickens' fiction the perversion of what I have called the humble realities of daily life betokens the sins of the soul and the emptiness of the heart. Thus the Dickensian ethic is found most vividly in pictures, not in argument. And this constant opposition between the good and the bad, norm and deviation, so strikingly sets off both the natural standard and the abnormal departure from it that one is surprised to hear Monroe Engels say that in *Dombey and Son* "the world . . . is a hell in which . . . un-nature has become the rule." [19]

THE HAND AND THE FACE. This revelatory play of contrasts applies also to the handshake, the embrace, and other affectionate gestures which constitute a kind of language, all the more useful because verbal expression fails some characters. Here I am led to controvert, or at least to qualify, the sweeping assertion of that most perceptive critic, Dorothy Van Ghent: "Dickens' technique is an index of a vision of life that sees human separatedness as the ordinary condition, where speech is speech to nobody and where human encounter is mere collision." [20] Of course Dickens was as aware as any of the solitude inherent in man's fate. But he also showed, as I have tried to demonstrate, that one can, as it were, people one's solitude and find, if not happiness as a mode of being, at least joy as a frame of mind and the yeast of existence. "Speech is speech to nobody"; even if it were so, speech is not the only language of men.

It is true that Ned Cuttle's interlocutors do not always understand his idiosyncratic idiom with its many words whose denotation and connotations are clear to him alone: Florence, for example, "did not quite understand this, though the Captain evidently thought it full of meaning" (xxiii). " 'Exactly so, Captain Gills,' said Mr. Toots, whose fervour of acquiescence was greatly heightened by his entire ignorance of the Captain's meaning" (lvi). Even Walter and Rob the Grinder do not succeed in comprehending him all the time. The Captain himself cannot always detect the real intention underlying other people's words, and sometimes even fails to catch the surface meaning: "Captain Cuttle, without quite understanding this, greatly approved it and observed in a tone of strong corroboration that the wind was quite abaft" (l). And yet, all understand the spirit which informs his jargon: everyone could say with Mr. Toots, " 'You've a way of saying things that gives me an agreeable warmth all up my back' " (lvi).

To revert to a point I made before, Dickens' characters have a language other than speech: the expression of the face. Emotional and ethical human relationships find a surer inspiration and foundation in the face than in discourse. This is why "le face à face demeure situation ultime" [21] in the Dickensian universe. One needs only to remember Walter and Florence, Mr. Dombey and Edith, Edith and Carker, and, best of all, at the end of the book, Mr. Dombey and Florence, whose love melts his ice and, if I may use biblical language, "causeth . . . the waters to flow." [22] Words are often like screens between people, but the expression of the face opens the way to the heart. "There was glory and delight within the Captain that spread itself over his whole visage and made a perfect illumination there" (xlix). Moreover, in what Dorothy Van Ghent has called "a universe that is nervous throughout," affectionate greetings are sometimes "violent," as when Sol Gills returns to the Midshipman:

> The Captain recovered himself with a great gasp, struck the table a tremendous blow, cried in a stentorian roar, "Sol Gills ahoy!" and tumbled into the arms of a weather-beaten pea-coat

that had come with Polly into the room. In another moment, Walter was in the arms of the weather-beaten pea-coat. In another moment, Florence was in the arms of the weather-beaten pea-coat. In another moment, Captain Cuttle had embraced Mrs. Richards and Miss Nipper, and was violently shaking hands with Mr. Toots. (lvi)

Because for these simple-hearted characters, a handshake or an embrace is so clearly an avowal of affection and a pledge of faithfulness, by contrast they set off the unreliability of the hypocrite's and selfish man's greetings. Sometimes the latter are even pathetic because they betray a failure to communicate. Mr. Dombey could not shake hands convincingly even if he tried. Now he takes Florence's hand "loosely in his own" (iii), now he transforms what should be a sign of welcome into one that repulses: " 'Florence,' said her father, putting out his hand so stiffly that it held her off" (xxviii). Carker and Bagstock would like their handshake to appear frank and cordial, but it so badly conceals their hypocrisy that it is merely grotesque and despicable. Thus, gestures, whether sincere or not, are always a telltale language: Dombey and Edith "standing together arm in arm . . . have the appearance of being more divided than if seas had rolled between them" (xxvii).

In *Dombey and Son* not only the story and the general structure of the novel but every detail convey the author's moral intention and his philosophy of life. As he himself remarked with a perceptiveness unusual in his literary criticism, "fiction is a way of organizing man's experience in the world so that he can comprehend it." [23]

TIME. The importance of time in this novel has often been remarked. It would be useless to repeat what has been said before about the frequent mention of clocks and watches, the fast-running river, and the rhythmic voice of the sea. But I should like to underline what seems to me to have escaped notice: the good and the bad live time differently, the former accepting its natural flow, whereas the latter try to hasten it. Thus, under a new form, there appears once again the opposition between norm and deviation.

Those whom the steady flow of time irritates are all goaded by excessive ambition and acquisitiveness. Carker endeavors to accelerate events so as the sooner to obtain complete independence as well as the woman he lusts after. Bagstock and Mrs. Skewton respectively urge Dombey and Edith to marry, for both look forward to the day when they can share "the elegance and wealth of Edith Dombey's establishment" (xxvi). Mrs. Skewton, like Mrs. Brown at the other end of the social scale, has denied a childhood to her daughter: " 'A child! . . . When was I a child! . . . You gave birth to a woman!' " (xxvii).

All the selfish parents who hope to satisfy their vanity vicariously through their children wish to speed up the flight of time. They send their boys to Dr. Blimber's school where the poor lads are treated like vegetables in a hothouse. (This reification of human beings is one aspect of one of the themes of the novel.) "Mental green peas were produced at Christmas and intellectual asparagus all the year round" (xi). Cornelia Blimber "regarded the young gentlemen as if they were born grown up" (xii). In front of his son's cradle Mr. Dombey dreams of the boy's "becoming qualified without waste of time for the career on which he is destined to enter" (v). It does not occur to him that everyone must order his life as he likes, and, therefore, that Paul's future should be his own, not his father's, property. In fact, he never sees the child in little Paul but the adult he ought to become (viii).

It is only the time of others that the selfish wish to speed up, not their own. Dombey never thinks that his son's maturity might well mean his own infirmity, senile decay, or death. It never occurs to him that the name of the firm may well be as derisively inaccurate tomorrow as today, with its conjunction of coordination which has nothing to coordinate. Today, the father and no son for partner; tomorrow, perhaps the son and no father. Mrs. Skewton too exemplifies this insane desire for a kind of temporal dichotomy, in a manner at once pathetic and comic, since she has always wished Edith to grow older while she remains young, or even grows younger. In this respect, Mrs. Skewton, that relic of the Regency, is a very "modern" character, for she anticipates our contemporaries' own brand of the refusal of time: the nonacceptance of senescence, the cult of youthfulness.

Time is a different thing indeed for the good characters. They also experience the present as anxiety and expectation, but it is anxiety about a friend and expectation of the day when they can see him again. To them the future means the service they wish to render, the help they propose to provide, the welcome they hope to give. These simple-minded people have an understanding of life that is lacking in characters better endowed with intellect: the good do not wish to disintegrate time, nor do they want it to run differently for themselves and for others. For them, self-concern and concern for others do not open up two diverging paths in the field of time, but two parallel ones which are indeed indistinguishable one from the other in the fullness of their *caritas*.

The good are always present when they are needed. Each could say with Mr. Toots, " 'I am entirely to be relied upon' " (l). The future of their duty is always the immediate future. Captain Cuttle is always ready to give his watch, his sugar tongs, his two teaspoons, and his tin canister containing "thirteen pounds and half-a-crown" (ix). Susan is willing to serve Florence without wages. Cousin Feenix goes to France to offer his "accomplished relative . . . such protection as a man very much out at elbows could offer" (lxi). Polly Toodle is always ready to do the Dombeys a good turn, for, as her husband puts it, " 'favour past . . . is never to be forgot.' " And thus, for the good, the present is and the future will be faithfulness to the past and generosity of being. Their time is that of the moral life.

To do Mr. Dombey justice, let us acknowledge that, in his own way, he is generous too. He lends Sol Gills money readily enough, but with such vulgar ostentation! Whether he grants a loan or presents his wife with jewels, he is wrapped in self-admiration and full of the importance of the gift. To him, to give means *donum*. But for Mr. Toots, Ned Cuttle, or Susan, to give is to express at once self-forgetfulness and love for others through one's action. To them, to give means *datio*.

DOMBEY AND THE MIDSHIPMAN. It has been said that Dombey incarnates modern capitalism and that all those who revolve round the Midshipman stand for an outdated image of society. But is this true? It would have been odd if Dickens had chosen to give a fast-dying conception of social life such young representatives as Walter, Florence, Susan, and Mr. Toots, not to mention the Toodles. To begin with, both Toots and Gills are "capitalists" too, since they live on unearned income. Moreover, had Dickens wished to make his readers sensitive to the vices and dangers inherent in the capitalism of the industrial age,[24] he would have given it a truly menacing representative, a man of wide-ranging mind and ambition, whereas Dombey is a poor muff after all, an incompetent businessman, incapable of seeing through his manager, let alone Bagstock. But Dombey is not the incarnation of an economic system; he, together with Carker, Bagstock, and Mrs. Skewton, is the incarnation of egoism and pride as destructive elements.

It is true that Dombey deals with Mrs. Richards, Walter, his staff, indeed everybody, as if they were things, but are we to infer from this that Dickens wished to expose the workers' alienation in mid-nineteenth-century economic organization? After all, Mrs. Skewton and Major Bagstock, whom one may regard as surviving specimens of the preindustrial era, also treat others, particularly their domestics, as objects. In Dickens' view, it is not capitalism nor even necessarily money which reify human beings, but pride, class-prejudices, unconcern for others. And the victims of this preposterous, dehumanizing mentality are the masters as well as the servants. Dombey, Carker, Bagstock, Mrs. Skewton, even Miss Tox to some extent, illustrate this reification.[25] Mrs. Skewton, Cleopatra, always assuming the same posturing and attitudinizing, with so little of her that is real once her curls, teeth, and other "juvenility" have been removed, is the most frightening *exemplum* of reification. She also shows the waste occasioned by greed and selfishness in one who has always tried to deceive others and to give herself out to be "an inestimable parent," "an incomparable mother," and who finally has come to believe it. As

Wladimir Jankelevitch has remarked, the hypocrite, who has obliterated and forgotten his real being and yet is not what he pretends to be either, is indeed nothing at all, a kind of ghost.[26] Mrs. Skewton's spectral appearance is a metaphoric image of her inner unreality.

Contrasting with these hollow and harsh characters, the friends of the Midshipman do indeed represent something of the past, but it is the past of a moral order which has always had its contemners and deviants, but which is still fully alive in Gills and Cuttle, Walter and Florence, Toots and Susan, and the Toodles. Symbolically, it is to these supporters of the ancient Christian values that the future belongs, since the Gays have one child already and the Toots are expecting one.

Little Paul gives another proof that Dickens wished to oppose a moral tradition to the perversion or disregard of that tradition, and not capitalism to some other economic system. He is said to be "old-fashioned," and he wonders "what could that old fashion be that seemed to make people sorry" (xiv). In one respect he is old-fashioned because he is about to die: Death is "the old, old Fashion" (xvi). But above all he is old-fashioned because of his kindness in a milieu and a world where harsh exigencies prevail. He attends to everybody, to his school friends as well as to Cornelia and Mrs. Blimber (xiv). And in the affection he wins from all, one may perhaps see a form of Dickens' wishful thinking or utopian dream: that of a world regenerated by love. In a way, this child is "the good spirit" Dickens invokes in a passage that has nothing to do with Paul, the good spirit who is to remind men that, "like creatures of one common origin, owing one duty to the Father of one family," they ought "to make the world a better place" (xlvii).

Thus *Dombey and Son* has a kinship with moralizing allegories and even with fairy tales [27] in which Cinderellas find charming princes, kindness and virtue their reward. Dickens himself often drew attention to this kinship, so one or two examples will suffice. Florence and Captain Cuttle chat by the fireside like "a wandering princess and a good monster in a story-book" (xlix). To Florence, her father's house is as lonely as "a magic dwelling-place in a magic story, shut up in the heart of a thick wood" (xxiii). Walter is another Dick Whittington. But the unusual, the bizarre, the marvelous, in Dickensian fiction gives expression and organization to man's experience in the world, from which it is sometimes far removed but never cut off: the unrealistic tale refers us back to reality.

ESSENCE AND EXISTENCE. Thus, in order to hold our attention, Dickens does not ask from us a willing suspension of disbelief in the same way as most great novelists do. When reading him we never forget for a moment that we have entered a world which is not ours. Not for a moment do we believe in the existence of Ned Cuttle, or Carker, or Florence, but this does not preclude us from feeling sympathy, or scorn, or pity: as Étienne Gilson has said, Dickens' characters do not exist, they *are*.[28] It is their energy of being which fascinates us. As several speak what G. H. Lewes called "the mother-tongue of the heart," [29] this community of feeling between them and ourselves contributes to the removal of all doubt in the reality of their being.

But this distinction between *esse* and *existere* is too subtle for many readers. "What pleasure can you take," some students have asked me, "in a caricatural world peopled with automatons?" Those who have read Santayana wonder how he could seriously write that Dickens does not exaggerate. Using the very words of the philosopher they go on to say: "It is precisely because 'we have eyes and ears' that we contend that in Dickens' universe all is falsified, the general prospect as well as all the details." They are not entirely wrong. Of course Dickens exaggerates, and thus often gives relief to features that are familiar enough in the world, but that we are apt to forget. In this case exaggeration is the revealing agent of truth. Actually we have never seen a Mrs. Skewton, but we have all seen old women with furrowed faces, sporting gaudy miniskirts, showing spindle shanks, looking like walking Death masquerading as Youth. Undoubtedly Mrs. Skewton is a caricature, a kind of *reductio ad absurdum* of people's vanity and self-delusion—but the reference to the truth of reality is undeniable. There are no Dombeys or Carkers among our acquaintances, but "the man of wood, without a hinge" and "the cat-like man" who is all teeth are only magnified portraits of *superbia,* the root of evil, in the first instance, and ineradicable cruelty in the second. We cannot forget them; the novelist forces us to face what we would prefer to ignore, compels us to look when we would rather avert our eyes.

Just as little Paul could see in the patterns of the wallpaper "things which no one else saw" (xii), Dickens sees, as no one else does, the one moral feature that characterizes a personality. And because he feels that there is to be found the hard ontological core which makes a man what he is, he keeps on mentioning it with ever-renewed fascination and gusto. The foundation of the Dickensian universe is an ontology of essence. If his characters keep making the same gestures and using the same turns of speech, if their behavior never surprises us, it is because all they say and do is the expression of their essential being. Their liberty consists in necessarily expressing what they are. If they are so often funny, that is because the comic springs forth from repetitive behavior and from the sameness of identity.

E. M. Forster calls them flat characters, but does not "flat" mean lack of individuality? Most of the people we meet daily are flat, whereas Dickens' characters are chock-full of individuality—in a way they do surprise us after all in being so completely, so boisterously, and always so unselfconsciously themselves. It is in order to convey his characters' haecceity, the perseverance of one and all to go on being what they are, that Dickens uses repetition of words and phrases and often resorts to the superlative of the qualifying adjective or to phrases carrying superlative meaning. Thus Mr. Toots is "the devotedest and innocentest infant" (lvi), and "no child could have surpassed Captain Cuttle in inexperience of everything but wind and weather. . . . Faith, hope and charity shared his whole nature among them" (xlix). Not only humans, but animals, things, and events are what they are to the utmost. Diogenes is caninity itself. A spring-cleaning day at Mrs. MacStinger's is superlative spring-cleaning, with superlative thoroughness and the housewife's superlative self-satisfaction. Continually, however, this superlative fictional exaggeration refers us to the nonsuperlative world in which we live, in which contingency holds sway and essential reality is unattainable. The repetitiousness that characterizes the Dickensian universe is regarded by many as proof of its creator's superficiality, whereas it reveals the acuity of his vision: life is repetitious, most people change very little. The same patterns of behavior recur time and again, the same habits and mannerisms; sameness prevails likewise in people's conversation, since the stock of favorite words and phrases is small. Indeed, reiteration is one of the main characteristics of the modern city.

But why is it that what is so dull in real life is so vivid and amusing in fiction? Perhaps this is because Dickens' own enjoyment of repetitive exaggeration is infectious, perhaps because he rouses us from somnolence and makes us see what we prefer to disregard. But the major reason is perhaps to be found in the unwonted transparency of his characters which is a feast to us since, in real life, doubt is part of our very knowledge of people. Of Captain Cuttle and others we want to learn nothing more: they are as wholly intelligible to us as Mr. Toots is to Susan Nipper. She bursts out with laughter when he says he'll go "into the silent tomb" immediately and comfortably now that Walter and Florence are reunited. "Bless your heart, my dear Miss Floy," says Susan, "he won't; he's a great deal too happy in seeing other people happy" (lvi). All Mr. Toots is summed up in this observation. There is indeed essential intelligibility!

Practically, there can be no change in a world resting on an ontology of essence. What, then, of Mr. Dombey, who does change when he finally welcomes the Florence he has neglected all his life? Even then, however, the man's master-passion asserts itself: lonely though he is, he would not have gone to Florence if he had heard her voice in the adjoining room or passed her in the street (lix). Thus even a character susceptible of change does not really develop. His change is no "becoming." It is willed by the novelist because he firmly believes that the child can and must redeem the parent—but there is no process of growth.

As Dombey reminds us of the stubbornness of pride and egoism, and Carker of the mystery of absolute evil, so Captain Cuttle and Mr. Toots help us to realize the other great mystery of the world of Dickens, that of absolute goodness. Again, the character's conduct is but the ever-recurring manifestation of his essential being, not a process of growth. The good *are* good, they do not become so. Much as he liked popular mythology, the author of *Dombey and Son* would not have appreciated that fine Talmudic legend which says that, when a man is born, angels decide whether he will be handsome or ugly, rich or poor, but not whether he will be good or evil, for that depends on him alone.[30]

But why make Cuttle and Toots not merely naïve but rather obtuse? Let me first remark that the lack of "sense" which Toots acknowledges (lx) is the source of so many comic effects that it endears him. The fun they occasion tempers the satirical bitterness prevailing in the portrayal of some other characters. Thus humor qualifies irony, extends the scope and deepens the resonance of the comic. More important, Cuttle's and Toot's behavior is always essentially right in spite of surface foolishness and a limited intelligence. Thus the intuitions of the heart and the spontaneous response of human kindness to human distress are made to seem more valuable both in private and social relations than the calculations of the intellect. The worldly-wise Carker and the would-be-shrewd Dombey ruin their own lives and bring about much misery, whereas the simple-minded Cuttle and Toots attain happiness and make others happy. Most readers would not change them for "the clearest-headed, longest-sighted" intellectuals. With Dickens they accept the fundamental belief: all men are of the same family. In their modest way they contribute to making the world a better place. When love holds sway in the world, both God and man are happy: as Alice Marwood puts it, "If man would help some of us a little more, God would forgive us the sooner perhaps" (xxxiii).

Michael Steig

ICONOGRAPHY OF SEXUAL CONFLICT IN
DOMBEY AND SON

DESPITE THE story-book romance of Florence and Walter, the dominant view of relations between the sexes in *Dombey and Son* is that they
involve a continuing struggle for power in which the female is the more
aggressive antagonist, and most often the victor. This view is brought out
vividly by certain of the original illustrations which bear upon the
Dombey-Edith-Carker triangle, and by two others that have to do with
Mrs. MacStinger's campaign to subject Captain Cuttle to permanent
marital thralldom. A study of the evidence of Dickens' professional relationship with Hablot K. Browne has led me to conclude that while one
may safely attribute the choice of subject for virtually all of Phiz's illustrations to Dickens, the minor details, and in particular those that comment allegorically (in the form of paintings, posters, sculpture, and the
like) upon the text, can generally be assumed to be the artist's own
contribution.[1] Such details thus have the status of contemporary critical
commentary of an especially pertinent kind, since they were created
while the novel was in progress and the illustrator in repeated communication with the author. At the very least, we can reasonably assume
that such details are consonant with the author's intention, and at times
they serve to clarify that intention.

Since I am concerned here with the contribution of incidental, allegorical details to an understanding of the novel, I shall pass over the first
illustration (Plate 13, "Major Bagstock is delighted to have that opportunity") that depicts Dombey's wooing of Edith. The next relevant
plate, Plate 17, "Joe B is sly Sir; devilish sly," illustrates the dinner in
chapter xxvi attended by Dombey, Carker, and Bagstock, and specifically
the Major's twitting Dombey about his lack of appetite, which is followed
by a toast to "angelic Edith." The one allegorical detail in this plate is
a most telling one. On the wall at left is a framed picture of a rather

comical looking gentleman in intimate conversation with a lady. The picture is labelled "TOBY WAD," with various dots and lines indicating that the legible part is incomplete; unquestionably the full title is something like "Toby and the Widow Wadman." Now, surely the two most memorable facts about Uncle Toby Shandy's wooing of the Widow Wadman are his total ignorance of women and her suspicion that the wound he received at Namur has made him impotent; and it is difficult to believe that whoever thought of putting this detail into the illustration was not somewhat conscious of these points and their bearing on *Dombey and Son.* Dombey is of course not technically impotent, since he has fathered two children, but at least one critic has argued that he is emotionally impotent,[2] and it should be stressed that Edith is in any case quite a different woman from the first Mrs. Dombey—the latter was all submission, while Edith is all defiance. The etching which appeared together with this one in Number XI of the monthly installments is "Mr. Dombey introduces his daughter Florence" (Plate 18), and although it contains no allegorical details (unless we count the first Mrs. Dombey peering out from beneath the cloth which partly covers her portrait), its conjunction with Plate 17 further emphasizes the relevance of that *Tristram Shandy* episode to Dombey's approaching marriage.

The next illustration with thematically significant details is Plate 27, "Mr. Dombey and his 'confidential agent,' " but here the details are no more than Browne's faithful rendering of the text: on the wall, in addition to what is presumably a picture of "voluptuous cast" (as described in the third paragraph of chapter xxxiii), there is the portrait of a woman said to resemble Edith, which allows Carker to "leer" mentally at the new Mrs. Dombey while he is acting the obsequious servant to Dombey (xlii). Carker features again in Plate 29, "Abstraction and Recognition," which shows Alice Marwood and her mother, "Mrs. Brown," watching him as he rides by on his horse, lost in thought. Here allegorical details, in the form of tattered posters on a wall, come fast and thick. Like all the *Dombey* plates this one was etched in duplicate; insofar as they are legible, the posters in the plate designated 29A by Albert Johannsen read, "THEATRE / CITY MADAM"; "TO THOSE ABOUT TO MARRY"; "CRUIKSHANK / BOTTLE"; "MOSES"; and "LULL / BAL MASQUE." Plate 29B adds "OBSERVE" and "DOWN AGAIN!"[3] "OBSERVE" must refer to Alice's watching Carker, while "BAL MASQUE" suggests either the concealment involved in this watching, or perhaps Carker's constant hypocrisy toward Dombey. Moses is the tailor whose poetical advertisements appeared in the parts to *Dombey* from the third number onwards,[4] but I can discern no particular relevance to the novel. Three others of these posters suggest ominous events brooding over Dombey and Carker: "TO THOSE ABOUT TO MARRY" alludes to the recent wedding of Dombey and Edith, and probably automatically suggested to many readers, the *Punch-*

line, "Don't"; Cruikshank's *The Bottle* (1847), an enormously popular picture-story of a fall from wealth to poverty and degradation, and "DOWN AGAIN" (which I have not been able to identify specifically) would seem to allude both to Alice's present condition, and Carker's and Dombey's future fates.

Massinger's comedy *The City Madam,* revived on the London stage in 1844,[5] is by far the richest of the allusions in the posters in Plate 29, for the play contains a number of parallels to *Dombey and Son:* a wealthy city merchant, Sir John Frugal, whose lack of a male heir is referred to at the outset as a "great pity" (I,i,11),[6] has a wife who, like Mrs. Skewton, fancies herself much younger than she is, and who, like Edith, is more than a match for her husband's dominance. There is, further, such a close parallel to the James Carker-John Carker relationship that one might suspect Massinger's play is Dickens' source: Sir John has a younger brother, Luke, who has squandered the fortune that was left to him instead of the rightful heir; Sir John, who has made his own fortune in the meantime, has paid off Luke's extensive debts to keep him out of prison, but Luke is now as a consequence treated as a kind of servant in the family, and is made aware constantly of his former disgrace and present dependence, recalling the way in which John Carker is kept down by his brother. There may be a further parallel in the fact that Luke (who, unlike John Carker, turns out to be a thorough villain) at one point speaks of himself as an "example" for others (I,ii,120), and later in the play urges his brother's clerks to embezzle money; we recall that Walter Gay was originally supposed to go bad in the same way as had John Carker, though not, of course, through John's efforts. Finally, there are in the play a mother and daughter, the bawd Secret and the prostitute Shave'em, who foreshadow the conflict between Mrs. Brown and Alice, in Shave'em's reproach to her mother that "you care not / Upon what desperate service you employ me, / Nor with whom, so you have your fee" (III,i,39–41).

The symbolic iconography of Edith begins in the other illustration to Number XV, Plate 30, "Florence and Edith on the Staircase." To the left, at the bottom of the stairs, is a statue of Agamemnon sacrificing Iphigenia. The most direct reference is to Dombey's rejection of and physical brutality towards Florence, but it should be remembered that this particular sacrifice in Greek legend led to a horrible retribution by wife against husband, as Dombey's treatment of Florence is the immediate cause of Edith's desertion of her husband. At the top of the stairs there is a statuette, under glass, of a half-naked woman riding a bear (primly sidesaddle) ; the most likely identification is Atalanta, who was suckled by a she-bear, and if this is correct the relevance for Edith is considerable, since Atalanta's best-known quality is her defiance of men, in particular her challenge to all men to try and best her in athletic feats. The statue to the lower right of the staircase is identified by Johannsen as Venus,[7] but it is as likely, again, to be Atalanta, since the statue holds some apple-like objects as though she is preparing to drop them. By casting Edith in the roles of Clytemnestra and Atalanta, the illustration thus implies that Edith's defiance is a combined result of Dombey's personality and her own. The view implied here of Edith as a castrating female is, as we shall see, further developed in another plate, but three other details in Plate 30 imply opposite qualities in Edith, which remain only potential. Two of these details are panels showing female angels carrying little children aloft; the third is a picture, above Atalanta, of a young girl holding a dove to her bosom. All three would seem to refer to Edith's potential as a loving stepmother.

Plate 32, "Mr. Dombey and the World" makes clearer what is already implied in the text, that Dombey's outrage at Edith's desertion is not the result of any feelings of tenderness towards her, but rather of injured pride, since his marriage has been prompted not by sexual feelings, but by a desire for ego-satisfaction through the production of a new son. In this etching, the portrait of Florence's mother truly seems to be peering out at Dombey from under a cloth; this effect is underlined by another portrait, of an old gentleman, who appears to be glancing sideways at Dombey. But Browne's most ingenious means of stressing Dombey's paranoia is the inclusion of a few peacock feathers above the mirror behind him. The "eyes" in these feathers seem to allude to Dombey's feeling that the whole world is observing his shame, while the proverbial pride of the peacock suggests the psychological origin of that shame. This detail may possibly have been suggested to Browne by Susan Nipper's earlier remark to Dombey, "I may not be a Peacock; but I have my eyes" (ch. xliv), but Browne has in any case used the symbol for his own purposes. This plate should be linked with a later one, Plate 37, " 'Let him remember it in that room, years to come!' " which shows Dombey in the state to which he has been reduced by his wounded pride, his fear of the "world's" opinion, and his growing feeling of having lost Florence. The bust of Mr. Pitt on the bookcase, which has been present in a number of the illustrations, looks down upon Dombey with its most disapproving expression; behind the bust is a rolled-up map which just reveals its title, "The World"; the first Mrs. Dombey's eyes now peer over the top of a folding screen, upon which are depicted a shepherd playing the flute to a shepherdess, and two couples dancing, both details which contrast strongly with Dombey's sullen, brooding state; these decorations and another on the screen, which appears to depict a wedding, also appear to look ahead to Dombey's coming transformation through the love of Florence, who is in this illustration entering Dombey's room, as yet unseen by her father.

To return to the events that have reduced Dombey to this condition,

Plate 34, "Mr. Carker in his hour of triumph" further develops the icon-ographical interpretation of Edith as a domineering, even castrating woman, and the novel's vision of sex as primarily a battle. Edith has just told Carker that she is merely using him as a means of escape from her marriage and has no intention of becoming his mistress. Behind her is a painting of Judith about to slay Holofernes, and below the painting and to the right is a statuette of an Amazon upon a horse, about to deal a deathblow to a fallen, male warrior. That this latter detail is certainly Browne's idea and not Dickens' is indicated by the artist's having used a similar motif, for similar, though comic purpose, in one of the plates to G. P. R. James's *The Commissioner* (Dublin, 1843 – plate entitled, "The Revolt of the Petticoats," facing p. 218). One of the two plates etched for the *Dombey* illustration (34B) shows a detail in a picture at right angles to the Judith one which may also be significant: most of the picture is invisible, presumably because of the reflection in its varnish of the bright candles, but there is discernible the figure of a woman who appears to be holding yet another instrument of destruction.[8] Professor John R. Reed has argued that the position of the characters—Edith with hand out-stretched in the general direction of Carker's spread legs—may further emphasize Edith's castrating tendencies, and that the Amazon's spear and Judith's sword both seem to point at Edith herself, implying that her emotional hardness is ultimately self-destructive;[9] these points are certainly plausible as a part of Browne's unconscious intention, if not his conscious one.

There are other castrating women in the novel besides Edith, such as Mrs. Chick, whose domination over her husband has produced his tic of whistling in place of verbal expression; and Mrs. Pipchin, who is a "child-queller." Apart from Florence, the real contrast to these women is afforded by Miss Tox. While neither Mrs. Chick nor Mrs. Pipchin is shown in Browne's allegorical frontispiece to the novel (Plate 39 – etched for the last number, when the book was substantially completed), Miss Tox, like several other characters, has her moral fate allegorically de-picted in relation to the sea. Thus, Dombey is rescued from drowning by Florence and Paul, while Major Bagstock, whose actual fate is not re-lated in the novel, is seen floundering on his back in the water, about to go down for good. Miss Tox is shown twice, standing on the shore expres-sing horror at the Major's condition, and being rescued by a Cupid in a boat. The intended point is clear: Miss Tox is saved, morally, by her unselfish love for Dombey, though her soul was perhaps in danger through her initial interest in the Major.

Other characters' fates are given somewhat more literally: Walter crawls up on the shore to embrace Florence, Sol Gills is saved by mer-maids from the watery element (half-literal, anyway), Death and Time come for an unprepared Mrs. Skewton, and Carker is run down by a train, while a supernatural figure aims a lightning-bolt at him. Paul is wafted to heaven by mothering angels, though several angels also beckon from a boat in the sea below him.[10] Of the major characters shown in this frontispiece, only Edith is not assigned a literal or allegorical fate. She is depicted twice, embracing Florence, and standing haughtily between the wily Carker and the obdurate Dombey, while Major Bagstock lasciviously points his walking-stick at the bustle of her gown. This all suggests the unsettled nature of Dickens' attitude towards Edith, or perhaps one could say it reflects the genuine moral complexity of her character. On the one hand, she is a dangerous, predatory female, destructive to men and emotionally hard; on the other hand, she is the product of her mother's attitude towards marriage as an economic bargain, and she shows a capacity for deeper emotions in her response to Florence. Dickens' unwillingness to pass final moral judgment upon Edith is underlined by the lack of a pictorial fate for her in this etching.

But we have not finished with the castrating women in this novel. Another pair of illustrations suggests a comic parallel to Edith and the other dominant females in *Dombey and Son*. Plate 25A, "The Midshipman is boarded by the enemy," gives the title "Medusa" to the picture on the wall of a ship foundering in a storm,[11] thus allusively emphasizing the destructiveness of Mrs. MacStinger's kind of femininity, as she attacks her former boarder (there is probably a pun in the illustration's title) in his retreat. The consequences of this "boarding" for Captain Cuttle's friend Bunsby are depicted in Plate 38, "Another wedding" in which Bunsby is led to the altar against his will, and which contains an unusually large number of allegorical details. The significant signs, posters, and billboards visible at the wedding procession of Mrs. MacStinger and Jack Bunsby are as follows: "JOLLY TAR"; "CITY THEATRE / SHE STOOPS TO CONQUER / BLACK EYED SUSAN"; "CLIPPER / SCHOONER / WASP" (Plate 38A; in 38B "TRIUMPH" is substituted for "WASP") ;[12] "REWARD! / LOST! / STOLEN"; "FRENCH PLAYS / ST. JAMES / LA MARRIAGE [sic] FORÇE"; and "WANTED / SOME FINE / YOUNG MEN / HECTOR / AMAZON." William F. Axton has pointed out the significance of Douglas Jerrold's *Black-Ey'd Susan* (1829) for *Dombey and Son*: Susan Nipper's black eyes are repeatedly emphasized in the text, but she directly parallels Dolly Mayflower in Jerrold's play, who has her own Toots, expressively named Gnatbrain.[13] The more specific relevance for Plate 38 is the genre of "nautical melodrama" into which the play fits; if Walter Gay was, as Axton argues, originally intended as an "ironically realistic treatment of the 'Jolly Jack Tar.' "[14] Cuttle and Bunsby are comic treatments of the same stereotype. I can discover no direct relevance in the plot of Goldsmith's *She Stoops to Conquer,* but the female as conqueror is certainly the main subject of Plate 38. Moliere's *La Mariage forcé,* however, is clearly relevant in its plot of a domineering woman keeping an unwilling, middle-aged bachelor true to his promise to marry her, through threats of violence.

Perhaps of greatest interest is the implicit characterization of Mrs. MacStinger as a powerful "Amazon," who has vanquished a valiant "Hector," for it parallels the designation of Edith as an Amazon in Plate 34. So far apart are Mrs. MacStinger and Edith in social class, demeanor, and appearance, that from the text alone one would scarcely draw any parallels between them. Yet these illustrations indicate the pervasiveness of the theme of woman as predatory and powerful; and the allusion in Plate 25A to "Medusa" further suggests the effect of such women upon men—if the sight of the Medusa turned men to stone, Edith in her way, and Mrs. MacStinger in hers, paralyze the masculinity of the men they encounter.[15] Dombey and Carker are both morally and sexually defeated by Edith, and Jack Bunsby is reduced to total helplessness by Captain Cuttle's former landlady. Only Cuttle's preternatural innocence saves him from the Medusa's spell, and it is a close escape at that.

Julian Moynahan has gone so far as to argue that Florence herself threatens and ultimately drowns Dombey's "firmness," his masculinity and sense of self, and from this standpoint she too could be considered as a castrating female.[16] However, this is too unconscious a part of Dickens' purpose to be reflected in the illustrations. What Browne's etchings do reflect and make vivid, in such a way that they must be considered an integral part of the novel, is the theme of love and marriage as a continuous battle in which the female usually triumphs.

J. Miriam Benn

A LANDSCAPE WITH FIGURES

Characterization and Expression in Hard Times

THE WEEKLY serialization of *Hard Times* set Dickens new problems; [1] he chafed against the restrictiveness of the form:

> The difficulty of the space is CRUSHING. Nobody can have an idea of it who has not had an experience of patient fiction-writing with some elbow-room always, and open places in perspective.[2]

Some critics blame the faults of *Hard Times* on its brevity, finding it thin, cramped, too purposeful, too scrupulous, too little pleasing to the imagination—the last a serious indictment of a book which pleads for imaginative pleasures.[3] Others praise its power, coherence, concise logic, speed or clarity. F. R. Leavis was among the most influential of these; as early as 1947 he stressed the consistency of its effects, the relevance of its detail, and the concentration which resulted from its symbolic method.[4]

We know that, because his novel was so short, Dickens was forced to discipline his natural tendency to multiply characters and symbols in searching for a wider frame of reference.[5] He wished to make observations about Utilitarianism in schools and in the home; about a social anomaly in the divorce laws; about the reasons for defective relations between capital and labor; about conditions in industry, and about safety regulations. His technical problem was to integrate his themes, and extract from them generalizations which would combine into a unified moral picture.

Occasionally Dickens himself takes on the task of generalization, but relates his observations closely to plot or fable. Thus, his comments on Harthouse imply the wider defects of dilettantism, which he represents.

> And yet he had not, even now, any earnest wickedness of purpose in him. Publicly and privately, it were much better for the age in which he lived, that he and the legion of whom he was one

[168

were designedly bad, than indifferent and purposeless. It is the drifting icebergs setting with any current anywhere, that wreck the ships. (179) [6]

More commonly, it is metaphor which widens the scope of his particular criticisms and helps Dickens make his generalizations. Leavis in *The Great Tradition* noted that "the symbolic intention emerges out of metaphor and the vivid evocation of the concrete." [7] However vividly evoked, concrete detail is strictly limited to what is both characteristic and typical; there is little room in *Hard Times* for the idiosyncratic or unique. Dickens insisted that his novel was not narrowly based on affairs in Preston; even without his disclaimer, his techniques would have made this clear. He has produced an allegorical "landscape with figures": men of stone or brass in a town of machinery and tall chimneys. The OED tells us that allegory is a "description of a subject under the guise of some other subject of aptly suggestive resemblance; . . . a figurative . . . narrative, in which properties and circumstances attributed to the apparent subject really refer to the subject they are meant to suggest; an extended or continued metaphor." We can see that the definition comes very close to describing Dickens' techniques in his fable of Utilitarianism.

His method is to create a character (or characters) whose primary quality of mind is expressible through a metaphor; this metaphor is then translated into a concrete environmental parallel, and given further expression in Dickens' own narrative, in the speeches he puts into his characters' mouths, and in his ironic additions to those speeches, or echoes of them. Subsidiary qualities cluster round the primary quality of mind; each has its own metaphorical analogues to demonstrate what is wrong with it—what it lacks aesthetically, let us say, or morally; where it goes on psychological or educational grounds.

Thus, Dickens evokes the aridity of Gradgrind's Utilitarianism by the metaphor of a sterile garden or the spoiling of a fruitful one. "Plant nothing else, and root out everything else," says Mr. Gradgrind of facts— and chooses for this, Dickens notes sardonically, a teacher who has "taken the bloom off the higher branches of mathematics." The name of Gradgrind's house, the suggestions in his own name, and the children's rock specimens "broken from the parent substances by those tremendously hard instruments their own names," are all metaphorical parallels for the children's arid lives and the hardness of their parents' own substance. Mr. Gradgrind and his stony environment coalesce from the start; of the terms "square wall," "vault," "cellarage," "two dark caves," "warehouse-room," some images relate to his environment, some to his person. They are secondary metaphors, adding the ideas of passivity and storage to the main metaphor of stony hardness. They combine to condemn a system which makes the brain a storehouse for facts and children as passively receptive as stone jars.

Helpless passivity implies aggressive opposing forces: Gradgrind is a "galvanising apparatus" [8] or a cannon "loaded to the muzzle with facts" prepared to blow the children "clean out of the region of childhood at one discharge." The description of the third gentleman's educational methods relies heavily on the language of the prize ring (5–6). Both men are ready to take childhood captive and drag it into statistical dens by the hair, yet neither is really cruel. They simply fail to understand human nature: Gradgrind uses the reproach "you are childish" to a child.

Gradgrind's other friend, Bounderby, uses aggressive and violent language even when he speaks of himself:

> You may force him to swallow boiling fat, but you shall never force him to suppress the facts of his life. (16)

Naturally enough, these two aggressively self-opinionated men undervalue the rest of creation. Gradgrind's System teaches him to consider men "reasoning animals"; his children are lectured at, "coursed, like little hares"—the pun is a comment on the System and on the wretchedness of children under it. The two men group individuals into denigratory categories: noisy insects, vagabonds, young rabble—not circus-folk or children.

Such expressions demonstrate a tendency in Gradgrind and Bounderby which makes their friendship less incomprehensible. Both ignore individuals: to Gradgrind, men are statistical data; to Bounderby, they are Hands, or Power, or just machines. Dickens satirizes Bounderby's attitude when he echoes the metaphor: "The Hands were all out of gear." As with the address, Pod's End, Dickens is suggesting that to both men people are as alike as peas and as soulless as numbers or as machines. They become objects, to be used and classified.

Statistics is a powerful weapon for obliterating the differences between individuals; the metaphor of statistics shows how Gradgrind and Bounderby can voluntarily blind themselves to realities: rather than consider marital incompatibility nearer home, Gradgrind buries himself in marriage statistics about the Calmucks of Tartary (99). The related metaphor of calculation is centrally placed in the novel in order to link Bounderby, Gradgrind, and the various elements in their public and private worlds. Tom, "that not unprecedented triumph of calculation which is usually at work on number one," connects the two households; he is totally allegorized, being based on a single character trait expressed through a metaphor. Similarly, the attempted seduction of Louisa by her father's political ally, Harthouse, is told in the language of the countinghouse.[9] At their first meeting they assess each other's value. Louisa hardly takes him at his own valuation, but, like a bookkeeper, she casts him up, so much on the debit side, so much to his credit: "Mr. Harthouse, I give you credit for being interested in my brother." Harthouse profits from Louisa's love for Tom, and casts up his own progress with her like a balance sheet, "so much the more . . . so much the less"; he reckons up his advantages as a winner might count his gains (179). Yet in the end he errs in his calculations, for Louisa's real personality, unique and incalculable, evades his arithmetical process.

Within the allegory, the logical person to oppose Harthouse is Sissy, for she is totally uncalculating. Sissy loves her father loyally and selflessly; her undiminished hope of his return prevents her running away from Stone Lodge, and is "the result of no arithmetical process," being "self-imposed in defiance of all calculation." It is her disinterestedness which helps her to rout Harthouse; besides, she speaks in language he can understand, of "compensation," or "reparation," of whether these will be "much" or "enough," in short, as if he is a moral bankrupt or has engaged in some damaging business dealings (233). Calculation, which entered the ninth chapter as a metaphor, has now become an allegorical way of life, which Sissy is there to overthrow.

Such a mode of expression does more than link Dickens' themes and characters. It provides lines of demarcation between those for whom the System—in whatever sphere it operates—is infallible, and those who are its unwilling victims, like Louisa or Stephen. When they appeal against the System's obliterating statistical techniques, it is as individuals. They do not want to be made into machines, like Bitzers. Bitzer, the System's star pupil, has lost his humanity: insectlike, he can respond "correctly" to the stimuli of questions, but cannot evaluate them. The allegorical approach clarifies certain values, or moral issues (like the limits of arbitrary power, the rights of individuals, or the nature of responsibility); but it also tends to simplify them, until the resolutions offered appear naïve (Sissy's routing of Harthouse) or insufficient (Stephen's promise).

Not all Dickens' characters in this novel are allegories, whether wholly or in part. Not all his characters are successful. Yet it would be completely wrong to say that it is the allegorical treatment of character which makes the novel, however interesting, so unsatisfactory. A character may be successful precisely because it is consistently and satisfyingly allegorical; it may fail either because Dickens mixed some humanity in with the allegory, or some unfortunate allegorizing in with his psychological realism. It is also possible that a wholly allegorical character fails, not because at every point of the action he is symbolizing something, but for some quite different reason, such as the poor integration of his role in the plot or the fable, or for some defect in his manner of expressing himself. In two characters, Dickens is trying, at particular places in the story, to achieve some point of balance between the human and the allegorical; in a third, he wishes human nature and allegorical significance to stand out equally throughout.

One of the simplest and most effective characters in the novel, and one who is at the same time the most allegorical, is Bounderby. His first metaphor is metal; more particularly, as he is a north-country banker, brass.[10] He also represents the bullying bluster of the master-class; his second, more strongly developed metaphor, is wind. He is just coarse material stretched by much air: a windbag. He is a puffed-up boaster, his early poverty a windy lie, his final defeat a deflation.[11]

It is no criticism to say that Bounderby is a static character based on a humor;[12] there is no need for him to be subtle, to change or repent—it would be out of character and unnecessary. His traits are constants; his pretence about his origins adds a pseudo-rationality to his abuse of the poor and weak, and is therefore functional throughout the plot. His rejection of refinement and imagination provides a marital environment in which Louisa will suffer enough to turn gratefully to Harthouse's supposed kindness. Bounderby's home is a suitable setting for Mrs. Sparsit, because her exaggerated claims to breeding are complementary to his pretensions to none. His qualities are given: he is always hostile to Stephen, always attracting toadyism, always repelling love. They state as a datum the impossibility of communication between such masters and men. Bounderby's fiction of turtle soup and gold plate expresses metaphorically the barrier of suspicion which he deliberately erects; it is there, whether a Hand comes to get advice, or to complain; Bounderby never varies.

Certainly Bounderby is a caricature, if by that we mean that he shows exaggerated consistency, a patterned coherence of major and minor character traits. He is fictionally successful, however, because he is adequate for all that he is required to be and do in both plot and fable, and because he is active, energetic, and racy in his speech. When Stephen, fasting save for a piece of bread, stands before him while he sits lunching off chops and sherry, Dickens is successfully using a political cartoonist's technique: the broad, simple outline; the few telling, clearly visualized details; successfully, because Bounderby's part in the plot calls for no greater subtlety than does his allegorical role in the fable.

The scene of his deflation particularly illustrates the range and scope of this wholly allegorical treatment. In it, he acts strictly in character, blustering, blaming others, trying to carry off a hopeless situation. The crowd, real enough in itself, supports him in his allegorical role: it goes off, like Rumour with a thousand tongues, to publish his humiliation to the four winds (283). In organizing so poetic a justice, Dickens is harking back to his first description of Bounderby as a windbag; so neat a scheme cannot be despised, for if Bounderby is static, he is static as a setting, a climate, or an atmosphere is static.

A static character rarely in himself surprises the reader; Dickens achieves the unexpected by making it happen to Bounderby. When he goes to break the news of his engagement to Mrs. Sparsit, he expects her to faint, and comes prepared with a harsh restorative. Her sympathy utterly confounds him, for there is nothing in his character which tells him what to do with sympathy. The scene (I, xvi) is comic precisely because it finds him at a loss; deprived of the one role he knows how to play, he can call on no other. What is surprising in the scene belongs not to him, but to Mrs. Sparsit's psychological ingenuity; his rigidity can feel only bewilderment and irritability when confronted with the unexpected. It is a brilliant example of the possibilities of static characterization.

In Bitzer, static, unrealistic, devoid of simple humanity, we have a case parallel to Bounderby's: an allegorical character who never steps outside his role. As with Bounderby and Gradgrind, his allegorical nature is immediately indicated through metaphor. The perfect product of the System is dehumanized, drained of color, cold, looking "as though, if he were cut, he would bleed white." So formal is Dickens' treatment of Bitzer that we need only two characteristics to recognize him next time: absence of color and an insectlike knuckling of the forehead. He does not develop, save that the cunning child grows into a cunning adult with enough psychological subtlety to flatter Mrs. Sparsit. Always a toady, he becomes a place-seeker and spy. Logically enough, his cunning operates through the technique Gradgrind taught him: simple calculation. Thus, he tries to arrest Tom not through animosity or an outraged moral sense, but simply from a calculation regarding the profit to himself. Such a character neither demands nor receives naturalistic treatment. Apart from his plot-function, which requires certain characteristic actions from him, he has no purpose save that served by his allegorical role, i.e., to show the ultimate logic of the calculus and to act as foil to Sissy's uncalculating, loving kindness.

Dickens shows clearly, by the farcical manner of their defeats, that we are not to feel for Bounderby or Bitzer as if they were human. Bounderby's public deflating and Bitzer's defeat by a dancing horse are suitably absurd ends to pretension and cunning, maintaining the tone at a level where there is no danger of the reader's involvement through sympathy. They are not equally successful portraits, for Bounderby's energy and liveliness of speech amuse us more, despite Dickens' exaggeration of his foibles.

Gradgrind presents Dickens with a more difficult technical problem, for he plays a double role, the human father and the allegorical Utilitarian. Unhappily, *Hard Times* had to open with Gradgrind in his allegorical role. After that, Dickens had insufficient space to wipe out the first deep impression made upon the reader by his metaphorical "commentary" which associated the idea of hardness with the man as well as with the doctrine.

Dickens launches Gradgrind as if he were to be as static and allegorical as Bounderby. His business is to crush the imaginative side of a child's nature in order to develop its reason. It is not an agreeable part to play, and it puts him irremediably in the wrong. Even his appearance is allegorical: his square finger and forehead, square coat, legs, and shoulders do not combine to make a human being, but are merely attributes. Gradgrind remains curiously formless, a statue still imprisoned in stone. It becomes difficult for Dickens to develop in him a capacity for tragedy and disillusionment, for these are only appropriate to human beings.

Dickens saw the allegorical Gradgrind in terms of blindness, and his human role as the recovery of sight, through revelation. At first he is wilfully blind: "We don't want to know about that here," he says, and his prejudices manipulate the truth to suit themselves; a circus clown becomes "a veterinary surgeon, a farrier and horse-breaker." His eye rests on the surface when that is safer, so that he does not see Louisa's uncomfortable ironies in the proposal scene (I, xv). Because Bounderby appears to embody certain of his own ideals—he is self-made, hard-headed, industrious; a producer, not merely an owner of wealth— Gradgrind does not look beneath the surface, and readily accepts his friend's autobiographical boasting.[13]

Just as he is blind to defect where his System allows him to approve, so also is he unable to see virtue in people whose way of life finds no place in it. If they are entertainers, they must be idle; if itinerant, vagabonds; yet the first great hope for Gradgrind as a human being is that he is patient with the circus folk in order to help Sissy.

When Gradgrind communicates Bounderby's proposal to Louisa, he is still almost entirely allegorical. His fatherliness is dormant, and he is the mere embodiment of a doctrine. Louisa's ironic questions cannot make him throw off his role, though they make him uncomfortable and drive him to evasions among facts and statistics. He is not entirely blind to her problem, but can shut his eyes to it until disaster opens them finally. In the meantime he gropingly accepts certain insights, though remaining blind to their full significance. Seeing that Sissy is not a shining credit to his System, he comments: "You are an affectionate, earnest, good young woman—and—and we must make that do" (91). His vision is clearing, but his values are unchanged, and he has yet to find a place for a kind heart in his System. He finds qualities in Sissy, however, which cannot be comprehended in a tabular statement or Parliamentary return (92), and through this crack a little light begins to shine.

Given more of this, the allegorical might have modulated successfully into the fatherly, but in II, xii, Dickens ruins a whole scene by adopting a wrong tone for Louisa. Her mannered speeches mar the simplicity and directness of Gradgrind's response to her misery; her part is too heavy, his to light, to achieve Dickens' purpose. A little later, Dickens obliterates Gradgrind's new humanity with a group of metaphors too reminiscent of the old allegorical character, which starts up before us just when we should be forgetting it:

> In gauging fathomless deeps with his little mean excise-rod, and in staggering over the universe with his rusty stiff-legged compasses, he had meant to do great things. . . . He had tumbled about, annihilating the flowers of existence. (222)

It is, perhaps, an echo of Carlyle's "deeper than any of our Logic-plummets hitherto will sound"; [14] if so, it comes at an inopportune time. It intrudes, spoiling the effect of some genuinely moving moments, as when Gradgrind finds for the first time that he can express love and compassion: "he softly moved her scattered hair from her forehead with his hand" (222). His slow and painful acceptance of the flaws in his System, of the new facts of instinct, imagination, love, and gratitude, is in fact finely done; unhappily, Dickens irrevocably mars the effect by rubbing in the moral.

Gradgrind's own words, though formal, are not stilted; his mental turmoil shows through his metaphors, which suggest collapse, stunning shock, a blow at the foundations of his world (221). He shows patience with Bounderby (III, iii) and a tentative uncertainty about himself that sits better on him than his old strident didacticism; he even shows the ghost a sense of humor. He wants to mend, if he can, what he has "perverted" in Louisa, and the depth of his bitter disillusionment with his System is revealed in his use of the word. The scene prepares us to pity him as a father in his scene with Tom at the circus; we will feel for him as we would not have done earlier.

Dickens returns to his allegory with the entrance of Bitzer, and Gradgrind's new humanity is overshadowed by Bitzer's cold logic, a caricature of the System's own teaching. Discrediting Gradgrind at this late stage, and by his own logic, puts him back in his old schoolroom role. Although the confrontation provides a dramatic turn in the plot, it throws out the program of a gradual development of humanity in Gradgrind. As allegory gains control, his humanity dwindles; we are back to the moral fable, and stay there while Sleary sees that the rewards that Gradgrind gives for services rendered shall be allegorically appropriate.

On the whole, Gradgrind is a failure. Bounderby is a success because he is not asked to step outside his allegorical role; Gradgrind fails because of the uneasy tension between his allegorical and his human selves. The shifts between them are uncomfortable, and are hampered by defects in other characters. We can feel, perhaps, that suffering and reformation came to the second Gradgrind, but we can hardly envisage any change which would bring them to the first.

Louisa is a more credible heroine than Dickens usually achieved; it is all the more unfortunate that the scene with her father, on her return from Bounderby's house, is so artificial and stagey. Her mental development in the novel is unsentimental and extraordinarily interesting. From her early childhood she is unlike Dickens' normally docile heroines; she has an air of jaded sullenness, is too hardened to cry, and shows a facial expression which reflects her father's blindness as well as her own conflict and frustration.

> Struggling through the dissatisfaction of her face, there was a light with nothing to rest upon, a fire with nothing to burn, a starved imagination keeping life in itself somehow, which brightened its expression. Not with the brightness natural to cheerful youth, but with uncertain, eager, doubtful flashes, which had something painful in them, analogous to the changes on a blind face groping its way. (12)

Her father repels any free and spontaneous expression of her feelings and she is compelled, like Dorothea with Casaubon in chapter xlii of *Middlemarch,* to stand away from him in critical detachment. She throws him a look "remarkable for its intense and searching character," probing or judging his motives and actions. When Bounderby asks for a kiss, her cold obedience, insulting slowness and averted face are striking indications of her conscious and intelligent rejection of all he stands for. Her passionate attempt to scrub away his kiss suggests Maggie Tulliver rather that a Dickensian heroine; Bella Wilfer might have scrubbed it away, but not with Louisa's smoldering hatred.

Louisa, talking to Tom in the firelight, sees in the coals not the usual girlish visions but the somber contrast between their abnormal home and the graces of ordinary family life. She is not simply wishing she could sing ballads; she is voicing a longing for harmony, fulfillment, and imaginative self-expression; she awakes from her dream of normality to the reality of Tom's squalid, selfish notion of a sister's usefulness and scope. All Louisa's impulses are blocked, warped, and frustrated; cold on the surface, all her life is underground. Dickens has made a far greater attempt than is usual with him to express the inner workings of such a mind; there is something extremely moving about Louisa's wish to know what normality is. She asks about Sissy's life with a "strong, wild, wandering interest peculiar to her," and later in the novel her awkward words to Stephen and Rachael demonstrate that she knows she has no expertise with people, and regrets it. She knows no nuances of expression to set them at their ease, and works at her contacts with them as though by the book. She tries to understand life by observing it, so her glance is never demure or docile, but "quick" or "searching";

PICTURESQUE BUILDING BY CATTERMOLE FROM *Barnaby Rudge*
The ruined Warren (Jane Rabb Cohen, "Strained Relations")

DICKENS IN ONE OF BYRON'S CHAIRS
(Jane Rabb Cohen, "Strained Relations")

she discourages observation of herself by a distant, reserved manner. Nobody before Mr. Harthouse cares enough to penetrate her reserve, and her father accepts at its face value her "I am as cheerful, father, as I usually am," ignoring the disguised hope that he will inquire just how happy she is. Unaccustomed to the penetration of her emotions by others, she does not contradict his account of her nature at the beginning of the proposal scene, but her silences are in fact no more docile than her glance: they put a pressure on him like speech (I, xv) .

In this excellent scene, Louisa's defense is made in Utilitarian manner: she requires him to define his terms, to utter as hard fact what a father should be unable even to contemplate, much less put in words. It actually discomposes him; he stumbles, and falls back on conventional phrases that muffle the enormity he is suggesting. She is brutally terse, routing him from one false position to the next, hounding him down as he retreats: "Difficult to answer it, Yes or No, father?" It is a deadly undermining of his intellectual position, and it takes him twenty-five or so windy lines to smother her in a Utilitarian answer. Her last impulse to confide in him passes; she accepts Bounderby's proposal in words so insultingly cold that they would be repellent but for their clear expression of a hope that Bounderby would be stung by them into withdrawing it. The scene then loses impetus, but recovers with Mrs. Gradgrind's pre-Freudian insight into psychosomatic symptons: "Well, I'm sure I hope your health may be good, Louisa; for if your head begins to split as soon as you are married, which was the case with mine, I cannot consider that you are to be envied, though I have no doubt that you think you are, as all girls do" (102) . It is an uncomfortable hope, and Sissy's wondering, compassionate look is uncomfortable too. From now on, Louisa changes: she is impassive, withdrawn, proud, and cold; even Harthouse finds her baffling, full of contradictions. Precisely because she is an exceptional heroine, she is saved from a conventional seduction-plot, for it is hardly possible that such an ironical, cool intelligence should be "deceived." In Dickens' novels, a heroine who represents neither deceived innocence nor virtuous rejection of temptation is rare indeed.

Louisa is not only rare; she is abnormal. Gradgrind speaks of her as "perverted." If Mrs. Gradgrind was crushed, so also is Louisa, not to death, but to a point where words like "sterility" or "frigidity" become appropriate; her womanhood dies. Her crippled life moves us, for she never ceases to grope, in her characteristically half-blind way, for something lost, some key, some path to the normality she is so conscious of having missed; she works at life as at a puzzle. Her intelligence can strip Harthouse, Bounderby, or Gradgrind of their pretensions, but she lacks intuition—she cannot tell what her own feelings are, or whether she is in love.

Unhappily, Dickens fails to keep Louisa alive, human, and interesting. After her return home, her stiff and conventional speeches irrevocably blur her original uniqueness. At this point in his story Dickens is thinking of Gradgrind as the non-allegorical, humanly distressed character, and it is time for Louisa to point the moral. She becomes his mouthpiece, a demonstration of the shortcomings of the System. Dickens does not see her now as a human being, but as a character with a message, with a function in his moral fable. Her use of Dickens' central metaphor in this scene is out of character and contrived: "defying all the calculations ever made by man, and no more known to his arithmetic than his Creator is" (216). Clearly it is not Louisa, but Dickens speaking. Jealousy of Sissy brings back to Louisa flashes of humanity thereafter, but she really does not come to life again.

Although Louisa does not survive this late intrusion of allegory into her role, one further point can be made in Dickens' favor. If we look beneath his vision of her future, surrounded conventionally by happy children (the merest postscript, a tidying-up of the story), we will see that his real conclusion is grimly unsentimental, even tough-minded: Louisa is too warped ever to form normal attachments or find personal happiness. She will never remarry; the children belong to other people. Those qualities in herself which might have brought love were neglected, perverted for life; though she may achieve a certain balance and find compensations, she can never herself lead a normal life; behind the conventional facade of his ending, Dickens does not cheat.

Stephen Blackpool's name defines his allegorical role: he is a Lancashire saint and martyr. He has, throughout, to be both allegorical and realistic, to suffer personally, as well as to typify the passive suffering of the workers. Dickens went to Preston for local color, and he studied to create an accurate dialect for him. Stephen pleased Dickens,[15] but has suffered a second martyrdom at the hands of the critics.

Stephen is a product of Coketown; together they form both a realistic and an allegorical indictment of industrial conditions. The physical setting is reminiscent of Engels' Manchester of 1844,[16] where the upper classes enjoyed healthy country air and lived in comfortable dwellings (27–28); where the river stagnated, a narrow, coal-black, stinking river full of the fifth and rubbish from bone-mills, dye-works, sewers, and privies (32). Engels commented: "It is here that one can see how little space human beings need to move about in, how little air—and what air!—they need to breathe in order to exist" (38). He concludes: "Industry alone has been responsible for all this, and yet this same industry could not flourish except by degrading and exploiting the workers" (38). Dickens has used nearly identical detail for Coketown—an evil-smelling, dye-filled river, "killing airs and gases," labyrinthine courts pressing one another to death—to support a precisely similar conclusion. He has no wish in *Hard Times* to identify any given place, so his descriptions stress the general rather than the particular. Every street in Coketown reeks of hot oil, but no particular street is mentioned; the few details we have (a bell in a cage, a brass knocker, four pinnacles like wooden legs, some white steps) suggest the constraint of Coketown, its money, ugliness, or respectability. Occasionally we get a close-up: stokers wiping their hot faces, boys in a boat stirring up vile smells; they are doing what is characteristic or inevitable in any place like Coketown. The schoolroom in the first chapter has no inky rulers, broken windows, flowers in jamjars; it has qualities or properties: whiteness, monotony, bareness, regularity, bleakness. Coketown is an expression of sameness, greed, and narrowness, a climate of the mind which warps and cripples.

It is with the same generalizing intention that Dickens frames Stephen's indictment of industrialism:

> "Deed we are in a muddle, Sir. Look round town—so rich as 'tis—and see the numbers o' people as has been broughten into bein heer, fur to weave, an' to card, an' to piece out a livin', aw the same one way, somehows, 'twixt their cradles and their graves. Look how we live, an' wheer we live, an' in what numbers, an' by what chances, and wi' what sameness; and look how the mills is awlus a goin, and how they never works us no nigher to onny dis'ant object—ceptin awlus, Death. Look how you considers of us, and writes of us, and talks of us, and goes up wi' yor deputations to Secretaries o' State 'bout us, and how yo are awlus right, and how we are awlus wrong, and never had'n no reason in us sin ever we were born. Look how this ha' growen an' growen, Sir, bigger an' bigger, broader an' broader, harder an' harder, fro year to year, fro generation unto generation. Who can look on 't, Sir, and fairly tell a man 'tis not a muddle?" (149–50)

The speech does not refer to Coketown only, but to the whole industrial North. Professor Monod has called it vague,[17] but it is, in fact, perfectly precise and applicable. Phrase by phrase, it covers the influx of cotton workers into the towns, their increase, their overcrowding in poor homes, the instability of their lives, their long hours, and their little share in the profits of the rich mills. Stephen indicts the dilatory investigations by commissions and committees and the misrepresentation of the workers' complaints before the House. He points to the rapid aggravation of such problems during the Industrial Revolution. It is a methodical summary of causes of unrest throughout Lancashire; the concrete supporting detail it lacks has already been supplied in the representative descriptions of Coketown. Dickens has neither room nor need to repeat it here, but its absence does not make Stephen's criticism vague or shallow.

So much justice can be done to Stephen, yet the reader remains dissatisfied with his speeches. Dickens often puts important social truths into the mouths of his humbler characters, perhaps to increase the middle-class reader's respect for the working classes; there is a certain artistic contrast between the speakers' lack of education and their instinctive wisdom.[18] Stephen's dialect might have vouched for his authenticity, sincerity, and virtue.[19] Unhappily, readers have not greatly liked or respected Stephen, and his dialect has been criticized as both inaccurate and literary.[20] If Stephen's language supported his role, it would not matter that his dialect was impure in such a case; successful impersonation of a part is probably the only criterion. Stephen may need his larger vocabulary in order to be properly articulate in his role; it stresses his social inferiority to Bounderby. In fact, we do not reject Stephen because of his shallow opinions or because his dialect is not authentic, but because we distrust his rhetoric, which is unsuited to the humble simplicity of his allegorical role.

In II, v, Stephen is too much the orator, uttering his defense of his work-mates in a series of rhythmically patterned parallel clauses:

> "God forbid as I, that ha' known, and had'n experience o' these men aw my life — I, that ha' ett'n an' droonken wi' 'em, an' seet'n wi' 'em and toil'n wi' 'em, and lov'n 'em, should fail fur to stan by 'em wi' the truth." (148)

This soon develops into an even rhythm of syntactically parallel triple repetitions, with a final fourth element for a sense of climax:

> "They're true to one another, faithfo' to one another, fectionate to one another, e'en to death. Be poor amoong 'em, be sick among 'em, grieve amoong 'em, . . . an' they'll be tender wi' yo, gentle wi' you, comfortable wi' yo, Chrisen wi' yo." (148)

By the time Stephen makes the speech first quoted, the rhythms dominate over the ideas. This is the reason for its apparent shallowness: its social criticism is quite precise, but meaning is blurred by repetition. It is oratory masquerading as simplicity, as in Stephen's speech to Bounderby beginning: "Sir, if yo was t'tak a hundred Slackbridges" (150–51). This is a loosely metrical structure, built up primarily of iambs and anapaests; the clauses pile themselves up into an odelike shape, depending less on repetition than on the ebb and flow of long and short rhetorical units, like lines of unequal length within a stanza. It is odd that Dickens, grappling with his lack of space, should have conceived this almost liturgical series of speeches, their tone faintly biblical, and suggesting the deliberate artistry of the preacher. Their rhythms lend a suspect emotionalism to Stephen's arguments; they blur the sharpness of his criticisms, and falsify his allegorical role of suffering simplicity. Stephen is most authentic at his simplest:

> "I ha' not coom here, Sir . . . to complain. I coom for that I were sent for." (149)

> "My brothers . . . and my fellow-workmen—for that yo are to me, though not, as I knows on, to this delegate here." (142)

Such speeches support his human, as well as his allegorical role. Elsewhere Dickens handles both with tact and delicacy, as when Bitzer accosts Stephen, who is smarting from a "baseless sense of shame and disgrace" at being sent to Coventry:

> Stephen coloured to find himself with his hat in his hand, in his gratitude for being spoken to, or in the suddenness of it, or both. He made a feint of adjusting the lining. (145)

Stephen's isolation is due to his refusal to join the Trade Union; he has been criticized for his "inexplicable obstinacy" and for having "no better reason for not joining than a mysterious promise." [21] If that were all, Stephen would be inadequately motivated, and an important episode would be reduced to triviality. If Stephen is to suffer political martyrdom, it must be for a reason which makes psychological sense, not for a quite arbitrarily given promise. Dickens prepared the ground for this scene as far back as I, xii, and I, xiii, when Stephen, wandering in the rain, has in his mind a dreadful wish he dare not formulate:

> Filled with these thoughts—so filled that he had an unwholesome sense of growing larger, of being placed in some new and diseased relation towards the objects among which he passed, of seeing the iris round every misty light turn red—he went home for shelter. (81)

Later that night he is haunted by dreams of murder and the gallows, and comes close to conniving at his wife's death; he is saved by mere chance, not by any moral choice of his own. His horror at this revelation of his potentiality for violence makes him give the promise to Rachael; it will help him avoid all situations that might occasion violence. It is this which makes him reject Trade Unionism; he is repudiating a situation in which his own and his work-mates' violence might be released. It is active pacifism rather than a sentimental promise that prepares him to suffer for his opinions. The episode stems from Dickens' belief in the violence that sleeps in all men, violence that a chance event might awaken; it owes little to his own observation of the Preston strike. If the novel is weak at this point, it is not because Stephen's actions are psychologically implausible, but because Dickens' views on Trade Unionism are naïve. Nor can one, as he hoped, generalize easily from so idiosyncratic a case as Stephen's.

As a character, Stephen fails through dullness, not implausibility. As an allegory, he fails because he seems more victim than martyr: he is a natural unfortunate, to whom far too many things happen for no good reason. Dickens uses metaphor to link his various Utilitarian targets, but Stephen has to tie up anything left over, like divorce or industrial safety—two themes that are insufficiently developed for lack of space. It is damaging to the balance of the novel that Bounderby's desire to rid himself of his wife should not, as Dickens intended, further illustrate Stephen's discovery that, in divorce, there is one law for the rich and one for the poor.[22] It is damaging for Stephen also, for his troubles seem all the more narrowly applicable to himself; we are not helped to generalize from them, and the moral fable is weakened. Similarly, Dickens' harping on the death of Rachael's little sister harms Stephen; it seems a deliberate device to raise the emotional temperature, instead of a way of generalizing from their wasted lives to the need for safety regulations. Elsewhere a self-conscious irony demonstrates Dickens' uneasiness with this theme: "inspectors considered it doubtful whether they were quite justified in chopping people up with their machinery" (110). Although it was obviously his intention to treat safety under the general heading of industrial conditions, Stephen's contrived death brought it into too great and sudden prominence. It tried to achieve for industrial safety a belated thematic importance, but seems only to have been recently and deliberately contrived to pile more trouble on Stephen. It illustrates better than anything else the excessive and arbitrary nature of Stephen's martyrdom, which sets us against both him and his author. Dickens' failure with Stephen is due only in part to the uneasy balance of his human and allegorical roles. His sufferings are too personal, or too much a matter of mischance, to sustain the moral and political generalizations Dickens extracts from them, and his rhetoric of persuasion overlays his human and allegorical simplicity with a questionable oratorical expertise.

Trevor Blount

DICKENS AND MR. KROOK'S SPONTANEOUS COMBUSTION

AS A LITTLE boy in Ordnance Terrace, Chatham, Dickens was terrified and yet excited by the gory, dismal tales of Mary Weller who, as he lay in bed at night, filled his imagination with the atrocities of Captain Murderer and the torments of Chips the shipwright who sold his soul to the Devil.[1] Dickens never forgot these nightmarish fantasies, and perhaps they are of an importance in his work comparable with the seminal books of David Copperfield's "library." Forster tells us that Dickens "had something of a hankering after" ghost stories, while the evidence of Dickens' writings as a whole illustrates quite clearly how his love of the grotesque slid imperceptibly into an equally dominant attraction towards the horrific. One must acknowledge a curious ambivalence in Dickens, and it was noticed by G. K. Chesterton when he glimpsed "these two primary dispositions of Dickens, to make the flesh creep and to make the sides ache," and claimed that they were "a sort of twins of his spirit."[2] The horrific side of life is certainly incorporated into the Dickens world, and, as he got older and his disillusionment at man's failure to make adequate social and moral progress deepened, it began to cast a longer and blacker shadow. In this connection it is obvious that his interest in prisons was obsessive, outcropping as a recurrent symbol from *Pickwick Papers* to *Little Dorrit*. We notice that Quilp is always associated with mud. We are aware that characters as grotesque as Dennis the Hangman, Jerry Cruncher, Silas Wegg, and Mr. Venus continually find a place in his fiction. Mrs. Gamp is a supreme comic grotesque, purified by humor, yet the humor itself grows out of a horrid but actual sordidness.

R. D. McMaster[3] picked up Dickens' confession that, while a boy at Wellington House Academy, he read a penny weekly called *The Terrific Register: or, Record of Crimes, Judgements, Providences, And Calam-*

ities, which came out in numbers between 1824 and 1825. McMaster proceeded to draw parallels between what he called this "sanguinary journal" and Dickens' work as a whole. The periodical is, indeed, an extraordinary compilation, piously drawing attention in its Preface to the first volume to "the moral tendency of the work, to those (if there be any such,) to whom it is not apparent" (1). Dealing in nothing but sensationalism, it offers a hotchpotch of atrocities, tortures, earthquakes, shipwrecks, ghosts, duels, plots, frauds, robberies, conspiracies, piracies, rebellions, executions, and escapes—all presented with an enormous amount of circumstantial detail: torn limbs, lopped heads, boiling metal poured into open wounds, slit noses, garroting, exposed bowels, and so on *ad nauseam.* Occasional illustrations add to the specificity. It is distressingly monotonous, a martyrology unsustained by faith, that panders to some of the less defensible perversities. Yet the magazine prides itself, again in the preface to the first volume, on the documentary basis of the information it provides. This presumably applies to the sundry methods of execution described with careful particularity, the account of the human sacrifices made by the Incas, and the story of the brigand who blackmails a mother into cutting off her nose before he jumps into an abyss with her child in his arms. "The stories, giving an account of supernatural appearances, are surprisingly authenticated," we read, "and we have therefore thought it our duty to submit them." It is the conjunction of asseverated fact and the apparently incredible that we ought most to notice, though basically it is rather smug pornography. The magazine is not offering simple horror; it is offering true horror—that is, horror made more chilling than sickly fancy by the fact that the unthinkable really occurred. (I ignore the pious claims it makes for itself over and above this.) What, out of this anthology of quaint Gothic grisliness, is specially relevant to *Bleak House* is an article that appeared in 1825, offering attested evidence for the scientifically proved "truth" of spontaneous combustion.

Thus it offers the case of the Countess Cornelia Bandi of Cadena:

> At the distance of about four feet from the bed was a heap of ashes, in which could be distinguished the legs and arms untouched. Between the legs lay the head, the brain of which, together with half of the posterior part of the cranium, and the whole chin had been consumed; three fingers were found in the state of a coal; the rest of the body was consumed to ashes, and contained no oil; the tallow of two candles were melted on a table, but the wicks still remained, and the feet of the candlesticks were covered with a certain moisture. The bed was not damaged, the bed-clothes and cover-lid were raised and thrown on one side, as is the case when a person gets up. The furniture and tapestry were covered with a moist kind of soot of the colour

of ashes, which had penetrated in to the drawers, and dirtied the linen. . . . The infectious odour had been communicated to other apartments.[4]

An extraordinary case, we shall agree, with the flame evidently coming from within, and attended by moisture, soot, and a pervasive smell. It appears that the countess was no drunkard, but used to bathe her body in camphorated spirit of wine, a habit that was thought to have increased her susceptibility to the calamity that befell her. This is not, it appears, mere fiction, either. It "was confirmed to the Royal Society of London, by Paul Rolli." Similar evidence guaranteed the authenticity of an analogous instance, contained in "a letter of Mr. Wilmer" "preserved in the same work." Thus of Mary Clues, a female drunkard, we are told circumstantially: "One leg and a thigh were still entire, but there remained nothing of the skin, the muscles and the viscera. . . . The wall and every thing in it [i.e., the apartment] were blackened, and . . . it was filled by a very disagreeable vapour; but . . . nothing except the body exhibited any strong traces of fire" (*Terrific Register*, p. 341) . This has a double interest for the reader of *Bleak House*. There is the strange nature of the alleged phenomenon itself; and there is the long roll call of learned authorities giving a show of unimpeachable authenticity. The sheer weirdness of what is alleged is sufficient to account for the way the information (derived from whatever source) lodged in Dickens' imagination. But, in addition, it had once been a common superstition — part, no doubt, of the submerged folklore of which nursery rhymes, proverbs, and basic bawdy form part. McMaster quotes from De Quincey's *Confessions of an English Opium Eater,* which was first published in 1822:

> Nervous irritation forced me, at times, upon frightful excesses [i.e., of opium]; but terror from anomalous symptoms sooner or later forced me back. This terror was strengthened by the vague hypothesis current at that period about spontaneous combustion. Might I not myself take leave of the literary world in that fashion?[5]

It was, we see, a "vague hypothesis" current when Dickens was a boy, the same time as that when Mary Weller was filling his mind with creatures of nightmare. McMaster does well to support this with two references to spontaneous combustion which occur in Dickens' earlier writings.[6] The first occurs in a deleted passage from "The Prisoners' Van" in *Sketches by Boz,* which first appeared on 29 November 1835 in *Bell's Life in London:* "We revel in a crowd of any kind—a street 'row' is our delight—even a woman in a fit is by no means to be despised, especially in a fourth-rate street, where all the female inhabitants run out of their houses, and discharge large jugs of cold water over the patient, as if she were dying of spontaneous combustion, and wanted putting out." In this instance it is interesting to notice how the "we" manages to dissociate the writer from the scene he is describing. He apparently includes himself in the assumptions that lead to the sort of fracas that he is deploring, only to "distance" it all completely by the cool irony with which the whole passage is suffused. The second example cited by McMaster occurs in *A Christmas Carol* (1843), and shows Scrooge bathed in light, awaiting the second spirit, "apprehensive that he might be at that very moment an interesting case of spontaneous combustion, without having the consolation of knowing it." Both instances are witty, and use the reference to make unexpected comic comparisons. Yet, implicit all the time is the assumption that spontaneous combustion is perfectly possible. The two examples corroborate what is evident in Dickens' preface to *Bleak House:* that he himself took the possibility of the disaster for granted. This is so true that McMaster's conclusion seems overcautious: "When Dickens decided to incinerate Krook, not only was he exploiting a popular taste for grisliness, he was playing upon the general uneasiness attaching to a popular superstition." Obviously Dickens was using the horror to horrify; no doubt he was competing with the sensationalism of writers like Thomas K. Prest and G. W. M. Reynolds; very probably he was exploiting the notion that such a visitation constituted an un-Chadbandian divine "composition"; and it is more than possible that he was indulging a personal attraction towards the gruesome. But in addition we must bear in mind Dickens' utter credulousness. His preface is quite explicit: "I do not wilfully or negligently mislead my readers, and . . . before I wrote that description [i.e., of Krook's death] I took pains to investigate the subject. . . . I shall not abandon the facts until there shall have been a considerable Spontaneous Combustion of testimony on which human occurrences are usually received." Dickens, of course, can never resist a verbal fantasy, but his wit does not mask his sincerity, for the word he uses is "facts." We know that he was misguided, but we must try to imagine what the effect would be if, as Dickens himself devoutly believed, the phenomenon could really occur. For he was not concerned at the primary level with the witty appropriateness of spontaneous combustion as a metaphor—as a kind of "model" illustrating his meaning in action. The load of symbolical significance he wanted to put on the metaphor was only relevant if it was based in attested fact. As with the Chancery satire, the satire on graveyard abuses, the satire on the Fowell Buxton expedition and on Mrs. Caroline Chisholm through the figure of Mrs. Jellyby, the satire on the Ministerial Crisis through the novel's Oodling and Uffing, and so on, his allegorical intention had to operate through documented actuality. His symbolic generalization had to be sustained by the parallelism he found in these actual happenings, and in the way all of them were *true*. In this way, the use he wanted to make of spontaneous combustion would only be valid if the phenomenon itself really existed.

As Dickens saw the problem there was a simple remedy for the swamping layers of paper and yet more paper—all the folios, cross bills, rejoinders, affidavits, and interrogatories of Chancery; all the ceaseless surge of begging letters washing over John Jarndyce; all the paper obstructionism that clogged the machinery of organized philanthropy and of Parliament. The remedy he saw was brutally simple. If paper is the problem, burn it; put an end to the superstructure of administration; and in its place establish a personal, direct form of philanthropy that can never forget the human issues at stake. All this paper circumlocution was a positive evil and, like all evil, self-corrupting. Obviously Dickens could not objectify the self-destruction, through its self-engendered poisons, of the office of Lord Chancellor; but he could and did imply it through the destruction of the Lord Chancellor's squalid otherself. Krook, then, is more than an exercise in local horror or an indulgence in grotesque overdrawing. As the Chancellor's mirror-image, he suffers what Dickens wants, in one way, to say about the Lord Chancellor himself. Yet, even so, his end must not be unrealistically contrived, for the novel is not a fairy tale although (in Jarndyce as fairy godfather and Esther as waif) it has certain of the elements of fairy tale. The contrivance is not masked by Dickens; instead he specially tries to draw attention to it by the daring dexterity and witty aptness of the plot elements he uses. Thus the death of Krook had to be based on something as verifiable as juvenile vagrancy, the inadequacy of foreign missionary societies, and the abuses that existed in a child-farm like Drouet's. Dickens is not a realist pure and simple. *Bleak House* is compounded of fantasy, grotesque fancies, specific social satire, and unmistakable moral affirmations, but it is all firmly founded in actual historical incidents, ideas, and practices. In this way it is an important part of his method that Jerry Cruncher in *A Tale of Two Cities* should be a Resurrection Man in the sense of body snatcher so that he could also be a grim parody of the novel's main "resurrection" theme—Recalled to Life—that culminates in the words of comfort running through Carton's mind on the way to the scaffold. It is equally part of the Dickensian method that a taxidermist and bone-articulator like Mr. Venus should exist actually as a taxidermist and bone-articulator so that thematically he should parody and thicken the notion of Birds of Prey and Golden Dustmen. In precisely the same way it is important in *Bleak House* that his reader should realize that he thought, and expected his readers to think, that spontaneous combustion was affirmed truth and respectable science.

The parade of learned authorities in Dickens' preface, as again in chapter xxxiii, is significant. He claims "about thirty cases on record" and mentions Bianchini's account of the Countess Cornelia de Bandi Casenate, the same case as that described in *The Terrific Register*. He also cites Le Cat's description of an alleged instance that occurred at Rheims, and this too is mentioned in *The Terrific Register*, where we are told that Le Cat specifies two instances—one, the death of a certain woman on 20 February 1725; the other, the death of Madame de Boiseon, a lady of eighty, who for years had been living on spirits and who perished in so unorthodox a manner on 22 February 1749. Other instances are quoted in the article in *The Terrific Register*, and what is impressive is the list of authorities adduced to support all the cases mentioned. We are directed, for example, to Vicq d'Azyr's narrative in the *Encyclopedie Methodique* [sic], under "Pathologic Anatomy of Man," for the case of a fifty-year-old female drunkard. Similarly, we are offered the *Acta Medica et Philosophia Hafniensia*, where details are given of the combusted death of a certain woman, a drunkard for three years, whose body was completely destroyed save for her skull and fingertips. In the same way, in the Transactions of the Royal Society of London a certain Grace Pitt was reported to have been half-burnt by spontaneous combustion on 9 April 1744. A further reference—to the *Journal de Medecine* (LIX, 140) —offers the testimony of a certain Merille, a surgeon of Caen, who attested the death by internal fire of another old woman, a Mademoiselle Thuars, who for years had been addicted to spirits. What is specially relevant to our present discussion is the real bookish scholarship attaching to this muster of instances. Spontaneous combustion was self-evidently an extraordinary phenomenon, but, given the spurious yet persuasive semblance of proved fact, why should the young Dickens have had the sceptical insight to doubt its authenticity, even if he had in fact read of it in some such publication as *The Terrific Register*?

Dickens' preface, however, also tells us why in fact he included the "word of remark" on spontaneous combustion at all: "My good friend MR. LEWES (quite mistaken, as he soon found, in supposing the thing to have been abandoned by all authorities) published some ingenious letters to me at the time when that event [i.e., Krook's death: in chapter xxxii, "The Appointed Time," which appeared in the tenth number in December 1852] was chronicled, arguing that Spontaneous Combustion could not possibly be." We are fortunate in that G. S. Haight has explained the background to this "word of remark" by drawing attention to the "letters" mentioned by Dickens.[7] Thus in his "Literature" column in the *Leader* on 11 December 1852 Lewes upbraided Dickens for incorporating outmoded science into his fiction as though it was still valid, managing thereby through the enormous influence of his popularity to give a popular superstition a fresh lease of life. Lewes supposed that

Dickens "had doubtless picked up the idea among the curiosities of his reading. . . . Captain Marryat, it may be remembered, employed the same equivocal incident in *Jacob Faithful.*" The criticism sprang from the aptness of the matter to a line of thought that had at the time captured Lewes's full support. According to Professor Haight he was "now at the height of his enthusiasm for Auguste Comte, whose work he had been discussing in a series of papers in the *Leader,* reprinted in 1853 as *Comte's Philosophy of the Sciences.* Lewes made it his business to attack any superstition that raised its head." What Haight brilliantly establishes without putting it into a positive statement is that the shape of Dickens' novel was slightly altered to accommodate an answer to this challenge. It is an admirable instance of the to-and-fro interchange between writer and reader that serial publication not only allowed but seemed to encourage. This peculiar sense of *audience* must have contributed to Dickens' choice to write serial novels to a deadline even long after any financial necessity for it had disappeared. Like W. Challinor's pamphlet, *The Court of Chancery: Its Inherent Defects as Exhibited in Its System of Procedure and of Fees* (1849), which came to Dickens through the post after the first number of *Bleak House* appeared in March 1852 and which Dickens incorporated substantially as Gridley's case, a chance act caused a modification of plan. As a result, the passage to which the preface directs our attention was included in the January 1853 number.

> Out of the court, and a long way out of it, there is considerable excitement too; for men of science and philosophy come to look, and carriages set down doctors at the corner who arrive with the same intent, and there is more learned talk about inflammable gases of phosphuretted hydrogen than the court has ever imagined. Some of these authorities (of course the wisest) hold with indignation that the deceased had no business to die in the alleged manner; and being reminded by other authorities of a certain inquiry into the evidence for such deaths, reprinted in the sixth volume of the Philosophical Transactions; and also of a book not quite unknown, on English Medical Jurisprudence; and likewise of the Italian case of the Countess Cornelia Baudi as set forth in detail by one Bianchini, prebendary of Verona, who wrote a scholarly work or so, and was occasionally heard of his time as having gleams of reason in him; and also of the testimony of Messrs. Foderé and Mere, two pestilent Frenchmen who *would* investigate the subject; and further, of the corroborative testimony of Monsieur Le Cat, a rather celebrated French surgeon once upon a time, who had the unpoliteness to live in a house where such a case occurred, and even to write an account of it; —still they regard the late Mr. Krook's obstinacy, in going out of the world by any such by-way, as wholly unjustifiable and personally offensive. (xxxiii) [*Baudi* is *Bandi* in the preface.]

In this passage, it is typical of Dickens that he should reduce scholarship to personal testimony—as though a superstructure of subsequent investigation were to resemble the administrative obstructionism of the rapacious benevolent societies. The passage demonstrates, too, an extra use for the arch irony that characterizes the third-person narrator. The ironic tone manages to include Lewes and his objections in the phrase "and a long way out of it" without disrupting the even flow of the novel. In addition the "men of science and philosophy" and the "doctors" serve to swell the ranks of the minor figures in the novel: the "world" that gives context and dimension, in simile and half-dramatized pieces of business, to the characters like Esther and Richard and John Jarndyce who play their lives out in the forefront of the action. While yet again, in inserting doubters as characters in the novel itself, and trying to show them the error of their ways by means of a whole army of learned citations within the texture of the story, the "real" existence of spontaneous combustion is "proved" on the level on which the novel must primarily be read. Just as a playwright can control the responses of his audience by making a character on stage utter the sort of criticism which a scene or a situation might inspire in the minds of some of the onlookers (the Nurse in *Romeo and Juliet* is a good instance of this),[8] so here, by being forced by Lewes to defend himself, Dickens has given one aspect of his novel an added, if fortuitous and specious, "authenticity."

Right was on Lewes's side, and he tried to point out to Dickens the relative antiquity of his authorities: the *Philosophical Transactions* of 1750, Beck's *Medical Jurisprudence,* and Fodéré's *Médicine Légale.* Dickens, he alleged, often ignored vital evidence, such as the presence of a lamp. For his part Dickens trusted his friend Dr. John Elliotson, who had lent him a lecture on the subject—though, as Elliotson's credulousness in the case of mesmerism had forced him to resign his chair in the Practice of Medicine at University College, London, he had not chosen a safe guide. A long letter (first published by Haight) that Dickens sent Lewes on 25 February 1853 is particularly valuable. In it he wrote: "When I thought of the incident—which came into my mind, as having that analogy in it which is suggested at the end of the chapter —I looked into a number of books with great care, expressly to learn what the truth was." In other words, Dickens thought first of the incident—presumably prizing in its sensational dramatic value as much as its moral aptness—and then worked up the documentation. (He did something comparable with the East Anglian dialect he uses in *David Copperfield.*) [9] Yet if we look at the passage "at the end of the chapter" to which he directs attention it is obvious that its local excitement is subsumed in its wide generalized aptness as a burlesque mirror-image:

The Lord Chancellor of that Court, true to his title in his last act, has died the death of Lord Chancellors of all Courts, and of

all authorities in all places under all names soever, where false
pretences are made, and where injustice is done. Call the death
by any name Your Highness will, attribute it to whom you will, or
say it might have been prevented how you will, it is the same
death eternally—inborn, inbred, engendered in the corrupted
humours of the vicious body itself, and that only—Spontaneous
Combustion, and none other of all the deaths that can be died.
(xxii)

The thematic moral relevance is uppermost here, but it is the outgrowth
of the scientific particularity of the phenomenon as Dickens saw it. It
offers substantive proof of the generalizing nature of Dickens' allegorical
intention: "the same death eternally." Krook—gin-sodden, sordid, grasp-
ing, mean, petty, enclosed, squalidly evil—is not important in himself.
His death is the death of one of Dickens' eccentric recluses: a male
Miss Havisham. But he is the simulacrum of his brother Chancellor,
and the Rag and Bottle Emporium is a travesty of that other graveyard
of wasted usefulness, that other storehouse of wasteful papers and documentation, the Court of Chancery itself. But the symbolism extends
even beyond the specific Chancery satire. Dickens is prophesying self-
destruction to "all authorities in all places under all names soever,
where false pretences are made, and where injustice is done." The sweep
of Dickens' castigation derives its force and validity from the vividness
of character and incident—the dramatic impact of Krook as a personage, the filth of his Marine Stores (the dirt conflicting with the "sea"
reference), and the weirdness of his death—of which the whole novel is
composed. But each element supports and quickens the meaning of
every other component. Dickens talks of "false pretences," and we see
how the themes of self-deception, blindness, and hypocrisy (all related
together as a form of moral myopia) interfuse and intermingle. He
talks of "injustice," and it is Jo, Guster, Charley, Caddy, Prince, Richard,
and Miss Flite, and even the infant Esther, whom we link together.
The novel is organized in parallels and welded together with unmistakable correspondences. The death of Krook is important in itself in
terms of plot and mystery; yet it is even more important when combined
with its affiliated threads of significance. It "is the same death eternally
—inborn, inbred, engendered in the corrupted humours of the vicious
body itself." Evil will end by poisoning itself: this is the positive moral
standard underlying the specific satire in the novel.

Dickens told Lewes that "I looked into a number of books with
great care." The pseudo-science that Dickens consulted is remarkably
reminiscent of the Vulgar Errors that Sir Thomas Browne claimed to
correct while obviously relishing the quaint folklore he renders so
superbly. Browne is a poet and a fantasist aspiring to be a Baconian,
and in a contiguous way Dickens, overcredulous as he was, obviously
relished his "facts" for their fantasy. In chapter xxxiii of *Bleak House*,

in his long letter to Lewes quoted by Haight, and in the Preface of 1853, Dickens cites J. Bianchini's account of the death of the Countess Cornelia Bandi of Cesena, and it is easy to see why the detailed specificity of what was alleged stimulated his imagination. An easy digest in *The Gentleman's Magazine* [10] (which seems to have been behind part of the article in *The Terrific Register*) is headed "Of the Death of the Countess Cornelia Baudi of Cesena" and reproduces from Bianchini some picturesque hypotheses [11] as to the causes of the phenomenon:

> The fire was caused in her entrails by inflamed effluvia of blood, by juices and fermentations in the stomach, and many combustible matters abundant in living bodies, for the use of life; and lastly by the fiery evaporations which exhale from the settlings of spirit of wine, brandies, &c. in the *tunica villosa* of the stomach, and other fat membranes, engendering there (as chymists observe) a kind of camphor; which, in sleep, by a full breathing and respiration, are put in stronger motion, and, consequently, more apt to be set on fire.

In a similar way one's fat is combustible, while "our blood, lymph and bile, when dry'd by art, flame like spirit of wine at the approach of the least fire, and burn away into ashes." To us this antique chemistry is, perhaps, amusing; but we ought to acknowledge the impressive array of testimony. Some of Bianchini's evidence is explicable as static electricity: e.g., "by the testimony of John Fabri, M.D., a noted philosopher, who saw it, sparkles of light flash'd out of the head of a woman, while she comb'd her hair. *Scaliger* relates the fame of another, *Cardanus*, a *Carmelite* monk, whose head continued 13 years to flash out sparkles, every time he toss'd his cowl over his shoulders." Learned treatises are ransacked to yield items like this: " 'The bile, which is a necessary juice for our digestion, was observed by *P. Borelli,* when vomited up by a man, to boil like aqua fortis' [*Centur.* II. *Obs.* 1, p. 109]." There are even quaint footnotes, such as: *"Galen de Morb. Diss.* Pigeons dung take [sic] fire, when it is become rotten." Now, this sort of mixture of science-poetry was known to Dickens. Just how much importance it had in suggesting a macabre mood, a pervasive ambience of shadowy menace, is hard to assess. But there is no doubt that the details from sources such as this found their way into *Bleak House.*[12] I shall return to the actual use Dickens made of such details later; but first I want to glance at the way the phenomenon as a whole is used in the novel.

Krook makes his first appearance in chapter v, "A Morning Adventure," the first chapter of the second number, which first came out in April 1852. Esther is the storyteller, and she recounts how she and Caddy Jellyby and Peepy leave the chaotic Jellyby home in the company of Ada Clare and meet Richard Carstone "dancing up and down Thavies

Inn to warm his feet." Their steps lead them towards the region of Chancery Lane, and they meet Miss Flite once more. She shows them Lincoln's Inn Gardens, and then conducts them to her own home:

> Slipping us out at a little side gate, the old lady stopped most unexpectedly in a narrow back street, part of some courts and lanes immediately outside the wall of the Inn, and said, "This is my lodging. Pray walk up!"
>
> She had stopped at a shop, over which was written, KROOK, RAG AND BOTTLE WAREHOUSE. Also, in long thin letters, KROOK, DEALER IN MARINE STORES.

The opening words of the number had recalled the fog outside ("although the fog still seemed heavy"), and referred to the dirt on Mrs. Jellyby's windows ("so encrusted with dirt, that they would have made Midsummer sunshine dim"). Thus, with brilliant brevity, Dickens picked up a cross-link with his earlier equation of fog and Chancery and correlated it with his parallel equation of Jellyby neglect and muddle. Caddy, trying to escape from home restrictions, once again (as in chapter iv) makes a gesture of friendship to Esther, whose goodness must within the moral scheme of the novel attract goodness, and suggests a morning walk. Esther's fine nature, in calling forth Caddy's love, exemplifies the way in which, in stimulating people to make contact with each other, real outgoing benevolence can bind society into an effective brotherhood. Thus the opening paragraph of chapter v provides a clever summary of ideas, images, and equivalences established in the first number. Yet in addition the chapter proceeds adequately and interestingly on the purely "story" level. Dickens, in a way so typical of him, expands his points through specific detail: Mrs. Jellyby's neglect of her husband, her bad housekeeping, and her neglect of Peepy— concrete instances of the theme of muddle. There is the detail of the "pewter pots and a milk-can hung on the railings": a reference to the beer cans taken home at night and left for collection by the local potboy, and the milk cans—solidly made metal containers—left for the milkman. This implies a social context—an impression of a "world" enclosing and sustaining the characters whose lives occupy the forefront of the novel. There is the individualizing detail of the cook's euphemism for her trip to the public house, "to see what o'clock it was,"—an expression that arose when, after Pitt's clock tax of 1797, inns installed special clocks as a facility for their customers. But beyond this specificity, implying that life is going on all around the characters, the plot has simultaneously been developing theme. Thus Caddy's talk is too explicit to be accepted as "natural"—though we do, perhaps, accept it as such when we read it for the first time, because of the pace at which Dickens keeps the novel moving. Her criticism of Mrs. Jellyby is undisguised: "where's Ma's duty as a parent?" Dickens thus uses her as a means of making almost direct criticism of her mother. In a similar way the speech of Richard is manipulated just as deliberately for dual effect, whilst the oracular wisdom of Miss Flite is unmistakable. There is Richard's comment as Miss Flite joins them: " 'So, cousin,' said the cheerful voice of Richard to Ada, behind me. 'We are never to get out of Chancery! We have come by another way to our place of meeting yesterday, and—by the Great Seal, here's the old lady again!' " I suppose we are aware of a certain measure of manipulation on Dickens' part here even on first reading, but I doubt if we consider it more than the slight improbability we have to grant, rather like the convention of verse in poetic drama, in order to allow Dickens to bring his characters together and to take Esther to the scenes that he wants her to describe. On further reading, however, we ought not to notice the way in which he is actually contriving his plot-device so that the very medium of his storytelling forms part of the allegorical meaning. Thus Richard's comment picks up Miss Flite's comment in chapter iii: "I have discovered that the sixth seal mentioned in the Revelations is the Great Seal." But it is more than a comic exclamation—a typically Dickensian way of labeling Miss Flite with an idiosyncratic tag or turn of phrase, and nothing more. It exemplifies the truth of what he says: "We are never to get out of Chancery!", for it is evident that even Richard's mild oaths are linguistically imprisoned by the Court's ubiquitous influence. Perhaps less tenuous than the linguistic involution is the way in which they circle unwittingly in a symbolic anticipation of Richard's subsequent embroilment and decline. He and Ada are not to get out of Chancery, and with complete irony on Dickens' part he is made to put into words what Dickens has already planned for him. More subtly still, Dickens has made them walk in a circle, drawn it would seem by an irresistible attraction towards the Court and its attendant dangers, a paradigm of their fate. So, if the chapter begins with an economical recapitulation, it proceeds to economical anticipation.

But all the while Dickens has been preparing for Krook, the Rag and Bottle merchant and dealer in Marine Stores. As Krook is a macabre simulacrum of the Lord Chancellor, and as the theme of muddle and unconcern links the Jellyby elements to the Chancery satire, the sequence from the dirt, irresponsibility, and mismanagement of the Jellyby household to the hint that Richard is already marked down for destruction in the grinding mills of Chancery, has been telling us something on the symbolic level of the load of allegorical significance that the Krook travesty is made to carry, while on the naturalistic level the same sequence from dirt to dramatic anticipation has made a point about the dirt and squalor we are going to see repeated in Krook's emporium. The allegorical content is made more complex still by the part that

Miss Flite plays in all this. From one point of view she is to be seen as a burlesque anticipation of Richard—part of the system of parallels and parodies that structures the novel. (In this way Hortense is related to my Lady, "Deportment" Turveydrop to Sir Leicester Dedlock, and Harold Skimpole to John Jarndyce.) Their paths cross, but Richard's cheeriness—part of his charm and part of his inherent weakness—will not save him, though it will make his decline the more pathetic. The irony of what he says forms part of the themes of blindness and self-deception that run through the novel. It is therefore with grotesque aptness that Miss Flite, the deranged prisoner of her madness and of her compulsive infatuation with Chancery, should lead them to her doubly significant home, Krook's Marine Store.

The emporium is dirty, ill-kept, and the last home of significantly *empty* bottles and *discarded* law papers, and of clothing that has degenerated into mere rags. Just as in Chancery where, once in, there is no escape, in Krook's shop "everything seemed to be bought, and nothing sold there." The shop exemplifies its owner, whose *first* words are, "Hi hi! . . . Have you anything to sell?" Telling details from the first chapter are caught up and given a special resonance: "As it was still foggy and dark, and as the shop was blinded besides by the wall of Lincoln's Inn, intercepting the light within a couple of yards, we should not have seen much but for a lighted lantern." Thus the fog of chapter i, together with the concurrence of darkness and ignorance, reappears. Blindness, part of the theme of hypocrisy and self-deception, is applied to the shop itself—an example of Dickens' animism infecting atmosphere and objects and the people associated with them. Light, health, and goodness can scarcely enter the darkness of Krook's emporium, and the light Krook provides is artificial—that of a lantern, perhaps meant to recall the fog-filled louvre of Lincoln's Inn Hall in chapter i.

Krook's death from spontaneous combustion is anticipated in the first description we have of him:

> An old man in spectacles and a hairy cap was . . . in the shop. . . . He was short, cadaverous, and withered; with his head sunk sideways between his shoulders, and the breath issuing in visible smoke from his mouth, as if he were on fire within. His throat, chin, and eyebrows were so frosted with white hairs, and so gnarled with veins and puckered skin, that he looked from his breast upward, like some old root in a fall of snow.

The immediacy of the portrait is startling. It is achieved partly through the strong visual impact of the frost of white hairs and the barklike appearance of his skin. While remaining within the bounds of good taste, Dickens renders old age obscene. There is something bestial about a "hairy" cap. There is an inner weakness in Krook, a physical deformity emblematizing a spiritual defect, causing his head to subside into the shoulders. It is typical of Dickens' many-sided ingenuity that the sub-sidence should cause the head to sink "sideways" between Krook's shoulders, deliberately matching and intensifying the significance of the quite literally "sinister" name, Krook. The similes are organized around three epithets: *short, cadaverous,* and *withered.* His "short" stature implies his likeness to an "old root" with "gnarled" skin. His "withered" appearance carries on the *root*-image, but adds the notion of inner subsidence accounting for the sunken head. His "withered" appearance blends with associations of "cadaverous," an epithet that extends the log / subsidence associations to include the feeling of death hinted at by the "white" hairs, and perhaps a dim reminder that hair still grows on corpses. (Two lines in Dylan Thomas's "When once the twilight locks no longer" read: "Some dead undid their bushy jaws, / And bags of blood let out their flies.") There is a distasteful connection between the *hairy* cap and the grizzled countenance. But had we pre-dictive powers we should see the anticipations here of Krook's death (just as we saw the anticipations of Richard's in his meeting with Miss Flite) : "the breath issuing in visible smoke," "cadaverous," "frosted" (perhaps as though with ash?) , and "some old root." With superb duplicity Dickens offers immediate vividness and obscene menace, while preparing for what is going to happen in chapter xxxii.

The double level of narrative goes on with Richard, with "laugh-ing encouragement," accepting the mock-Chancellor's invitation to enter, and later "rather carelessly" saying that he is unable to imagine why Krook is called "the Lord Chancellor" and his "shop" the "Court of Chancery." It is noticeable in Dickens that gesture and manner em-blematize character, and Richard's charming carelessness is connected with a deeper irresponsibility and a more pervasive inability to come to terms with the realities of life and marriage. Miss Flite makes the Krook / Chancellor equivalence explicit, however, and yet shows her own self-deception (despite the oracular wisdom with which she is endowed) by claiming that Krook is "a little—you know!—M——!" His attraction towards Ada's beautiful hair is seen as corrupt and defil-ing, for perhaps we are meant to regard hair (as it often is) as a sex symbol. The three "sacks of ladies' hair below" in Krook's cellar ob-jectify wasted beauty, and perhaps correlate with the images of "padded ease" (associated with the Woolsack) of the first chapter of the novel. Krook is also given a rapacious cat, Lady Jane, as a sort of diabolical familiar—partly to complement Miss Flite's symbolically caged birds. Dickens' equations leave us in no doubt as to the response expected of us:

> "And I have so many old parchmentses and papers in my stock. And I have a liking for rust and must and cobwebs. And all's

fish that comes to my net. And I can't abear to part with anything I once lay hold of (or so my neighbours think, but what
do *they* know?) or to alter anything, or to have any sweeping, nor
scouring, nor cleaning, nor repairing going on about me. That's
the way I've got the ill name of Chancery." (v)

The thematic parallels with the paper obstructionism of Chancery, the
interminable correspondence of Mrs. Jellyby and Mrs. Pardiggle, and
the flood of begging letters swamping John Jarndyce are extended by
the "old parchmentses and papers." The dirt parallels that include
Tom-all-Alone's, Mrs. Jellyby's household, Tulkinghorn's cobwebbed
port, the "dusty" folios of Chancery, and the "mud" imagery running
through the novel are generalized further by Krook's liking "for rust
and must and cobwebs," while we see why Dame Durden likes to sweep
the cobwebs out of the sky. The accretiveness of the mud of chapter i,
the slow conservatism of what Sir Leicester stands for, the acquisitiveness
of the lawyers on Phiz's cover, and the predatoriness of the Smallweeds
are echoed in the way Krook cannot "abear" to part with anything he
lays hold of. The hostility of Chancery to reform, the reluctance of
Parliament to transform itself from "that dustheap" in Westminster
to something positive and efficient, and the dilatoriness of all circum-
locutional officials are reflected in Krook's reluctance "to alter anything,
or to have any sweeping, nor scouring." He and the Chancellor are
meant to be equated fairly exactly, for he goes on to say: "I go to see
my noble and learned brother pretty well every day, when he sits in the
Inn. He don't notice me, but I notice him. There's no great odds be-
twixt us."

By this time the sharply outlined grotesquerie is excellently established. Krook is a sinister parody of the Lord Chancellor, and his
emporium is a comment on Chancery muddle. Krook as allegorical
figure is a stronger element in the novel than Krook just as Krook, and
as we read we regard him on this double level simultaneously. Dickens
moves with such dexterity and rapidity from scene to scene, each caught
with incisive accuracy, that we do not ask for an inner life for Krook.
He is important for what his projection makes him and for what he
represents, not for what he feels. We accept him as an outline of a man,
boldly drawn, yet having no inward experience. We do not enquire
why, on the simply psychological level, he has a liking for dust and
must, or why he is impelled to buy and not to sell. He *is* useless acquisitiveness; and the inner emptiness almost represents the pointlessness of
what he does. But he is just one manifestation of the vice, and he forms
part of the intricate system of parallels and cross-references that dis-
tinguish the force, truth, and method of Dickens' maturer novels, with
their acute social analysis, from the high-spirited picaresque of his
earlier career. The system of cross-references achieves variety of impact

through plot manipulation, vivid visual portraiture, and an economical double-tiered frame of allusion. Dickens' scenes are, as regards meaning, rather reminiscent of a mediaeval "pageant," with one level of meaning a comic Heroding on the ground; on the cart, another level of serious satire; and up above, a third level of generalized moral relevance. Thus Krook's shop is an absurd flight of imagination—an exercise in the macabre. But it also equates with pernicious muddle, heartache and waste: the sins of Chancery. Beyond this again, moreover, is the implied attack on all obstructive systems, the true function of which is lost in formalities that have degenerated into senseless ends-in-themselves, whereas once they might have been means-to-an-end. The relevance of all this symbolical significance to Richard, Ada, and Esther is made plain when Krook learns Richard's surname. On the level of storytelling technique, this manages to provide a summary of what we learned in the first number (rather as Macbeth's letter to Lady Macbeth summarizes the fast-moving events that have swiftly occupied the stage up to that time). Krook brings certain names into conjunction:

> "Carstone," he repeated, slowly checking off that name upon his forefinger; and each of the others he went on to mention, upon a separate finger. "Yes. There was the name of Barbary, and the name of Clare, and the name of Dedlock, too, I think." (v)

In addition, it is related to Tom Jarndyce, whose suicide, up to now no more than a gabbled allusion in Mr. Tangle's discourse, is related circumstantially:

> "'For,' says he, 'it's being ground to bits in a slow mill; it's being roasted at a slow fire; it's being stung to death by single bees; it's being drowned by drops; it's going mad by grains.' He was as near making away with himself, just where the young lady stands, as near could be."
> We listened with horror.
> "He come in at the door," said the old man, slowly pointing an imaginary track along the shop, "on the day he did it—"

In this way the pattern is made unmistakable. The further developments (implied by the "parchmentses") are brilliantly prepared for.

As they come down from Miss Flite's room, past the room where Nemo is to die, Esther and her friends find Krook storing away a "quantity of packets of waste paper" (i.e., the "costly nonsense" of Chancery, and perhaps a will, and some letters) in a "kind of well in the floor" (v), which obviously recalls the "well" of the Court (i). He is working hard, with perspiration beading his forehead; but it is not wholesome toil, for even labor at Krook's hands becomes dishonest and dirty and wasteful. He is as illiterate as Jo, but, prompted by greed—a quality that shows in what way he is related to his Smallweed relatives— he is searching for something unspecified; for, like Tulkinghorn,

Bucket, Guppy, Jobling, and even Esther, he is a detective. Like every-one else in the novel, he responds to Esther's goodness and genuine benevolence, and he asks her to help him. If his motive in learning to read and write is perverse—both part of the sequence of inverted values threading the novel, and. an objectification of his lack of interest in his lodgers and neighbors and society in general—the fact is put into dramatic emblem for us in his manner of chalking the letter "J" on the wall-panel. "ᒐ," he writes—a hook, we might fancifully infer, or a "bend sinister" to match his Krookedness. (I am aware that, literally, it is a bend *dexter*, but I want to emphasize its reversal of what is normal.) It is a J written back to front, but otherwise "just such a letter as any clerk in Messrs. Kenge and Carboy's office would have made" (v). In his calligraphy, the mirror-image Lord Chancellor writes in a mirror-image law-hand. The weight of incidental aptness—the multi-functional appropriateness of Dickens' casual detail—presses heavily on such economically chosen facts. Krook spells out "JARNDYCE." He spells out "BLEAK HOUSE." Lady Jane, his familiar, assesses Esther as though the girl were one of Miss Flite's caged birds. Thus the menace of evil is conveyed with astonishing dexterity, using the simplest of means. The "circular" motion of the chapter—which started at the Jellyby house, gravitated to Chancery, became involved with Miss Flite, introduced Krook, touched on Nemo, filled in the details of Tom Jarndyce's end, and implied (did we but know) the interdependence of the legal litter, the Jarndyce will, the Krooked greed of lawyers, and the fate awaiting Richard—thus returns to Richard and Ada. Richard, who is to be bewitched by the lure of easy money, warns Esther not to trade her hair, symbol of her beauty—beauty that will, in fact, be disfigured because of the social irresponsibility of authority. Richard, who will be so misguided as to misprise the good advice of John Jarndyce, sees that Chancery is the heartless game of chess that Phiz rendered on the cover illustration. However, "Chancery will work none of its bad influences on *us*," he assures Esther, with unconscious irony. The novel as a whole will show that love and innocence are not proof against contagion and death, and that whereas Little Nell passed in-violate through sordid reality, Richard will be squeezed, weakened, and killed by the slow-grinding mills of Chancery—and, by implication, of the baleful influence of that larger evil of which the squalid reflec-tion of the High Court of Chancery, Krook's emporium, forms part.

The equation of the Court and the emporium is cleverly cemented together with street mud. We read in chapter x:

> It is quite dark now, and the gas-lamps have acquired their full effect.

We notice the darkness, the artificial light, and remember the conjunc-tion of haggard gas and obscuring fog in chapter i:

> Jostling against clerks going to post the day's letters and against
> counsel and attorneys going home to dinner.

We should notice the reference to the correspondence involved in the
operation of Chancery, and link it to the theme of wasteful effort and
that of obstructive paper work. Noticeable, too, is the way in which the
lawyers who, by day, act their official roles (as Dickens himself makes
the theatrical metaphor carry a weight of thematic significance) are
transformed into the common humanity binding all men:

> and against plaintiffs and defendants, and suitors of all sorts,
> and against the general crowd. . . .

It is significant that the servants of useless Paper press against the
general trend:

> in whose way the forensic wisdom of ages has interposed a million
> of obstacles. . . .

We can recall the dummy-book titles that Dickens devised for the Gad's
Hill library: "The Wisdom of Our Ancestors, Vol. I Ignorance, Vol. II
Superstition, Vol. III The Block, Vol. IV The Stake, Vol. V The Rack,
Vol. VI Dirt":

> has interposed a million of obstacles to the transaction of the
> commonest business of life—diving through law and equity. . . .

Thus it links up with the parallels of the opening chapter of the novel:

> and through that kindred mystery, the street mud, which is made
> of nobody knows what, and collects about us nobody knows
> whence or how:

(which is to say not even Parliament and those Born to Rule—hence
the need for Detectives)

> we only knowing in general that when there is too much of it, we
> find it necessary to shovel it away—

(that is, the remedy Dickens offers for all abuses of oversystematization)

> the lawyer and the law-stationer come to a Rag and Bottle shop,
> and general emporium of much disregarded merchandise, lying
> in the shadow

(quite literally and metaphorically)

> of Lincoln's Inn, and kept, as is announced in paint, to all whom
> it may concern

(the legal note yet again)

> by one Krook.

The paragraph serves to link both Tulkinghorn and Snagsby—the one greedy for secrets and devious power, the other a man of good heart engaged willy-nilly in a course of reeducation—with the mock-Chancellor.

It is Tulkinghorn who finds Nemo's corpse—yellow, just like Chadband and the color of Krook's combusted grease. Tulkinghorn's candle is extinguished, and his detective activities momentarily blackened out (x). Krook can no more relight the candle from the "red embers" in Nemo's grate than life can be revived in Nemo himself (xi). By process of association, Nemo—in the "foul and filthy" room, surrounded by "scum and mist" (another link with the fog of the opening) —for the time being actually *is* the fire in its dead, ashy state, just as at the end of chapter x his life is equated with the guttering candle which splutters out into its punningly apt "winding-sheet" (the spent candle-grease):

> He has a yellow look in the spectral darkness of a candle that has
> guttered down, until the whole length of its wick (still burning)
> has doubled over, and left a tower of winding-sheet above it.

It is interesting that Krook is so consistently associated with the macabre and sordid. Typically, he almost "smacks his lips" at the thought that Nemo may have committed suicide. Typically, too, he took no more interest in his lodger—who, as someone trying to dissolve his past identity must be, was "too close to name his circumstances"—than in the "ladies whose heads of hair" (as fundamentally a symbol of their identity and individuality and beauty as the shorn hair of Delilah's Samson) "I have got in sacks downstairs" (xi). It is part of Dickens' witty economy to make Krook acquire this symbolic beauty and selfhood and then merely to store it away uselessly underground, like the Chancery documents themselves. But Krook displays interest when Esther, Caddy, Allan, and John Jarndyce are together in Miss Flite's room (xiv). Krook has been identified with his rapacious cat: "'His room—don't look rich,' says Krook, *who might have changed eyes with his cat,* as he casts his sharp glance around" [My italics: xi]. Thus the menace embodied by Krook is externalized by the tearing claws of Lady Jane that threaten Miss Flite's birds—Hope, Joy, Youth, Peace, Rest, Life, Dust, Ashes, Waste, Want, Ruin, Despair, Madness, Death, Cunning, Folly, Words, Wigs, Rags, Sheepskin, Plunder, Precedent, Jargon, Gammon, and Spinach. The very names, in their mad disarray, have the promiscuity of the bottles in Krook's shop. In their mixture of abstract qualities and legal paraphernalia, they summarize Dickens' Chancery satire. In their movement from the human qualities ravaged by Chancery—Hope, Joy, Youth, Peace, Rest, and Life—the qualities that Ada and Richard enjoy for the time being but which they are destined to lose—to the ravages themselves (Dust, Ashes, Waste, Want, Ruin, Despair, Madness, and Death), on through to the motives for the abuses of the Chancery system (Cunning, Folly . . . Plunder), on further to the means by which the abuses are fostered (Words, Wigs, . . . Sheepskin, . . . Precedent, Jargon, Gammon, and Spinach) — these words provide a sort of "potted" biography of a Chancery victim like Miss Flite or Richard Carstone. The word "Sheepskin," referring to Krook's "parchmentses," also suggest the wolf's proverbial disguise and the fate of the animals it attacks. The word "Gammon" emphasizes the unnecessary, nonsensical aspect of Chancery dilatoriness. The list of names degenerates as Krook recites them ("all cooped up together, by my noble and learned brother") into the nursery rhyme rhythm of "A frog he would a-wooing go" (xiv). It is as though all the things associated with Miss Flite must degenerate into an echo of something meaningful once (like Sir Anthony Rowley and the Court of Charles II), but which at present is little more than an empty parody of sense.

The parallelism between the relationship of the cat to the birds, and the relationship of Krook to Flite (also implying the relationship of the Lord Chancellor to Richard), anticipates the method of William Holman Hunt's "The Awakening Conscience" of 1853, where the cat making for the bird under the table provides a visual comparison with "the woman recalling the memory of her childish home and breaking away from her gilded cage with a startled holy resolve while her shallow companion still sings on ignorantly intensifying her repentant purpose." [13] Dickens displays deftness in making Krook deny Lady Jane's rapacity in such a way that her visible menace is increased: "She'd never offer at the birds when I was here, unless I told her to do it." We wonder what circumstances would lead him to tell her to attack. The power Krook has over the cat stresses the way in which the rapacity of the animal is an extension of Krook's own ability to harm. But it is not only in this way that Dickens adds Krook to the novel's bestiary. Krook has a "sharp" eye; he is cunning. We recall the fox [14] menacing Ada from one direction in the left-hand panel of Phiz's cover-illustration. The fortunes of Ada are identified with those of Richard in the novel as a whole. Perhaps the Fox symbolizes guile, the threat that sniffs from one quarter, while the Will o'the Wisp (i.e., the blandishments of Chancery and easy money) beckons from another. Krook conducts Jarndyce, who makes a practice of avoiding the real Court like the plague, around the mock-Court, while observing him "with the slyness of an old white fox." It is ironic that Jarndyce, in being shown the place where Krook is trying to learn to read and write, should be so near to the place where the Jarndyce will is actually hidden. The craftiness of the old Fox has its limits, however. Krook is unwilling to entrust his teaching to anyone for fear "they might teach me wrong!" His suspicion and avarice are insulating devices, cutting him off from society. Because of them, locked as he is in the ignorance of how to communicate in writing with other human beings—the inner psychological darkness being externalized by his dirty, shadowy shop—Krook "buys" but cannot "sell": that is, acquires but cannot use—rather like Christ's parable of the hidden talent. He hides things away—beauty, usefulness, and everything that once had value and utility—and they grow rusty and sprout cobwebs. He corrupts what he acquires, perverting their natural functions and qualities. He cannot exchange, for that would be to communicate. Like Jo—who is also illiterate, and who also has a fur cap—Krook is separated from a large part of society. Blackness and chaos unite Tom-all-Alone's and Krook's emporium. But unlike Jo's exile from society, Krook's social insulation is self-imposed, a narrowness rather like the Smallweed concentration on accountancy, which banishes both fancy and health. Whereas Joshua is a money miser, Krook is a hair and paper miser. Krook is inward-looking and distrustful, and as such becomes a variation of the Pardiggle / Jellyby / Turveydrop theme of solipsism.

Like Richard and Ada, Miss Flite was a ward of Chancery. Kenge and Carboy still pay her an allowance. Guppy is once more their agent, and it provides him with access to the penetralia of Krook's emporium. His friend Jobling has proved as improvident as Richard (or Dick Swiveller). "It's the fashionable way," Jobling tells Guppy and "Chick Weed" in chapter xx; "and fashion and whiskers have been my weaknesses, and I don't care who knows it." Such improvidence is exploited by the sagacious Guppy. It is not very different, except in degree, from Joshua's advice to Barty: "Live at his [Guppy's] expense as much as you can, and take warning by his foolish example. That's the use of such a friend. The only use you can put him to" (xxi). Both Joshua and Guppy hasten to exploit the weaknesses of the people "foolish" enough to put themselves at their disposal. For Guppy, friendship—in much the same way as his proposal to Esther—takes second place to acquisitiveness and expediency; and the instance extends yet further the novel's range of perverted values. In this way his advice to Jobling serves his own ends as much at it relieves "Weevle." "There must be time," he says, "for these late affairs to blow over. You might live through it on much worse terms than by writing for Snagsby" (xx). The parallel, with relevance, hints at the train of thought that (as it were, before the novel begins) prompted Nemo to a similar line of action. Action in the novel is often imitative and emphasizes in dramatic form the communal oneness of humanity. Thus Guppy knows that Krook has a room to let: Nemo's old room. He knows that Krook will not try to make contact with Jobling: "He'll ask no questions." But Krook's mysterious rummagings and secret delvings have excited Guppy's curiosity: "always rummaging among a litter of papers, and grubbing away at teaching himself to read and write; without getting on a bit as it seems to me" (xx); for rumor has

it that Krook is immensely wealthy (a sort of fictional counterpart of
the real-life Jennings, perhaps). For Dickens is aware that dreams of
buried treasure, golden geese (like Tennyson's "The Goose"), and new-
found wealthy relatives touch the imaginations of all poor people. Thus
when the Smallweeds take up the search, all the neighbors burst into a
rash of money fantasies:

> What those treasures are, they keep so secret, that the court is
> maddened. In its delirium it imagines guineas pouring out of tea-
> pots, crown-pieces overflowing punch-bowls, old chairs and mat-
> tresses stuffed with Bank of England notes. It possesses itself of
> the sixpenny history (with highly-coloured folding frontispiece)
> of Mr. Daniel Dancer and his sister, and also of Mr. Elwes, of
> Suffolk, and transfers all the facts from those authentic narratives
> to Mr. Krook. (xxxix)

Wealth, coming fortuitously, is a great leveller. With the speed of magic,
it can transform Boffins and Dorrits into gentlemen. Today, so one
writer alleges,

> On the whole, people do not resent other people's possessions, if
> only because they might at any time "come up on the pools"
> themselves: but what does *stir* up jealousy and ill-feeling is the
> idea that someone might be, *in himself and for his own qualities,*
> superior to the general run.[15]

This sort of comment conflicts, of course, with Dickens' idea that genuine
saintly denial of self as exemplified in Esther will induce imitation. It
is more like George Bernard Shaw's view that, as he shows in the
Epilogue to *Saint Joan,* nobody can live with a saint and that a saint is
tolerable only after his death. However, Raven's claim does fit in with
Dickens' picture of the predatory Smallweeds (and the predators of the
novel generally; like Krook, Vholes, and the Chancery lawyers), and
hints at the realism Dickens shows in putting this rapacity in a context
where materialistic daydreams of "guineas pouring out of teapots" are
the daily fancies of ordinary people. Part of Richard's downfall is that
he mistakes this common daydream for reality.

In all of this Dickens has not lost sight of Krook's ultimate end.
The article that appeared in *The Literary Gazette* began categorically:
"The greater part of the persons who have fallen victim to spontaneous
combustion have made an immoderate use of alcoholic liquors." If Nemo
sought escape through opium ("The room is strongly flavoured with it,"
says the "dark young surgeon" [xi]), Krook solaces himself with gin.
Guppy remarks, "I don't believe he is ever sober" (xx). And when he
takes Jobling, now "Weevle," round to the emporium to be introduced
to his new landlord, they find the old man "sleeping like one o'clock;
that is to say, breathing stertorously with his chin upon his breast, and

quite insensible to any external sounds, or even to gentle shaking. On the table beside him, among the usual lumber, stand an empty gin-bottle and a glass" (xxi). In Phiz's wrapper-illustration, these things seem to be attributed to the Law Writer, which argues the presence of the common factor—escape from reality—in both of them, just as it exists in a comparable way in Mrs. Jellyby's concern with the Borrioboolans, Mrs. Pardiggle's with the Tockahoopo Indians, and Turveydrop's with the manners of a past epoch. Mention of the empty gin *bottle* gives a small extra relevance to Krook's emporium in its function as an extrapolation of the inner man. The dirty bottles that Esther describes in chapter v come back to mind with an added aptness. Krook's "Rag and Bottle Shop" becomes almost a rag and GIN bottle shop. And to make the connection even more positive, Dickens' third-person narrator goes on (as Guppy tries to rouse the old soak), "But it would seem as easy to rouse a bundle of old clothes." This emphasizes that the shop is a RAG and bottle shop, indeed. With brilliant wit, the clothes actually *become* the bottle: "to make a bundle of old clothes, with a spirituous heat smouldering in it." For Dickens knows what effect—both in the lives of the characters in the novel as they are enacted for us, and on the level of symbol and metaphor—this combustible gin is going to work in Krook's intestines. The old man's lips are "parched" and "dry," suggesting easy kindling. He is certainly insulated from the world as Guppy tries to rouse him. Guppy pronounces the positive proof: "Why, he might be robbed, fifty times over!" It tells us something of the constant orientation of Guppy's mind that he immediately thinks in terms of robbery and acquisitiveness. It is paradoxical, however, in Krook—who retires to the bowels of his shop, shows no interest in his lodgers, and is unwilling to be helped in his efforts to learn to read for fear he should be taught wrongly—that he should try to become oblivious of the world of his own choosing. Dickens' direction is unshakable. If the gin bottle looks back to Esther's description of the Marine Stores, the flavored atmosphere looks forward to the "Appointed Time": "The unwholesome air is so stained with this liquor, that even the green eyes of the cat upon the shelf, as they open and shut and glimmer on the visitors, look drunk." The *stained* air: for once we can quite literally claim Dickens as a master of *atmosphere*.

The chapter that details Krook's death is very cleverly placed. In one of the most suspenseful climaxes in the whole novel, Esther has just said, "I am blind" (xxxi). It brings to a close volume I of the two-volume limited edition of the novel forming part of the edition de luxe of 1882. It is the mid-point of the novel. In the next chapter (still part of the tenth number), the darkness that has overtaken Esther seems to be picked up in the picture of Lincoln's Inn at night: "perplexed and troublous valley of the shadow of the law, where suitors generally find but little day" (xxxii). Dickens is imposing the metaphorical Night of Chancery upon the actual nighttime of Chancery Lane. The echo of the Twenty-Third Psalm: "The Lord is my shepherd. . . . Though I walk through the valley of the shadow of death, I will fear no evil," throws into ironic relief the present use of sheepskin: so that one almost believes the skins to have been literally flayed off the backs of Chancery litigants. "In dirty upper casements, here and there, hazy little patches of candle-light reveal where some wise draughtsman and conveyancer yet toils for the entanglement of real estate in meshes of sheepskin, in the average ratio of about a dozen of sheep to an acre of land." The word "wise" is used, of course, ironically: the work is wasteful and immoral; but the draughtsmen are also men of talent, and this word "wise" is in one sense not misapplied to them, and this makes their squandered talents all the more regrettable. The word "meshes" harks back to Krook in chapter v: "all's fish that come to my net." Dickens in establishing an ambience of leaden anticipation in which any dreadful horror is possible. It is rather like what Shakespeare does when preparing the scene for the assassination of King Duncan. The heavy oppression afflicts Banquo:

> A heavy summons lies like lead upon me,
> And yet I would not sleep . . .
>   (*Macbeth,* II, i)

Just as things of evil stalk the night-imagery of *Macbeth* (and both *Macbeth* and *Bleak House* chance to have porters!), the curfew bell at Lincoln's Inn is given a dismal resonance in Dickens' art, and he turns badly tended lamps—and everything about Chancery does not function properly—into stage properties projecting monstrous anticipations: "clogged lamps like the eyes of Equity, bleared Argus with a fathomless pocket for every eye and eye upon it." By rendering the purlieus of Chancery in such terms as these, Dickens is—by association and reflection—attributing such qualities to the Chancery travesty: "the neighbouring court, where the Lord Chancellor of the Rag and Bottle shop dwells."

Nowhere in *Bleak House* does Dickens excel the consummate skill with which he here weaves threads of theme upon the loom of melodrama. As I have shown, he begins with a brief picture of Lincoln's Inn at night—with the scriveners hard at work on their useless, harmful paperwork—that recalls the beads of sweat on the brow of Krook when Esther found him frenziedly searching for the Jarndyce will. The narrative passes on to Krook's court, and fills in some of the activities of the neighborhood. In clever parody, the Piper children and the Perkins children and their friends "have been lying in ambush about the by-ways of Chancery Lane"—a comic parallel with Chancery's heartless Game. The Harmonic Meeting at the Sol's Arms, the conversation of Mrs.

Piper and Mrs. Perkins, the songs of Little Swills, and the sundry speculations about Miss M. Melvilleson's baby, provide a society in which to
"place" the action, and a comic context that can contain and control
the grotesque sensationalism that Dickens is employing. The policeman
on his rounds, the appearance of the potboy, and the smell of tobacco
imply a real community. Yet Dickens is careful to modulate from serious
satire into comic relief and then, further, into macabre humor, and then
back again, holding no note too long—or even very long. Paragraph one
has been "atmospheric" and thematic; paragraph two (with the hint of
Krook being "continually in liquor") has provided a context of comic
normality and of warm life being lived. Paragraph three, however, hints
at what Dickens is mainly about in the chapter, picks up the running
"fog" imagery and associations, and summarizes some of the knotted
themes: "a laggard mist, . . . a fine steaming night to turn the slaughter-
houses, the unwholesome trades, the sewage, bad water, and burial-
grounds to account, and give the Registrar of Deaths some extra business" (xxxii). (The importance of these cross-references to Tom-all-
Alone's and to Nemo's burial ground should not go unremarked.)
And just as Banquo was disturbed on a certain night of impending
disaster, "Weevle" is uneasy and Snagsby on edge. With successful comic
effrontery, Dickens does not *tell* us in so many words that an aroma of
burnt carrion is infecting the air (just as the smell of gin had filled
Krook's home on an earlier occasion, and just as pestilential diseases
rose, air-borne, from walled-in graveyards); but instead dramatizes it
in a short scene of macabre irony. He has Snagsby—horrid thought!—not
only sniff but actually *taste* the air:

> "Airing yourself, as I am doing, before you go to bed?" the
> stationer inquires.
> "Why, there's not much air to be got here; and what there is,
> is not very freshening," Weevle answers, glancing up and down
> the court.
> "Very true, sir. Don't you observe," says Mr. Snagsby, pausing
> to sniff and taste the air a little; "don't you observe, Mr. Weevle,
> that you're—not to put too fine a point upon it—that you're
> rather greasy here, sir?"
> "Why, I have noticed myself that there is a queer kind of
> flavour in the place to-night," Mr. Weevle rejoins. "I suppose
> it's chops at the Sol's Arms."
> "Chops, do you think? Oh!—Chops, eh?" Mr. Snagsby sniffs
> and tastes again. "Well, sir, I suppose it is. But I should say their
> cook at the Sol wanted a little looking after. She has been burning
> 'em, sir! And I don't think—not to put too fine a point upon it—
> that they were quite fresh, when they were shown the gridiron."
> (xxxii)

The passage makes an impression at first reading—providing fun about bad smells and tainted meat. The general context of unwholesome air sockets the extract as though it were no more than a little piece of funny by-play, restating the obvious in a comic mode. But on subsequent readings, the ingenious ambiguity can be properly relished. Like any good magician, Dickens has distracted our attention with intricate flourishes while, with supreme cunning, he pulls little doves from up his sleeve and from behind his waistcoat. The grease, the stench, the carrion odor: such necessary data are simultaneously given and disguised.

The thematic interweaving continues. Snagsby mentions Nemo. Mrs. Snagsby, with a pocket handkerchief tied ridiculously round her head, parodies the ghostly fate pursuing Lady Dedlock by tracking after her husband like a diabolical familiar. The waited-for Guppy appears; yet, with unobtrusive persistence, Dickens is still touching in a setting and a mood fit for frightful happenings. The candle's knotted wax is ironically given its colloquial name, "a long winding-sheet" (xxxii) — which is perhaps meant to recall the scene of Nemo's death: "He has a yellow look in the spectral darkness of a candle that has guttered down, until the whole length of its wick (still burning) has doubled over, and left a tower of winding-sheet above it" (x). Guppy's mysteriousness elicits an ambiguous exclamation from Jobling: "By George, if we were going to commit a murder, we couldn't have more mystery about it!" But Dickens does not harp on one string. He recalls Lady Dedlock; he recalls Guppy's affection for the (disfigured) Esther—providing an opportunity for this sort of Swivelleresque language: "You really ought to be careful how you wound the feelings of a man, who has an unrequited image imprinted on his art." Of course, in his pretended affection for Esther, which is proof of both Esther's innate attractiveness of personality and of his own subservience to expediency, Guppy is to some extent playing a part, acting a role—just as the Chancery lawyers act out roles— with himself and Jobling as the audience. It is a minor example—rather like Mrs. Pardiggle's belief that she is constantly allowing people to catch her out doing good works ("I lay myself open to detection, I know," she tells Esther in chapter viii) —of the day-dreaming narcissism of many of the characters in *Bleak House* who play-act in front of some private mirror in their minds and thereby fail to look squarely at what monstrous abuses exist in real life and fail to appraise correctly what ethical standards ought to guide their activities. It is done in a variety of ways in the novel, but in no instance is Dickens concerned solely with dissecting theme. As here, it is done simultaneously with passing on information, or adding to the novel's flow of humor, or helping to establish character, and so on. Thus in this case we see Dickens thickening the mystery by divulging the time—the Appointed Time (itself a pun) —that Krook arranged to pass over the vital bundle of letters which Guppy promised

"FLORENCE AND EDITH ON THE STAIRCASE"
(Michael Steig, "Iconography of Sexual Conflict in *Dombey and Son*")

"Mr. Dombey and the World"
(Michael Steig, "Iconography of Sexual Conflict in *Dombey and Son*")

Lady Dedlock he would procure for her. Guppy demonstrates his detective ability by analyzing the mirror-accuracy of Krook's copy of Honoria's handwriting. "A woman's. Fifty to one a lady's" (xxxii) —though at least one graphologist of our own time would deny that it is possible to "sex" handwriting in this way.[16] But while the two of them whisper like conspirators in Jobling's room, a strange occurrence has taken place down below, and its obscene physical evidence begins to punctuate the narrative.

As we saw, Snagsby sniffed and tasted the greasy smell of combusted chops. A sootflake—reminiscent, perhaps, of the snowflakes in mourning for the death of the sun of the miry scene with which the novel opened— has attached itself to Guppy's coat sleeve. "See here, on my arm!" he cries (xxxii). "See again, on the table here! Confound the stuff, it won't blow off—smears, like black fat!" Time crawls on, and Nemo's presence is felt. More "hateful" soot gets in, and Guppy feels compelled to open the window to get "a mouthful of air." But as he talks, his fingers are hideously defiled by a "thick yellow liquor" from the window sill, a "stagnant, sickening oil"—perhaps akin to that of Chadband!—and nauseously repellent. The bell of Saint Paul's, a sort of passing-bell at that witching hour, eventually rings midnight. Tony goes down to call Krook, yet he complains: "I couldn't make him hear, and I softly opened the door and looked in. And the burning smell is there—and the soot is there, and the oil is there—and he is not there!" (xxxii, xiv). The pair of them descend to Krook's chamber, and Dickens organizes the scene with his customary dramatic tact. Lady Jane is snarling at something before the fire, for we are not *told* outright that charred remains cover the hearth. Instead, our attention is directed to a creature "registering" surprise; and from that we are meant to work back to what occasions the shock and disgust rendered in the cat's attitude. Dickens still does not *say* directly what has happened. He offers us the evidence: "the smouldering suffocating vapour," the "dark greasy coating" on the walls, the old man's cap and coat suggesting that he is near. From such sordid data we, the readers, are meant to deduce what has happened as though we, like Bucket, were detectives faced with a mystery. There is great cunning in this. In handling grossly improbable material, Dickens adopts a strictly "factual" approach. Has Krook hanged himself perhaps? Guppy and Jobling "act" the tentative explanation by looking up and finding that the answer is no. Then they catch sight of the thin red cord that was used to tie the love letters of Honoria and Hawdon together. It is a "clue" to Krook's whereabouts. It is soiled, however—just as love, in the case of Lady Dedlock and her first love, became itself defiled, and Esther (the result of it) a "disgrace" in the eyes of Miss Barbary. The grubby, grubbing attentions of Krook have added further stains to what once must have been not without honor. In the upshot, the purity of their love—something mutual,

close, unforced—has proved inviolable. Krook has met his fate before
the love affair can be sordidly traded in any more.

Gradually our eyes are brought to bear on the "something" that has
bemused Lady Jane: "The cinder of a small charred and broken log of
wood sprinkled with white ashes, or is it coal?" (xxxii). Dickens does not
let the mystery go unexplained, however. Having led up to the "fact" of
spontaneous combustion "factually," he now diagnoses the physical phenomenon itself and goes on to press its metaphorical significance. For fear
we should not carry the analogue as far as he intends it to be taken, he
makes the function of Krook's mock-Court of Chancery as a travesty of the
real Court even more explicit and thereby dramatizes his remedy for all
dilatory organizations, for all paper-clogged obstructionism, for all systems
that have degenerated into legalized tyrannies. What he does not press
quite so hard, however, but what we should also notice, is the irony that,
in that ghost-haunted emporium, where "Weevle" had felt the presence
of Nemo to be still strong, the literal death of Krook and the attendant
destruction of Lady Dedlock's incriminating evidence imply the inevitable
self-annihilating poisons of evil and the corresponding blotting-out of
the testimony of man's indiscretions. Evil is self-destructive; and the
weaknesses that betray ordinary people into making mistakes that in
various ways put them at the mercy of unscrupulous villains will, by its
own inherent corruptness, eventually be wiped out and forgotten.

What is extraordinary in all of this—and, as I have shown, Dickens
thought he was making use of harsh, scientific fact—is the way he has
taken the salient points from the learned accounts he consulted and incorporated them so smoothly into his scenes and episodes. But they are
made multifunctional: story material in themselves, at once startling and
vivid, and yet splendidly appropriate to the thematic concerns of the
novel as a whole. Thus, referring back to the article in the *Gentleman's
Magazine* for 1746, we can now see what details he decided to incorporate
and what weight of meaning he made them bear. There is the "heap of
ashes"; the "greasy and stinking moisture"; the "moist ash-coloured soot";
the probing nature of the sootflakes that "penetrated the drawers" and
"even got into a neighbouring kitchen," so that "in the room above the
said soot flew about"; the "greasy, loathsome, yellowish liquor"; "the
unusual stink." Dickens' account even parallels the mention in the article
of the liquor trickling down the "lower part of the windows," and the
"gluish moisture" spread over the room were the combustion itself took
place. But what he has borrowed, he has improved on. The gradual hinting of what is happening—the stench, the soot, the grease, the state of the
actual room—is made by turns darkly comic and startlingly horrific. By
humor, by plot-matter, and by touching-in the normal life of the neighborhood, Dickens "places" and controls the sensationalism. The associated
details—the white ash and the black log—of the charred remains, hark
back to the original description of Krook, with his froth of white stubble

and his gnarled skin. The alcoholism that must "cause" his combustion is made functional, too, that is, made part of the recurrent theme of isolation and insulation, and the related theme of escape. The gin-bottles are made part of the idea of Krook's trade in rags and bottles, while, at times, Krook is thought of as a bundle of rags. So, in running imagery, thematic parallels, "externalized" characterization, and suspenseful narrative, the materials of "science" are transmuted into multifunctional, artistic elements. Beyond even this, however, it is necessary for us to suspend our disbelief temporarily and to try to imagine that the phenomenon of spontaneous combustion can actually occur. It is rather like making the jump back to the world of Geoffrey Chaucer, where in order to appreciate (for example) the tale of Chanticleere and Dame Pertelote, we have to know about, and even "believe" in, mediaeval astrology and mediaeval physiology and mediaeval dream-theories if we are not to miss the tender ironies in the animal-human ambiguities that Chaucer so wittily exploits. If we can do this in the case of Dickens and spontaneous combustion, we can shadowily recapture—even if we are unable, in Keatsian phrase, to "feel on the pulse"—the actual horror that is heightened so enormously at the idea that the strange, monstrous happening could really happen. Even more important, however, is the weight and force that the symbol acquires if we do, in fact, make the necessary imaginative leap. Dickens makes the connection quite plain. It is an instance to add to his use of topical materials like the burial ground scandals, Chancery abuses, and the Ministerial Crisis involving Lord John Russell. For Dickens, his metaphors and symbols had to work on the level of pure, firm-based fact if their wider metaphorical and symbolic significance was to be truly valid. If we make the leap of imagination in the case of spontaneous combustion, therefore, and not only admire Dickens' art but "believe" in his "science," the power of the Krook simulacrum as a parody of the High Court of Chancery derives added force. What Dickens dramatized in the case of Krook he means to apply equally to Chancery itself—and even, by implication, to all the parallels with Chancery (such as Parliament, child-farms, benevolent societies, and missionary organizations) which are focused in *Bleak House* as a whole. The Krook travesty has a generalized relevance, therefore, and it represents in its extreme form the moral affirmation the novel makes in the face of evil. Thus the assertion that the self-engendered poisons of evil will eventually work their own destruction is given positive, yea-saying authority. Such a positive commitment on the part of Dickens is necessary to balance and qualify the objective realism—for which Dickens still lacks his due— that clearly records, though with tender compassion, the death of a romantic idealist like Richard Carstone [17] and of a victim of neglect like Jo, in a world where acquisitiveness prospers and petty treachery secures a "fypunnote."

Lance Schachterle

BLEAK HOUSE AS A SERIAL NOVEL

MODERN CRITICS have an understandable tendency to regard Dickens' *Bleak House* as if it were designed to be read all at once from cover to cover, without any interruptions save those of fatigue. But of course the original audience for *Bleak House* did not encounter the novel in this way. For them (and for Dickens) *Bleak House* was not a book, but rather a serial, carefully arranged to appear in nineteen monthly installments.[1] Unfortunately, those of us who today ignore the consequences of the novel's serialization miss some qualities vital to Dickens' art: the slow, deliberate pace of publication, and the suspense which the monthly interruption of the narrative naturally aroused. We can, however, attempt to recapture the effect Dickens intended monthly part-issue to have by scrutinizing the techniques of Dickensian serial publication. By investigating the novel from the hitherto little-explored avenue of its serial form, we can throw new light upon its structure, and examine some of the implications of its serial form.[2]

Bleak House provided the original serial reader with a year and a half of suspenseful fascination, for he read the novel in nineteen carefully constructed installments spaced out over as many months, rather than in one of the massive book editions now available. Each installment, printed in its own thirty-two page pamphlet (about forty-five pages in the New Oxford Illustrated Dickens edition), contained three or four chapters of varying mood and texture—a not unduly long or monotonous amount of reading for a single sitting. Dickens thus rigidly controlled the pace at which his serial audience read *Bleak House*. Moreover, he published three or four chapters each month which were arranged carefully to provide precisely the plot material he wished to reveal at that stage of the serial's development. Suspense was painstakingly prorated on a monthly basis. The Victorian reader, who, like Thackeray, judged

a novel by looking at the conclusion to see if the protagonists were suitably disposed of, was not offered the opportunity in a serial to shorten
his imaginative labors by turning immediately to the last chapter. Rather,
for nineteen months he had to "live with" *Bleak House* in a state of extended curiosity. Reading in this fashion is perhaps foreign to many
moderns who, caught in the contemporary spirit of "here today-gone
tomorrow" best sellers, skim quickly through any "big" novel—thus ignoring in *Bleak House* the arousal of suspense and the leisurely exposi-
tion basic to Dickens' art.

As we shall see, monthly part-issue, which at first glance might seem
a refractory vehicle for any complex work of fiction, proved in Dickens'
hands a superb medium for publishing *Bleak House*. A less able serialist
might easily have reduced the suspense of "what happens next" to mere
sensationalism. But by 1852 Dickens was a master of his serial art; in
Bleak House the suspense which monthly part-issue engenders directed
the reader's interest to the novel's principal issues, and engaged his imagination in the task of working out the elaborate pattern of symbols
and juxtapositions which bind the installments together.

It is no accident that *Bleak House* is both Dickens' first "anatomy
of society" and his first detective story.[3] In this novel the author wished
to demonstrate on a scale not before attempted one of his favorite beliefs, that "the world . . . was so much smaller than we thought it; we
were all so connected by fate without knowing it; people supposed to be
far apart were so constantly elbowing each other; and to-morrow bore
so close a resemblance to nothing half so much as to yesterday."[4] To insure that the reader learned this truth about society for himself (rather
than passively taking the author's word for it), Dickens created a complex of themes, images, and plot lines which are parceled out over the
nineteen months, but which together—after the reader has joined them—
figure forth the novel's significance. Over the months the reader slowly
pieced the novel's segments together, making *Bleak House* come alive
by means of his own imaginative effort.

— *I* —

Dickens was thoroughly aware of the special nature of publication in
parts and anticipated its difficulties by developing appropriate techniques.
His letters as editor of *Household Words* and *All the Year Round* often
advise contributors about the requirements of serial publication.[5] Again
and again Forster's biography bears witness to Dickens' envisioning his
works as a succession of installments, though without losing sight (at
least in his mature works) of an overall plan.[6] Evidence for his composing *Bleak House* installment by installment may be found in the
number plans and memoranda for that novel: each part received a sepa-

rate sheet of notes, suggesting that Dickens thought the novel through one monthly number at a time. The sketches show that Dickens was especially anxious to maintain continuity from part to part and to keep the reader in suspense throughout the appearance of the serial.[7] Finally, in several prefaces Dickens speaks of the special nature of serial publication, often assuring his audience that he is at all times in control of the unfolding parts.[8] The implication of this evidence is clear. Though Dickens never forgot the need for his installments to form a continuous narrative, at least in the process of composition he considered his novels as serials to be published in parts, not as conventional novels printed seriatim—a quite different fictional mode.

The author of *Bleak House* was, of course, not the first to write a serial novel, though, as Mrs. Tillotson remarks, he was the first to make the publishing of novels in parts both popular and respectable.[9] Dickens was faced with the same problems of variety-within-unity which afflicted earlier serialists.[10] The serial writer must establish unifying themes or plots which embrace all the parts while at the same time he must make each installment an artistic whole in itself.[11] Since each part of *Bleak House* was published and read separately, every number had to stand by itself; a weak installment might imperil continued sales. On the other side of the coin, each installment had to relate to all the rest so as to provide an integrated novel which could appear in volume form after its serialization was complete.

Most novels, of course, are divided into units, usually chapters, which must follow one another without loss of continuity. The natural unit, however, for the serial novel is not the chapter, but rather the installment (which may consist of several chapters). The reader tends to regard the installment as a much more independent unit than the chapter, not only because of its greater size and complexity, but also because it appears physically by itself, either as a certain number of magazine pages or as an independent pamphlet. Furthermore, each installment stands out more clearly as a self-contained unit since in the intervals between publication the reader has ample opportunity to forget precisely what has passed in the narrative of the previous number. Because of this striking independency of the installment part, the serial novelist is faced with an urgent need for techniques to maintain continuity throughout his numbers. The devices which Dickens used to achieve serial unity—carefully constructed installments, reiterated symbols, and juxtaposed themes—have been studied separately, but their function in bringing the serial numbers together has often been ignored.

— 2 —

An examination of Dickens' methods of serializing *Bleak House* falls naturally under two closely related heads: techniques used to connect the parts together, and techniques used to make each number stand by itself. These techniques are different sides of the same coin, for often serial devices serve both functions. Perhaps the best way to begin investigating the serialization of the novel is to look in detail at a single installment, the tenth number, in terms of its design as an independent fictional whole.[12] The December 1852 installment of *Bleak House* (No. X) contained three chapters (xxx, xxxi, and xxxii), the first two of which are part of Esther Summerson's narrative. At the end of the ninth installment, the reader has learned—if he has not already guessed—that Esther is Lady Dedlock's child. The Lady's shell of hauteur and family pride, manifested throughout chapter xxix in her interview with Guppy, has finally been shattered by her anguished realization that her child is alive. The sequel, the tenth installment, begins with Allan Woodcourt's mother praising her own family in Esther's presence: "This, you see, is the fortune inherited by my son. Wherever my son goes, he can claim kindred with Ap Kerrig. He may not have money, but he always has what is much better—family, my dear" (No. X, xxx, 411).[13] "Family, my dear" should ring false in the reader's ear. Though Mrs. Woodcourt's worship of family is comical, Honoria Dedlock's is not. Pride has divided her from Esther's father, Hawdon; Dedlock family pride has proven a poor substitute for the natural sympathies it has cut off.

By beginning the tenth number with Mrs. Woodcourt's display of family pride, Dickens has delicately recalled the reader's attention to the far more blighting family pride which Lady Dedlock has shown in the previous installment. Thus the gentle comedy of Mrs. Woodcourt's "family, my dear" is both an appropriate introduction to chapter xxx, which records Caddy Jellyby's marriage, and a recollection of the end of the preceding installment. Furthermore, the juxtaposition of family pride in Lady Dedlock and in Mrs. Woodcourt offers an example of Dickens' skill in viewing the same theme in two different numbers from two different viewpoints—a most useful device for insuring both continuity and variety.

Despite the touch of satire in the appearance of both "telescopic philanthropists" (Mrs. Jellyby and Mrs. Pardiggle) at Caddy's wedding, the tone of chapter xxx is prevailingly humorous. Little happens in this chapter; it is not (as are many of the other chapters) devoted to a businesslike advance of the various plots. Rather chapter xxx acts as a comic interlude, in which the author and reader alike pause in amused contemplation of a descriptive genre scene, before getting on to more serious matters.

Chapter xxxi, again from Esther's pen, continues her personal history, but here the tone is pathetic, not comic. This chapter, unlike the one before devoted to Caddy's wedding, is a quick-moving, terse narrative whose primary function is to advance the plot rather than to entertain. The plot lines involving Esther, Jo, the brickmakers, Skimpole, and Jarndyce are all carried forward; the central event is Esther's contracting a fever from Jo, whom she has been trying to aid. In another line of action, Harold Skimpole is revealed as a heartless man who can sing a pathetic ballad "about a Peasant boy

> 'Thrown on the wide world, doom'd to wander and roam,
> Bereft of his parents, bereft of a home,'

—quite exquisitely" (No. X, xxxi, 436) —after having advised Jarndyce to turn just such a youth (Jo) out of his house. The chapter ends with Esther stricken blind, the victim ultimately of a "blind" social system which hopes to ignore problems like Jo by ordering him to "move along," or, at best, giving him (as Mr. Snagsby does) an occasional charitable half crown. Yet, quick-moving as it is, chapter xxxi is not without symbolic overtones. In the description of Jo's illness, Dickens joins together suggestions of extreme heat and cold, which often separately adumbrate the hostility of *Bleak House*'s world: " 'I'm a-being froze,' returned the boy, hoarsely, with his haggard gaze wandering, . . . 'and then burnt up, and then froze, and then burnt up, ever so many times in a hour' " (No. X, xxxi, 430) .[14]

Chapter xxxii, "The Appointed Time," the last chapter of the tenth number, is one of Dickens' best constructed, a virtuoso piece with a slow, suspenseful crescendo. The sensational descriptions which prefigure the discovery of Krook's remains are not mere Gothic trappings; they repeat throughout the constellation of mud-cold-darkness-fog images which the first chapter establishes so memorably. A comparison of a few passages from chapter xxxii with those from chapter i which they recall will demonstrate Dickens' recurring imagery:

> It is a close night, though the *damp cold is searching* too; and there is a *laggard mist* a little way up in the air. (No. X, xxxii, 444)
> *Fog* cruelly *pinching* the toes and fingers of his shivering little 'prentice boy on deck. (No. I, i, 1)
>
> It's a *tainting* sort of *weather*. (No. X, xxxii, 445)
> *Implacable* November *weather*. (No. I, i, 1)
>
> See how the *soot's falling*. . . . Confound the stuff, it won't blow off—smears, like *black fat*. (No. X, xxxii, 450)
> *Smoke lowering* down from the chimney-pots, making a soft *black drizzle*, with flakes of *soot* in it as big as full-grown snow-

flakes—gone into mourning, one might imagine, for the death of the sun. (No. I, i, 1; *italics mine throughout*)

Such resonances between the language in chapters i and xxxii serve to lift the discovery of the combusted Krook (which climaxes both the chapter and the installment) out of the realm of the sensational. Krook's death is not a perversion of reality; it is the fulfillment of a set of actions and symbols, present from the first number, which foreshadow "the death of all Lord Chancellors in all Courts, and of all authorities in all places under all names soever, where false pretences are made, and where injustice is done" (No. X, xxxii, 455–56).

The tenth number, assessed by the multiplicity of its tones and techniques, is almost a novel in little. It contains the humor of Caddy's wedding, the pathos of Esther's blindness, the irony of Skimpole's selfishness, and the melodrama of Krook's death. As in all the other numbers, certain chapters in this installment serve to advance the plot, but in others this advance is arrested for a lengthy humorous description (xxx) or a richly resonating symbolic scene (xxxii). Beginning with Mrs. Woodcourt's "family, my dear" which establishes a connection with the theme of family pride in the previous installment, the middle number ends with the discovery of Krook's ashes, adumbrating the purification of society by spontaneous combustion at some future "Day of Judgment" (to use Miss Flite's term). The tenth number is thus both progressive and regressive: the discovery of Krook's death looks back in its language to the first number (thus maintaining overall continuity), while at the same time it leads to the eleventh which describes the comic inquest conducted over Krook's ashes. Dickens has thus succeeded brilliantly in composing an installment which stands by itself as a pleasingly variegated fragment, yet which has running through it the themes, images, and juxtapositions which are the life-blood of all the other numbers.[15]

Although the installments vary in composition, their effect is roughly the same as that of number X. Each part of *Bleak House* is strikingly diverse, often displaying in its carefully-contrasting chapters the familiar moods and tones of Dickens—suspense, pathos, irony, indignation, melodrama, and comedy. Dickens' installments neither fall apart internally nor seem disconnected when read together because each number encompasses so full a range of emotions that it stands as a satisfying little fictional world in itself. Yet the suspenseful plot always whets the reader's appetite for more of the same, compelling him to read on until the whole story has been revealed.

— *3* —

Having given his installments a life of their own, Dickens had also to interrelate them so that each part meshed with those before and after it. Dickens had at his command an array of devices to sustain continuity

among his different serial parts. Each of the five serial devices examined
below—1) the installment conclusions, 2) the transitions between installments, 3) the dual narrative, 4) the thematic juxtapositions, and
5) the symbolic images—clearly may function both to interconnect the
numbers and to make them independent. For example, the installment
conclusion may contribute to the form of the number by bringing it to a
rousing close, while at the same time, the reader's curiosity which the
conclusion stimulates may help to connect the number to its sequel.

1)   Installment conclusions offer a serial author the tempting opportunity to arouse suspense simply by putting one of the principal characters in jeopardy at the end of a part. This trick soon becomes shopworn,
and Dickens rarely used it. After sixteen years' experience with serialized
novels, he had developed a variety of installment conclusions which
function mainly to suggest future actions, and which arouse suspense
without being sensational. Furthermore, the numbers of *Bleak House*
do not end clumsily as had many parts in earlier novels. No longer is
the smooth flow of the narrative interrupted to call the reader's attention
to the need to await the sequel for the action to continue.[16]
  In contrast to the conclusions used in previous novels, the installment
conclusions of *Bleak House* are not abrupt or arbitrary interruptions of
the narrative. Most frequently, by spotlighting significant themes, they
subtly suggest the principal concerns of the novel.[17] For example, the last
paragraph of the first installment does not jar the narrative flow: "The
purblind day was feebly struggling with the fog, when I opened my
eyes to encounter those of a dirty-faced little spectre fixed upon me.
Peepy had scaled his crib, and crept down in his bedgown and cap, and
was so cold that his teeth were chattering as if he had cut them all" (No. I,
iv, 45). Using the images of the novel's opening chapter—"the purblind
day," "the fog," and the "cold"—the conclusion of the first installment
calls attention to the "cold" and "blind" Jellyby household.
  Less frequent than the endings which emphasize principal themes
are those which give the reader important hints concerning the plot—
as, for example, Esther's references to Allan Woodcourt at the conclusion
of numbers IV and XI. Occasionally installment endings act as a rousing
climax, as does Lady Dedlock's realization that Esther is her daughter
(No. IX), or the death of Krook (No. X). Only twice, at the end of
number III (entering the room of the dead Nemo) and number XVI
(Bucket's discovery that Lady Dedlock was out the night of Tulkinghorn's murder), did Dickens use the installment conclusions to force the
reader to await the sequel for the solution of a mystery. Despite the different ways in which Dickens employed the installment conclusions, in none
did he break through the convention of the unobtrusive narrator to remind the reader that he must wait a month to learn what happens next.
The reader must wait, but he is not subjected (as in *Pickwick Papers*)

to a clumsy reminder that he is at the mercy of the serial form. Instead the installment conclusions summarize present action, and often encourage the reader to speculate in the monthly intervals between publication about future events.[18]

2)   In beginning a sequel, Dickens must immediately secure the reader's attention for the new events, while maintaining continuity with the preceding number. The simplest transition is to continue in the first chapter of the sequel the action left at rest or unfinished in the preceding installment. The reader's suspense is thus rapidly relieved, and the lines to the preceding number are made clear.[19] A more subtle transition occurs when the sequel begins with a chapter concerning characters and situations different from those of the preceding chapter. This transition often occurs when the sequel (as is frequently the case) begins with the alternate narrator. If the reader recalls the end of the previous installment, he may be jolted at first by what seems a discontinuity, but if he uses his wit, he will soon comprehend that the apparently incongruous transition continues the central concern of the previous installment, but in a new vein. As we have seen, the transition between numbers IX and X (which move from Lady Dedlock's family pride to Mrs. Woodcourt's) employs this method.

   Still more interesting are the transitions in which the action concluding the preceding number is continued in a different tone in the sequel. We have just seen such a case, in numbers X and XI, where number XI carries on in a comic vein the death of Krook which had been treated melodramatically in number X. Such a transition shows how serialization allowed Dickens to juxtapose contrasting expositions of the same event (e.g., Krook's death). Comedy follows on the heels of melodrama, and the reader experiences the enlightening shock of seeing the same event treated a month apart in two radically different ways.[20]

3)   The dual narrative is yet another device Dickens employed to knit together the nineteen numbers of *Bleak House*. In all save five installments, at least one chapter is from the pen of Esther Summerson. Unlike Dickens' earlier novels, *Bleak House* contains no main character about whom the entire novel revolves, for the real protagonist is the "bleak house" of English society. Faced with the problems of avoiding a lack of sympathetic involvement in a novel whose main thrust (in the omniscient narrative) is a satiric and objective portrait of a whole society, Dickens hit upon the solution of allowing one character to tell her story in the first person. By means of the inevitable sympathy which first-person narrative elicits, Dickens hoped to engage the reader's sympathy for Esther, who provides an emotional point of contact for the reader as he explored the panorama laid before him in monthly installments.

   In terms of the serialization, the dual narrative is significant for the way in which the reader's curiosity is aroused as he moves back and forth between Esther's and the omnisient narrative. Facts which he learns in Esther's limited narrative are not put into the full perspective until the omniscient narrative in the sequel provides the bakground. Esther's and the omniscient narrator's chapters alternate in three-quarters of *Bleak House*'s installments because Dickens realized how useful such a proce-dure was in keeping suspense up.[21] Themes, symbols, clues, and events which turn up in one narrative may occur in quite a different context in the other. Part of the pattern of the novel the reader learns in one narra-tive, and part in the other. As he reads on, his ingenuity is challenged to piece the two parts together, and this task, which rivets his attention to the novel, leads him from number to number. Throughout the nineteen months of *Bleak House*'s serialization, the reader's insight is constantly supplemented, but not until the last number is it complete. The reader mediates between the personal, "Esther" chapters and the impersonal, satiric chapters, until, ultimately, by the last installment, the two narra-tives merge, and the creative tension which has carried him through the nineteen months of suspenseful mystery collapses.

4)   Juxtaposition is another of the principal techniques in Dickens' serial art.[22] Not only does the novelist juxtapose materials presented in the two narratives, but he also sets side by side comparable scenes or events drawn from different installments. Central themes in *Bleak House* are reinforced by presentation through more than one character and in more than one number, so that two or more people or related incidents figure forth the same theme. As in a cinematic montage, events at first seem discrete, but are later comprehended as interrelated.[23] The reader is drawn into the process of creating the novel for himself as he grasps these juxtapositions among the different installments. He fathoms the bleakness of *Bleak House* when he realizes the complementary significance of the Lord Chancellor in the first installment and Krook, his comic double, in the second. Both the Lord Chancellor and Krook suggest the absurd faith in formalities and legal documents which lies near the novel's core of corruption. Krook's mirroring of the Chancellor in the second number serves to keep the hor-ror of Chancery before the reader's eyes, and thus draws the two numbers together. Legal obfuscation is everywhere.

     In the same way, the social snobbery of Sir Leicester (No. I) is re-peated on a ridiculous level in old Turveydrop (No. V), and in Jobling (No. VII). The succession of installments provides Dickens with ample opportunity to repeat in differing ways the same essential points without wearying his readers with patent repetition. Yet such repetition as there is contributes significantly to the serial's overall unity.

     An example of Dickens' juxtaposition of similar actions among his numbers is the repeated detective searches. The first of these is Guppy's, whose efforts (in Nos. II, III, VI, VII, IX, and X) to ingratiate himself with Esther leads him to uncover her relationship with Lady Dedlock. Working with an interest in Lady Dedlock rather than in her daughter, Tulkinghorn discovers the same secret (in Nos. III, IV, VII, IX, XI, XII, and XIII). Krook and his legatees, the Smallweeds, are searching constantly for secrets; though Krook fails, Grandfather Smallweed (along with the Chadbands) also learns of Lady Dedlock's attachment to Captain Hawdon (in No. XVII). Mrs. Bagnet solves a mystery too; with an acuity of observation worthy of Sherlock Holmes himself, she deduces (in No. XVI) that George has recently seen his mother, and sets out to bring her to London. Paramount among all these detectives is of course Inspector Bucket, who (in Nos. XVII and XVIII) traces Lady Dedlock to the dismal site of Hawdon's grave. Even Mrs. Snagsby indulges a bent for detection, which leads her to the absurd conclusion that her husband is Jo's father (No. VIII, in a chapter aptly entitled "Mrs. Snagsby Sees It All").

With the exception of Mrs. Snagsby (whose efforts provide comic relief from the seriousness of the other detectives' investigations), all these characters, acting separately and in different numbers so as to maintain interest, keep the reader involved in the unfolding serial by revealing fragments of the pattern of relationships. No month passes without the reader learning something new from one of these detectives. None of these characters—not even Bucket—sees the whole pattern, but each aids the reader over the nineteen months to "see it all" for himself.

5)   A final significant device used by Dickens to unify his numbers is his symbolic imagery. Perhaps nothing about *Bleak House* has been praised so widely as the first chapter, in which the central themes and symbolic images—the court, the fog, the darkness, and the cold—are set forth. With conscious artistry almost Shakespearean, Dickens repeated these themes and images in different numbers to make evident the inner similarities among events which at first seem quite unrelated. The images of the novel's two opening paragraphs—"implacable November weather," "mud in the streets," "smoke lowering," "soft black drizzle," "flakes of soot . . . as big as full-grown snow-flakes," "slipping and sliding," "crust upon crust of mud," "fog everywhere"—recur in the description of Chancery (No. I), Chesney Wold (Nos. I, II, IX, and XIII), the death of Krook (No. X), and the pursuit of Lady Dedlock (No. XVII and XVIII). The fog-mud-darkness-cold constellation of images in the first chapter has often been praised, but its many repetitions, which act to show the encrustations of human selfishness everywhere present in the other installments, have been undervalued.[24]

A few examples of one recurring image—fog—will demonstrate how Dickens permeated the separate numbers with repeated symbolic im-

agery.[25] We have already seen above how in chapter xxxii Dickens used
fog imagery to figure forth the death of Krook. But, as early as the
conclusion of the first installment, images of fog have been employed:
"The purblind day was feebly struggling with the *fog*, when I opened
my eyes to encounter those of a dirty-faced little spectre fixed upon me.
Peepy had scaled his crib, and crept down in his bedgown and cap, and
was so cold that his teeth were chattering as if he had cut them all"
(No. I, iv, 45; italics mine). The second installment opens with a similar
invocation of "implacable November weather": "Although the morning
was raw, and although the *fog* still seemed heavy—I say seemed, for the
windows were so encrusted with dirt, that they would have made Midsummer sunshine dim—I was sufficiently forewarned of the discomfort
within doors at that early hour" (No. II, v, 46; italics mine). To establish
a link between the two parts, Dickens has begun his second installment
with muted references to the fog (and the dirt and coldness) with which
he began and closed his first number.

Fog (in the presence of its first cousin mist) reappears, as we have
seen, in the chapter devoted to the death of Krook: "It is a close night,
though the damp cold is searching too; and there is a laggard *mist* a little
way up in the air" (No. X, xxxii, 444). Fog or mist again and again
envelops Chesney Wold in gloom: "All that prospect, which from the
terrace looked so near, has moved solemnly away, and changed . . . into
a distant phantom. Light *mists* arise" (No. XIII, xl, 564). Esther visits
the declining Richard on a morning when "the sea was heaving under a
thick white *fog*" (No. XIV, xlv, 618); four installments later Esther and
Bucket track Lady Dedlock through a day and night in which "the sleet
fell . . . unceasingly, a thick *mist* came on early, and . . . never rose or
lightened for a moment" (No. XVIII, lvii, 781); later "the *mist*, and the
sleet into which the snow has all resolved itself, are darker" (No. XVIII,
lviii, 795; italics mine throughout). These passages are not mere descriptions; they all use the symbolic imagery of the first chapter to suggest a
central theme in *Bleak House*—that selfishness, like fog, cuts man off
from his fellows. All these disparate events and descriptions, spread over
many installments, are brought together by the web of repeated images
which permeates the novel, and sustains its pattern of relationships.

— *4* —

In any novel divided into units the author must take care to prevent
the separate parts from becoming unrelated. Clearly in a novel in which
these units are individually published at monthly intervals the problems
of coherence are still greater than those in a story which appears seriatim.
Employing the five serial devices discussed above, Dickens sustained
continuity among his installments. By concluding each number with

suggestions of future actions, and reiterating principal images and symbols throughout the parts, Dickens prevented his installment units from falling into unrelated episodes. Moreover, by publishing *Bleak House* over a period of nineteen months, he gave his audience time to reflect on the novel as it appeared piece by piece, and thus to consider at length the truth of its picture of society. *Bleak House* was not presented as a transient best seller; it remained for months the topic of conversation among the reading public—time enough to make a deep impression.[26]

Each month a new part was published, presenting new clues and fresh mysteries which led the reader further into the fictional puzzle. Each eagerly-awaited number, to which the reader applied his ingenuity in tracing themes and symbols, rewarded him with an incremental comprehension of the novel. Anyone who takes the time to mark out the novel's monthly part divisions will be struck with the extraordinary skill the author used to parcel out the necessary hints and revelations, always enriching the reader's comprehension, yet always keeping up suspense by transferring his curiosity from one mystery to another.[27] As soon as the mystery of Esther's birth is cleared away in number IX, Dickens shifts the reader's interest to Tulkinghorn as he closes in on Lady Dedlock (climaxed in No. XIII). Tulkinghorn's death and the possibility that Lady Dedlock was the murderer follow (Nos. XV and XVI). The final exciting chase after Esther's mother (Nos. XVII and XVIII) insures the continuance of suspense through the penultimate part. The reader's interest thus never flags as he pursues mystery after mystery through the installments of *Bleak House*.

Yet the primary reason for arousing the reader's curiosity is not to pander to his desire for ever-greater thrills: Krook's death, like Milton's Sin and Death, is allegorical rather than sensational. Publishing the serial at monthly intervals permitted Dickens to arrange the plot so as to stimulate the reader's imagination. By stopping the installments at salient points and throwing out suggestions for future events, the author encouraged his readers to reflect on the novel's past actions, and to speculate about future ones. Mrs. Tillotson has suggested that serial publication fostered a "concreative" reciprocity between author and reader: monthly part-issue permitted an ease of response between author and audience which encouraged the readers to express themselves actively in the novelist's creativity.[28] Not only did "concreativity" facilitate the writer's expression, but it also, through the agency of the suspense which serialization engendered, secured the reader's imagination more firmly, and involved him more closely with the issues of the novel.

In *Bleak House* Dickens not only overcame the difficulties of publishing a unified narrative in monthly installments, but he learned furthermore to create a plot whose effect on the reader depends in part on its being serialized. Without the suspense which part-issue aroused, the reader would have been less encouraged to enter into the "concreation" of *Bleak House*. The "anatomy of society" and the detective story thus work hand in glove: over nineteen months the reader must put together these installment fragments in his imagination to form the elaborate pattern of interrelationships which stretch from the top to the bottom of society in the novel.

Fragment by fragment, month by month, the reader found his way into the novel's web of connections. Aided by the clues uncovered by the detectives in the various parts, and drawn on by the suspenseful interruptions basic to serial publication, the reader *himself* became the preeminent detective, for only he, unlike any of the novel's characters, came to understand how (to use Forster's words again) "people supposed to be far apart were so constantly elbowing each other; and to-morrow bore so close a resemblance to nothing half so much as to yesterday." [29]

Leonard Manheim

A TALE OF TWO CHARACTERS

A Study in Multiple Projection

DICKENS SCHOLARS have never been able to forgive *A Tale of Two Cities* its popularity—its very special kind of popularity. *Pickwick Papers* has survived the adulation of the special Pickwick cult; *David Copperfield* has survived the sentimental biography-hunting of the Dickensians; even *Great Expectations* may survive its selection as the Dickens work to be presented in "service courses" on the lower college level. But *A Tale of Two Cities* will never wholly live down the fact that it has received a kiss of death by its almost universal adoption as the Dickens work to be presented to secondary school students, usually during the tenth year of their formal education. Several factors have contributed to the persistence of the high-school syllabus-makers in prescribing the reading of *A Tale of Two Cities*. The first reason seems to be its compactness; it is not as long as most other Dickens works. In my own experience, it has been preferred even when *David Copperfield* was permitted as an alternative, purely because *David Copperfield* was so much longer. A second reason, which stems from the era when all novels were suspect, is the fact that *A Tale of Two Cities* is an historical novel, and the curse was considered removed from the "novel" because of the "history." But the factor which probably loomed largest in the minds of the syllabus-makers was the "purity" of *A Tale of Two Cities*. It is wholly without the taint of immorality; it seems to be practically free of sexuality. (Can the account of the rape of Madame Defarge's sister in Doctor Manette's secret narrative be called sexuality? It is easy enough to pass over it—it is so hazily referred to; and in any event, it is a story of an occurrence in a benighted foreign country and hence a horrible example of "foreign" morality.) There is no Little Em'ly, no Martha Endell. There is no Hetty Sorrel; indeed *Adam Bede* was never permitted to sully the adolescent mind. Silas Marner's Eppie had the advantage of having it both ways since she was legally legitimate but, for the purposes of the story, a bastard; the legal legitimacy was enough to satisfy the academic censor. Let it not be thought that I exaggerate; I speak from experience, and although there is no time or place here for a complete documentation of my conclusions, I submit that the criterion for high school reading is usually—or at any rate used to be—one of superficial absence of any "immoral" element. Yet it is ironically noteworthy that *A Tale of Two Cities,* on a less superficial level, is the product of a great sexual crisis in the author's life, an upheaval in his psychosexual pattern which has been but dimly comprehended. Perhaps it would be as well to recount once again the facts as they have been clarified by recent scholarship.

On 10 February, in 1851, Dickens wrote to Wills, his long-suffering editorial assistant on *Household Words,* asking Wills to play the part of a servant in the comedy *Not So Bad as We Seem,* a typical nineteenth-century play written by the prolific Bulwer Lytton for production by Dickens' semi-permanent company of amateur actors. Dickens hastened to assure Wills that he would be in good company—among talented literary amateur actors. He playfully assumed the character of Sairey Gamp:

> "Mrs. Harris," I says to her, "be not alarmed; not reg'lar play-actors, hammertoors."
> "Thank 'Evens," says Mrs. Harris, and bustiges into a flood of tears! [1]

The over-burdened Wills found it impossible to add participation in his principal's theatrical ventures to his other duties, and he politely declined the offer. A little while later, Dickens wrote to his friend Augustus Egg, scenic designer of many of the productions, asking him if he could induce Wilkie Collins to accept the role. Collins did accept and thus began the friendship with Dickens which was to last until the latter's death. There was nearly fifteen years' difference in age between the two; their temperaments were fundamentally dissimilar; yet the influence of Collins on every phase of the latter years of Dickens' life and work is most marked, and there was ample indication that he tended, as time went on, to usurp the confidential position formerly held exclusively by John Forster, to the no small annoyance of that worthy gentleman.

In Collins, Dickens found an admirable traveling companion, one who introduced him to phases of life at home and abroad with which he had formerly been familiar by hearsay only, one who was reasonably free from Victorian prejudices so dear to the heart of John Forster. In Collins he found an equally enthusiastic devotee of the theatre, a competent and thorough deviser of complex plots (frequently of a most melodramatic character). It was Collins who put together the melodrama *The Lighthouse,* with a highly emotional leading role which Dickens delighted to play. It was he who was entrusted with the task of dramatizing the very worst of the Dickens Christmas numbers, *No Thoroughfare,* for professional production; and it was he who concocted *The Frozen Deep,* that queer melodrama in which Dickens played his last performance on the amateur stage. This play opened at Tavistock House on the twentieth birthday of Dickens' oldest son. It was a most elaborate affair, with one set designed to represent a scene near the North Pole, "where the slightest and greatest things the eye beheld were equally taken from the books of the polar voyagers." It was repeated several times, one outstanding series of performances being given in Manchester. Dickens writes of it in his preface to *A Tale of Two Cities:*

> When I was acting, with my children and friends, in Mr. Wilkie Collins's drama of "The Frozen Deep," I first conceived the main idea of this story. A strong desire was upon me then, to embody it in my own person; and I traced out in my fancy, the state of mind of which it would necessitate the presentation to an observant spectator, with particular care and interest.
>
> As the idea became familiar to me, it gradually shaped itself into its present form. Throughout its execution, it has had complete possession of me; I have so far verified what is done and suffered in these pages, as that I have certainly done and suffered it all myself.[2]

Much of the idea of *The Frozen Deep* seems to have originated with Dickens himself rather than with Collins. It was Dickens who inserted the "comedy relief," Dickens who wrote the verse prologue which Forster spoke from behind the curtain before the opening, closing with these words:

> But, that the secrets of the vast Profound
> Within us, an exploring hand may sound,
> Testing the region of the ice-bound soul,
> Seeking the passage at its northern pole,
> Soft'ning the horrors of its wintry sleep,
> Melting the surface of that "Frozen Deep."[3]

The plot of the play whose hero Dickens so greatly longed to "embody in his own person" is worthy of being examined closely, when we consider how much it meant to him during his composition of *A Tale of Two Cities* and how clearly it constituted a turning point in his life.

> The first act makes us acquainted with four young ladies living in Devon, each of whom has a lover serving with a Polar expedition. Clara Burnham not only has her betrothed out in the icy regions, but the rejected lover who was sworn to kill him wherever and whenever they meet, though he does not even know the name of his rival. Clara, haunted by the fear that some mysterious influence may reveal them to each other, tells

her story to Lucy Crayford. As she does so, a crimson sunset
dies away to grey and Nurse Esther goes about the house mur-
muring of scenes that come to her from "the land o' ice and
snaw." She stands, as night falls, by the misty blue of the window,
describing to the young ladies her bloody vision from the Northern seas. Lucy Crayford shudders and calls for lights: Clara
Burnham swoons.

   The second act is set in the arctic regions. The stranded men
are in a hut deciding who is to go and seek relief. Frank Aldersley is chosen by lot, and when somebody else falls out, Richard
Wardour has to accompany him. Just before they start Wardour
discovers that Aldersley is his hated rival.

   The third act takes place in a cavern in Newfoundland. The
girls, smartly dressed in crinolines, their Scotch nurse, and some
members of the expedition are present, but neither Wardour nor
Aldersley. Presently a ragged maniac rushes in and is given food
and drink. He has escaped from an ice-floe but is not too demented to recognise and be recognised by Clara Burnham, who
suspects him of having murdered her Frank. As soon as he under-
stands this he goes off, returning a few minutes later with Aldersley in his arms to lay at Clara's feet. "Often," he gasps, "in supporting Aldersley through snow-drifts and on ice-floes have I been
tempted to leave him sleeping!" He has not done so and is now
exhausted to death.[4]

   Dickens played Wardour; and Collins, Aldersley. Purposely for the
"part," each of them grew a substantial beard which he kept in later life.
During the early private showings and at the special performance for the
Queen, the women's roles were played by lady amateurs. However, when
it was decided to repeat the play at Manchester for the benefit of the
late Douglass Jerrold's family, it became apparent that the size of the
house (it held three thousand spectators at one performance) would require the engagement of professionals for the women's roles. It was on
the recommendation of a friendly theatrical manager that Mrs. Ternan
and her two daughters, Maria and Ellen, were engaged for the production.
Mrs. Ternan played the Scottish nurse; Maria Ternan played the leading
role of Clara Burnham; and Ellen played one of the other girls, probably
Lucy. Now it must become at once apparent that the tale which pictures
Ellen in tears in the wings of the theatre, in agony over the scanty costume she was to wear in *The Frozen Deep* (!) must be apocryphal. As a
matter of fact, Dickens had known Ellen at least since the spring of 1857
when he had met her, really in tears in her dressing room because she
was to play the role of Hippomenes in Talfourd's *Atalanta,* a part in
which she might well be alarmed at having "to show too much leg." However, it was during the brief period of rehearsals at Tavistock House, with
Maria and Ellen rushing in and out of his study, Ellen perching on the
arm of his chair and turning soulful eyes upon him as he instructed her

in the interpretation of her role, that young love began to spring anew in the breast of the forty-five-year-old author. Collins was enthralled by Dickens' brilliance during the Manchester performances. "Dickens," he wrote, "surpassed himself. He literally electrified the audience." [5] And well he might, for the clock had turned back. He was once again the eighteen-year-old who was going to make his fortune as an actor in Covent Garden.

Aghast for a moment after the first emotional shock had passed, Dickens tried to run away from himself again, this time with Collins. The trip is the one described in their joint literary effort known as *The Lazy Tour of Two Idle Apprentices*. When it was over, the problem was solved and Dickens had cast Victorian morality to the winds and was an ardent suitor for the favors of the young lady. A word as to the choice between the two sisters. It was Maria whose acting ability had most impressed the critical director, and he wrote of her performance in the glowing emotional orgy of a letter to Miss Burdett-Coutts. Yet it was to Ellen that he was sexually attracted. After all, there are limits to the extensions of a real-life *Maria*. Two of them (Maria Beadnell and Mary Hogarth) had passed into agonizing oblivion. The Mary-figure, the virgin-mother, was still the dominant image, but a little disguise, a little displacement of the emotional tone was clearly needed—and the choice fell upon the sister-image, Ellen. After all, the Superego in the irrational Unconscious might be lulled into a sense of security by the pretense that it was to *Mary's sister* that he was still being "true"!

It was in such troubled days that *A Tale of Two Cities* was conceived and, for the most part, written. It was the work used to launch the new publication *All the Year Round,* which succeeded *Household Words* after Dickens' break with his former publishers, occasioned by his frantic desire to suppress the Ternan scandal. The whole work is impregnated with the spirit of the theatre. Its structure is dramatic and Dickens is reported to have sent proof sheets to Henri Regnier with a view toward immediate dramatization for the French theatre. The work has a complicated plot-structure which yet stands up better under analysis than any novel since *Barnaby Rudge,* with which it at once compels comparison. Like that former work, it is markedly deficient in humor. There seems to be no room in it for both the old comedy and also the new Collins-inspired melodrama. There is not even as much comedy in the new work as in *Barnaby Rudge,* the former novel of revolutionary days, for Miss Pross and Jerry Cruncher cannot bear even so much of the burden as was formerly shared by Miss Miggs and Sim Tappertit.

The compulsive quality of the writing of *A Tale of Two Cities* is revealed in the preface quoted as moment ago. Whenever we find an author stressing such compulsions, we can safely conclude that we are dealing with "repressed" inspiration from unconscious sources. The most striking effect upon the novel of the emotionally disturbed period which produced it lies in the Dr. Jekyll-Mr. Hyde aspect of its leading male character. The word "character" is used in the singular intentionally, for in *A Tale of Two Cities* Dickens developed even more fully than was usual for him the tendency to embody his own ideal of himself, his own Fantasy-Hero in two or more characters *(multiple projection)*. Charles Darnay and Sydney Carton are two plainly delineated faces of the same coin. Their names are extensions of a familiar pattern. The fortunate-unfortunate French nobleman bears his author's Christian name with a surname which uses the first initial of *Dickens* to bear out the fantasy of noble birth in disguise, since Charles is said to have assumed the name Darnay upon dropping the hated appellation Evrémonde, adapting his new surname from his mother's noble name of D'Aulnay, eliding the aristocratic *de* in deference to British taste. In the name Sydney Carton the trend is more hidden; yet it too is a simple cipher, easily susceptible of solution—as it is meant to be. The *Charles* element is transferred to the *Car-* syllable of the last name; in the first syllable of *Sidney,* we have the same softening of *Dick-* which may be noticed in the name *Jarndyce* (pronounced Jahn-diss) in *Bleak House,* here reversed (another reversal) to form Syd. The implication is apparent. Both Carton and Darnay are Dickens (not literally, of course, but in fantasy); the point is further stressed by the fortuitous fact that they look alike.

Consider this last point for a moment. Carton, during Darnay's English trial for treason, points out the resemblance between himself and Darnay to his senior counsel, Mr. Stryver, who uses it (so it is said) to discredit the testimony of a witness, a witness who had testified that he had seen the defendant Darnay descend by stealth from the Dover mail in order to spy upon a garrison and dockyard, admitting that he had never seen the accused upon any other occasion.

> "You say again you are quite sure that it *was* the prisoner?" The witness was quite sure.
>
> "Did you ever see anybody very like the prisoner?" Not so like (the witness said), as that he could be mistaken.
>
> "Look well upon that gentleman, my learned friend there," pointing to him who had tossed the paper over, "and then look well upon the prisoner. How say you? Are they very like each other?"
>
> Allowing for my learned friend's appearance being careless and slovenly, if not debauched, they were sufficiently like each other to surprise, not only the witness, but everybody present, when they were thus brought into comparison. My Lord being prayed to bid my learned friend lay aside his wig, and giving no very gracious consent, the likeness became much more remarkable. My Lord inquired of Mr. Stryver, (the prisoner's counsel), whether they were next to try Mr. Carton (name of my learned

friend) for treason? But Mr. Stryver replied to my Lord, no; but he would ask the witness to tell him whether what happened once, might happen twice; whether he would have been so confident, having seen it; and more. The upshot of which was, to smash this witness like a crockery vessel, and shiver his part of the case to useless lumber. (II, iii)

Now any competent trial lawyer will recognize that this is very bad cross-examination. The fact that Mr. Darnay resembled Mr. Carton does not really impeach the credibility of the witness' testimony, unless, as the presiding judge suggested, it had been counsel's intention to show that Mr. Carton was also in the neighborhood at the time. An identification by a witness may be impeached far better by his inability to pick the prisoner out of a group of people (a "line-up," for example) who do *not* in any way resemble one another. Yet for Dickens it fits into a set pattern. Darnay is first accused of treason in England (treachery, betrayal of his country, let it be remembered—parallel in fantasy-life to a man's "betrayal" of his wife). He is saved by his *alter ego,* Carton. Seventeen years later the accusation of betrayal is renewed before another, "foreign" tribunal—foreign both geographically and in the standard of loyalty which it imposes. Now Carton is impotent. He cannot plead in the new court. He cannot answer the fatal and misguided denunciation of the destructive father-image, the Law. But he can assume the place of his double and die in his stead, making a propitiatory sacrifice of himself by which he clears and saves the innocent person of the favored hero. Never was there a more felicitously contrived scapegoat pattern.

All of the virtue which would make the favored lover worthy of his virgin is embodied in Jekyll-Darnay. All of the vice—gloomy, Byronic, objectively unmotivated and unexplained—is concentrated in Hyde-Carton (who, of course, never gets the girl), for whom it is purged away by his "full, perfect, and sufficient sacrifice," not for the sins of the whole world, to be sure, but for the sinful love of one Charles Dickens for one Ellen Ternan. Even the self-satisfying sense of resurrection, an "undying" after death, is accomplished by the final picture of Sydney's mind just before the guillotine falls, envisaging the rosy future which is to follow for all concerned, even his own rebirth in his child-namesake. How can Ellen hesitate now? Her middle-aged lover is not only the most fascinating of men; he is also (by a vicarious propitiatory sacrifice) the most guiltless, and she will share that pristine state of innocence with him forever!

Lucie is basically only one more in the line of Dickensian virgin-heroines whom the critic Edwin Pugh felicitously called "feminanities."[6] Yet, as Professor Edgar Johnson clearly saw, there was a subtle distinction.

Lucie . . . is given hardly any individual traits at all, although her appearance, as Dickens describes it, is like that of Ellen, "a short, slight, pretty figure, a quantity of golden hair, a pair of blue eyes," and it may be that her one unique physical characteristic was drawn from Ellen too: "a forehead with a singular capacity (remembering how young and smooth it was), of lifting and knitting itself into an expression that was not quite one of perplexity, or wonder, or alarm, though it included all the four expressions." . . . The fact that Lucie and Dr. Manette at the time of his release from the Bastille are of almost the same age as Ellen and Dickens does not mean that the Doctor's feeling for his daughter is the emotion Dickens felt for the pretty, blue-eyed actress, although the two merge perhaps in his fervent declaration [in his letter protesting the scandal, a letter which he "never meant to be published"] that he knows Ellen to be as "innocent and pure, and as good as my own dear daughter." [7]

But Lucie fails to fit into the pattern of the unattainable dream-virgin of the earlier novels in at least one other respect. Most of Dickens' earlier heroine-ideals do not marry until the last-chapter summation of the "lived-happily-ever-after" pattern. Lucie is married, happily married, through much of the book. She maintains a household for her husband and her father, and she finds room for compassion, if not love, for the erring Carton. What is more, she has children, two of them. Yet she seems never to grow older. She was seventeen in 1775; she is, to all intents and purposes, seventeen in 1792. In the interim she has allegedly given birth to two Dickens-ideal infants, two of the most sickening little poppets we could possibly expect from one who, despite his experience as the father of ten children, still sought desperately to re-create infancy and childhood in an image which would affirm his own concept of unworldly innocence. Let the reader take a firm grip on himself and read the dying words of the little son of Charles and Lucie Darnay, who died in early childhood for no other reason, it must seem, than to give the author another opportunity to wallow in bathos.

> "Dear papa and mamma, I am very sorry to leave you both, and to leave my pretty sister; but I am called, and I must go!"
> . . . .
> "Poor Carton! Kiss him for me!" (II, xxi)

Poor Carton, indeed! Poor Dickens! Little Lucie is not much better, for in Paris, after her father's condemnation, when her mother is mercifully unconscious and unaware of Carton's presence, she cries out in sweet childish innocence to friend Sydney:

> "Oh, Carton, Carton, dear Carton! . . Now that you have come, I think you will do something to help mamma, something to save papa! Oh, look at her, dear Carton! Can you, of all the people who love her bear to see her so?" (III, xi)

Out of the mouths of babes! At this point there is obviously nothing for Sydney to do but head straight for the nearest guillotine.

But Sydney is not to be left wholly without his own dream girl. Just as the purified Darnay is permitted to live out his life with the "attained" (and untainted) Lucie, so the dying Carton is accompanied to his execution by the virgin-victim, the innocent seamstress whom he solaces and strengthens until the final moments of their love-death, although her first glance had revealed that he was not the man Darnay whom she had previously admired.

Since the pattern of attainability is characteristic of the primary "virgin" in this novel, the figure of the *decayed virgin,* the older freak and enemy, is markedly absent from it. A few novels back, Dickens had had such characters in the immortal Sairey Gamp (*Martin Chuzzlewit*) and Mrs. Pipchin (*Dombey and Son*) ; he was to have the most horrifying of them all in his very next novel (*Great Expectations*) in the person of Miss Havisham. Here Miss Pross, although she has many of the elements of the "freak" in the best Dickensian tradition, is all benevolence, with her red-headed queerness overshadowed by her devoted love and affectionate care of the virgin-queen to whom she is a substitute mother, with no flaw except her unconquerable belief in the virtue and nobility of her erring brother Solomon. Just as she, the benevolent mother-protectress, is herself merely an aged virgin, so her counterpart and rival is the childless wife (also a devoted, albeit vindictive, sister), Thérèse Defarge. The word *rival* is used advisedly, for while there is no sign of overt rivalry between the two during nine-tenths of the novel, Dickens goes out of his way to bring them face to face at the end. He strains all of his plot structure to bring Mme. Defarge to the Manette dwelling on the day of the execution to have Miss Pross left there alone to face her. Then a melodramatic physical encounter ensues between the two women, neither of whom can, in any sense of the words, speak the other's language. Lucie's bad angel falls dead (accidentally, of course, by her own hand), but the good angel is not unscathed, and if, in her later life, her "queerness" is augmented by the ear-trumpet which she will no doubt use, yet all will know that she came by this crowning, though no doubt humorous, affliction in a good cause.

Although the category of mother-figure is limited, there is no lack of father-counterparts, for the law-as-father has become blended with the fear of condemnation by society, which thereby also becomes a symbolic father-figure. Society and its moral sanctions constitute the only fly in the ointment of adolescent happiness in a sinful love. We have noted that, as a propitiatory gesture, Charles's wicked father-enemy is not his father (as he well might have been) but his thoroughly aristocratic twin-uncle, who, being French, is more villainous than any British father-enemy might

have been. Mr. Stryver, in his vampirish relationship with Carton, is
another figure of the worthless "father" who sucks the blood of his
talented "son." And since Dickens almost always maintains a balance
between evil and virtuous figures in all categories, we have, on the
benevolent side, Mr. Lorry, another unmarried "father," the only living
figure in the gallery of scarecrows who inhabit Tellson's Bank. Midway
between the two classes is the hagridden Ernest Defarge, whose every
attempt at benevolence is thwarted by his vengeful wife and her abettors,
the allegorically named *Vengeance* and the members of the society of
Jacques. This last-named group produces one brilliantly sketched
psychopath, the sadistic, finger-chewing Jacques Three.

The one remaining father-figure is the most interesting, complex, and
well-developed character in the whole novel, Dr. Manette. Since he could
not have been much more than twenty-five years old when he was torn
from his newly-wedded English wife to be imprisoned in the Bastille for
nearly eighteen years, he must have been less than forty-five when we
first met him in Defarge's garret. And Dickens, let it be remembered, was
forty-five when he wrote of him. Here is his portrait:

> A broad ray of light fell into the garret, and showed the
> workman, with an unfinished shoe upon his lap, pausing in his
> labour. His few common tools and various scraps of leather were
> at his feet and on his bench. He had a white beard, raggedly cut,
> but not very long, a hollow face, and exceedingly bright eyes. The
> hollowness and thinness of his face would have caused them to
> look large, under his yet dark eyebrows and his confused white
> hair, though they had been really otherwise; but they were
> naturally large, and looked unnaturally so. His yellow rags of
> shirt lay open at the throat, and showed his body to be withered
> and worn. (I, vi)

Of course the appearance of great age in a middle-age man is rationally
explained by the suffering entailed by his long, unjust imprisonment. Yet,
nearly eighteen years later (the repetition of the number is meaningful),
when he has become the unwitting agent of his son-in-law's destruction
and has been unable to use his special influence to procure Charles' release, he is pictured as a decayed mass of senility.

> "Who goes here? Whom have we within? Papers!"
> The papers are handed out and read.
> "Alexandre Manette. Physician. French. Which is he?"
> This is he; this helpless, inarticulately murmuring, wander-
> ing old man pointed out.
> "Apparently the Citizen-Doctor is not in his right mind? The
> Revolution-fever will have been too much for him?"
> Greatly too much for him. (III, xiii)

Carton envisions his complete recovery, but we have some difficulty in believing it.

In the interim, however, he is pictured as a stalwart, middle-aged medical practitioner. His sufferings have caused a period of amnesia, with occasional flashes of painful recollection, as in the scene in which he hears of the discovery of a stone marked D I G in a cell in the Tower of London. We never know, by the way, whether his recollection at this moment is complete and whether he has, even furtively, any recall of the existence of the document of denunciation found by M. Defarge. The aspects of conscious and repressed memory are here handled with great skill by Dickens. Generally, his amnesia is reciprocal; he cannot recall his normal life during the period of relapse, or vice versa, especially when his relapses are triggered by events and disclosures which bring up memories of his old wrongs. His reversion to shoemaking for a short time after Charles proposes marriage to Lucie and again for a longer time following Lucie's marriage and Charles's final revelation of his long-suspected identity foreshadow the great disclosure which is to make him the unwitting aggressor against the happiness of his loving and beloved daughter.

When we consider Dr. Manette's conduct, however, we find that, whether Dickens consciously intended it to be or not, the doctor of Beauvais is a good psychiatrist, at least in the handling of his own illness. His shoemaking is superficially pictured as a symptom of mental regression and decay, but in its inception it must have been a sign of rebellion against madness rather than a symptom thereof. He relates that he begged for permission to make shoes as a means of diverting his mind from its unendurable suffering. Shoemaking, truly an example of vocational therapy, was the only contact with reality that his distracted mind, otherwise cut off from reality, possessed. It was, therefore, a means of bringing about his recovery. Lucie fears the shoemaking, but she realizes that her loving presence, coupled with the availability, if needed, of the vocational contact with reality, will serve to draw him back to normal adjustment. It would seem, then, that the act of Mr. Lorry and Miss Pross, carried on furtively and guiltily, of destroying his shoemaker's bench and tools after his spontaneous recovery from the attack following Lucie's wedding, was a great error, an error against which the doctor, giving an opinion in the anonymous presentation of his own case by Mr. Lorry, strongly advises. For when he once again falls into a state of amnesia and confusion, after the realization of the damage he has done to Charles and his impotence to remedy that damage, he calls for his bench and tools, but they are no longer to be had, and he huddles in a corner of the coach leaving Paris, a pitiful picture of mental decay from which we can see no hope of recovery despite the optimistic vision of Carton's last moments.

The basic aim of this paper has been, of course, psychological interpretation; but the psychological critic has sometimes been accused of neglecting the critical function of evaluation, and possibly a few concluding words might be added on that score.

In a lecture on criticism given at Harvard in 1947, E. M. Forster distinguished beautifully between the function and method of creation and the function and method of criticism.

> What about the creative state? In it a man is taken out of himself. He lets down, as it were, a bucket into the unconscious and draws up something which is normally beyond his reach. He mixes this thing with his normal experience and out of the mixture he makes a work of art. . . . After this glance at the creative state, let us look at the critical. The critical state has many merits, and employs some of the highest and subtlest faculties of man. But it is grotesquely remote from the state responsible for the works it affects to expound. It does not let buckets down into the unconscious. It does not conceive in sleep or know what it has said after it has said it. Think before you speak, is criticism's motto; speak before you think is creation's. Nor is criticism disconcerted by people arriving from Porlock; in fact it sometimes comes from Porlock itself.[8]

What Mr. Forster has set forth can best be understood in the light of the road which has been taken by psychological, particularly psychoanalytic, criticism in the more than twenty years which have elapsed since the delivery of that lecture in 1947. The psychoanalytic critic of today would like to think that he comes from Xanadu rather than Porlock. He cannot claim that he consistently writes before he thinks, but his thinking is to some extent based on material which the bucket lowered into the depths has brought up for him.

What can he say about the permanent literary value of the work which he is discussing? He cannot of course undertake to give any absolute final judgment; it will hardly be suitable for him to do what so many academic critics do, that is, to report the state of critical opinion in the "in-group" that usually passes critical judgment in academic circles. I have suggested elsewhere that the function of the psychoanalytic critic in evaluation is to prognosticate rather than to judge. I can do no better than to quote here my preferred authority, Norman Holland:

> Saying a literary work is "good," then, from the point of view of our model, is predicting that it will pass the test of time; that it "can please many and please long"; that it is a widely satisfying form of play; or, more formally, that it embodies a fantasy with a power to disturb many readers over a long period of time and, built in, a defensive maneuver that will enable those readers to master the poem's disturbance.[9]

A Tale of Two Cities does, it seems to me, give every indication, even apart from its past history, that it "can please many and please long." Its use of the dynamic scapegoat pattern with the employment of the pattern of multiple projection, which it has been my aim to point out in this essay, does indeed embody a fantasy, a fantasy which was disturbing to Dickens and is still undoubtedly disturbing to many readers, and has used that device of multiple projection as the defensive maneuver that enables readers to master that disturbance. In that sense, there seems to be little doubt about the continuance of the perennial popularity of this often maligned but still frequently read novel of Dickens' later period.

But all of that is really by the way. Criticism of the kind which I have attempted is designed to furnish information rather than critical judgment, even of a prognostic nature; it is the kind of criticism which was described by Arthur Symons in his introduction to the *Biographia Literaria* of Coleridge:

> The aim of criticism is to distinguish what is essential in the work of a writer. It is the delight of the critic to praise; but praise is scarcely part of his duty. . . . What we ask of him is that he should find out for us more than we can find out for ourselves.

Robert Barnard

IMAGERY AND THEME IN
GREAT EXPECTATIONS

THE ALL-PERVASIVE theme of *Great Expectations* is not money, but guilt—guilt imposed, guilt assumed, guilt transcended. The ambiguities and implications of this theme have been most persuasively analyzed by Dorothy Van Ghent.[1] The second major theme, to my mind, is that of perverse—usually parasitic—relationships, and this theme embraces the portrayal of the corrupting power of wealth which occupies so much of the story on its literal level. While these two themes represent the moral quicksands in which Pip lets himself be entrapped, the third major theme, Christian love and "true fatherhood," suggests the means by which he, and not he alone, may be redeemed.

It has been commonly recognized that, with the possible exception of the prison, *Great Expectations* contains no all-informing symbol such as the fog in *Bleak House* or the river in *Our Mutual Friend*. John H. Hagan, Jr.'s suggestion that the marshes and the graveyard are comparable symbols is not a convincing one.[2] Nevertheless I wish to suggest in this essay that by a series of reiterated images and motifs Dickens adds new dimensions to the themes adumbrated above, in particular throwing a cloak of ambiguity over the question of guilt and innocence by his use of images connected with crime and prison, and illuminating the nature of the human relationships in the novel by the use of the animal imagery which pervades the whole book.

It becomes clear through a variety of subtle means in the early chapters of *Great Expectations* that the young Pip soaks up guilt like a sponge. From the moment he knows he has to rob the larder, everything around him takes on an accusatory or revengeful air. The very coals in the household fire seem to him "avenging," he dreams of pirates who summon him to be hanged, the boards on the staircase cry "Stop thief," the cattle (especially one with a clerical air) accuse him, and even the gates and dykes run at him as if they were pursuers (8–14). The whole picture of a guilty and terrified childish mind is remarkably vivid, so much so that the reader is never tempted to stop and ask himself whether the depravity Pip feels in himself is commensurate with the offense he has committed. He has deprived himself of a piece of bread and butter, and stolen random items of food from the family larder—no very enormous sins in the mind of the average child. Even granting the distorted vision of a terrified boy, it would seem that Pip is exaggerating his crime.

But of course the guilt he feels on the score of this minor theft is only part of a larger guilt—congenital, as it were, since it seems to have been generally regarded as criminally stupid in him to allow himself to be born at all—fostered in him by his sister, his sister's friends, and his surroundings. To Mrs. Joe he is not just a burden; he is a delinquent, to be treated as such. As a suitable topic for conversation during that most appallingly unmerry Christmas dinner which follows the second meeting with the convict, she regales the company with a catalogue of "all the illnesses I had been guilty of, and all the acts of sleeplessness I had committed, and all the high places I had tumbled from, and all the low places I had tumbled into, and all the injuries I had done myself, and all the times she had wished me in my grave, and I had contumaciously refused to go there" (24). When, after the convict-hunt, he is sleepy, she removes him as "a slumbrous offence to the company's eyesight" (38). The very food she allows him is given "a mortifying and penitential character" (49). The rest of the company follows suit. It is Pip's misfortune, both in childhood and in adulthood, to be brought into contact with overbearing characters whose most usual method of conducting a conversation is inquisitorial. His position vis-à-vis Pumblechook and Jaggers is at best that of a slippery witness, at worst that of a criminal in the dock. Whether it is Pumblechook sticking the point of the conversation into him as if he were "an unfortunate little bull in a Spanish arena" (22), or Jaggers, gnawing his forefinger and throwing it at him, Pip's position is as abject as that of any nineteenth-century delinquent, before the court on a trivial but capital charge.

The notion that Pip's fallen condition requires constant repentance and moral "touching up" is metaphorically expressed through the clothes he is forced into. They, like his diet, are of a "penitential" character:

> As to me, I think my sister must have had some general idea that I was a young offender whom an Accoucheur Policeman had taken up (on my birthday) and delivered over to her, to be dealt with according to the outraged majesty of the law. I was always treated as though I had insisted on being born in opposition to the dictates of reason, religion, and morality, and against the dissuading arguments of my best friends. Even when I was taken to

have a new suit of clothes, the tailor had orders to make them
like a kind of Reformatory, and on no account to let me have the
free use of my limbs. (20)

The intensive concentration on Pip's feelings of guilt and delin-
quency culminate in the extraordinary suggestion that he himself is in
some way responsible for the attack on his sister. Orlick, the real attacker,
puts it bluntly during the scene in the sluice-house by the lime kiln:
"It was you as did for your shrew sister." The more conventional Pip of
those days replies: "It was you, villain" (404). The younger Pip would
have had a more ambiguous reaction. The attack occurs after two scenes in
which the imaginary guilt is very obviously laid on Pip's shoulders. First
we have the scene where he is "bound" to Joe, and treated as a criminal
by court, family, and by-standers alike—especially by Pumblechook, who
held him "as if we had looked in on our way to the scaffold" (98). Then
the reading of *George Barnwell* fixes on him, in his own eyes as well as
Wopsle's and Pumblechook's, the role of ungrateful and murderous ap-
prentice. The feeling that he had "had some hand in the attack
upon my sister" (113) is intensified when the weapon is found to be
the convict's leg-iron, the symbol of Pip's "criminal" connection with
the convict.

In all these ways, some with comic overtones, some completely serious, a degree of uncertainty is given to the question of guilt and innocence
in this novel. With the exception of Joe, who is still in a paradisaic
state of grace and innocence, the guilt of one character tinges the other
characters, just as the moral regeneration of one character tinges the
others. Thus all the characters participate in the fallen state of the others,
and participate in their redemption too. Sin and crime are complex,
both in their causes and in their consequences. In this novel the involved
coincidences and connections, the gradual revelation of past wrongs which
provide guilty links between disparate characters—in short the creaky
machinery of a Dickens novel, so clumsily handled in *Little Dorrit,* for
example—have an artistic purpose which totally justifies them. Magwitch,
Miss Havisham, Pip, and Estella are connected by chains of guilt and
corruption, and their roles as betrayers and betrayed, corruptors and
corrupted, are deliberately allowed to become ambiguous. Miss Havisham,
betrayed by Magwitch's associate, herself corrupts both Pip and Estella;
Pip's childish pity for the convict starts a process of regeneration in him
which itself contributes materially to the process of corruption in Pip.
Guilt is infectious: Jaggers compulsively washes it off with scented soap;
Pip feels contaminated by Newgate; when Magwitch is spied on after his
return, it is Pip who gets the "haunting idea" (360) of being watched, and
who feels that, if the convict is caught, he, Pip, will in some way be his
murderer. In this matter of guilt and crime the characters are members
one of another.

"Mr. Carker in His Hour of Triumph"

(Michael Steig, "Iconography of Sexual Conflict in *Dombey and Son*")

"ANOTHER WEDDING"
(Michael Steig, "Iconography of Sexual Conflict in *Dombey and Son*")

This fact, of course, explains why Newgate Prison has so often been felt by readers to have an importance in the novel quite incommensurate with the space devoted to it. Corruption spreads outwards from there, and almost all the major characters are affected by that corruption. In addition, a real prison is necessary to reinforce the many "images" of prison in the novel. Prison is no mere "overspill" theme from Dickens' previous novels; it is an inevitable concomitant of the main theme. Miss Havisham's crazy self-immolation is no mere repetition with variations of Mrs. Clennam's grim voluntary imprisonment in *Little Dorrit;* it is a still more powerful symbol of man's propensity to cherish his emotional wounds, distort them to mere theatricality, use them as an excuse to pervert others. In all the scenes involving Satis House, strong emphasis is placed on keys, bars, chains, and blocked windows. And throughout the novel the windows of rooms Pip is in give no view of the world outside: they are shuttered, dirty, damp, "patched like a broken head" (154). One comes down "like a guillotine" and nearly beheads him as he tries to look through (163). Everywhere he goes Pip feels shut in, "caged and threatened" as he describes himself in the little causeway inn on the Thames (419). Innocence provides no escape from the prisons; indeed, the only way Wemmick can keep his innocence free from the contamination of Newgate is by shutting himself off from the world in his miniature castle at Walworth. Prisons, then, permeate the book, though not quite so completely as in *Little Dorrit.*

And, unlike *Little Dorrit,* the novel is also saturated with other aspects of punishment and legal repression, used symbolically. For example, Pip's "guilty" connection with the convict leads to his metaphorically bearing his leg-iron as well. The bread and butter he secretes becomes a "load on my leg," and that "made me think . . . of the man with the load on *his* leg" (11). The cold morning earth rivets itself to the young Pip's feet "as iron was riveted to the leg of the man" (14). The convict, and his messenger at the Jolly Bargemen who "rubs his leg" (70), never appear but that we are reminded again of the iron and the associations it has for Pip.

Chains, too, pervade the novel: on a literal level, obviously enough, on the door of Satis House and attached to Jaggers' watch, sign of his mastery of the underworld characters he deals with. The symbolic use is more interesting. In a Dickens novel we usually have a symbol of "destiny," the complex interweaving of people, events, and past actions which provides the plot of the novel and makes the characters what they are. Often this symbol is quite a conventional one: in *Little Dorrit* it is a road; in this novel we have the river and the ships on it, which are several times identified with Miss Havisham and Pip's delusions concerning his expectations from her (120, 103, 307). But Pip's real destiny is connected with a chain:

Think for a moment of the long chain of iron or gold, of thorns
or flowers, that would never have bound you, but for the formation of the first link on one memorable day. (67)

The significance of the symbol becomes more explicit when Magwitch returns. Now he is no longer a man, to be pitied, but an object: "what I was
chained to" (313). When Pip comes to contemplate the realities of his
situation, as opposed to the rosy vision of a calm sea and prosperous voyage with which he had been deluding himself, he realizes that Magwitch
has been "loading me with his wretched gold and silver chains" (307).

Similarly the "traps" which have sealed Magwitch's destiny catch
Pip as well. The traps are set both by the law and Compeyson. Early in
the novel the convicts are described as game "trapped in a circle" (28);
Compeyson's criminal activities involve the entrapping of others: "All
sorts of traps as Compeyson could set with his hand and keep his legs out
of . . . was Compeyson's business" (330). Magwitch sees these traps as
an occupational hazard of his kind: "I'm an old bird now, as had dared
all manner of traps since he was fledged" (315). Pip is less adept at
keeping out of them; indeed, he makes his own. Jaggers is compared to
a man who sets a trap—"Suddenly—click—you're caught" (188)—and
Pip is a victim of his legalistic equivocations. The sluice-house is described
as a trap, which indeed it is, set by Orlick. But his delusions concerning
Estella are at least partly of his own construction: "You made your own
snares," says Miss Havisham (341).

Perhaps the most subtle way Dickens suggests the transference of guilt
from one character to another is by his use of the image of the dog. In
chapter iii, while Pip, with the pity for his desolation which is to have
such momentous consequences, is watching the convict eating the food he
has brought him, a comparison occurs to his mind which is to reverberate
through the novel:

> I had often watched a large dog of ours eating his food; and I now
> noticed a decided similarity betwen the dog's way of eating, and
> the man's. The man took strong sharp sudden bites, just like the
> dog. He swallowed, or rather snapped up, every mouthful, too
> soon and too fast; and he looked sideways here and there while
> he ate, as if he thought there was danger in every direction of
> somebody's coming to take the pie away. He was altogether too
> unsettled in his mind over it, to appreciate it comfortably, I
> thought, or to have anybody to dine with him, without making
> a chop with his jaws at the visitor. In all of which particulars he
> was very like the dog. (16)

It is a comparison which has been hinted at on the convict's first appearance in the churchyard—"a man . . . who limped and shivered, and glared
and growled" (2)—and which is maintained throughout the early chap-

ters in which he appears. The soldiers growl at the captured pair "as if to dogs" (36), as Pip is to remember when he travels home from London in the company of the two other convicts. It is, indeed, an identification which Magwitch himself accepts, using it as a description of himself only less frequently than his favorite "warmint." When he hears of the existence of the escaped convict Compeyson he vows to "pull him down like a bloodhound" (18). When he reappears to reveal to Pip the source of his expectations, he refers to himself as "that there hunted dunghill dog wot you kep life in" (304). At this time, in spite of his resolution to keep "a genteel muzzle on," he disgusts Pip not only by his low talk, but by his eating:

> He ate in a ravenous way that was very disagreeable, and all his actions were uncouth, noisy and greedy. Some of his teeth had failed him since I saw him eat on the marshes, and as he turned his food in his mouth, and turned his head sideways to bring his strongest fangs to bear upon it, he looked terribly like a hungry old dog. (312)

Though the novel is full of animal imagery, the identification of the convict with a dog, by implication a miserable, starved cur, is interesting because no other character, except perhaps Pumblechook, is so surely and continuously identified with any one species. The comparison is not a particularly surprising or unusual one, but what makes it especially significant is that it spills over onto the young Pip. The convict himself calls him "young dog" (2) and "fierce young hound" (16), and this last phrase is remembered with anguish by Pip when he fears that the convict will imagine it was he who betrayed him. But it is later in the book, when Pip himself is in the position of the despised outcast, that the comparison comes through most clearly. Curiously enough, it comes in a scene in which he is being fed:

> She came back, with some bread and meat and a little mug of beer. She put the mug down on the stones of the yard, and gave me the bread and meat without looking at me, as insolently as if I were a dog in disgrace. I was so humiliated, hurt, spurned, offended, angry, sorry—I cannot hit the right name for the smart —God knows what its name was—that tears started to my eyes. (57)

It is through his treatment by Estella, so different from the spirit in which he himself watched the convict, that he comes to find himself in the position of the hunted convict whom he had feared and compassionated: a spurned outcast, despised, almost beneath contempt, his humanity degraded or denied, reduced to the level of a beast.

It is through the use of this image that we see most clearly that, as

Pip takes over the same metaphor as the convict, he assumes his share in his guilt and emotionally comprehends his position in society. The child can both pity the convict and put himself imaginatively in his position. The young man with "expectations" and a horror of crime can do neither, which makes doubly ironical Magwitch's part in bringing about this change in character.

The emotional lives of these characters who share guilt and share redemption are lived on a fairly basic level, and it is appropriate that the images which describe them should be drawn so frequently from the animal world. In *Little Dorrit,* where the action takes place on a more sophisticated social plane and where the level of emotion is consistently low, the characters are most often compared to inanimate things—buildings, vehicles, pieces of machinery. Here they are compared to dogs, horses, spiders, snakes. So persistent is the imagery that hardly a character escapes identification with an animal; most of them are compared, at one time or another, to a variety of species, for in this book the emotions are primitive, raw, and barely under control. Life is a Darwinian struggle for survival and supremacy.

There is no carefully worked-out scheme to be traced in this imagery. The characters are not given specific animal identifications or roles to play, and the novel does not become a neatly-planned bestiary. The value of the imagery is mainly in its suggestion of strong, basic passions, of life lived at a less than human level. Nevertheless, certain loose patterns do emerge. For example, in the earlier parts of the novel, Pip and Joe, as befits their childish and dependent condition, are likely to be compared to domestic animals—horses, pigs, lambs, and so forth—just as later the Pocket children are compared to a flock of sheep. Apart from the consistent identification of Magwitch with a cur, the comparison most usually used for the convicts—both the pair on the marshes and the pair on the coach—is with "wild beasts" (32) and "lower animals" (214), with the hulks as a "wicked Noah's ark" (36) to imprison them in. Like most of the images and objects associated with them, this rubs off onto Pip, especially in scenes of violence. After the fight with Herbert he regards himself as a "savage young wolf or other wild beast" (86), and much later in the book he is consistently addressed as such by Orlick in the melodramatic scene in the sluice-house: "Now, wolf, . . . afore I kill you like any other beast . . ." (404) and so on. All these patterns are suggestive, but by no means rigid. Perhaps the most interesting of these fairly consistent comparisons is the association of Satis House with insects and repulsive animals. The association is made most explicitly when Pip first sees the decayed splendor of Miss Havisham's bridal feast:

> It was spacious, and I dare say had once been handsome, but every discernible thing in it was covered with dust and mould,

and dropping to pieces. The most prominent object was a long table with a table-cloth spread on it, as if a feast had been in preparation when the house and the clocks all stopped together. An épergne or centre-piece of some kind was in the middle of this cloth; it was so heavily overhung with cobwebs that its form was quite indistinguishable; and, as I looked along the yellow expanse out of which I remember its seeming to grow, like a black fungus, I saw speckled-legged spiders with blotchy bodies running home to it, as if some circumstance of the greatest public importance had just transpired in the spider community.

I heard mice too, rattling behind the panels, as if the same occurrence were important to their interests. But the blackbeetles took no notice of the agitation, and groped about the hearth in a ponderous, elderly way, as if they were short-sighted and hard of hearing, and not on terms with one another. (78)

The description of the beetles in human terms completes the intentional confusion in this novel between things human and things animal.

No scene at Satis House is complete without a reference back to the mice, beetles, and spiders, until the rottenness and the insects are finally disturbed by Pip's attempt to save Miss Havisham by dragging the great cloth from the table—the first generous action in this house for a generation. In the earlier stages of his fortune, Pip has seen his delusions confirmed in "the crawlings of the spiders on the cloth, in the tracks of the mice, . . . the gropings and pausings of the beetles" (289), but to him the insects and rot signify little more than wealth unused, and future glory promised him:

She reserved it for me to restore the desolate house, admit the sunshine into the dark rooms, set the clocks a going and the cold hearths a blazing, tear down the cobwebs, destroy the vermin—in short, do all the shining deeds of the young Knight of romance, and marry the Princess. (219)

In fact the insects are symbolic of the repulsive desires and ambitions nurtured by the psychopathic woman who has laid waste the house. The effects of her moral and mental sickness spread outwards, and the insect imagery in the novel spreads wherever the influence of Satis House is felt. For example, we can guess that Bentley Drummle is to be connected with this aspect of Pip's life by his nickname of "The Spider." It is not a comparison that would come readily to mind for such a heavy, dull, brutal character—the comparison of him with "some uncomfortable amphibious creature" (192) seems to suit him better—but Dickens makes it appropriate by his elaborations on the resemblance: he is described as a "blotchy, sprawly, sulky fellow" (200); his victory with Estella is ascribed to the "patience of his tribe" since he "outwatched many brighter insects,

and would often uncoil himself and drop at the right nick of time" (295).
Estella's other suitors are, of course, moths around a candle.

Among the first fruits of what Pip believes to be Miss Havisham's
generosity is residence at Barnard's Inn, described throughout in terms
reminiscent of Satis House, and particularly notable for "dry rot and wet
rot and all the silent rots that rot in neglected roof and cellar—rot of rat
and mouse and bug and coaching stables near at hand besides." [3] And
again the insidious influence of Newgate Prison, whose connection with
Satis House is mysteriously yet clearly suggested throughout the book, is
conceived as a "cobweb" from which it is impossible totally to extricate
oneself.

The rank nature of Miss Havisham's mind and ambitions, and the
repulsive nature of the few human relationships she still keeps up are also
reflected in the ruined garden around Satis House. The very color of
the weeds, green and yellow, are the colors always associated with Sarah
Pocket when she contemplates what she regards as Pip's good fortune at
the expense of herself. The picture of nature we get from the garden,
desolate and poisonous, invades the interior of Satis House, with its
"wintry branches" of candles, and its épergne growing out of the cloth
"like a black fungus" (78). It spreads, too, to Newgate, Wemmick's "con-
servatory" of dead plants, malignant growths nurtured to destroy or be
destroyed.

One of the consequences of Miss Havisham's moral sickness is that
the only relationships she is capable of are tinged with parasitism, a parasitism which works two ways: Miss Havisham feeds on Estella—she looks
at her "greedily" and "as though she were devouring the beautiful creature she had reared" (288), and kisses her "with a ravenous intensity that
was of its kind quite dreadful" (226). On the other hand a host of relatives battens on her like parasites and looks forward to the time when, as
she puts it, they will "come to feast" on her (82). The word "toady"
which is always used to describe them retains a lot of its original animal
significance in Dickens' usage, as it does later when he describes Mrs.
Coiler, the "snaky and fork-tongued" (181) toady to Mrs. Pocket.

But Miss Havisham and her associates are not by any means the only
parasites in the novel, and this important theme is illustrated not only
through images involving repulsive animals, but also through the many
suggestions of people actually feeding off each other. Of course food and
eating play a large part in the book, and the many meals consumed are
made richly significant. As we have seen, Pip first becomes conscious of his
degraded social position through his doglike feeding at Miss Havisham's.
Similarly he first realizes the glories and perils of his new prosperity
through his meal at the servile Pumblechook's ("none of those out-of-the-
way No Thoroughfares of Pork now") (145) and his first meal with Herbert where his table manners are corrected. This last meal recurs to the

reader's mind when Magwitch displays similarly uncouth table manners on his return from Australia, arousing disgust in the correct young man Pip has now become. But above all the novel suggests that human beings may destroy each other by eating them up emotionally. Repulsive pictures of people eating each other are fairly common. The tone is set right at the beginning:

> "You young dog," said the man, licking his lips, "what fat cheeks you ha' got."
> I believe they were fat, though I was at that time undersized for my years, and not strong.
> "Darn me if I couldn't eat 'em," said the man, with a threatening shake of his head, "and if I han't a mind to't." (2)

And of course this terrifying first scene culminates in the story of the young man and the threat that Pip's heart and liver may be "tore out, roasted and ate" (3). The reader may not be wrong if he senses a link between this scene and that in which Miss Havisham commands Pip to love Estella.

> "If she wounds you, love her. If she tears your heart to pieces— and as it gets older and stronger it will tear deeper—love her, love her!" (226)

At the Christmas dinner the company compare Pip to the pork they are eating, and the thought seems to increase their appetite rather than put them off. Later, the convict hunt provides a "terrible good sauce" for their dinner, just as contemplation of Drummle "actually seemed to serve as a zest to Jaggers' wine" (203). Human relationships in this novel frequently descend to the parasitic or cannibalistic—for example, the scenes between Miss Havisham and Estella finally become so disgusting they are hard to read calmly—and the roles of cannibal and victim are deliberately kept ambiguous.

Yet, while so much of the novel occupies itself with life at an animal level, with brute loyalties and brute grudges, a more positive and generous attitude to life's possibilities is suggested from the start, and it remains in the background throughout as the only option which will enable Pip to break out of the net of dependence and corruption which he has let himself be snared in. Such an attitude is centered, of course, on Joe, who throughout the novel represents Pip's true father, contrasted to the false father figures of Pumblechook, Miss Havisham, and (at least initially) Magwitch.

The Christian virtues of humility and charity are the essence of Joe's "true father" relationship with Pip. Christianity, present primarily as a repulsive perversion in *Little Dorrit*, pervades this novel as a force strong and vital, purged of the sentimentality which tinges the Christian references of the early novels. It is the absence of Christian influences that has made Magwitch what he is, and allows him to regard his black Testament "as a sort of legal spell or charm" (315). Like Jo in *Bleak House*—"moved on" where Magwitch is "took up"—he is continually associated with Christian objects and allusions, to emphasize the shameful indifference of the Church towards him and his kind. It is surely a Christian faith, among other things, that Pip is thinking about when he talks of "the thousand natural and healing influences" that Miss Havisham shut herself off from when she retired from the world, for he goes on to say that her mind became diseased "as all minds do and must and will that reverse the appointed order of their Maker" (378). The least attractive characters pervert the gospel message. The toady Raymond Pocket asks: "If a man is not his own neighbour, who is?" (75). When the clergyman reads "those noble passages . . . which remind humanity how it brought nothing into the world and can take nothing out," the "worldly-minded" Pumblechook is heard to "cough a reservation in the case of a young gentleman who came unexpectedly into a large property" (267). Pip's sister's cleanliness, more uncomfortable than dirt, is compared to the ostentatious Godliness of the falsely religious (20).

The Christian aura which surrounds Joe is created subtly and gradually. The passage where he most explicitly endorses Christian standards is the splendid passage where he explains to Pip why he doesn't "rise" against his wife's tyranny (45). But Dickens' usual method is to associate Joe with certain religious words: for example, Joe "sanctified" home when Pip was a child (100), though Pip later grew so "ungracious" as not to believe in it any more; Pip feels the soft touch of Joe's hand on his arm "as if it had been the rustle of an angel's wing" (133); he thinks of the wreaths from his pipe as "a blessing from Joe" (138). Pip never doubts his own inability to come up to Joe's higher code, but he is always conscious of it, and affected by it whenever he is brought into close contact with it:

> It was not because I was faithful, but because Joe was faithful, that I never ran away and went for a soldier or sailor. It was not because I had a strong sense of the virtue of industry, but because Joe had a strong sense of the virtue of industry, that I worked with tolerable zeal against the grain. It is not possible to know how far the influence of any amiable honest-hearted duty-doing man flies out in the world; but it is very possible to know how it has touched one's self in going by, and I know right well that any good that intermixed itself with my apprenticeship came of plain contented Joe, and not of restless aspiring discontented me. (101)

God is not often on Joe's lips, but God and Heaven are always on Pip's lips when he thinks of Joe, Biddy, and the forge.

The story of the novel is the story of the forces which prize Pip away from Joe and his code, of the false fathers who lead him to false goals. Miss Havisham implants the wish for social betterment and the glitter of wealth, corrupting him as surely as she corrupts Estella with the jewels. Pumblechook assumes the role of benefactor after the expectations materialize and it is then that we understand why Dickens has so insisted on the words "swindler" and "imposter" in his descriptions of him. We see that, as soon as he comes into his expectations, Pip is likely to be corrupted into the Pocket-Pumblechook view of life: he wonders whether "the clergyman wouldn't have said that about the rich man and the kingdom of Heaven, if he had known all," and he determines to buy the respect of the obscure inhabitants of the village (for whom he feels an emotion which he mistakes for compassion) with "a dinner of roast-beef and plum-pudding, a pint of ale and a gallon of condescension" (139). We need no authorial prodding to remember Pumblechook's savory pork pie and the bottles of port and sherry. Thus it is no surprise that, when Pip meets Pumblechook for the first time since the news broke, he accepts the imposter's ludicrous "well-deserved" complacently, and thinks it "a sensible way of expressing himself" (145), and under the influence of the wine and the flattery even momentarily thinks he had been mistaken in his opinion of him, and that he was "a sensible practical good-hearted prime fellow" (147). The false father, it seems, has won.

When Magwitch returns it seems that we are to see a further false assumption of fatherhood. His actions and words bespeak the authentic Pumblechook. His "favourite action of holding out both his hands for mine" recalls Pumblechook's similar gesture at the momentous breakfast just referred to; Pumblechook's "but do I see afore me him as I ever sported with in his times of happy infancy" (145) finds an echo in Magwitch's similarly proprietorial "and this is the gentleman what I made!" (313). His "air of an Exhibitor" (320) recalls Pumblechook too, as does his misuse of his Testament.

But Magwitch changes, or, as Pip expresses it, softens. We need not look too closely into the causes of this, and indeed, Dickens tells us nothing whatsoever about it, except that it has happened. This is not a novel where character and motivation are explored at a subtle level, and no more than a minimal psychological consistency is necessary. Pip himself is an adroit conjuring trick on Dickens' part, at one and the same time the miserable snob who despises Joe's manners and the perfectly neutral "nice young chap" narrator of the Copperfield stamp, who can enjoy Wopsle's Hamlet and ask him home afterwards, and toast sausages with the Aged P. The reader simply accepts Magwitch's softening, which is depicted symbolically as well as stated as a fact. Once again Dickens uses clothes with rich significance, as he has done earlier wth Pip and Joe: where before it was impossible to disguise him, since, whatever he dressed in, he still looked the convict he once had been, after the softening he looks "as like a river pilot as my heart could have wished" and "a natural part of the scene" (413–14). What is interesting about the softening is not how it came about, but the fact that as soon as it has come about those Christian references which hitherto have been associated mainly with Joe begin to cluster around Magwitch. "Faithful dear boy, well done" (413), he says as he steps into the boat, recalling the parable of the talents. The ripples of the river make in his ears "a sort of Sunday tune" (415). After his capture the language of the Gospels becomes very insistent indeed:

> The kind of submission or resignation that he showed, was that of a man who was tired out. I sometimes derived an impression, from his manner or from a whispered word or two which escaped him, that he pondered over the question whether he might have been a better man under better circumstances. But he never justified himself by a hint tending that way, or tried to bend the past out of its eternal shape.
>
> It happened on two or three occasions in my presence, that his desperate reputation was alluded to by one or other of the people in attendance on him. A smile crossed his face then, and he turned his eyes on me with a trustful look, as if he were confident that I had seen some small redeeming touch in him, even so long ago when I was a little child. As to all the rest, he was humble and contrite, and I never knew him complain. (432)

At this point of the novel Dickens allows the language of the Christian religion to pass Magwitch's lips for the first time—in his words to the Judge at his trial—and when he dies Pip "knew there were no better words that I could say beside his bed, than 'O Lord, be merciful to him a sinner'" (436).

Thus it is through Magwitch, who had been to him "a better man than I had been to Joe" (423), that Pip casts off his corruption and comes back to the values and ideals of the forge. With Joe's return to nurse Pip in his illness Christianity becomes more and more explicitly part of the novel's theme: "O God bless him! God bless this gentle Christian man" prays Pip, when he recognizes his nurse (439). It never leaves the book now, and on the last page of the book—at least in the revised version, which is often found unacceptable, especially by those who imagine they have been reading a realistic novel—Estella begs Pip to say "God bless you, God forgive you!" (460) and the two go off into the rising mists amid the echoes of *Paradise Lost* last heard at the end of Part I.

Great Expectations should surely be seen, therefore, as a study of guilt, corruption, and redemption, seen in predominantly Christian terms. The role of money and social rank as corruptors is important but still subsidiary, and Dickens' most ambitious study of their influence is to be reserved for his next novel. Here the emphasis is not on society but on the individual, the nature of his relationships with others, and the most basic passions of the human heart. The emphasis throughout is on man's fallen condition, on the monstrous power of sin, on man's limitless ability to delude himself into taking the wrong course of action. But the guilt Pip so strongly feels, both for his own crimes and those of others is not only a consequence of man's fallen state; it is also a precondition of his regeneration. The mood of the novel is not so totally despairing as in some of the other late novels, and Dickens allows the possibility that a grain of human goodness and nobility may survive a long exposure to evil and corruption, that human decency and love may win at least some small, private victories.

In treating these themes Dickens gives them depth and complexity by his subtle use of related images and connecting links. Though there is no one linking symbol in the novel which, like Jarndyce and Jarndyce, can demonstrably connect a variety of disparate characters and themes, Dickens' use of smaller links and similarities to suggest the interrelatedness of everything in the novel is just as great an achievement. Because of its apparent simplicity many readers are reluctant to admit to a preference for *Great Expectations* over the more complex symbolic structures. Yet one suspects that most of them do prefer it, and in view of the complexity of Dickens' moral vision, his sensitive portrayal of close personal relationships (never his strongest point), and the masterly grasp of structure, it may be that they are right to do so.[4]

Annabel M. Patterson

OUR MUTUAL FRIEND: DICKENS AS THE COMPLEAT ANGLER

OUR MUTUAL FRIEND is not a book which satisfies all of Dickens' admirers. Those who appreciate Dickens mainly for the exuberance of his characterization and his gift for caricature feel a certain flatness in this last novel but one, and interpret Dickens' statements about the difficulty of its development as signs of failing powers.[1] Those who appreciate Dickens for his remarkable anticipation of surrealist or symbolist techniques feel, on the contrary, that *Our Mutual Friend* shows a greater imaginative freedom than the earlier novels, and a metaphysical daring which more than makes amends for the subservience of character to theme. This paper, rather obviously, is going to align itself with the second attitude, and is based on the assumption that when Dickens speaks of his difficulties in writing *Our Mutual Friend,* it is not because of age and exhaustion, but because he was aiming at something different, something which required greater concentration both of memory and foresight, and greater attention to the structural relevance of almost any phrase.

The structural pattern which Dickens so labored to maintain in *Our Mutual Friend* depends on the central fact and image of the river Thames, which, like the story of John Harmon's drowning, flows through the novel, linking together the lives of almost all the characters as if they were tributary streams. The fundamental metaphor which explains the dominance of the river is given by Dickens in two parts, both equally explicit, one early in the novel and one late. When Lizzie Hexam first hears that her father is suspected of the murder of John Harmon and is "cut adrift" from the waterside community, as represented by the Six Jolly Fellowship-Porters Inn, she stands in lonely misery on the river bank; and

> as the great black river with its dreary shores was soon lost to her
> view in the gloom, so, she stood on the river's brink unable to see

into the vast blank misery of a life suspected, and fallen away
from by good and bad, but knowing that it lay there dim before
her, stretching away to the great ocean, Death. (I, vi)

Much later, the train taking Jenny and Lightwood to the apparently dying
Eugene is described as "spurning the watery turnings and doublings" of
the river it crosses, and

> going straight to its end, as Father Time goes to his. To whom
> it is no matter what living waters run high or low, reflect the
> heavenly lights and darknesses, produce their little growth of
> weeds and flowers, turn here, turn there, are noisy or still, are
> troubled or at rest, for their course has one sure termination,
> though their sources and devices are many. (IV, xi)

In both passages the basic metaphorical statement is that life, the river,
flows inexorably into death, the sea; but Dickens protects both his characters and his readers from the simplistic nature of this statement by the
superb indirection of his omniscient narrator. In the first passage the symbolic perception is partly Lizzie's and partly the narrator's, but, since it
does not become explicit until the last word, "death," the reader is encouraged to move on before resolving this ambiguity. In the second passage also one is left to wonder how much of the perception belongs to
Lightwood and Jenny, as they travel towards what they believe to be a
deathbed, and at the same time one appreciates the Miltonic control of
the narrator: a simple comparison between the direct train and Time leads
to a complex analogy, not just between life in general flowing death-
wards and the river flowing towards the sea, but between different lives
and rivers of varying character. Taken together, as they were surely meant
to be taken, the two passages represent two of Dickens' most sophisticated
and suggestive techniques in *Our Mutual Friend:* the intuitive perception, or part-perception, of his most interesting characters that the river
operates at some level above or below normal experience; and the principle of moral differentiation between characters, according as they "reflect
the heavenly lights and darknesses, produce their little growth of weeds
and flowers, . . . are troubled or at rest." Throughout the novel, his people are made known to us either by their actual relationship to the river,
and their degree of sympathy with it (the Hexams, Eugene Wrayburn,
Rogue Riderhood, Bradley Headstone, Betty Higden, John Harmon himself) , or by some figurative judgement on their activities made in watery
terms.[2]

A good deal of the work on these water metaphors, symbols, and still
more mysterious relationships has already been done. In an essay in 1949
Robert Morse drew attention to the theme of drowning in *Our Mutual
Friend,* and remarked, "as it has been said of Shakespeare that each play
follows a consistent imagery, it is easy to point out in *Our Mutual Friend*

a poetic revelry in water associations." [3] Perhaps in response to this encouragement, J. Hillis Miller's chapter on the novel explores exhaustively
the symbolism of death by drowning, and all the water metaphors for psychological process or stasis.[4] I propose therefore to limit myself to one
part only of this complex of associations—the role of fishing and fishermen in *Our Mutual Friend;* and I shall consider this fishing theme primarily as evidence of a technique not usually attributed to Dickens at all.
The technique is that of literary reference, on a large scale, to a single
work which he could assume at least some of his readers would know and
recognize. The terms of reference are ethical and structural; Dickens is
not interested in illustrating or authorizing particular moments of
his novel, but in providing it with a whole moral context from an earlier
work and world. The work so referred to is, I suggest, Isaak Walton's
Compleat Angler, first published in 1653, and reprinted so many times
since then that, as one modern editor has said, "at least in name, it is almost as well known as the Bible or Shakespeare." [5] Dickens' use of images
and concepts from the *Compleat Angler* in *Our Mutual Friend* enforces a
more serious reading of the novel than its romance ending might imply,
just as his use of Sidney's *Astrophil and Stella* in *Great Expectations*
makes Estella and Miss Havisham more sinister than they would otherwise be.[6] In both these late novels, Dickens has supplemented his own
sense of decency and social justice by importing into his work the signs
and structures of a more naïve ideal; in *Great Expectations* it is the Petrar-
chan love ethic, and in *Our Mutual Friend* it is the pastoral ethic, expressed in fisherman's terms. This is a highly sophisticated technique; and
it is less like Shakespeare's image-grouping in the plays than it is like
Eliot's use of Shakespeare in *The Waste Land* to create a moral context in
which the London of his own day and the Thames of his own London
are seen in demonic parody of their function in the Elizabethan Golden
Age.

In view of the rather limited notion of Dickens' reading which has
recently been proposed,[7] it is important to note that Dickens *had* read
the *Compleat Angler.* In a light-hearted essay on "The Great Interna-
tional Walking Match," dated February 1868 (three years after the completion of *Our Mutual Friend*), Dickens observed of one of the contest-
ants that he was "of the rubicund and jovial sort, and has long been
known as a piscatorial pedestrian on the banks of the Wye." And he adds,

> But Isaac Walton hadn't pace—look at his book and you'll find
> it slow—and when that article comes in question, the fishing-rod
> may prove to some of his disciples a rod in pickle.[8]

It is not at all clear in what sense Dickens is here using the word "disciples," and since the "article in question" is literary as well as ambula-
tory pace, it may well be that Dickens is thinking of literary rather than

piscatorial instruction and guidance. No one would argue against Dickens that the *Compleat Angler* is a racy book, but perhaps not all remember how much more it is than a fisherman's handbook, and how full it is of concepts and images which are of relevance to *Our Mutual Friend*.

The *Compleat Angler* is set initially in the form of a debate between Auceps, the fowler, Venator, the hunter, and Piscator, the fisherman, on the respective merits of their crafts. It is not until Piscator, using arguments from philosophy, natural history, legend, and the Scriptures, has won the debate that the technical aspects of the craft of fishing are set out. The technical part, too, has a dramatic function, for it is given in the form of instruction to Venator, who has become the fisherman's scholar, in order to become a fisherman himself. In other words, there is a quiet conversion; and the change from hunter to fisherman is made laudable by the conceptual argument on which Piscator rests his case, namely, that fishing is the best occupation to improve a man's disposition and morals, since it combines the active and the contemplative life, in a pastoral setting of innocence and peace.

As is clear from the commendatory verses which precede it, the "Afterword" which suggests that Walton might have called his book the *Arcadia of Angling,* and the references to Virgilian pastoral which it contains, the *Compleat Angler* was intended to be an original variation on the pastoral genre, with its ethic of innocent leisure held up in contrast to the corruptions of the Court or the business world. It is not by accident that Piscator begins his case for the supremacy of fishing by setting fishermen apart from the world of action as it is normally conceived:

> Sir, there be many men that are by others taken to be serious grave men, which we contemn and pity. Men that are taken to be grave, because Nature hath made them of a sowre complexion, money-getting-men, men that spend all their time first in getting, and next in anxious care to keep it; men that are condemned to be rich, and then always busie or discontented: for these poor-rich-men, we Anglers pity them perfectly, and stand in no need to borrow their thoughts to think our selves happy. (29)

Also, as Renaissance pastoral sometimes made use of the scriptural meaning of "shepherd" to give its ethic a Christian sanction, as in Spenser's *Shepheardes Calender* or Milton's *Lycidas,* so the *Compleat Angler* goes to the Scriptures for a Christian definition of "fisherman." Venator says that he is willing to be called simple, "if by that you mean a harmlessness, or that simplicity which was usually found in the primitive Christians, who were (as most Anglers are) quiet men, and followers of peace" (29–30). Later he comments on the significant fact that when Christ came to choose his disciples, he chose first "four that were Fishermen, whom he inspired and sent to publish . . . a new way to everlasting life" (46). One of the commendatory verses takes the symbolism a stage further by re-

minding Walton's readers of the old mysterious pun on the word *piscis;* [9]
and the point is finally made in the "Anglers Song," that in a Christian
context fishing usually carries the symbolic meaning of fishing-for-men.

> For so our Lord was pleased when
> He Fishers made fishers of men:
> Where (which is in no other game)
> A man may fish and praise his Name.

And all this conversation is set in the quiet countryside, where one gives
away part of the day's catch to the poor, where the honest milking-woman
speaks of the "golden age" of her youth, and where, if one was a fisherman,
one could sit "viewing the silver-streams glide silently towards their center,
the tempestuous Sea; yet sometimes opposed by rugged roots and pebble-
stones, which broke their waves and turned them into foam: and sometimes . . . viewing the harmless Lambs, some leaping securely in the cool
shade, whilst others sported themselvs in the chearful Sun" (70).

It is in this context, I suggest, that Dickens set the theme of fishing,
and fishing-for-men, which runs through *Our Mutual Friend.* In the first
place, it hardly needs pointing out again that Dickens focuses virtually
all the social criticism of the novel on "men that are taken to be grave,
because Nature hath made them of a sowre complexion, money-getting-
men, men that spend all their time first in getting, and next in anxious
care to keep it." The real avarice of Fascination Fledgeby and Silas Wegg,
and the pretended avarice of Mr. Boffin, modeling himself on all the
most miserable misers of the past, are merely naïve figures of the larger
configuration, the money-orientated society which meets to dine at the
dinner tables of the Veneerings and the Podsnaps. It is from this world,
which has its focus in the city, that all of Dickens' "good" characters
have, in one way or another, to escape; and it is important to notice how
often this escape is not only a moral one, but a geographical one also.
The world to which they escape is that of the upper reaches of the
Thames, a world which is still, miraculously, a place of pastoral innocence and peace.[10]

The second of Dickens' people to leave the city and enter the pastoral
world is the old woman, Betty Higden. (The first is Lizzie Hexam, but
it is not until after Betty Higden's death that we learn where Lizzie has
gone.) When the old woman sets out on her pilgrimage towards an
honorable as opposed to an institutional death, she "had taken the up-
ward course of the river Thames as her general track" (III, viii). One
wonders whether it is purely by accident that Dickens mentions her
appearance in "the pleasant towns of Chertsey, *Walton,* Kingston, and
Staines." But there is certainly nothing left to the reader's ingenuity in his
description of the character of these towns:

> In those pleasant little towns on Thames, you may hear the fall
> of the water over the weirs, or even, in still weather, the rustle of

the rushes; and from the bridge you may see the young river, dimpled like a young child, playfully gliding away among the trees, unpolluted by the defilements that lie in wait for its course, and as yet out of hearing of the deep summons of the sea.

For Betty Higden, death in this unspoiled landscape is an act of innocence and freedom, an assertion of individual resistance to the economic assumption that she ought to be handed over "safe to the parish," an assertion of the individual's right to be both poor and solitary. And it is her funeral which brings John Harmon and Bella Wilfer into the pastoral environment, and we see for the first time signs in Bella that the awful example of Mr. Boffin turned miser is having its intended softening effect. As John and Bella walk by the river after the funeral, Dickens gives Bella a new mirror to look into, instead of the looking glass into which she has looked so often and received so little good advice:

> Perhaps the old mirror was never yet made by human hands, which, if all the images it had in its time reflected could pass across its surface again, would fail to reveal some scene of horror or distress. But the great serene mirror of the river seemed as if it might have reproduced all it had ever reflected between those placid banks, and brought nothing to light *save what was peaceful, pastoral, and blooming.* (III, ix)

It is in this pastoral setting, where the river is still unpolluted, that fishing is possible. When Eugene Wrayburn comes up the river in search of Lizzie, it is on the excuse of going on "a solitary fishing excursion," and we learn that, before reaching his destination, he "had put up for the night, at an Angler's Inn" (IV, i). As he stands waiting for Lizzie, observing the "silver river" and the sheep that are in Walton's landscape also, he remarks to himself on the quietness of the place:

> It was very quiet. Some sheep were grazing on the grass by the river-side, and it seemed to him that he had never before heard the crisp, tearing sound with which they cropped it. . . . "What's here to do?" he asked himself, leisurely going towards the gate and looking over. "No jealous paper-miller? *No pleasures of the chase in this part of the country? Mostly fishing hereabouts!"* (IV, vi)

The irony is, of course, that he does not really come as a fisherman into fishing country, but as a hunter in pursuit of Lizzie, and bringing behind him in pursuit of himself the mad schoolmaster, Bradley Headstone. Surely Dickens is here remembering, among other things, the debate between Piscator and Venator in the *Compleat Angler,* and the quiet remark of the fisherman that "in the Scripture Angling is always taken in the best sense; and that though hunting may be sometimes so taken, yet it is but seldom to be so understood" (47). The double-entendre so politely referred to by Piscator is present in Dickens' novel also; and when Eugene enters the pastoral world he brings with him as well the influence of all those dark nights in the London streets, when he himself enjoyed the "pleasures of the chase" tormenting Bradley Headstone. In this respect he is almost as guilty as Headstone, who is at one moment explictly described as "a scholastic huntsman clad for the field, with his fresh pack yelping and barking around him" (III, ii), and whose visits to the pastoral world only serve to spatter him in blood and later to bury him under the "ooze and scum behind one of the rotting gates" of Plashwater Weir Mill Lock. Both Eugene and Headstone, then, are hunters, and their entry into fishing country precipitates one of those scenes of horror which the "great serene mirror of the river" had seemed to refuse to reflect. Fortunately for Eugene, he is also involved unconsciously in the deeper theme of fishing-for-men, which complicates the pastoral ethic, and makes it much more than a simple statement of innocence.

The novel, of course, opens with the gruesome chapter in which Gaffer and Lizzie Hexam are out on the river close to London Bridge, literally fishing for men. Their activity is the darkest antithesis possible to the true act of fishing-for-men, in its scriptural sense and in the sense of Walton's "Anglers Song," since it is only for dead men that they fish, and only for financial gain. The symbolic meaning of the apostolic fishing-for-men is both implied and denied in young Charlie Hexam's comments on the state of the man so retrieved:

> Pharaoh's multitude, that were drowned in the Red Sea, ain't more beyond restoring to life. If Lazarus were only half as far gone, that was the greatest of all the miracles. (I, iii)

In one sense, since the body is believed to be that of John Harmon, he is restored to life, and the reader discovers he has little compunction in consigning George Radfoot to the state of a badly-decayed piece of Gaffer Hexam's "luck." However, there is no question but that Gaffer's trade is designed by Dickens to be horrifying, and no question but that Lizzie is simultaneously repelled and fascinated by the search, which she identifies with the river itself. In the dialogue between them, Lizzie declares her antipathy to the river, while Gaffer, in improbable rhetoric, insists on her dependence on it:

> How can you be so thankless to your best friend, Lizzie? The very fire that warmed you when you were a baby, was picked out of the river alongside the coal barges. The very basket that you slept in the tide washed ashore. (I, i)

Ironically, it is Hexam's words which prove to be the more true, for it is ultimately Lizzie's loyalty to the river which gives her the opportunity to cancel out the sinister aspects of the old occupation, and make the river her best friend indeed.

The irony is made the more terrible by Dickens' description of how Gaffer Hexam's body is brought ashore as a piece of his own "luck," and played by Mr. Inspector as if it were a cunning fish on the line:

> "Come!" he added, at once persuasively and with authority to the hidden object in the water, as he played the line again; "it's no good this sort of game, you know. You *must* come up. I mean to have you."

And in case anyone should fail to see the metaphor, Dickens adds:

> It was an awful sort of fishing, but it no more disconcerted Mr. Inspector than if he had been fishing in a punt on a summer evening by some soothing weir high up the peaceful river. (I, xiv)

It is in this passage that Dickens shows explicitly how the different kinds of fishing are related, and how the fishing for dead bodies in the London Thames is to be seen as a demonic parody of the true occupation in the pastoral world upstream. It is also probable that some of the nastiest aspects of the parody—the use of the word "luck," the coolness of Mr. Inspector's tone, and the pedagogical manner in which he explains to Mortimer and Eugene how the accident must have happened—come from the *Compleat Angler* itself. When Venator is learning his new craft, for example, he complains that he has been waiting for two hours, and has not seen a fish stir; to which Piscator replies:

> Well Scholar, you must indure worse luck sometime, or you will never make a good Angler. But what say you now? There is a Trout now, and a good one too, if I can but hold him, and two or three turnes more will tire him: Now you see he lies still, and the sleight is to land him: Reach me that Landing Net: So (Sir) now he is mine own, what say you now? (p. 69)

It is surely not by coincidence that Piscator instructs his student in the catching of trout by marking off the points for observation, thus: "And next you are to take notice . . . And you are to note . . . and so you may observe . . . Now you see . . ." and that Mr. Inspector instructs Eugene and Mortimer in the various stages of how Gaffer Hexam was caught by similarly marking his points: "Now see . . . And you will have observed before, and you will observe now . . . Likewise you will have observed . . . Now see . . . Now see!" If this is indeed the source for Mr. Inspector's manner and style, there is a particularly unpleasant analogy between the way in which Piscator refers familiarly to the trout as "him," and Mr. Inspector's insistence on retaining the personal pronoun for Gaffer Hexam, long after his personality has left him:

> "What is to be done with the remains?" asked Lightwood. "If you wouldn't object to standing by him half a minute, sir," was the reply, "I'll find the nearest of our men to come and take

charge of him;—I will call it *him,* you see," said Mr. Inspector, looking back as he went, with a philosophical smile upon the force of habit. (I, xiv)

This is the more striking when it is compared with the narrator's technique, necessary for maintaining suspense, of calling Eugene's body "it" throughout his rescue, although, as we learn later, he is still alive.

It is this bitter parody of true fishing, then, in both the lifetime and the death of her father, that causes Lizzie Hexam's antipathy to the river, and to some extent to her father himself, since her dependence for livelihood on the river is really synonymous with her dependence, during childhood, on him. It is Lizzie's voice that the winds imitate when they mock Gaffer Hexam's corpse, caught in his own line:

> Father, was that you calling me? . . . Was it you, the voiceless and the dead? Was it you, thus buffeted as you lie here in a heap? Was it you, thus baptized unto Death, with these flying impurities now flung upon your face? Why not speak, Father? Soaking into this filthy ground as you lie here, is your own shape. Did you ever see such a shape soaked into your own boat? Speak, Father. (I, xiv)

But since it is also the voice of the winds, it is possible for them to say, as Lizzie herself never could have said, even in her bitterest moment, "Was it you, thus baptized unto Death"; for this is demonic parody of Romans 6 : 3–5, "Know ye not that so many of us as were baptized into Jesus Christ were *baptized into his death?* Therefore we are buried with him by baptism into death: that like as Christ was raised up from the dead by the glory of the Father, even so we should walk in newness of life."

But the ambivalence of Lizzie's response is indicated by the fact that after her father's death, she stays beside the river, against all advice to the contrary, hoping in some unstated way to be able to clear her father's name. When Charlie begs her to leave the river, she replies, "I can't get away from it, I think. . . . It's no purpose of mine that I live by it still" (II, i). When she is finally persuaded by Riah to escape from Eugene, she does not leave the river, but goes upstream into the pastoral world, where even such an industrial object as the paper mill can be seen as a row of lighted windows reflected in water. And there she is given the opportunity to cancel out the demonic parody, to redeem the old corrupt practice of fishing for corpses, by rescuing a man who still lives, and whom she does not, until she catches him, recognize as Eugene. Dickens makes it perfectly clear how important it is to Lizzie that her old skills can at last be put to clean use, and in her spoken or breathed prayers as she handles the boat we are being informed that the passage from Romans is being restored to its proper sense:

> Now, merciful Heaven be thanked for that old time, and grant,
> O Blessed Lord, that through thy wonderful workings it may
> turn to good at last! To whomsoever the drifting face belongs,
> be it man's or woman's, help my humble hands, Lord God, to
> raise it from death and restore it to some one to whom it must be
> dear! (IV, vi)

And Dickens may also be remembering the statement in Walton's "Anglers Song" that in fishing-for-men, as "in no other game, / A man may fish and praise his name."

This is the main theme of fishing, and fishing-for-men, and in it there appears most clearly Dickens' reasons for using the *Compleat Angler* as his point of reference. Not only does it supply the pastoral ideal against which the money-orientated society can be measured, but its very naïvete makes possible the kind of parody which shocks profoundly, by being not merely a distortion, but a complete inversion of something simple and good. This is what I have been calling demonic parody, in the sense in which black magic operates by inverting the name of God.

There are other forms of parody fishing, however. The effectiveness of Dickens' definition of Podsnappery is much improved by our understanding of the theme of fishing-for-men. Mr. Podsnap is a man who "had thriven exceedingly in the marine insurance way" (I, xi), and Mr. Veneering, we are told, "had prospered exceedingly upon the Harmon murder, and had turned the social distinction it conferred upon him to the account of making several dozen of brand-new bosom-friends." In other words, they both prey, as Gaffer Hexam had done, on the victims of sea and river, including the so-called Harmon drowning itself, but they manage to do so in a manner well-protected from the social ignominy which followed Hexam; and whereas Hexam had made at best a skimpy living out of the business, they "had thriven exceedingly" and "had prospered exceedingly," phrases in which the parallel structure is surely not accidental. It is not therefore meant to be entirely comic, nor merely a measure of the superficiality of the dinner talk at the Podsnap's table, when Dickens informs us that Mr. Veneering means again to plunge into the subject of the Harmon drowning, and proceeds to develop the metaphor of plunging in:

> addressing himself to the most desirable of his neighbours, while
> Mrs. Veneering secured the next most desirable, he plunged into
> the case, and emerged from it afterwards with a Bank Director
> in his arms. In the meantime, Mrs. Veneering had dived into the
> same waters for a wealthy Ship-Broker, and brought him up, safe
> and sound, by the hair. . . . And this she did with such a success-
> ful display of her eight aquiline fingers and their encircling
> jewels, that she happily laid hold of a drifting General Officer,

his wife and daughter, and not only restored their animation
which had become suspended, but made them lively friends
within an hour. (I, xi)

We have to turn from this passage to Lizzie's rescue of Eugene to appreciate how it parodies *in advance* her prayer for help and her seizing of
his body by "its bloody hair." In the world of Podsnappery, fishing-for-
men means fishing for wealthy associates with a spicy subject matter as
bait, without any regard for the internal gravity of that subject matter;
and what is worst about this combination of veniality and superficiality
is that it cannot, unlike the craft of Gaffer Hexam, be redeemed by proper
use. The nearest Mr. and Mrs. Veneering can come to the true purpose
of fishing-for-men is by way of what one might call a delayed-action pun.
Where Lizzie prays that she may be given strength to catch hold of "the
drifting face" and "to raise it from death and restore it to someone to
whom it must be dear," Mrs. Veneering "happily laid hold of a *drifting*
General Officer, his wife and daughter," but only *"restored their animation"* within the social circle.

Dickens' adaptation of the theme here is not demonic parody, although it has sinister implications. The tone of the passage is closer to
the kind of parody Pope achieves in *The Rape of the Lock,* where superficial social encounters are dressed up to look like serious literary or
historical events. The element of the macabre in this passage is controlled by humor, and also, of course, by the fact that this fishing-for-men
is only a metaphor for an unworthy activity, rather than the activity
itself. This is not true, however, of the last occasion on which Dickens
introduces the fishing theme, producing another kind of distortion and
a still different tone. The third parody is achieved by Rogue Riderhood,
who has a special relationship with the river, having been once himself
drowned in its lower reaches, and restored to life by artificial respiration.
The faint hope of his daughter Pleasant that "the old evil had been
drowned out of him" is proved to have been the delusion she really
knew it was by his behavior in the pastoral world. When Rogue Riderhood is relieved of the necessity of skulking about the river and dwelling
"deep and dark in Limehouse Hole," he is sent upstream to take charge
of the pleasant-sounding Plashwater Weir Mill Lock. But his only
response to this new environment is to watch with grim humor the hunting of Eugene by Bradley Headstone, and then in turn take up the hunt
of Headstone, in order to blackmail him. It is all the worse, therefore, that
when he goes hunting Headstone, he uses fishing as a means of his
destruction.

After Headstone has thrown his blood-stained Bargeman's outfit into
the river, Riderhood, who has watched him change back into a schoolmaster, has the following conversation with himself:

"Now, . . . shall I foller you on, or shall I let you loose for this once, and go a-fishing. . . . If I wasn't to go a-fishing, others might.—I'll let you loose this once, and go a-fishing." (IV, vii)

Later we are told that "Rogue Riderhood had been busy with the river that day. He had fished with assiduity on the previous evening, but the light was short, and he had fished unsuccessfully. He had fished again that day with better luck, and he carried his fish home to Plashwater Weir Mill Lockhouse, in a bundle" (IV, vii). It is this bundle, of course, which contains Bradley Headstone's Bargeman's outfit, which is identical with Riderhood's own clothing; and there is a bitter echo here of the "luck" which Gaffer Hexam used to have when fishing further down the river. It is this bundle which Riderhood carries under his arm to Bradley Headstone's school, in order to torment the schoolmaster by his mock-catechism of those most unpastoral lambs, his pupils:

"Wot's the diwisions of water, lambs? Wot sorts of water is there on the land?" Shrill chorus: "Seas, rivers, lakes, and ponds." . . . "Wot is it, lambs, as they ketches in seas, rivers, lakes, and ponds?" Shrill chorus (with some contempt for the ease of the question) : "Fish!" . . . "Wot is it, besides fish, as they sometimes ketches in rivers? Well! I'll tell you. It's suits o' clothes." (IV, xv)

But it is more than a suit of clothes that Riderhood has caught. It is the Bargeman's identity, which matches his own—a fact recognized with terrible clarity by Bradley Headstone as he erases his own name from the blackboard. The motive for Riderhood's fishing is thus doubly corrupt: it is a means to blackmail, and therefore he fishes, like Gaffer Hexam, for financial gain; and it is also the hunt to death. But, as Headstone, by copying his clothes, took Riderhood's identity upon him, and as Riderhood's response is to threaten him with continual pursuit ("I mean as I'll keep you company, wherever you go, when you go away from here"), so they go down together, girded by Headstone's "iron ring" and trapped between the two iron gates of the Lock.

This dark relationship is bad enough in itself, but it becomes considerably darker if we compare it, as I believe Dickens did, with the relationship established at the end of the *Compleat Angler* between Piscator, the teacher, and Venator, the hunter-turned-fisherman. In place of Riderhood's mockery of Headstone's teaching abilities ("though not a learned character my own self, I do admire learning in others, to be sure!") Walton makes the hunter-turned-fisherman humbly grateful for the instruction he has received. In place of Riderhood's ironic threats ("but he is most excellent company, that man, and I want him to come and see me at my lock") Walton presents Venator as looking forward eagerly to the next fishing season, when he may have Piscator's company once again. "Indeed," says Venator, as he bids farewell to his master,

> your company and discourse have been so useful and pleasant, that I may truly say, I have only lived since I enjoyed them, and turned Angler, and not before. Nevertheless, here I must part with you, here in this now sad place where I was so happy as first to meet you; But I shall long for the ninth of May, for then I hope again to enjoy your beloved company, at the appointed time and place. . . . And let the blessing of St. Peter's Master be with mine.

And Piscator replies, "And upon all that are lovers of Vertue, and all that love to be quiet, and go a fishing." What more subtle condemnation could there be of Rogue Riderhood's attitude to the quiet occupation, when we remember his muttering: "If I wasn't to go a-fishing, others might.—I'll let you loose this once, and go a-fishing"?

If this demonstration of craft on Dickens' part is convincing, then some of the remarks that he himself made about *Our Mutual Friend* make more sense. It is not necessary to read only exhaustion and depression into his statement about the slowness of its growth:

> I have grown hard to satisfy, and write very slowly. And I have so much—not fiction—that *will* be thought of, when I don't want to think of it, that I am forced to take more care than I once took.[11]

Exhaustion and depression were undoubtedly influential; but one of the possible responses to such feelings is a retreat into the shapeliness of formal pattern. The fine threefold structure of *Great Expectations* is one example of the impulse towards pattern; the manipulation of the fishing theme in *Our Mutual Friend* is another. Plot and personality stimulate, but pattern consoles; and one would think that it must have been particularly consoling to be able to maintain a pattern, with such Miltonic or providential power of recall or anticipation, in a novel written in serial form.

Paul Gottschalk

TIME IN *EDWIN DROOD*

ABOUT A third of the way through *The Mystery of Edwin Drood,*
Mr. Grewgious pauses by the door of Cloisterham Cathedral and peeps
in. "Dear me," he says, "it's like looking down the throat of Old Time." [1]
It is a rather imaginative notion for such a singularly angular man. It
is also only one of many instances in the novel in which the architecture
and people of Cloisterham are set against the background of things past
and passing and to come. The revolutions of time, indeed, are a major
leitmotif in *Edwin Drood;* the purpose of the present essay is to examine
the nature and significance of this motif.

The novel itself is carefully set in time, a time that Dickens sees as
extending from out of the almost immemorial past into the workaday
present. Our first view of Cloisterham, the major scene of the book,
establishes this continuum as the town's chief feature:

> An ancient city, Cloisterham, and no meet dwelling-place for
> anyone with hankerings after the noisy world. A monotonous,
> silent city, deriving an earthy flavour throughout from its Ca-
> thedral crypt, and so abounding in vestiges of monastic graves,
> that the Cloisterham children grow small salad in the dust of
> abbots and abbesses, and make dirt-pies of nuns and friars; while
> every ploughman in its outlying fields renders to once puissant
> Lord Treasurers, Archbishops, Bishops, and such-like the atten-
> tion which the Ogre in the story-book desired to render to his
> unbidden visitor, and grinds their bones to make his bread. (18)

The passage does more than establish Cloisterham as an immemorially
old town: it shows the impingement of the past on the present, as the
dead literally provide sustenance for the living in accordance with the
natural cycle of decay and growth, and as the dead peacefully intrude
themselves upon their successors—a theme to which the discovery of

[265

Edwin's body will provide a singular and horrifying variation.[2] The architectural transfusion of past into present, so common in English towns, extends even into the souls of the townspeople:

> In a word, a city of another and a bygone time is Cloisterham, with its hoarse Cathedral bell, its hoarse rooks hovering about the Cathedral tower, its hoarser and less distinct rooks in the stalls far beneath. Fragments of old wall, saint's chapel, chapter-house, convent and monastery, have got incongruously or obstructively built into many of its houses and gardens, much as kindred jumbled notions have become incorporated into many of its citizens' minds. All things in it are of the past. (19)

Stones, notions, and even the very sounds carried through the air link the town serenely with its past. And, in addition to the Cathedral and the ancient gatehouse, which is the residence of Jasper, one of the chief settings of the Cloisterham chapters is Rosa's school, the Nuns' House, "a venerable brick edifice, whose present appellation is doubtless derived from the legend of its conventual uses" (19) —note that these uses are legendary: again, the past is not cold history but part of the "notions" of the townsmen. Cloisterham is the natural habitat of Durdles, the bibulous sexton who lives among the dead—the "old 'uns,"—treating them with the familiarity of everyday professional acquaintances.

The England of *Edwin Drood,* then, is an England of shifting history with an underlying permanence. The people of Cloisterham go about their daily business in the comfortable shadow of the past; Mr. Grewgious, Rosa's guardian, goes about his with exemplary regularity in London under the sign of P. J. T. 1747. Even that great symbol of change, the railroad, has not yet reached Cloisterham (and when it does, Dickens observes, the trains will not stop there) :

> Some remote fragment of Main Line to somewhere else, there was, which was going to ruin the Money Market if it failed, and Church and State if it succeeded, and (of course) , the Constitution, whether or no . . . . (54–55)

Plus ça change, plus c'est la même chose.

In this world of continuity, Jasper is at once in time and out of it. In a town where the citizens fear ghosts, have that "innate shrinking of dust with the breath of life in it from dust out of which the breath of life has passed" (134), his very dwelling, the old gatehouse between the high street and the ancient cathedral close, places him on the borderline between the present and the past, the living and the dead. At night in Cloisterham, the close is deserted, cut off from life:

> One might fancy that the tide of life was stemmed by Mr. Jasper's own gatehouse. The murmur of the tide is heard beyond; but no

wave passes the archway, over which his lamp burns red behind
his curtain, as if the building were a Lighthouse. (135) [3]

His own personal life shows this double time. On the one hand, as
choirmaster he lives in the tempo of Cloisterham and literally keeps the
ecclesiastical hours of the Church. On the other, off in the city, he lives
in the timeless world of opium. (The midnight scene in the crypt with
Durdles, as Jasper scouts the territory for his murder and obtains the
key for Mrs. Sapsea's monument under the pretense of seeking the
picturesque, is a horrible combination of the diabolic and the ecclesiastical in the figurative seas beyond the tide of life.) While most men's
memories are continuous, Jasper's breaks into two different parts, that
of the choirmaster and that of the opium addict, neither of which holds
communication with the other. He is, of course, the classic example of
the divided self that Dickens mentions in the oft-quoted passage on
animal magnetism, and at the end, it has been argued convincingly, it
will take hypnosis to make him realize what he has done.[4] This discontinuity sets him apart from his fellow townsmen, who live unseparated
from their own past. And we never know when he conceives the murder:
it seems present in his mind from the very first ambiguous encounter
with his nephew; it is the creation of his other, timeless self, a scheme
imposed upon life from an existence outside of time. "Well; I have
told you that I did it here hundreds of thousands of times," he says to
the old opium seller. "What do I say? I did it millions and billions of
times. I did it so often, and through such vast expanses of time, that
when it was really done, it seemed not worth the doing, it was done so
soon" (266).

In this context, it is especially interesting that Edwin Drood himself
is characterized as a young man with a future—not that he has particularly great expectations, but that Dickens stresses over and over what
lies ahead for him. Most obviously, he is betrothed to Rosa—a betrothal
established by their respective parents, now dead, and one more example of the past's impingement on the present and the future. (It is
a benevolent scheme, designed for the young people's happiness: if, as
Grewgious hastens to make clear, they do not want to marry after all,
they are not obliged to, and Edwin's one major act is to cut himself
off from what is arbitrary in the past, to free himself for the future.)
It is this tie with the past and future that links Edwin to Cloisterham
and to the plot itself. In addition, over and over again in his conversation and his actions, his thoughts turn habitually to what is supposed
to come, to the future that, for him, will never be. When we first see
him, he is about to turn twenty-one and inherit the future laid out for
him in the past. His conversation with Jasper and with Rosa turns
naturally upon his impending marriage, upon his domestic and profes-

sional establishment in the Egypt that he will never see. In addition, he continually makes small plans for the immediate future. Ironically, he plans to break the news gently to Jasper that his engagement is off. He plans to return to Grewgious the ring that instead will be buried with his corpse. He has the Cloisterham jeweler wind and set his watch, though he will not live the time it will take for it to run down again. And Dickens goes even futher by hinting several times of Edwin's growing interest in the newly-arrived Helena Landless, thus establishing a whole series of conventional romantic expectations on the part of the reader himself,[5] expectations that are abruptly cut short just as Edwin's expectations are cut short: the hints are red herrings drawn across the path of the experienced novel-reader to involve him in a conventional future that is not, in fact, to occur.

We are accustomed to learning a great deal about an important character's past the first time we see him in a novel—especially if the character is to be the victim in a murder mystery—but Edwin has no past to speak of, only a future, near and distant, which he has partly laid out himself and partly received, tentatively, at the hopeful and loving hands of the past. He has no achievements, only promise. Jasper, on the other hand, has a great deal of past. What lies behind Edwin is irrelevant; behind his uncle, however, lies something dark and evil and —the refrain of chapter i—"unintelligible," a prior existence that the unfinished part of the novel would have brought to light. But Jasper has no future. "The cramped monotony of my existence grinds me away by the grain," he tells his nephew, in the same conversation in which his nephew elaborates his future plans. "I must subdue myself to my vocation. . . . It's too late to find another now" (14).[6] The murder of Edwin Drood is horrible not simply because the villain is cruel and cunning and the victim charming and innocent, but because it is the murder of a young man with a future by a man who has none. In killing Edwin, Jasper murders time.

Other details of the murder bring out this theme still more clearly. The murder occurs on Christmas Eve—itself a symbolic crisis in time, a commemoration of a moving from old to new, just as Edwin is about to enter into a new life. The murder is shortly after midnight, and, symbolically, it stops time itself. A fierce storm rages that night that only subsides early Christmas morning:

> It is then seen that the hands of the Cathedral clock are torn off; that lead from the roof has been stripped away, rolled up, and blown into the Close; and that some stones have been displaced upon the summit of the great tower. Christmas morning though it be, it is necessary to send up workmen to ascertain the extent of the damage done. These, led by Durdles, go aloft; while Mr. Tope and a crowd of early idlers gather down in Minor Canon

Corner, shading their eyes and watching for their appearance up
there.

This cluster is suddenly broken and put aside by the hands
of Mr. Jasper; all the gazing eyes are brought down to the earth
by his loudly inquiring of Mr. Crisparkle, at an open window:
"Where is my nephew?" (168)

The hands of Jasper have, figuratively, stopped the hands of the Cathedral
clock—and the hands of Edwin's watch, so recently set and wound and
now, its owner dead, once more allowed to run down. Jasper has immured
Edwin's body in Mrs. Sapsea's monument and covered the body with some
of Durdles' quick-lime: he hopes to *annihilate* Edwin, to put him outside
of time, into the irrecoverable world of the "old 'uns," to violate the
natural cycle of death, decay, and life that Dickens establishes at the outset of the novel. It is thus, perhaps, that Jasper reacts with scorn and apparent reluctance to Durdles' assertion that he once had heard a mysterious cry:

> "What do you mean?" is the very abrupt, and, one might say,
> fierce retort.
> "I mean that I made inquiries everywhere about, and that
> no living ears but mine heard either that cry or that howl. So I
> say they was both ghosts; though why they came to me, I've never
> made out."
> "I thought you were another kind of man," says Jasper,
> scornfully.
> "So I thought myself," answers Durdles with his usual com-
> posure; "and yet I was picked out for it."
> Jasper had risen suddenly, when he asked him what he
> meant, and he now says, "Come; we shall freeze here; lead the
> way." (136)

If, as Dickens hints, Jasper's reaction here is rather in excess of the facts
as they appear, the reason is that he plans to commit a murder, to put
Edwin Drood out of time; in his own mind, he must insist on the discontinuity of time, of the dead and the living. And to get the key to Mrs.
Sapsea's monument, Jasper must ply Durdles with liquor until he loses
all sense of time, until he falls asleep, dreaming that he counts Jasper's
footsteps and "that the footsteps die away into distance of time and of
space" (138); when Durdles at last awakens, he must ask:

> "What's the time?"
> "Hark! The bells are going in the Tower!"
> They strike four quarters, and then the great bell strikes.
> "Two!" cries Durdles, scrambling up; "why didn't you try
> to wake me, Mister Jarsper?"
> "I did. I might as well have tried to wake the dead." (139)

Cloisterham—and the moral universe of the novel—lives comfortably with its past, and its future is just as comfortably secure in the hands of its young citizens, who, at the end of the novel, will be paired off to continue the natural cycle of life, death, and new life that Dickens has established at the outset. But meanwhile, one of these young people has been murdered, the cycle interrupted, and the unfinished half of the novel must have dealt with its reestablishment. Meanwhile, the *leitmotif* of time has served one of its purposes: we can see that the storm that accompanies the murder is not simply melodramatic embellishment, any more than the storm that accompanies the murder of Duncan in *Macbeth* or even the trembling of nature that accompanies the original sin in *Paradise Lost*. The murder of Edwin Drood is not simply repulsive in itself: it is a violation of the natural order.

Finally, the natural cycle will be reestablished; time will be fulfilled. The ring that Edwin receives from Grewgious and that is buried with his corpse is at once the means and the symbol of this fulfillment. Through the ring, of course, the body will be identified and justice ultimately accomplished. Dickens develops the theme in his own comment on Edwin's decision not to mention the ring to Rosa, a decision that means that it will remain hidden in his inner pocket, where Jasper will not find it:

> Let them [the jewels of the ring] be. Let them lie unspoken of, in his breast. However distinctly or indistinctly he entertained these thoughts, he arrived at the conclusion, Let them be. Among the mighty store of wonderful chains that are for ever forging, day and night, in the vast iron-works of time and circumstance, there was one chain forged in the moment of that small conclusion, riveted to the foundations of heaven and earth, and gifted with invincible force to hold and drag. (151)

Time is not simply a matter of coincidence—it is a moral force.[7] The image of the chain, of course, is a recollection of *Great Expectations:*

> That was a memorable day to me, for it made great changes in me. But it is the same with any life. Imagine one selected day struck out of it, and think how different its course would have been. Pause you who read this, and think for a moment of the long chain of iron or gold, of thorns or flowers, that would never have bound you, but for the formation of the first link on one memorable day.[8]

Here even more, there is the feeling that the course of time is more than merely consequential, that the past will come full circle in the future, that it is "gifted with invincible force to hold and drag." *Drag:* Rosa has used the same word only a few pages earlier, explaining her relief that the prearranged engagement is at last broken off:

> "And you know," said Rosa innocently, "you couldn't like me
> then; and you can always like me now, for I shall not be a drag
> upon you, or a worry to you." (147)

Rosa uses the word in abnegating her hold on Edwin, in freeing him from
an unnatural situation that the past has laid on him — for among the good
people of the novel, what is unnatural in the past can ultimately be laid
aside. The chief unnatural act, however, and one that cannot be laid
aside, is the murder, and now the ring will be a "drag" on Jasper as his
past catches up with him. Edwin has been charged "by the living and by
the dead" to return the ring should his engagement to Rosa be broken
off (125). Ironically, gruesomely, he will keep this charge, and the ring
will return again to Mr. Grewgious' keeping, where it will take its place
among the bitter-sweet memories of things dead until, like the many
other ghosts in *The Mystery of Edwin Drood,* it once more rejoins the
living, returning "into circulation again, to repeat [its] former round"
(151).[9]

In *Great Expectations* the metaphysical chains that bind day to day
are man made, just as are the physical chains that bind Magwitch or that
stretch across the door of Satis House. And in other Dickens' novels in
which the evil lies predominantly in some social institution, the central
symbol will commonly be a symbol of that institution, such as the disease-
ridden fog that represents Chancery in *Bleak House* or the prison in
Little Dorrit. His last novel, however, takes place out of the mainstream
of Victorian society, in a universe that is morally ordered, and where evil
is the act of individual men. The central symbol, then, is of this order
itself, this force which underlies those acts of men and by which those
acts are to be judged. Against the background of time the tale of Jasper
and Edwin Drood unfolds. Against the background of time we see Jasper's
unnaturalness and the particular unnaturalness of the murder he commits. And time itself will bring about the solution to the mystery of
Edwin Drood.

The keynote to the completed half of the novel is sounded at the end
of the first chapter when, "awakening muttered thunder" (4), a passage
from Proverbs is intoned in the Cathedral. Dickens cites (incorrectly)
only the first four words, but the rest of the verse and the one following
are what he evidently had in mind:

> When a wicked man dieth, his expectation shall perish: and the
> hope of unjust men perisheth. The righteous is delivered out of
> trouble, and the wicked cometh in his stead. (11 : 7–8)

The keynote to the unwritten half of the novel, I think, comes in another
Cathedral scene and another, less somber biblical allusion; it is on almost
the last page that Dickens wrote:

> A brilliant morning shines on the old city. Its antiquities and ruins are surpassingly beautiful, with a lusty ivy gleaming in the sun, and the rich trees waving in the balmy air. Changes of glorious light from moving boughs, songs of birds, scents from gardens, woods, and fields—or, rather, from the one great garden of the whole cultivated island in its yielding time—penetrate into the Cathedral, subdue its earthy odour, and preach the Resurrection and the Life. The cold stone tombs of centuries ago grow warm; and flecks of brightness dart into the sternest marble corners of the building, fluttering there like wings. (277)

"I am the resurrection, and the life: he that believeth in me, though he were dead, yet shall he live" (John, 11 : 25). The Gospel is describing the greatest miracle: the raising of Lazarus. In Dickens' hands, however, the specifically miraculous disappears, replaced by the recurrent, cyclical pattern of time, as spring comes to Cloisterham Cathedral, where past and present daily meet, at a moment when the novel begins hastening toward the deliverance of the righteous out of trouble and the coming of the wicked in his stead.

Earlier, a man of the church had confronted and consoled a righteous man in trouble:

> "And you must expect no miracle to help you, Neville," said Mr. Crisparkle, compassionately.
> "No, sir, I know that. The ordinary fulness of time and circumstances is all I have to trust to." (197)

It is the sort of thing an earnest young minor canon might well say to his earnest young charge; in the context of *Edwin Drood,* however, it makes far deeper sense than a casual eavesdropper would suspect.

NOTES

INDEX

HARRY STONE: *The Unknown Dickens*

¹ I have recently collected Dickens' hitherto unidentified and uncollected contributions to *Household Words*. See *Charles Dickens' Uncollected Writings from "Household Words" (1850–1859)*, ed. Harry Stone, 2 vols. (Bloomington: Indiana University Press, 1968).

² Professor K. J. Fielding and Alec W. Brice have recently done valuable work on the *Examiner*.

³ Professor Philip Collins is interested in some of these problems.

⁴ For a discussion of these means see the headnotes and footnotes to the portions of the extra Christmas numbers retrieved in my edition of the *Uncollected Writings*. See note 1.

⁵ The title varies. Some copies contain the following title page: *The Nine Christmas Numbers of All the Year Round, Conducted by Charles Dickens*. In all copies that I have seen, the spine bears the following legend: *Christmas Stories from All the Year Round Conducted by Chas. Dickens*. There are variations also in the original cloth bindings and in other matters not affecting the text.

⁶ The first seven extra Christmas numbers of *All the Year Round* were issued anonymously, the last two, *Mugby Junction* (1866) and *No Thoroughfare* (1867), listed the authors on the wrapper and on the first page. I have also seen advertisements dated 1864 which list the contributors to each of the first five extra Christmas numbers of *All the Year Round*. These ads simply list each number and its contributors, however; they do not specify who wrote what.

⁷ All letters, unless otherwise noted, are quoted from *The Letters of Charles Dickens*, ed. Walter Dexter, 3 vols. (Bloomsbury: The Nonesuch Press, 1938). Rather than give volume and page references, I include the date and recipient of each letter cited.

⁸ John Hollingshead, *My Lifetime*, 2nd ed., 2 vols. (London: Sampson Low, Marston & Company, 1895), I, 110.

⁹ *The Minor Writings*, p. 161.

¹⁰ *My Lifetime*, I, 110–12.

¹¹ I am grateful to Mrs. Madeline House and the Clarendon Press for information concerning these letters.

¹² Carl Ray Woodring, *Victorian Samplers: William and Mary Howitt* (Lawrence: University of Kansas Press, 1952), p. 203.

¹³ William Howitt, *The History of the Supernatural*, 2 vols. (London: Longman, Green, Longman, Roberts, & Green, 1863), II, 440.

¹⁴ Dickens' encounters with Howitt were preceded and followed by many other Dickensian dealings with spiritualists. These dealings, covering a period of many years, included Dickens' attendance at séances, a good deal of

correspondence with spiritualists and their supporters, much reading on spiritualism and allied subjects, many antagonistic articles on spiritualism by Dickens and others in *Household Words* and *All the Year Round,* and much attention to Dickens (often erroneous or abusive) in spiritualist periodicals. In all these matters, Dickens' attitude was always skeptical or hostile, and his skirmishes with Howitt should be seen as a battle in a much larger war. For a brief history of that war, see N. C. Peyrouton, "Rapping the Rappers: More Grist for the Biographers' Mill," *Dickensian,* LV (January 1959), 19–30; (May 1959), 75–89.

[15] Kitton, p. 161, says that Dickens was responsible for the openings of all the segments not his own "except 'The Ghost in the Picture-Room,' which is in rhyme." He is clearly in error here, apparently having for-

gotten that there is a brief prose introduction.

[16] This, of course, is further evidence of Dickens' authorship. Other members of the "society" at the haunted house can also be linked to Dickens' circle, and it seems likely that Dickens incorporated these details into *The Haunted House* as a kind of Christmas *jeu d'esprit.* For example, the narrator's chief companion, a "maiden sister . . . I venture to call her eight-and-thirty, she is so very handsome, sensible, and engaging"—seems a version of Georgina Hogarth, Dickens' maiden sister-in-law, then thirty-two, and since his recent separation from his wife, the manager of his household. And "Turk," the bloodhound the narrator and his sister bring with them to the haunted house, seems a version of Dickens' own bloodhound, also named Turk.

MARGARET GANZ: *The Vulnerable Ego*

[1] "Remonstrance with Dickens," *Blackwood's Edinburgh Magazine,* LXXXI (January–June 1857), 497; Henry James, *The Future of the Novel* (New York, 1956), p. 75.

[2] For instances of early praise see "The Pickwick Papers," *Quarterly Review,* LIX (1837), 484–518, and "The Pickwick Papers," *London and Westminster Review,* XXVII (July 1837), 194–215. In 1864 the *Westminster Review* reaffirmed its earlier judgment of Dickens in "Modern Novelists: Charles Dickens" by calling his humor the "first . . . most important . . . most distinctive of his attributes (N.S. XXVI, 417). *Fraser's Magazine* in "The Early Life of Charles Dickens" (N.S. V [January–June 1872], 112) noted with disappointment "an increase of mannerism . . . and in the self-complacence of an actor sure of applause, the most artificial efforts at humor and pathos [being] produced without any gauging of their worth." In 1874 *Temple Bar* deplored "the

mere mannerisms without novelty, and the grotesqueness without humor, into which Dickens, once so fresh, so original, and so matchlessly humorous, was already slowly lapsing" in his last years; see "Bulwer and Dickens. A Contrast," XLIII (1874–75), 176.

[3] John Gross, "Dickens: Some Recent Approaches," *Dickens and the Twentieth Century,* ed. John Gross and Gabriel Pearson (London, 1962), p. xii.

[4] See Monroe Engel, *The Maturity of Dickens* (Cambridge, 1959), pp. 80–82; J. Hillis Miller, *Charles Dickens: The World of His Novels* (Cambridge, Mass., 1959), pp. 36–84; Edgar Johnson, *Charles Dickens: His Tragedy and Triumph* (New York, 1952), I, 325–27. In a more recent study devoted to the early novels, *Dickens: from Pickwick to Dombey* (New York, 1965), Steven Marcus is concerned with the function of Mr. Pickwick and Tony Weller as representatives of "the self still secure and

undisturbed by internal conflicts" rather than with the humorous reverberations of their innocent grapplings with the world of experience. Emphasizing the theme of "true prudence" in *Nicholas Nickleby,* Marcus adduces Mrs. Nickleby's cavalier treatment of reality as evidence of imprudence but, beyond a reference to Dickens' "comic intelligence" at work, is not impelled to explore the humorous function and impact of her divagations (see pp. 38, 35-39, 99-100). In two very recent articles on *Oliver Twist* and *David Copperfield* in which the emphasis does fall on the comic aspects of Dickens' work, the approach is self-consciously cerebral in its application of the insights of Bergson (whose relevance to English humor is in many ways dubious) to Dickens' art. For further comments on James R. Kincaid's two essays, "Laughter and *Oliver Twist*," PMLA, LXXXIII (March 1968), 63-70, and "Dickens' Subversive Humor: *David Copperfield*," *Nineteenth-Century Fiction,* XII (March 1968), 313-29, see my article "Humor's Alchemy: The Lesson of *Sketches by Boz*," *Genre,* I (October 1968), footnote 5, pp. 300-301.
5   See for example Chesterton's praise of "the really great comic characters of Dickens" in *Charles Dickens, The Last of the Great Men* (New York, 1942), p. 85. George Gissing's conviction that "humour is the soul of his work," and David Cecil's view the Dickens' " 'pure' humour" is "intoxicatingly funny" are other cases in point. See Gissing's *Charles Dickens: A Critical Study* (London, 1903), p. 166, and Cecil's *Early Victorian Novelists* (London, 1934), p. 43. A. O. J. Cockshut's distinction of two types of humor in Dickens, the "negative" resting on and the "positive" transcending "moral categories," bears some resemblance to Cecil's distinction between "pure" and "satirical" humor (*The Imagination of Charles Dickens* [New York, 1962], pp. 16-18). It is the "pure" or "positive" humor to which

we refer as *humor* proper, assigning to it a greater importance than Cecil or Cockshut have done, in the conviction that, transcending the narrow didacticism of satire in its genial exploration of universal incongruities and paradoxes, it is capable of offering a rich and complex criticism of life.
6   Quoted by John Forster in *The Life of Charles Dickens* (London, 1927), II, 273. This apology is one of the many instances given by George Ford of Dickens' reactions to charges of improbability in his novels (see *Dickens and his Readers: Aspects of Novel-Criticism since 1836* [Princeton, 1955], pp. 129-55).
7   Cockshut astutely points to a weakness in the handling of symbols as he refers to the "conveniently symbolical" "pile of rags and bones" in the home of Mrs. Brown in *Dombey and Son,* and goes on to comment wryly that "few prostitutes, still less their mothers, would have the symbolic requirements of novelists so much at heart so as to put up with the inconvenience of piles of rags and bones on the floor" (*The Imagination of Charles Dickens,* pp. 106, 107). Dickens' most successful use of symbols (of the fog in *Bleak House,* for example) is related to the inspired power of observation and description which, from the start, made him a masterly creator of atmosphere; merely by describing the fog or the river Thames, he already enhances and transfigures their importance.
8   See "Le mécanisme de l'humour," *Études de psychologie littéraire* (Paris, 1913), pp. 97-160. This brilliant essay is essential to any study of humor.
9   Without specifically mentioning humor, Chesterton makes a similar point in finding the actions of Mrs. Nickleby quite secondary to the "inexhaustible fairyland" of her past memories, so wonderful for her "to whom relevancy is nothing." "There is no particular necessity," Chesterton tells us, "that we should know what happens to Madeline Bray. There is a

desperate and crying necessity that we should know that Mrs. Nickleby once had a foot-boy who had a wart on his nose and a driver who had a green shade over his left eye" (*Charles Dickens*, p. 84).

10 Ibid., p. 63.

11 Sigmund Freud, "Humour," trans. Joan Riviere, *Collected Papers*, ed. James Strachey (New York, 1959), V, 217.

12 Ibid.

13 See Edgar Johnson, *Charles Dickens*, I, 241–53.

14 For Edgar Johnson, "the period of *Dombey and Son* represents a turning point both in Dickens' life and in his literary art" and witnesses the expression of a "discontent" that "had roots in personal emotion, but . . . was reflected too in his changing outlook on society." He was now led to question "the share the solid member of society had in allowing and fostering evils of which he was often smugly unaware" (*Charles Dickens*, II, 626–27).

15 See Ford, *Dickens and his Readers*, pp. 111–13. Lionel Stevenson sees the alteration of mood, structure, style, and characterization in the three novels that follow *David Copperfield*—*Bleak House, Hard Times*, and *Little Dorrit*—as evidence of Dickens' attempts to meet the challenge of Charlotte Brontë, Thackeray, Mrs. Gaskell, and Kingsley ("Dickens's Dark Novels, 1851–1857," *Sewanee Review*, LI [1943], 397–409).

16 John Butt and Kathleen Tillotson, *Dickens at Work* (London, 1957), p. 25. According to them, "the sparseness of notes in the first complete manuscript, that of *The Old Curiosity Shop*" suggests that those for the preceding novels "are likely to have been very slight indeed." See pp. 25–34 for their discussion of Dickens' use of notes in the novels that follow.

17 *The Letters of Charles Dickens*, ed. Walter Dexter (London, 1938), II, 747. All references to Dickens' texts in this study are from *The Nonesuch*

Dickens, 23 vols. (Bloomsbury, 1937–38).

18 So original in fact was the style of his greatest humorous creations that it endowed them with a greater authenticity than those characters who spoke and acted in a realistic manner. As Ford puts it, Dickens' "really flat characters," such as "his insipid heroes and heroines," "are more ordinary, more natural, and hence should supposedly be more probable" than the "highly stylized, strongly-colored individuals," yet in contrast with them, "they are pale and insignificant, and, paradoxically, improbable" (*Dickens and his Readers*, p. 137).

19 See "Preface to The First Cheap Edition" in *Martin Chuzzlewit* (London, 1937), p. xii.

20 Ibid., p. 472.

21 Gissing, in his perceptive discussion of the resemblance between the two characters, notes that "the same perfect method of idealism is put to use in converting to a source of pleasure things that in life repel or nauseate; and in both cases the sublimation of character, of circumstance, is effected by a humor which seems unsurpassable" (*Charles Dickens*, pp. 171–72).

22 *Martin Chuzzlewit*, p. 755.

23 Ibid., p. 763.

24 Ibid., p. 629.

25 Ibid., p. 409.

26 Ibid., pp. 628, 760, 763. The best confirmation of some of my suggestions regarding the power of Mrs. Gamp's language is to be found in Cockshut, *The Imagination of Charles Dickens*, pp. 20, 21.

27 There are of course other examples of it in *Martin Chuzzlewit* itself, in young Bailey's impudent remarks, in Mrs. Todgers' pronouncement on gravy, in the early insolent discourses of Montague Tigg, and in the wild rhetoric of General Clarke and Elijah Pogram. Though we will see a clear instance of the power of expression in Flora Finching of *Little Dorrit*, many of the characters in the

novels that follow *Chuzzlewit* exhibit a certain quaintness of style: Susan Nipper in *Dombey and Son*, Betsey Trotwood in *David Copperfield*, Boythorn in *Bleak House*, Mr. Plornish, John Chivery, and Mrs. Tickit in *Little Dorrit*, Joe Gargery in *Great Expectations*, and "the Billickin" in *The Mystery of Edwin Drood*.

28 To a certain extent the character of Pecksniff prepares us for this shift in emphasis. Though he is a far more prominent figure in *Martin Chuzzlewit* than Mrs. Gamp, she easily overshadows him because of the inventiveness of her expression which stamps her with personality. He is merely an emblem of hypocrisy who reveals himself in a prolix, mannered, and platitudinous style, calculated to arouse mockery and indignation, but often only unbearably tedious. His whimsical reference to the babyhood of his daughter Cherry, whom he "carried . . . in [his] arms, when she wore shapeless worsted shoes—I might say mufflers—" is a rare instance of inventive grotesquerie. His standard mode of expression is exemplified in this hypocritical speech to Tom Pinch: "If it comes to pass that either of us be run over, in any of those busy crossings which divide the streets of life, the other will convey him to the hospital in Hope, and sit beside his bed in Bounty!" (*Martin Chuzzlewit*, pp. 81, 475). Dickens' moral indignation already here vitiates his delight in the eccentricities of the mind which had made Squeers and Bumble appealing; this muting of his humor will again be evident in the rhetoric of the Reverend Chadband in *Bleak House*, and the pompous pronouncements of Mr. Sapsea in *The Mystery of Edwin Drood*.

29 *David Copperfield*, (London, 1937), pp. 155, 173.

30 Ibid., p. 696.

31 Ibid., pp. 747–48. Dickens' attitude to the Micawbers may also have been influenced by his own ambivalence towards his parents. For the re-

semblances between the Micawbers and Mr. and Mrs. Dickens, see Johnson, *Charles Dickens*, II, 680–84.

32 *David Copperfield*, p. 757. Just before Micawber's departure, David notices that "he had acquired a bold buccaneering air, not absolutely lawless, but defensive and prompt. One might have supposed him a child of the wilderness, long accustomed to live out of the confines of civilization, and about to return to his native wilds" (p. 796).

33 The character of Mrs. Pardiggle is another case in point. See *Bleak House* (London, 1938), pp. 99–106.

34 *Hard Times*, (London, 1937), pp. 502, 588, 713, 642.

35 Ibid., p. 730.

36 Ibid., p. 731.

37 Ibid., p. 760. The seriousness of Dickens' purpose is evident, as, in a letter to Charles Knight (March 1854) he calls attention to Sleary's speech in *Hard Times*, in which he has "jocosely suggested" the need for diversions from toil. He goes on to say: "The English are, so far as I know, the hardest-working people on whom the sun shines. Be content if, in their wretched intervals of pleasure, they read for amusement and do no worse. They are born at the oar, and they live and die at it. Good God, what would we have of them!" In a letter to his son, Henry Fielding (March 1870), he quotes part of Sleary's speech to enforce his conviction "that narrow-minded fanatics, who decry the theatre and defame its artists, are absolutely the advocates of depraved and barbarous amusements" (*The Letters of Charles Dickens*, II, 548; III, 769).

38 *Little Dorrit*, (London, 1937), pp. 163, 164, 177.

39 Ibid., p. 554.

40 Ibid.

41 Ibid., pp. 277, 292, 294.

42 Ibid., p. 159.

43 Ibid., p. 160.

44 We know of course that Dickens had endured a disappointment similar

to that of Arthur in meeting again after many years his earliest love—Maria Beadnell—and in witnessing in her some of the appalling changes displayed by Flora. For the details of his personal death of an illusion, see Edgar Johnson, *Charles Dickens*, II, 830-39. Yet Dickens' sense of the universality of disillusionment is conveyed in a letter to the Duke of Devonshire (July 1856) in which he states: "It came into my head one day that we have all had our Floras (mine is living, and extremely fat), and that it was a half serious half ridiculous truth which had never been told" (*The Letters of Charles Dickens*, II, 785).

JOHN R. REED: *Confinement and Character in Dickens' Novels*

1   For W. H. Auden, the movement in *The Pickwick Papers* is from the uncommitted world of games to the involved world of the real, and it is his "encounter with the world of the Fleet [that ends] Mr. Pickwick's innocence." "Dingley Dell & the Fleet," in *Dickens: A Collection of Critical Essays*, ed. Martin Price (Englewood Cliffs, N. J., 1967), p. 81.

2   Of course, Dickens exercised throughout his career a strict hand over illustrations for his books and therefore close coordination between text and illustration is not unusual.

3   I believe Albert Johannsen, in *Phiz Illustrations from the Novels of Charles Dickens* (Chicago, 1956) is incorrect in identifying the female figure as Miss Tox (p. 306).

4   There are several illustrations in *Pickwick* that encourage a spatial reading, especially that showing Pickwick in the pound and the one picturing Grubb with the goblin. In both, a church steeple looms in the background, shrinking the center of the illustration to claustrophobic proportions.

5   Lionel Trilling, "Introduction," *Little Dorrit* (London, 1953).

6   See *Little Dorrit*, I, ii, ix; II, xii; and elsewhere.

7   Edgar Johnson, *Charles Dickens: His Tragedy and Triumph* (Boston, 1952), I, 46.

8   Dickens was, for example, deeply concerned with prisons as social realities and visited them in England or while traveling abroad. He was constantly aware of the spatial limitations of living accommodations. Sylvère Monod has suggested that Dickens desired to put undesirable persons (including his own children) at a distance from himself, and even Dickens' parents found themselves exiled to the little Exeter cottage which did not suit their needs so well as their son's. This spatial fascination might appear darker in tone if we considered Dickens' need to escape from the restraints of his work by long rides or walks, and later by extensive and prolonged trips abroad. Dickens' intimate understanding of London as space—as neighborhoods, streets, chambers contingent upon one another—might explain his "craving for streets" that constantly haunted him when he was away from the city. Though Dickens was impressed by American distances, he was at home among the involved turnings of London's more controlled spaces. It would even be possible, if one chose, to suggest a more sinister shade in Dickens' spatial concerns by noting his fascination with the hidden regions beneath Venice when he visited that city, or his desire to share Mary Hogarth's burial space.

9   George H. Ford, *Dickens and His Readers: Aspects of Novel-Criticism since 1836* (New York, 1965), p. 143. Sylvère Monod also regards Dickens' novels as "spatial rather than temporal," as journeys or roads rather than movements in time. Time itself is rendered "into visible distances." *Dickens the Novelist* (Norman, Okla., 1968), p. 79.

10   Dorothy Van Ghent, "The Dick-

ens World: A View from Todgers's," in Price, p. 34.

[11] J. Hillis Miller, *Charles Dickens: The World of His Novels* (Cambridge, Mass., 1965), p. 43. Miller develops the implications of the labyrinth metaphor in Dickens' novels, and, in a different manner from my own, concerns himself with Dickens' search for identity.

[12] See chapter five of Steven Marcus' *Dickens: From Pickwick to Dombey* (New York, 1965) for discussion of pressures in *Barnaby Rudge.*

[13] The other emblematic ship in *David Copperfield* is the one that carries Emily and Mr. Peggotty away to begin a new life. "A sight at once so beautiful, so mournful, and so hopeful, as the glorious ship, lying, still, on the flushed water, with all the life on board her crowded at the bulwarks, and there clustering, for a moment, bareheaded, and silent, I never saw" (lvii).

[14] See Gwendolyn B. Needham's "The Undisciplined Heart of David Copperfield," *Nineteenth-Century Fiction,* IX (1954), 81–107, for a discussion of this aspect of David's development.

[15] In David's attempt to form Dora's mind, Dickens may have been recognizing an impulse in himself to direct others. He was, after all, an enthusiastic and demanding director of theatrical performances, took a sincere interest in reshaping the lives of fallen women, and required absolute control over his business ventures when he could demand it.

[16] Dickens' villains are often counter-images of what he probably conceived himself to be, though his heroes are rarely self-imitations. Barbara Hardy is correct in saying that, for Dickens and other nineteenth-century novelists, the typical conversion is "a turning from self-regard to love and social responsibility" ("The Change of Heart in Dickens' Novels," in Price, p. 39). For Dickens, this conversion follows some form of constraint or

confinement, often not only metaphorical, as the proliferation of quasi-institutions such as the Fleet, Fagin's den, or Dotheboys Hall, where the children resemble "malefactors in a jail," testifies (NN, viii).

[17] But see below in this study: David equates the discipline of his life with the discipline of art.

[18] Such discoveries are described in Johnson, II, 689; and Monod, pp. 303 and 454. Dickens' own literary career moved in a pattern similar to those in his novels, for his early writings appeared under the name Boz; he then assumed his proper identity as Charles Dickens; and ultimately merged his identity with his works in his theatrical readings. Similarly, space was continually a preoccupation not only in his fictional world, but in the world of composition itself: from his penny-a-line reporting, to serial publication, wherein he worked from one self-contained unit to another toward a gradual liberation, to his sense of constraint under Bentley and other publishers, to his frustration with small numbers. "The difficulty of the space," he complained of writing *Hard Times,* "is CRUSHING," and "the small portions" of *A Tale of Two Cities,* drove him "frantic" (Johnson, II, 796 and 950). And he admitted to "an enormous outlay in the Father of Marshalsea chapter, in the way of getting a great lot of matter into a small space" (Johnson, II, 847).

[19] Monod, p. 69.

[20] Archibald C. Coolidge, Jr., *Charles Dickens as Serial Novelist* (Ames, Iowa, 1967), pp. 144–45, touches on this subject.

[21] Robert Garis, in *The Dickens Theatre: A Reassessment of the Novels* (Oxford, 1965), sees Dickens' concern with character as shaped by a "theatrical" view. Thus, although for him the novel is not a character, it is the space in which characters perform. But also, see note 25 below.

[22] Johnson, II, 603.

[23] Ibid., I, 295.

[24] Ibid., I, 43.
[25] Garis sees the novels themselves as performance. Hence, Dickens' performance of them later was almost an inevitability. Of Dickens the author, Garis says: "This describer, this artist, is present before us not as a personality, with particular personal feelings, attitudes, and habits, but as a performer, as a maker and doer" (p. 9).

DUANE DEVRIES: *Two Glimpses of Dickens' Early Development as a Writer of Fiction*

[1] Published in December 1836. The original version is reprinted in " 'In All the Glory of Print,' " *Dickensian*, XXX (1933-34), 1-10, and in F. J. H. Darton's *Dickens, Positively the First Appearance* (London, 1933), pp. 53-68. Darton deals briefly with the revisions that Dickens made in "A Dinner at Poplar Walk" (better known to readers as "Mr. Minns and His Cousin," the new title that Dickens gave it in 1836), as do John Butt and Kathleen Tillotson in Chapter II ("*Sketches by Boz:* Collection and Revision") of *Dickens at Work* (Fair Lawn, N. J., 1958), and Siegfried Benignus in his early and largely neglected *Studien über die Anfänge von Dickens* (Ph.D. dissertation, University of Strasbourg, 1895; published Esslingen, 1895). "A Dinner at Poplar Walk" is, as Butt and Tillotson indicate, "the most thoroughly revised of all the tales" (p. 43).
[2] In December 1833, Dickens proudly wrote to his friend, Henry Kolle, that the *London Weekly Magazine* (still known to Dickens by its former title, *The Thief*) had pirated "A Dinner at Poplar Walk" for publication and that he had received "a polite and flattering communication from The Monthly people requesting more papers." See *The Letters of Charles Dickens*, ed. Madeline House and Graham Storey (Oxford, 1965), I (1820-39), 33.
[3] In "Comic Viewpoints in *Sketches by Boz*," *English*, XII (1958-59), C. B. Cox states that the important theme of the tale is implicit in the contrast that Dickens draws between the coldness and drabness of Minns' "ordered existence" and the "exuberant joy in life" of Bagshaw (pp. 133-34). In addition to the evidence that I have already given in the text, one need only contrast the relationship between Scrooge and his nephew in *A Christmas Carol* (which does, it seems to me, illustrate the contrast of which Cox speaks) with that between Minns and his cousin to realize that Dickens does *not* favor the Bagshaws to Minns.

LOUIS JAMES: *Pickwick in America!*

[1] "On the Genius and Character of Hogarth," in *Life, Letters and Writings of Charles Lamb*, ed. Percy Fitzgerald (London, 1903), IV, 288.
[2] Madeline House and Graham Storey, eds., *The Letters of Charles Dickens* (London, 1965), I, 431 n.
[3] LXVIII (1838-39), 77.
[4] Louis James, *Fiction for the Working Man 1830-1850* (London, 1963), pp. 47-49. (Revised edition pending.)
[5] John Butt and Kathleen Tillotson, *Dickens at Work* (London, 1957), p. 64.
[6] Dion Boucicault, "The Art of Acting," in *Laurel British Drama, the Nineteenth Century*, ed. Robert Corrigan (New York, 1967), p. 32.
[7] Ibid., p. 18. See also Gary J. Scrimgeour, "Nineteenth Century Drama," *Victorian Studies*, XII (September, 1968), 91-100. Anyone writing on Dickens and the drama is today indebted to Robert E. Garis, *The Dickens Theatre* (Oxford, 1965), and William F. Axton, *Circle of Fire* (Lexington, 1966).

8   Edgar Johnson, *Charles Dickens* (New York, 1952), I, 60.
9   Earle Davis, *The Flint and the Flame* (Columbia, 1963), pp. 37–53.
10 Charles Mathews, *Sketches of Mr. Mathews' Celebrated Trip to America* (London, 1825), p. 17.
11 *Life in London* (London, 1821),

p. 9.
12 J. Franklin, *The Cockney* (London, 1953), p. 9
13 W. H. Auden, "Dingley Dell and the Fleet" in *The Dyer's Hand* (London, 1962).
14 Pierce Egan, Sr., *Life in London*, pp. xiii–xiv.

JANE RABB COHEN: *Strained Relations*

   All citations to the work of Charles Dickens and George Cattermole, given parenthetically in the text of this paper, refer to their locations in *The Nonesuch Dickens*, ed. Arthur Waugh, Hugh Walpole, Walter Dexter, and Thomas Hatton (Bloomsbury, 1939), n.v.n. When relevant, the original date and place of a work is supplied in a separate footnote, as are all the sources of Dickens' correspondence and of the reproduced illustrated matter. Abbreviations of titles, used both in the text and in the footnotes are listed as follows:

SBB	*Sketches by Boz* (which contains the portions of *Master Humphrey's Clock* other than OCS and BR)
NN	*Nicholas Nickleby*
OCS	*The Old Curiosity Shop*
BR	*Barnaby Rudge*
NL, I, II, III	*The Letters of Charles Dickens*, ed. Walter Dexter (Bloomsbury, 1938) which will be superseded by
Pilgrim, I–	*The Letters of Charles Dickens*, ed. Madeline House and Graham Storey (Oxford, 1965–). Only Volume I, covering the years 1820–39, has appeared at this date of writing.
Unpub. Pilgrim	"MS. Files of the Pilgrim Edition of Charles Dickens's Letters," ed. House and Storey, which the editors kindly made accessible to the writer.

1   John Ruskin, "Modern Painters," *The Works of John Ruskin*, ed. E. T. Cook and Alexander Wedderburn (London, 1903–12), III, 220–21. See also William Rossetti, *Fine Art Chiefly Contemporary* (London, 1867), p. 162, for another estimate of Cattermole as "an artist of real talent much cankered by flimsiness."
2   William Makepeace Thackeray, quoted in Lewis Marvy, ed., *Sketches after English Landscape Painters* (London, 1850), n.p.n.
3   Pilgrim, I, 277–78, Forster [26 June 1837], Cattermole's presence on the prison tour is not mentioned by John Forster, *The Life of Charles*

Dickens, ed. J. W. T. Ley (London, 1928), p. 132, but is noted by William Charles Macready, Diary Entry for 27 June 1837, *The Diaries of William Charles Macready, 1833–51*, ed. William Toynbee (New York, 1912), I, 401–2. See also Thackeray, *The Letters and Private Papers of William Makepeace Thackeray*, ed. Gordon N. Ray (Cambridge, Mass., 1945), I, 413, Letter to Mrs. Carmichael-Smyth, 19 January 1840: Thackeray's observation that Cattermole's manner of speech was "full of Walter Scottisms" is doubtless relevant to Dickens' comment here.
4   Pilgrim,   I,   375,   Cattermole

[?February 1838]; and see Pilgrim, I, 637; Diary, 12 December 1838.

5 Mrs. George Cattermole, quoted in Frederic G. Kitton, *Charles Dickens by Pen and Pencil* (London, 1889–90), II, 181–82.

6 Pilgrim, I, 576, Cattermole [21 August 1839].

7 Mrs. George Cattermole, quoted in Kitton, *Dickens by Pen and Pencil*, II, 182.

8 Pilgrim, I, 583, Cattermole, 21 September 1839. The artist's presence is not noted by Forster, p. 127, but is by Macready, Diary Entry for 5 October 1839, II, 25.

9 NL, I, 245–46, Cattermole, 13 January 1840.

10 Cf. Robert Buss, "My Connexion with *The Pickwick Papers*," in Walter Dexter and J. W. T. Ley, *The Origin of Pickwick* (London, 1936), p. 134.

11 NL, I, 251–52, Cattermole, 9 March 1840 and NL, I, 252, Cattermole, March, 1840.

12 NL, I, to Cattermole: 349, 12 September 1841; 269, 14 August 1840; 342, 28 July 1841; 293, 14 January 1841; 251–52, 9 March 1840; 269, 14 August 1840; and 346, 19 August 1841.

13 Cf. W. A. Fraser, "The Illustrators of Dickens. III. George Cattermole," *Dickensian*, II (September 1906), 237–39; and see Pilgrim I, 589, Cruikshank [?3 October 1839]: Cruikshank was to have illustrated BR when it was first conceived, but, by the time Dickens finally wrote the novel in 1841, Cruikshank was preoccupied with other works; Kitton, *Dickens and His Illustrators* (London, 1899), p. 133.

14 NL, I, 269, Cattermole, 14 August 1840 and NL, I, 297, Cattermole, 28 January 1841; NL, I, 298, Cattermole, 30 January 1841 [Browne did the raven] and NL, I, 350, Cattermole, 12 September 1841 [Browne did the frontispieces for MHC, II and III and the final illustration]. See also Browne, Letter to Dickens, undated, in Kitton, *Dickens and His Illustrators*, p. 83; NL, I, 251–52, Cattermole, 9 March 1840.

15 See MHC, I, frontispiece;

[Thomas Hood], "Master Humphrey's Clock, Volume I," *The Athenaeum*, No. 680 (7 November 1840), 887–88.

16 William Dean Howells, *Heroines of Fiction* (New York, 1901), I, 121. Many sophisticated readers, including Sydney Smith, Thomas Hood, Carlyle, Jeffrey, and Edgar Allan Poe, were overwhelmed by the scenes of her death, according to George H. Ford, *Dickens and His Readers* (New York, 1965), pp. 56–57. In contrast, Hopkins kept "a thoroughly dry eye," according to his letter of 18 August 1888 to Robert Bridges in *The Letters of Gerard Manley Hopkins to Robert Bridges*, ed. Claude Colleer Abbott (London, 1935), p. 279.

17 Macready, II, 116, 21 January 1841, quoted in Kitton, *Dickens and His Illustrators*, p. 127 n.

18 See NL, I, 283, Cattermole, 21 December [1840]; see NL, I, 283–84, Cattermole, 22 December 1840 and development of "Nell dead" from Sketches, reproduced in Kitton, *Dickens and His Illustrators*, Plate XI, facing p. 126, to the published woodcut in MHC, part X, p. 210; and NL, I, 293, Cattermole, 14 January 1841.

19 NL, I, 298, Cattermole, 30 January 1841.

20 NL, I, 495, Cattermole, 20 December 1842.

21 NL, I, 275, Cattermole, 13 October 1840 and see Macready, II, 90, 20 October 1840.

22 NL, I, 309, Cattermole, 27 March 1841. See also Dickens' letter to Edward Marjoribanks, 8 April 1841, in Charles Dickens, *Letters from Charles Dickens to Angela Burdett-Coutts*, ed. Edgar Johnson (London, 1952), pp. 28–29.

23 NL, I, 301, Cattermole, 22 February 1841; NL, I, 302, Cattermole, 26 February 1841; see Forster, p. 133, for description of the Shakespeare society whose members included Dickens and several of his illustrators besides Cattermole: Maclise, Stanfield, Frank Stone, and Leonardo Cattermole, quoted in Kitton, *Dickens by Pen and*

Pencil, II, 178, who, together with his elder brother nicknamed Forster, Thackeray, Bulwer, Edwin and Charles Landseer, Mark Lemon, John Lane, Macready, Maclise, Dr Quinn and other frequent guests as "Portwiners."

24 See Thackeray, *Letters*, I, 413, Mrs. Carmichael-Smyth, 19 January 1840; 329, Frank Stone, 20 January 1837; 282, Diary, 20 April 1835; and 287, Fitzgerald, May 1835.

25 Forster, pp. 497–98 n. See Leonardo Cattermole's sketch of "Sloppy" reproduced in Kitton, *Dickens by Pen and Pencil*, II, 179.

26 See Leonardo Cattermole and Mrs. Cattermole, quoted in Kitton, *Dickens by Pen and Pencil*, II, 178–80 and 182, and Lane's portrait of Dickens, reproduced I, facing p. 37, as is one of Cattermole, I, facing p. 37, and Leonardo Cattermole's drawing of Dickens in one of Byron's chairs, reproduced II, 177.

27 NL, I, 293, Cattermole, 14 January 1841. The "Maypole" is the artist's fanciful representation of the Chigwell Inn mentioned in Forster, p. 166 and 168 n, and see "Maypole Inn," MHC, Part II, p. 229. As Kitton, *Dickens and His Illustrators*, p. 129, notes, Cattermole's picture of "The Boot," the inn where the rioters resort (BR, p. 426) is a direct transcript from an old print c. 1780.

28 NL, I, 297, Cattermole, 28 January 1841; NL, I, 298, Cattermole, 30 January 1841; and see NL, I, 299, Forster, 9 February 1841: Dickens has "just written to Browne enquiring when he will come and confer about the raven"; as Forster, p. 165, notes: "the invitation to the artist was for a conference how best to introduce him graphically."

29 Ruskin, "Ariadne Florentina," *Works*, XXII, 467–68; NL, I, 302, 26 February 1841.

30 NL, I, 299, Cattermole, 9 February [1841]: the delayed block may have prevented the artist from taking on the raven; n.b. that Dickens wrote Browne about doing the raven the same day. See "The Watchman," the plate in which the Locksmith's House appears, in MHC, Part XIII, p. 251.

31 NL, I, 342, 28 July 1841 and 19 August 1841.

32 Robinson, *Henry Crabb Robinson On Books and Their Writers*, II, 599, 4 September 1841.

33 NL, I, 344, Cattermole, 6 August 1841, and see P.S. quoted in Kitton, *Dickens and His Illustrators*, p. 130; Cattermole, Letter to Dickens, 12 August [1841], quoted in Kitton, *Dickens and His Illustrators*, p. 130, and see "The Turret" of the ruined Warren in MHC, Part XVII, p. 264; and NL, I, 346, 19 August 1841.

34 NL, I, 349, Cattermole, 12 September 1841; and 354, Cattermole, 21 September 1841.

35 Ruskin, "Modern Painters," *Works*, III, 221–22.

36 NL, I: 680, Forster, 2 June 1845; 699, Cattermole, 27 August 1845; 703, Macready, 18 September 1845.

37 See Unpub. Pilgrim, Cattermole, 26 October 1845; NL, I, 717, Cattermole, 6 November 1845; NL, II, 84, Frederick Dickens [April 1848]—perhaps misdated as there is no record of Cattermole's having acted in any production in 1848; if he did, there would be little need for such assistance by that time; Unpub. Pilgrim, Lady Blessington, 7 November 1845; J. W. T. Ley, *The Dickens Circle* (New York, 1918), p. 67: cf. Kitton, *Dickens by Pen and Pencil*, II, 108, who does not list all of the performances of *Every Man* nor list Cattermole in any of the ones listed.

38 NL, II, 370, Cattermole, 15 January 1852.

39 Forster, p. 130.

40 NL, II, 781, Beard, 21 June 1856.

41 NL, III, 648, Mrs. Cattermole, 16 May 1868.

42 Unpub. Pilgrim, Miss Cattermole, 26 July 1868; NL, III, 660, Wills, 26 July 1868.

43 NL, III, 659, Mrs. Cattermole, 22 July 1868.

44 See NL, III, 667, Mrs. Cattermole,

13 September 1868, and Unpub. Pilgrim, Mrs. Cattermole, 19 October 1868; NL, III, 678, Frith, 16 November 1868; Unpub. Pilgrim, Mrs. Cattermole, 6 January or 14 April 1869; NL, III, 648, Mrs. Cattermole, 16 May 1868; and Unpub. Pilgrim, Mrs. Cattermole, 28 October 1868.
45 See Unpub. Pilgrim, Frith, 21 March 1869 and NL, III, 715, Henry Bicknell [not Browne's brother-in-law who had died in 1861], 30 March 1869.
46 Unpub. Pilgrim, Mrs. Cattermole, 15 April 1869, and 13 May 1869.
47 Mrs. Cattermole, quoted in Kitton, *Dickens by Pen and Pencil*, II, 182.

ANGUS EASSON: *The Old Curiosity Shop*

1 *Pilgrim*, II, 187–88. The following abbreviations are used: *Pilgrim = Letters of Charles Dickens*, ed. Madeline House and Graham Storey (Oxford, 1965– in progress); Dexter = proof sheets of *The Old Curiosity Shop* in the Dexter Collection, British Museum; Forster = proof sheets of the novel in the Forster Collection (48 E 27); Number = weekly episode of *Master Humphrey's Clock* (the novel ran in Number IV, then Numbers VII and VIII and continuously until its last episode in Number XLV); f. = number given to proof sheet in Forster volume or number of sheet in Dexter Collection. In quoting from the manuscript, spelling and punctuation have conservatively been altered; to key in quotations, the relevant words at beginning and end are given from the *Master Humphrey* text *in italics;* square brackets enclose deletions in the manuscript and pointed brackets additions. References to the printed text of the novel are to the original three-volume issue of *Master Humphrey's Clock*, 1840–41. Material in the Victoria and Albert Museum and British Museum appears by permission.
2 As follows: Dexter, xxix and xxxvii (complete); xxxi (in part). Forster, xxxiii, xxxiv, xl–xliv, xlvi, xlvii, l–liii, lvi–lvix, lxii, lxiii, lxv, lxvi (complete); xlv, xlviii, xlix, lx, lxi, lxiv, lxvii (in part).
3 See S. J. A. Fitz-Gerald, *Dickens and the Drama* (New York, 1910); and see *Pilgrim*, II, 337 fn. 2, where the change in the furnace-man is touched on with reference to Stagg in *Barnaby*

Rudge.
4 I, 213, "a child of the Devil" becomes "a child of the devil"; but this seems to depend on individual printers rather than policy, since elsewhere the Devil keeps his capital: "We all said he had the Devil's luck and his own, and as it was the kind of night for the Devil to be out" (I, 257).
5 "Heaven" was originally "God"; changed in the manuscript, as is II, 213, l. 7; other changes between manuscript and *Master Humphrey* are II, 189, l. 6; 192, l. 40; 201, l. 34.
6 The expansions began by accounting for a group of characters not already assigned to their fates: List, Jowl, Groves, and Frederick Trent, making Fred the cause of their downfall—though Fred is already accounted for in ch. l, where he is reported "in a locomotive gaming-house." In the list of characters bound with the manuscript, Groves, List, and Jowl are bracketed together near the end, followed by (the final name): "qʸ Young Trent"; the only people on the list not accounted for are the Sexton, marked by a query, and Miss Monflathers, marked with a decided "NO." Space was filled also by listing the additions to Kit's family, so that from the bald statement: "When Kit had children six and seven years old, the little group would often gather round him," Dickens expands the circle to include a Barbara and a Jacob, an Abel and a Dick (II, 222, ll. 40–45). These two additions made up some twenty lines (nearly half a page); the new version of Master Humphrey's

remarks completed another four and a half pages.

7   In the Number plan Dickens had included the Sexton: "snow—hard weather—travelling by night. at last arrive—late—Sexton—cottages—people abed—lights in windows—The bird."

8   See Joan Stevens, " 'Woodcuts dropped into the Text': The Illustrations in *The Old Curiosity Shop*," *Studies in Bibliography*, XX (1967), 113–34, for discussion of the relation of text to pictures.

9   In *The Old Curiosity Shop* two original passages were added (in i and iv) in the 1841 volume issue of the novel separate from *Master Humphrey;* John Butt (p. 188) says the first of these was introduced "in the first revised edition." It is not clear whether he means by "revised" the 1841 issue or (a more proper description) the Cheap Edition of 1848, which was revised in the usual sense of that word.

10   Another literary echo, suggesting Gray's *Elegy*, comes in the schoolmaster's meditation upon Nell's endurance (II, 52 between ll.12 and 13): *"full of such heroism.* How many thousands with no other motive to exertion or endurance, and with no other reward, live unregarded, and die unnoticed and unknown! What humble churchyard, but has many such heroes mingling with its dust! *Have I yet to learn. . . ."*

11   Normally Dickens begins a new chapter on a new slip, which would make the former supposition more likely; but there are other examples (e.g., lxxi and lxxii) where the new chapter begins just after a short paragraph. On balance it appears that the final part of the chapter was written before lxviii was begun.

12   See Gerald Grubb, "Dickens's Marchioness Identified," *Modern Language Notes* LXVIII (1953), 162–63, where the passage is quoted in full; I do not fully agree with Grubb on the significance of the omission (see my forthcoming note "Dickens's Marchioness Again," in the *Modern Language Review*). *Pilgrim*, II, 167 fn. 3 points out that in December 1840 Dickens was probably considering this revelation, and points (rightly, I think) to the hints that remain (*Pilgrim*, II, 176 fn. 4) as evidence that we should still be aware of the connection between Sally and the Marchioness, and that Quilp knew the truth.

JEROME MECKIER: *The Faint Image of Eden*

1   See Archibald Coolidge, *Charles Dickens as Serial Novelist* (Ames, Iowa, 1967), and John Butt and Kathleen Tillotson, *Dickens at Work* (London, 1957).

2   J. Hillis Miller, *Charles Dickens: The World of his Novels* (Cambridge, Mass., 1958), p. 87.

3   In his *The Life of Charles Dickens*, ed. J. W. T. Ley (London, 1928), p. 121, Forster remarks that *Nickleby* had "the advantage of a better laid design" than *Pickwick*.

4   See Chesterton's Introduction to *Nicholas Nickleby* in the Everyman's Library edition (London, 1957).

5   Coolidge gives a helpful list of the installments for all of Dickens' serial novels, pp. 183–86.

6   Almost everyone who writes about this novel treats Squeers as a character confined to the Yorkshire section of the novel, a section that ends quite early, by the fourth installment, chapter xiv.

7   Since she is to be one of the elect, Dickens must have her refuse her brother when he offers her a place in his family (xxxi).

8   Steven Marcus argues in a footnote in *Dickens from Pickwick to Dombey* (New York, 1964), p. 99 n, that these two stories are about prudence and thus that they are integral

to a novel built around that theme. Obviously, the stories can serve more than one purpose.

9   A. O. J. Cockshut is thus accurate when he detects in the early Dickens "a religion in transition from supernatural belief to humanism": see his *The Imagination of Charles Dickens* (New York, 1962), p. 94. Steven Marcus echoes this (p. 94) when he talks of Dickens' effort "to apply the morality of the Gospels to the state of England."

10   The novels of Aldous Huxley and Evelyn Waugh often follow Dickens' lead by creating a pocket of sanity where the hero finds a chance for survival.

11   Squeers was more successful in reducing Smike to the dimensions of Dotheboys Hall. The schoolmaster tyrannizes boys and Smike will never advance mentally beyond the schoolboy's level.

12   Miller, p. 87. Similar objections to the novel can be found in Edgar Johnson's *Charles Dickens: His Tragedy and Triumph* (New York, 1952), I, 287. Professor Johnson claims that the novel lacks "essential unity" and is full of "gratuitous interludes" that have "anarchistic vitality."

13   Aldous Huxley, *Point Counter Point* (London, 1928), Quarles wrote: "A novelist modulates by reduplicating situations and characters. He shows several people falling in love, or dying, or praying in different ways

—dissimilars solving the same problems. Or, vice versa, similar people confronted with dissimilar problems" (ch. 22).

14   There is even a hint that Crummles has used the stunting value of gin to keep the Infant Phenomenon within his world (xxiii) just as Squeers contributed to Smike's retardation.

15   Thus when the short sailor duels his taller counterpart he "always had the best of it" because he "was the moral character" (xxii).

16   The struggle between good and evil in the early Dickens often involves a generation gap. The older person (Fagin, Ralph, Quilp) consciously combats and persecutes the younger. When Ralph debates Nicholas, he chooses "the taunts best calculated to strike deep into a young and ardent spirit" (xx).

17   See Bernard Bergonzi's article on *Nickleby* in *Dickens and the Twentieth Century* ed. John Gross and Gabriel Pearson (London, 1962), p. 76.

18   In "The Young Dickens," Greene speaks of the "Manichean world" of *Oliver Twist* where he finds "the nightmare fight between the darkness where the demons walk and the sunlight where ineffective goodness makes its last stand in a condemned world." See *The Lost Childhood and Other Essays* (New York, 1966), p. 56.

HENRI TALON: *Dombey and Son*

1   "Dickens. La philosophie de Noël," *Le roman social en Angleterre, 1830–1850* (Paris, 1931).

2   As, for example, Philip Collins has done in his *"Dombey and Son— Then and Now," Dickensian,* LXIII (May 1967): "Dickens is making a traditional moral point about pride and riches, not a specifically nineteenth century one about a particular economic system."

3   Quoted in *The Dickens Critics*,

ed. by George H. Ford and Lauriat Lane, Jr. (Ithaca, N. Y., 1961), p. 137.

4   Or rather systems. See Dagobert D. Runes, *Dictionary of Philosophy* (Ames, Iowa, 1960), p. 44: "Capitalism is a very loose term which covers a host of actually different economic systems."

5   Ford and Lane, p. 148.

6   Étienne Gilson, *L'être et l'essence* (Paris, 1962), p. 235.

7 Gastón Bachelard, *La poétique de l'espace* (Paris, 1958), esp. chapters 1 and 2.

8 Martin Heidegger, "Batir, Habiter, Penser," "L'homme habite en poète," *Essais et conferences* (Paris, 1958). See also his *Hebel, l'ami de la maison* in *Questions IV* (Paris, 1966).

9 Emmanual Lévinas, *Totalité et infini* (La Haye, 1961), especially "La demeure," pp. 125–42.

10 Ibid., p. 128.

11 Bachelard, p. 28.

12 Lévinas, p. 131.

13 J. P. Richard, *Littérature et sensation* (Paris, 1954), p. 119; H. A. Talon, *Two Essays on Thackeray* (Dijon, n.d.), p. 16.

14 *The Imagination of Charles Dickens* (London, 1961), p. 60.

15 As quoted by Dedalus in the library scene in *Ulysses*.

16 Thomas Malthus, *An Essay on the Principle of Population* (London, 1803), book 4, chapter 6, p. 531. For this quotation I am indebted to my colleague Mme. Sadrin.

17 *Novels of the Eighteen-Forties* (Oxford, 1956), p. 196.

18 *Dickens, Money and Society* (Berkeley, Calif., 1968), p. 110.

19 *The Maturity of Dickens* (Cambridge, Mass., 1959), p. 112.

20 *The English Novel: Form and Function* (New York, 1953), p. 127.

21 Lévinas, p. 53.

22 Psalm 147.

23 "The Spirit of Fiction," *All the Year Round*, XVIII (27 July 1867), p. 119.

24 Capitalism in the 1840's had not yet assumed its "modern" impersonal character, which did not appear until the 1860's and 1870's, after the Limited Liability Act of 1853–56.

25 John Lucas, "Dickens and *Dombey and Son*: Past and Present Imperfect," in D. Howard, John Lucas, and J. Goods, *Tradition and Tolerance in Nineteenth Century Fiction* (London, 1966), pp. 109–10.

26 Wladimir Jankelevitch, *Du mensonge* (Lyon, 1942), p. 37. He has extended his analysis in his monumental *Traité des vertus* (Paris, 1949).

27 Tillotson, pp. 174–75.

28 Gilson, p. 32: "Pour lui, comme pour nous, leur realité [des personnages de Dickens] est celle de types, ou, pour parler la langue de Platon, d'Idées. Mrs. Gamp, Scrooge, Tartuffe et Harpagon ne nous semblent si réels que parce qu'ils 'possèdent toujours en même façon leur identité à eux-mêmes.' Bref, ils sont, bien qu'ils n'existent pas."

29 "Dickens in Relation to Criticism," *The Dickens Critics*, p. 62.

30 E. Amado Lévy-Valensi, *Le temps dans la vie morale* (Paris, 1968), p. 201.

MICHAEL STEIG: *Iconography of Sexual Conflict in* Dombey and Son

1 Evidence is given in my article, "Dickens, Hablôt Browne and the Tradition of English Caricature," *Criticism*, XI (1969), 219–33; it may be noted here that three of the *Dombey* plates show variations of allegorical details in the duplicate steels (see discussion, below), suggesting clearly that these details were not specified by Dickens.

2 Steven Marcus, *Dickens: From Pickwick to Dombey* (London, 1965), p. 343.

3 Albert Johannsen, *Phiz Illustrations from the Novels of Charles Dickens* (Chicago, 1956), pp. 288–89.

4 Bernard Darwin, *The Dickens Advertiser* (London, 1930), p. 140.

5 Allardyce Nicoll, *History of English Drama, 1660–1900* (London, 1960), IV, 442.

6 Philip Massinger, *The City Madam*, ed. Cyrus Hoy (Lincoln, Neb., 1964). Subsequent references are to this text.

7 Johannsen, p. 289.

8 Johannsen, p. 296. And compare the (possibly allegorical) detail of Judith in Hogarth's *Marriage-à-la-Mode*, I.

9 "Emblems in Victorian Literature," *Hartford Studies in Literature*, II (1970), 28–31.

10 Cf. John Butt and Kathleen Tillotson, *Dickens at Work* (London, 1957), p. 95 n, on the relation between the frontispiece and the cover to the monthly parts.

11 Johannsen, p. 281.

12 Ibid., pp. 304–5.

13 "*Dombey and Son:* From Stereo-type to Archetype," *Journal of English Literary History*, XXXI (1964), 313.

14 Ibid., 309.

15 That Dickens, two numbers later, describes Edith as looking at Dombey "as if she were a beautiful Medusa" (ch. lxvii) suggests not only a parallel, but a possible influence of illustrator upon author.

16 "Dealings with the Firm of Dombey and Son: Firmness *versus* Wetness," *Dickens and the Twentieth Century*, ed. John Gross and Gabriel Pearson (London, 1962), pp. 121–31.

J. MIRIAM BENN: *A Landscape with Figures*

1 See John Butt and Kathleen Tillotson, *Dickens at Work* (London, 1957), chapter 8.

2 *The Letters of Charles Dickens*, ed. Walter Dexter, 3 vols. (London, 1938), II, 543.

3 As Monroe Engel, *The Maturity of Dickens* (Cambridge, Mass., 1967), p. 172, points out.

4 "The Novel as Dramatic Poem," *Scrutiny*, XIV, No. 3 (Spring 1947), and reprinted as chapter v of *The Great Tradition*.

5 Here I differ from Robert Garis, who sees brevity, equally with unity and economy, as resulting from the method of logical refutation of Utilitarianism: *The Dickens Theatre* (Oxford, 1965), p. 144. The weekly serial makes brevity the method; it is a cause, not an effect.

6 Page references are to the Oxford Illustrated Edition, 1966, unless otherwise stated.

7 F. L. Leavis, *The Great Tradition* (London, 1948), p. 253.

8 Carlyle used this metaphor while writing of "that brutish godforgetting Profit-and-Loss Philosophy": "Ah me, into what waste latitudes have we wandered; . . . where the men go about as if by galvanism, with meaningless glaring eyes, and have no soul, but only a beaver-faculty and stomach!" *Past and Present*, Everyman Edi-tion of 1941, pp. 180, 199.

9 See R. Quirk, *Charles Dickens and Appropriate Language* (Durham, 1959), p. 20.

10 See David Lodge, "The Rhetoric of *Hard Times*," in Paul Gray, ed., *Twentieth Century Interpretations of Hard Times* (Englewood Cliffs, N. J., 1969), for an interesting analysis of the "brass" metaphor and Bounderby's "brazen" deceit.

11 The word is aptly used in *Dickens at Work*, p. 208.

12 Leavis several times draws attention to the Jonsonian character of *Hard Times*, e.g. on p. 257, and says that "Bounderby turns out to be consistently a Jonsonian character in the sense that he is incapable of change."

13 Cf. Leavis: "Dickens here makes a just observation about the affinities and practical tendency of Utilitarianism," p. 251.

14 Thomas Carlyle, *Past and Present* (London, 1941), p. 159.

15 "I have done what I hope is a good thing with Stephen": letter to Forster, 14 July 1854, quoted by him in his *Life of Charles Dickens* (London, 1966), II, 429.

16 *The Condition of the Working Class in England*, included in W. O. Henderson, ed., *Engels: Selected Writings* (Pelican, 1967). The next four page references in parentheses

are to this volume.

[17] Sylvère Monod, *Dickens the Novelist* (Norman, Okla., 1967), p. 445.

[18] Stanley Gerson, *Sound and Symbol* (Stockholm, 1967), p. 339.

[19] Monod, p. 445.

[20] E.g., A. H. Smith and R. Quirk, "Some Problems of Verbal Communication," *Transactions of the Yorkshire Dialect Society*, part LIV, vol. IX (1955), pp. 18–19. They quote Stephen's words: "I read in the paper every 'Sizes, every Sessions—and you read too—I know it!—with dismay —how th' supposed unpossibility o' ever getting unchained from one another, at any price, on any terms, brings blood upon this land."

[21] Humphry House, *The Dickens World* (London, 1942), pp. 206, 210.

[22] *Dickens at Work*, p. 211.

TREVOR BLOUNT: *Dickens and Mr. Krook's Spontaneous Combustion*

[1] Cf. "Nurse's Stories" in *The Uncommercial Traveller* (8 September 1860).

[2] *Charles Dickens* (London, 1956; 1st ed. 1906), p. 86.

[3] "Dickens and the Horrific," *The Dalhousie Review*, XXXVIII (Spring 1958), 18–28.

[4] *The Terrific Register*, II (1825), 340–43.

[5] Thomas De Quincey, *Confessions of an English Opium Eater* (London, 1949), p. 244.

[6] Ibid., p. 23.

[7] Gordon S. Haight, "Dickens and Lewes on Spontaneous Combustion" *Nineteenth-Century Fiction*, X (June 1955), 53–63. My debt to this article for what follows is self-evident, not least for the first publication of a relevant Dickens' letter. However, I take the liberty of using Haight's findings to support certain points of my own.

[8] Cf. with how Benedick in *Much Ado About Nothing*, hiding in the arbor, anticipating deception on the part of the good-natured deceivers, hears answers to all the sceptical questions that must have passed through his mind (*Much Ado*, II, iii). He eventually trusts the evidence of his ears and eyes—part of the theme of appearance and reality sustaining the play (hence so many instances of eavesdropping, etc.)—because the gray-bearded Leonato, who *seems* incapable of such trickery, has guaranteed the truth of what has been said.

[9] Vide [K. J. Fielding], "*David Copperfield* and Dialects," *The Times Literary Supplement*, No. 2,465 (30 April 1949), p. 288.

[10] "Of the Death of the Countess Cornelia Baudi of Cesena," *The Gentleman's Magazine*, XVI (1746), 368 ff.

[11] It has been pointed out to me by my friend Mr. J. C. Dow in conversation, that a common factor in the severe burning which from time to time occurs in the case of young children wearing inflammable nightdresses that catch fire, and also in the case of old people and invalids who fall forwards into a fire, is the way in which the fatty substances of which the abdomen is composed, tend to melt in the great heat and to form a small pool under the fallen body. Eventually this pool of grease catches alight, and as a result much of the combustible tissue in the body is destroyed. This sort of grisly accident is not, unfortunately, at all rare, and many cases have been documented by pathologists. Mr. Dow suggested that this sort of happening may lie behind some of the cases attributed by the pseudo-scientists to spontaneous combustion.

[12] For example, *The Literary Gazette: and Journal of Belles Lettres, Arts, Sciences* etc., No. 587, p. 414, published "SOME NOTES UPON THE PHENOMENON CALLED 'SPONTANEOUS

COMBUSTION'" on Saturday, 28 June 1828.

[13] Holman Hunt. Quoted in *Illustrated Catalogue of the Loan Exhibition of Victorian Painting 1837–1887* (London: Thos. Agnew & Sons, 22 November–16 December 1961), p. 34.

[14] Cf. Vholes vis-à-vis Richard: "So might an industrious *fox*, or bear, make up his account of chickens or stray travellers with an eye to his cubs" (my italics: xxxix).

[15] Simon Raven, *The English Gentleman: An Essay in Attitudes* (London, 1961), p. 16.

[16] Cf. "It is agreed among graphologists that sex and age cannot be assessed from handwriting. The reason is that mentally we all have qualities of both sexes." Eric Singer, *A Hand-writing Quiz Book: Graphological Exercises* (London, 1953), p. 18.

[17] Cf. Jobling to Guppy as they watch Richard cross the Square: " 'William,' says Mr. Weevle, adjusting his whiskers; 'there's combustion going on there! It's not a case of Spontaneous, but it's smouldering combustion it is' " (xxxiv). A page or two earlier another echo has been heard: "All the while, Vholes, buttoned up in body and mind, looks at him attentively. All the while, Vholes's official cat watches the mouse's hole" (ibid.). Just as Lady Jane is a sort of extrapolation of an aspect of Krook's character, Vholes's cat represents a part of Vholes. It seems a deliberate cross-reference.

LANCE SCHACHTERLE: Bleak House *as a Serial Novel*

[1] *Bleak House* appeared in nineteen monthly parts (or installments, or, to use Dickens' favorite term, numbers) from March 1852 to September 1853. Readers who wish to know which chapters fall into each installment of *Bleak House* (or any other Dickensian novel) should consult Thomas Hatton and Arthur H. Cleaver, *A Bibliography of the Periodical Works of Charles Dickens* (London, 1933); K. J. Fielding, "The Monthly Serialisation of Dickens's Novels," *Dickensian*, LIV (1958), 4–11, and "The Weekly Serialisation of Dickens's Novels," *Dickensian*, LIV (1958), 134–41; or the convenient table in Archibald Coolidge, Jr., *Charles Dickens As Serial Novelist* (Ames, Iowa, 1967), pp. 183–86.

[2] Even the critics who lately have discussed Dickens' literary techniques have not examined *Bleak House* closely as a serial. The chapter in John Butt and Kathleen Tillotson, *Dickens At Work* (London, 1957), pp. 177–200, is concerned with *Bleak House's* topicality. In discussing the novels, Sylvère Monod in *Dickens Romancier* ([Paris, 1953], tr. as *Dickens the Nov-elist* [Norman, Okla., 1968]) makes use when possible of the Forster Collection of memoranda and number plans, but *Bleak House* receives relatively scant attention. Archibald Coolidge, Jr.'s, *Charles Dickens As Serial Novelist* is devoted entirely to Dickens' serial techniques, but usually prefers generalizations to a careful examination of individual novels; *Bleak House* is mentioned passim. Finally, H. P. Sucksmith, "Dickens at Work on *Bleak House*: A Critical Examination of his Memoranda and Number Plans," *Renaissance and Modern Studies*, IX (1965), 47–85, examines the implications of the skeletal number plans (which are also printed in the article), but does not discuss the larger issues of the serial form of the text itself.

[3] The phrase "anatomy of society" is Edgar Johnson's; puzzles of detection had occurred in Dickens' novels before *Bleak House* (e.g., *Oliver Twist*), but never before had a principal character (Inspector Bucket) been a detective agent.

[4] John Forster, *The Life of Charles Dickens*, ed. A. J. Hoppé (London,

1966), I, 59.

5 See, for example, his letter to Mrs. Brookfield of 20 February 1866, in which he mentions (in reference to weekly serialization) the need for a "special design to overcome that specially trying mode of publication" (Nonesuch Dickens, *Letters*, [Bloomsbury, 1938], III, 461).

6 For example, Forster records Dickens' comments concerning *David Copperfield*: " 'Copperfield half done,' he wrote of the second number on 6 June. 'I feel, thank God, quite confident in the story. I have a move in it ready for this month; another for the next; and another for the next. . . .' 'Copperfield* done (20 November) after two days' very hard work indeed; and I think a smashing number. . . .' 'Work in a very decent state of advancement (13 August) domesticity notwithstanding. I hope I shall have a splendid number' " (Forster, II, 90–91). Similar passages occur bearing on the month-by-month composition of *The Old Curiosity Shop* (Forster, I, 117–25), and *Dombey and Son* (Forster, II, 21–35). Unfortunately, Forster did not preserve any account of Dickens' remarks on *Bleak House*, though he did praise it as "in the very important particular of construction, perhaps the best thing done by Dickens" (Forster, II, 114).

7 Sucksmith's examination of the number plans and memoranda for *Bleak House* (p. 49) traces Dickens' foreshadowing of Tulkinghorn's death —the hint concerning the "pointing Roman" is noted in the plan for Number V, though Tulkinghorn's death does not occur until Number XV. A study of the plans themselves shows Dickens' similar attention in the various numbers to keeping up suspense about Lady Dedlock, Richard, and Hortense.

8 See, for example, the original preface to *Little Dorrit*: "As it is not unreasonable to suppose that I may have held its [the novel's] various threads with a more continuous attention than any one else can have given to them during its desultory publication, it is not unreasonable to ask that the weaving may be looked at in its complete state, and with the pattern finished" *Little Dorrit*, National Edition, XXIV (London, 1907), xiii.

9 Kathleen Tillotson, *Novels of the Eighteen-Forties* (Oxford, 1954), pp. 27–30.

10 Serialized prose fiction began appearing in the Restoration and continued throughout the eighteenth century, but on such a minor scale that, perhaps with the exceptions of Ned Ward's *The London Spy* (1698–1700), several of Johnson's longer essays (in the 1750's), and Smollett's *Sir Launcelot Greaves* (1760–61), most modern readers are unaware of the existence of part-issue fiction before the Victorians. In the nineteenth century, however, before the appearance of the first part of *Pickwick Papers* in April 1836, several magazines (among them the *New Sporting Magazine*, the *Metropolitan Magazine*, and *Blackwood's*) had offered serial fiction by John Galt, Michael Scott, Robert Surtees, D. M. Moir, Frederick Marryat, and others.

11 See Sucksmith's discussion (pp. 63–65) of the first number of *Bleak House*, which Dickens carefully revised before publication to include the present chapter ii, "In Fashion." The new chapter reinforces chapter i, "In Chancery"; its inclusion suggests that Dickens was aware that the first installment had to contain a substantial parallel between the world of Chancery and the world of society, upon which parallels in the succeeding months might be based.

12 For a lucid account of the significance of the middle installments of Dickens' novels, see William Axton, " 'Keystone' Structure in Dickens' Serial Novels," *UTQ*, XXXVII (October, 1967), 31–50. Mr. Axton's suggestion that "in *Bleak House* . . . the . . . principle of keystone structure operates across the centre of the

narrative to bridge and equate the literal and figurative levels of meaning, to precipitate the novel's symbolic system out of its naturalistic materials" (p. 43) is, however, open to question, for the "symbolic system" of *Bleak House* is established firmly in the first chapter. Hence there is little need in the tenth number for it to be precipitated "out of its naturalistic materials," since from the very beginning of the novel, figurative and literal levels have existed (to shift the metaphor) symbiotically.

[13] All references to Dickens' texts are to the New Oxford Illustrated Dickens.

[14] In a note, J. Hillis Miller has called attention to another symbolic overtone (blindness) in the tenth number, which spans chapters xxxi and xxxii. Unfortunately, these chapters do *not* "stand at the juncture of two monthly parts," as Mr. Miller claims; the serial juncture falls between chapters xxxii and xxxiii. Mr. Miller's remarks are quite true in regard to the transition between chapters, but in error regarding the installment transition. See *Charles Dickens: The World of His Novels* (Cambridge, Mass., 1958), p. 177 n.

[15] Brief as it is, the number plan for the tenth installment shows Dickens at work thinking through this unit of *Bleak House*. His notes on the left-hand side of the sheet list potential characters and events for the number, followed by a "yes" or "no" depending on which he finally decided to include. Richard is abandoned for the month, but Esther's connection with Jo ("Connect Esther & Jo? YES.") and her illness are included. The right-hand side of the plan breaks the installment into its three chapters, with a list of the salient events in each under the proper chapter title. The plan for chapter xxxii, for example, begins "Weevle uneasiness" and emphasizes the "soot—oil from the window" which figure so largely in the chapter. See Sucksmith, p. 75.

[16] Note, for example, the clumsiness of the conclusion of Number VIII of *Pickwick Papers:*

> "But when is this to be done, Sam?" inquired Mr. Pickwick.
> "All in good time, sir," replied Sam.
> Whether or not it was done in good time, or not, will be seen hereafter. (xxiii, 321)

In the conclusion to the numbers of *Bleak House*, Dickens never used such obvious appeals to the reader's curiosity.

[17] See *Novels of the Eighteen-Forties*, p. 45.

[18] Often the number plan makes a note of the installment conclusion, perhaps as a reminder to the author of the goal of the installment, and of the effect he wanted to leave the reader with at the part's end. The number plan for the sixth installment ends with the germ of Jo's vision of the cross atop St. Paul's (with which the sixth number closed); both memoranda and plan for the thirteenth installment remind the author to "work up to—FRENCHWOMAN" (Sucksmith, p. 78), and the possibility that Lady Dedlock killed Tulkinghorn (which is raised in the conclusion of Number X) is recorded tersely as "BUCKET & MERCURY" (Sucksmith, p. 81).

[19] This kind of transition occurs nine times, between Numbers I and II, III and IV, IV and V, X and XI, XI and XII, XIV and XV, XVI and XVII, XVII and XVIII, and XVIII and XIX.

[20] Admittedly only readers who looked back at the end of the last month's number before beginning the current number would be likely to appreciate such transitions. Yet these subtle connections between parts are undeniably in the text, and stand as evidence of Dickens' skill in serial construction, whether or not all his original readers caught them.

[21] Mr. Sucksmith has remarked (p. 63) that the number plan for the

eighteenth part shows that Dickens considered doing all of that installment from Esther's point of view, but decided to retain the dual narrative as being more suspenseful.

22 Mr. Coolidge, especially in his eighth chapter, has discussed the novelist's *alternation* between tragic and comic scenes. He has paid less attention to a more significant serial technique: the *juxtaposition* of the same theme or similar events among the various numbers. Alternation provides variety within a single number by contrasting different moods. Juxtaposition, on the other hand, provided continuity between two or more numbers by setting side by side different treatments of the same event, character, or theme. For example, the inquest into Krook's death (Number XI) which follows his death (Number X) is not mere alternation between any melodramatic scene and any comic one; it is the purposeful juxtaposition of the same event (Krook's death) treated in two different ways in two different numbers. Such juxtapositions provide excellent transitions between numbers, and contribute greatly to the serial's overall continuity.

23 The famous director Sergei Eisenstein was one of the first to notice the resemblance between cinematic montages and Dickens' plots. See his "Dickens, Griffith, and the Film Today," in *Film Form* (Cleveland, 1957), pp. 195–255.

24 Perhaps the best examination of *Bleak House*'s symbolism is J. Hillis Miller's, pp. 160–79.

25 A similar examination of the different numbers could be made in terms of images of coldness, disease, legal documents, or iron barriers.

26 In a letter to John Blackwood of 4 August 1872, George Eliot remarked on this effect of serialization: "the slow plan of publication has been of immense advantage to the book [*Middlemarch*] in deepening the impression it produces." See *The George Eliot Letters* (New Haven, 1955), V, 297.

27 Again, the number plans reveal how month by month Dickens kept suspense alive from part to part. For example, the memoranda for Number XIII (in which Tulkinghorn confronts Lady Dedlock about her child) first suggests "Wind up with Esther's Narrative?", but adds immediately "No—Frenchwoman. *Lay that ground*" (Sucksmith, p. 77); the number plan also remarks "Begin grim shadow on him [Tulkinghorn]" (Sucksmith, p. 78). The sketches thus show Dickens bringing Tulkinghorn's pursuit of Lady Dedlock to a climax, while at the same time preparing for a new mystery, Tulkinghorn's murder.

28 *Novels of the Eighteen-Forties,* p. 36.

29 After an examination of Tulkinghorn and Bucket, J. Hillis Miller comes to the parallel conclusion that "the real detective is the narrator himself, attempting through mere passive perception and exercize of constructive intelligence to discover the laws of the world he sees" (Miller, p. 176). It is, however, more accurate to insist that the reader is the true detective, since the narrator has from the very beginning comprehended the whole novel, which it is his function to tell in suspenseful monthly parts so as to encourage the reader's detective search.

LEONARD MANHEIM: *A Tale of Two Characters*

1 See Laurance Hutton, ed., *The Dickens-Collins Letters* (New York 1892), p. 6.

2 Preface to the First Edition (November 1859), reproduced in Walter Allen's Perennial Classic Edition of *A Tale of Two Cities* (New York, 1965), p. xvi. His text is taken from

the Charles Dickens Edition of 1868–70.

[3] Quoted in Dame Una Pope-Hennessy, *Charles Dickens* (London, 1945), pp. 361–62.

[4] Ibid., pp. 362–63.

[5] *Dickens-Collins Letters*, pp. 78–80 (2 August 1857).

[6] *The Charles Dickens Originals* (London, 1925), p. 68.

[7] *Charles Dickens: His Tragedy and Triumph* (New York, 1952), II, 973.

[8] V. S. Pritchett, article on E. M. Forster, *New York Times Book Review*, 29 December 1968, VII, p. 1.

[9] Norman N. Holland, *The Dynamics of Literary Response* (New York, 1968), p. 203; originally published in *Literature and Psychology*, XIV, No. 2 (1964), 43–55.

ROBERT BARNARD: *Imagery and Theme in* Great Expectations

[1] Dorothy Van Ghent, "The Dickens World: A View from Todger's," *Sewanee Review*, LVIII (1950), 419–38.

[2] John H. Hagan, Jr., "Structural Patterns in Dickens' *Great Expectations*," ELH, XXI (1954), 54–66.

[3] Though these associations seem constant when Dickens describes buildings associated with the law. (cf. the description of Clifford's Inn in *Our Mutual Friend*, ch. viii: "That gentleman glanced into the mouldy little plantation, or cat-preserve, of Clifford's Inn, as it was that day, in search of a suggestion. Sparrows were there, cats were there, dry-rot and wet-rot were there, but it was not otherwise a suggestive spot.")

[4] The author wishes to acknowledge his great indebtedness to Mr. Björnar Lund-Nilsen, and to the stimulus provided for this article by work done with him during the supervision of his A.M. thesis on *Great Expectations* presented at the University of Bergen, 1969.

ANNABEL M. PATTERSON: *Our Mutual Friend*

[1] The classic example of this attitude is found in John Forster's biography of Dickens, first published in 1872–74:

> The book thus begun and continued under adverse influences, though with fancy in it, descriptive power, and characters well designed, will never rank with his higher efforts. It has some pictures of a rare veracity of soul amid the lowest forms of social degradation, placed beside others of sheer falsehood and pretence amid unimpeachable social correctness, which lifted the writer to his old place; but the judgment of it on the whole must be, that it wants freshness and natural development.

The Life of Charles Dickens, rev. ed., A. J. Hoppé, ed. (London, 1966), II, 294–95. A modern version of this same attitude, qualified by some account of the intervening criticism, is found in K. J. Fielding, *Charles Dickens: A Critical Introduction* (Boston, 1964).

[2] The most obvious method of character discrimination by water is in terms of depths and surfaces, as J. Hillis Miller has shown. It seems, however, that Dickens was willing to allow some characters to sail upon the surface of life without its doing them any harm. It is typical of Mr. Veneering that he bases his political speech on the original metaphor of the ship of state; but presumably Dickens is only defining a simple-minded happiness when he describes the old pensioner at Bella's wedding as being "stranded . . . in a harbour of everlasting mud, when all in an instant

Bella floated him, and away he went
. . . a slow sailer on the wind of happiness" (IV, iv). Similarly Bella's own happiness and playfulness constantly expresses itself in terms of boats, actual voyages to Greenwich, imaginary ships with cargoes full of precious things, the fabulous ship's captain who will name a boat *The Bella,* and finally, the boat which will bring the baby Bella home. Tiresome as this may be to an unsentimental reader, and though it compares badly with Lizzie Hexam's relationship to the river, it is clearly not intended by Dickens to be uncomplimentary.

³   Robert Morse, "Our Mutual Friend," *Partisan Review,* XVI (1949), reprinted in *Dickens: Modern Judgements,* ed. A. E. Dyson (Toronto, 1968), p. 264.

⁴   J. Hillis Miller, *Charles Dickens: The World of His Novels* (Cambridge, Mass., 1958), pp. 279–327.

⁵   John Thompson, ed., *The Compleat Angler* (New York, 1962), p. 5. All quotations are taken from this edition, which is based on the 1676 text of the *Compleat Angler,* the last to be revised by Walton.

⁶   See my article, "Pip, Philip and Astrophil: Dickens's Debt to Sidney?" *Dickensian,* LXIII (1967), 158–62.

⁷   Philip Collins, "Dickens's Reading," *Dickensian,* LX (1964), 137–39. The general impression left by Collins's article is that Dickens was not particularly interested in the literature of the Renaissance, with the notable exception of Shakespeare, and that he read mainly prose fiction.

⁸   Charles Dickens, *Miscellaneous Papers,* ed. B. W. Matz, (Vol. XXXV of the Gadshill Edition of the *Works*), p. 64.

⁹   The following Latin verses, by Henry Bayley, appear at the end of the complimentary apparatus:

Unicus est Medicus reliquorum
     piscis, et istis
Fas quibus est Medicum tangere,
     certa salus
Hic typus est Salvatoris mirandus
     Jesu,
Litera mysterium quaelibet hujus
     habet.

Hunc cupio, hunc capias (bone
    frater Arundinis) ἰχθύν;
Solveret hic pro me debita, teque
     Deo.
Piscis is est, et piscator (mihi
     credito) qualem
Vel piscatorem piscis amare velit.

¹⁰   Steven Marcus, in *Dickens from Pickwick to Dombey* (New York, 1965), argues convincingly that, by the time Dickens came to write *Martin Chuzzlewit,* and partly as a result of his experiences in America, "the promise the pastoral idea once held for him has given way to a view of the Pastoral as a microcosm of the corruptions of society, disguising the disingenuousness of Pecksniffery, and tending to a denial of history and our condition in it. This denial is represented in Martin's chief experience in America, the journey to the settlement of Eden" (pp. 253–54). The "terrestrial paradise" turns out to be a "hideous swamp." Since Marcus' promised second volume on the later novels is not yet published, I do not know what explanation he would give for Dickens' return to the pastoral idea as a genuine ideal. Possibly he felt the American dream of a New World to be a particularly dangerous branch of pastoralism; and it is true that in *Our Mutual Friend,* to really benefit from the pastoral experience, one must return with it into society and the city, as Eugene and Lizzie intend to return.

¹¹   Forster, II, 293.

PAUL GOTTSCHALK: *Time in* Edwin Drood

¹   Charles Dickens, *The Mystery of Edwin Drood* (London: Oxford University Press, 1956), p. 93. All subsequent page references to *Edwin*

Drood are enclosed within parentheses after the citation and refer to this edition.

2   I do not propose any new speculations on the ending of the novel. I assume that John Jasper has murdered Edwin Drood shortly after midnight on Christmas morning, that he has hidden the body in Mrs. Sapsea's monument, covering it with quicklime, and that when the remains are discovered, their identity will be established by means of the ring that Mrs. Grewgious had given Edwin and that Edwin had secreted in an inner pocket, this identification being the first link in the chain that will lead Jasper to the gallows. So much is generally accepted.

3   Dickens repeats the image on p. 167: "The red light burns steadily all the evening in the lighthouse on the margin of the tide of busy life"; it is the evening of the murder.

4   See Aubrey Boyd, "A New Angle on the Drood Mystery," *Washington University Studies,* IX (October 1921), 35–85, especially 77 and 83–84; and Edmund Wilson, "Dickens: The Two Scrooges," *The Wound and the Bow* (New York, 1965), pp. 75–77. Both writers take their hint, of course from Forster's famous remark: "The originality of the story was to consist in the review of the murderer's career by himself at the close, when its temptations were to be dwelt upon as if, not he the culprit, but some other man were the tempted": *The Life of Charles Dickens,* rev. ed., A. J. Hoppé, ed. (London, 1966), II, 366.

5   The young man pursuing his true love despite his parents' plans for him to marry another is, of course, a stock theme of romantic comedy.

6   Jasper harps on the fact, repeating it to Durdles (45) and to Neville (75).

7   This same point has been well made in relation to Dickens' previous works by John Henry Raleigh, "Dickens and the Sense of Time," *NCF,* XIII (September 1958), 127–37; however, Professor Raleigh does not discuss *Edwin Drood,* where this theme receives its most powerful and explicit treatment.

8   The passage concludes chap. ix.

9   Just as Cloisterham is perpetually returning "into circulation"; see especially the description of Minor Canon Corner:

> Swaggering fighting men had had their centuries of ramping and raving about Minor Canon Corner, and beaten serfs had had their centuries of drudging and dying there, and powerful monks had had their centuries of being sometimes useful and sometimes harmful there, and behold they were all gone out of Minor Canon Corner, and so much the better. Perhaps one of the highest uses of their ever having been there, was, that there might be left behind, that blessed air of tranquillity which pervaded Minor Canon Corner, and that serenely romantic state of the mind—productive for the most part of pity and forbearance—which is engendered by a sorrowful story that is all told, or a pathetic play that is played out. (50–51)

The last sentence might almost be a comment on the novel itself.

INDEX

All the Year Round: composite writings in, 3, 5; Christmas numbers in, 6; articles on psychic phenomena, 8; attack on Howitt in, 12

American Broad Grins (R. Tyas), 74

American Turf Register and Sporting Magazine, 73–74

Barnaby Rudge: lack of humor in, 28; enclosed space of, 48; illustrations for, 87–89; concern for tyranny in, 135

Battle of Life, The: spatial framework of, 53

Bell's Life in London: appearance of "The Prisoner's Van" in, 185–86

Blackwood's Magazine: review of Little Dorrit in, 23

Bleak House: symbolism in, 24; dark novel, 28; stylization in, 35–36; horror element in, 183–92, 209–11; reading for, 183–92; spontaneous combustion in, 184–211; symbolic function of Krook, 186–87, 191, 197–201; Dickens' defense of, 188–92, 210–11; presentation of Krook, 192–210; as serial novel, 212–24; the number as unit, 213–14, 215–17; themes of, 223–24

"Bloomsbury Christening, The": as revision of "A Dinner at Poplar Walk," 55–64

Browne, Hablôt K. (Phiz): plates in Dombey and Son, 45, 161–67; plates in Master Humphrey's Clock, 81, 83, 89; wrapper to Bleak House, 205

Bulwer Lytton, Edward, 24, 205

Burdett-Coutts, Angela, Baroness, 29, 229

Carlyle, Thomas: echoes of in Hard Times, 175, 290

Cattermole, Clarissa, Mrs., 82, 91–92

Cattermole, George: personal relations with Dickens, 81–83, 86–87, 89–91; illustrator of Master Humphrey's Clock, 83–86; plans for Barnaby Rudge, 87–89

Chesterton, G. K.: on Dickens' humor, 25–26; on Nicholas Nickleby, 130; on horror in Dickens, 183

Christmas Carol, A: reference to spontaneous combustion in, 186

Christmas Numbers of All the Year Round Conducted by Charles Dickens, 6

Christmas Stories, 6

City Madam, The (Massinger): parallels in Dombey and Son, 162–63

Cockshut, A. O. J.: on Dombey and Son, 277

Collins, Wilkie: writing for The Haunted House, 6, 11, 13, 17–18; as dramatist, 226–29

Combe, William, 68

Commissioner, The (G. P. R. James), 165

Compleat Angler, The (Walton): parallels in Our Mutual Friend, 254–64

Confinement theme in Dickens: in Pickwick Papers, 41–43; in Little Dorrit, 42, 43, 45–48, 49; in Great Expectations, 43–44, 238–47; in Dombey and Son, 44–45; in Oliver Twist, 48; in Nicholas Nickleby, 49–50; in Our Mutual Friend, 50; in Martin Chuzzlewit, 50–51; in David Copperfield, 51–54; in Battle of Life, 53; general, 81

Coolidge, Archibald C., 129

Court of Chancery, The: Its Inherent Defects as Exhibited in Its System of Procedure and of Fees, 189

Critic: letter of Howitt in, 11

Cruikshank, George: illustrations in Life in London and Oliver Twist, 68–